Nirvana

Nirvana

A Detailed Guide to the Band that Changed Everything

Marc Burrows

WHITE OWL
AN IMPRINT OF PEN & SWORD BOOKS LTD.
YORKSHIRE – PHILADELPHIA

First published in Great Britain in 2024 by
White Owl
An imprint of Pen & Sword Books Limited
Yorkshire – Philadelphia

ISBN 978 1 39905 339 6

A CIP catalogue record for this book is available from the British Library

Typeset by Mac Style
Printed in the UK by CPI Group (UK) Ltd, Croydon, CR0 4YY.

MIX
Paper | Supporting responsible forestry
FSC® C013604

Pen & Sword Books Limited incorporates the imprints of After the Battle, Atlas, Archaeology, Aviation, Discovery, Family History, Fiction, History, Maritime, Military, Military Classics, Politics, Select, Transport, True Crime, Air World, Frontline Publishing, Leo Cooper, Remember When, Seaforth Publishing, The Praetorian Press, Wharncliffe Local History, Wharncliffe Transport, Wharncliffe True Crime and White Owl.

For a complete list of Pen & Sword titles please contact

PEN & SWORD BOOKS LIMITED
47 Church Street, Barnsley, South Yorkshire, S70 2AS, England
E-mail: enquiries@pen-and-sword.co.uk
Website: www.pen-and-sword.co.uk
or
PEN AND SWORD BOOKS
1950 Lawrence Road, Havertown, PA 19083, USA
E-mail: uspen-and-sword@casematepublishers.com
Website: www.penandswordbooks.com

Dedication

For Kurt, and everyone else we've lost along the way.
And for everyone who has ever written 'NIRVANA' on their pencil case or scratched it into a desk.

Contents

Acknowledgements

I couldn't have written this book without the incredible journalists and music writers who have tackled Nirvana's story before. Right out of the gate, I'd like to acknowledge Michael Azerrad, Charles R. Cross[1], Gillian G. Gaar, Carrie Borzillo and Everett True, whose books helped me find the spine for this work, and whose contradictions with each other made straightening out the timeline feel so necessary and so satisfying. I'd also like to acknowledge the oral histories put together by Mark Yarm and Nick Soulsby, which have both been invaluable sources. If you enjoyed this book, I urge to you to seek out work by all of the above, whether it's about Nirvana or anything else.

Much gratitude is owed to the team at White Owl/Pen & Sword – Jon, Laura, Charlotte, Lori, Victoria and everyone else, both for their patience with this volume, and their support of my other madcap ventures.

Ceaseless gratitude is also due to my friend Rich Jennings for the two home-copied white cassettes, one with *Nevermind* and *In Utero*, one with *Bleach* and *Incesticide*, and for the years of swapping our CD collections. I think he might still have my Nirvana singles box set. Thanks to Lou up the road for lending me *Nevermind* and changing my life. Thanks to my parents for sitting through endless hours of me learning Nirvana basslines in my room, and to Biff for being right there with me. Thanks to Rob Wilkins for the suspicious orange drinks.

Finally, I need to acknowledge my darling Melanie, who not only scrubbed up this work with her impeccable editorial eye, but who has made me, honestly, the happiest I have ever been in my entire, woebegotten life. And to Oscar and Felix – thank you for letting me in.

1. Shortly after the first draft of this book was delivered I received the awful news that Charles Cross had passed away, at the age of just 67 — which is no age at all. Cross's book *Heavier Than Heaven* was considered by many to the definitive biography of Kurt, and he has written many subsequent books on Nirvana and the Seattle music scene which, as the editor of the city's music paper *The Rocket* he was also an intrinsic part of. I couldn't have written this book if I hadn't read *Heavier Than Heaven* many, many years ago. It's a book that meant a lot to many people. I hope he knew that.

Foreword
By John Robb

It's July 13, 1989.

A weary young band is playing the second to last date on their debut coast-to-coast American tour. The kind of jaunt where you play out of-the-way towns in beaten-up venues to a handful of people. There are about thirty hardy souls in the back room of the long-defunct Maxwells venue in Hoboken across the Jersey River from Manhattan. I'm there to cover if for the long-defunct music paper *Sounds* having championed the band since their debut 'Love Buzz' single at the tail end of the year before conducting their first-ever British press interview over the phone.

The audience are transfixed by the explosive energy on the stage. The sheer volume and the power of the band is mesmerising but so are the tunes that somehow grapple their way through the tsunami of sound.

The singer is a skinny young kid who flails like a raging rag doll in a wind tunnel of blissful noise. He has the voice of a broken old blues man, a rasping connection that screams and howls its way through the songs or slips into a croaked intensity.

It's like John Lennon in Hamburg, it's like John Lydon's peak psychodrama, The Pixies' Black Francis stripped of his artful intensity and it's down to a core of flesh-ripping angst and melancholic howl...it's like nothing else.

I'm stood at the back of the venue and a woman from Virgin records in France is shouting down my ear, 'this will be the biggest band in the world in two years,' she boldly claims and I nod my head vigorously thinking she means they will be as big as Sonic Youth who have become the yardstick for Alt rock success in the past couple of years.

Before the gig, the band's Sub Pop record label were conspiratorially filling me in on their ambitions and again we feel they can reach the Sonic Youth ceiling for underfed underground groups. Already Nirvana have the tunes and Cobain has that waif-like charisma that will score with a portion of the lost tribes of American youth.

The rest of the band have something as well – bassist Chris (later Krist) Nosovelic is a flailing hyperactive beanpole who hovers protectively behind his smaller home town buddy before sticking his bass through the venue roof. The about-to-be-sacked drummer Chad Channing is actually a pretty decent stickman and the briefly employed second guitar player Jason Everman is a mass of curls and flailing stage moves who wanders around New York City streets with me over the 4 days we stay with the band in the tiny Lower East Side flat they are ensconced in. Five years later he will be an American paratrooper in Afghanistan in one of the most unlikely career twists I can think of.

Later that evening we crawl back into the cramped flat we are staying at with the band and headliners TAD. There are fourteen of us back to back on the floor and we talk into the night about music and life and the intensity of the last tendrils of Punk Rock played out in its last incantation – grunge.

On the way back my photographer had broken his leg after getting hit by a bus and the band ferry cheese sandwiches back to him as he can't stay in the hospital overnight due to the curious way the 'land of the free' treats fellow humans.

The young band is Nirvana and their singer is Kurt Cobain who is months away from becoming the mascara'd Jesus Christ on a million T-shirts and the doomed rag doll James Dean of his generation unintentionally leading a youthquake that will turn rock music onto its head and reverberate through the decades forever as one of the great rock bands of them all.

Nirvana was always a band though.

Cobain may eventually be an exalted latter-day saint, a grunge icon and one of the key signifiers for his generation but he was never a solo performer despite writing most of the songs. Even the early lineup underlined this and as it morphed into the classic trio after Channing and Everman were ditched and Dave Grohl stepped in on drums, each corner of rock's perfect triangle was holding its own.

Fast forward just over two years later and a song the band were talking about in my half an hour interview is about to be released.

Anyone who had already heard 'Smells Like Teen Spirit' knows that the future has arrived. Decades of it being played in every club around the world a zillion times have never watered down its visceral power. It still explodes from the ether and its earful of scouring vocal still breaks your heart. If rock music is about volume and intensity and voice masking an extraordinary poetic sensibility then Nirvana has got it all cranked through a big muff.

They are now signed to a major label and the clock is ticking on the band. They have had to graft a few years at the bottom on the grunge bills, touring with label mates TAD but they are now on Geffen and things are going to chnage.

Fast.

No-one expected what happens next and within weeks 'Teen Spirt' breaks the barriers and the dam is broken and the band's *Nevermind* album will help to define a generation. Every song is perfect – melody, melancholy and raw power somehow tempered by the mix to get it over the line and onto the radio – that impossible alchemy.

Post Nirvana, every underground rock band in America will get a record deal and those long years and long drives across the USA hit a payday for an unlikely brawl of other fellow musicians as Nirvana are thrust blinking into a limelight that they will never understand.

It's a mutual thing.

The power trio now armed with human dynamo and the best drummer of his generation Dave Grohl have cranked the power even further and producer Butch Vig has made sense of the sound and walked the tightrope between the raw power of the proto Nirvana and a pop sheen. He's done a great job and the wake-up call has gone around every mall in the USA. The band's detachment and slacker mentality strike a raw nerve with dislocated Gen X youth and the band are its soundtrack.

Being big though was never part of the equation for the young band steeped in the epic manifestos and sagas of Punk Rock. Instead of enjoying the trip Kurt Cobain and his merry men seem determined to pull the whole rotting edifice down. They look awkward on TV, deliberately fuck up miming on *Top Of The Pops* and rampage around the big circuit with a disdain for the fripperies of showbiz.

At first, its all great fun but the wheels are coming off and the follow-up third album, Sept 1993's *In Utero*, is a much darker affair albeit beautifully recorded by Steve Albini who adds a light and shade to the band dynamic as well as his trademark perfect drum sound. It's certainly not a tougher listen due to its sound – if anything there is an added clarity and there are moments of pure melodic pop bliss that ring out from the songs that get to breathe with Albini's brilliant ear for the true dynamic of a rock band.

The album barely disguises the inner turmoil and emotional wreckage of the singer who screams 'I Hate Myself And I Want To Die'. Yet there as many moments of beauty and sweet melody on the album as much as the anticipated noise fest Cobain had threatened.

The last time I interview them is in this period and even the perpetually effescenet David Grohl cannot mask a band falling apart at its emotional seams.

The album may not sell in the truck loads of the debut but it's still another enormous record. The band's disdain for the mainstream doesn't seem to have put the mainstream off them.

The last tour is a helter-skelter of drug overdoses and wheels falling off the carriage. Now married to Courtney Love, they may be an unconventional couple but like Sid and Nancy there is a genuine love there. The singer's in-built depression is now compounded by his heroin use and his life is falling apart.

On the morning of April 8 1994 news wire reports of his death by a self-inflicted gunshot wound. It's a tragic and heartbreaking full stop on a young life and a brilliant band.

Seven notes later the label release Unplugged – an acoustic album recorded for MTV at the tail end of their career. The acoustic nature of the album and added cello is full of heartbreak and the song's stripped-down arrangements only add to the intensity and emotion. The album has many of their finest moments on it like their cover of Lead Belly's 'In The Pines', a leftover from an aborted blues album that Cobain and his friend Mark Lanegan had toyed with, and a killer cover of Bowie's 'The Man Who Sold the World' which is oddly closer in style to the superior Lulu version. It's a haunting peak into a different future for the band – an ability to escape from the dense explosive rock that had made their name and a tantalising glimpse into the 'what ifs'

In the decades that followed, Nirvana have become a permanent fixture in rock's canon – one of the key bands in its journey. The surfeit of emotion added to the thrilling power and that gift for molten melody make them stand out forever.

Introduction

'Nirvana are the most perfect band there has ever been'. I've said that so many times over the years. I stand by it. Not the *best* band there's ever been. Not the most original. But the most perfect. A perfect meeting of musical styles. Of melodic sensibilities and genuine underground values. A mass of contradictions that merge and overcome one another to become something greater. Something ... perfect.

Maybe you had to be there. I don't remember the first time I heard 'Smells Like Teen Spirit' – I was ten when it was released, and I don't think I was paying much attention. It just became one of those songs you have known your entire life. It comes on and you think 'Oh! This!'. That's how I felt a few years later, now aged twelve, when I heard *Nevermind* properly. I'd recently assumed the identity of 'rock music fan' thanks to a chance encounter with a Guns N' Roses cassette in the school library. Looking for more, for anything, I'd asked a rock-inclined neighbour, who seemed to look the part. 'What about Nirvana?' she said. 'I don't know, are they good?' I replied. Later that day she handed me a cassette of *Nevermind*, and *that* I remember. 'Smells Like Teen Spirit', yes, but I already knew that one from the usual cultural osmosis. But 'In Bloom'? 'Come As You Are', 'Lithium'? These were dumbfounding. Gobsmacking. At twelve I had no idea what Kurt was singing about specifically, but like every young person who discovers that album I knew exactly what he wanted us to *feel*. Like no other album I can think of, *Nevermind* is a feeling. A ballooning in the chest. A sense of giddyness. Like guzzling fizzy lemonade straight from the bottle on the hottest day of the year. It sounds like running down hill feels. And I had been wasting my time on *Guns N' Roses*?![1]

There's a perfection to Nirvana. The choruses. The voice. The crisp and mesmerising bass lines. The way Dave Grohl can turn a drum kit into a factory floor. It went in on a primal level. And it changed, well ... *everything*. Nirvana weren't the most successful artist of their generation – Pearl Jam sold more records. Foo Fighters have sold way more tickets. But they were the most impactful. Almost overnight, Nirvana changed what it meant to be a credible

1. Actually, look, I really love Guns N' Roses. I'm aware of all the reasons not to, and I long ago decided I didn't care.

band. They made a million awful, spandex-clad rock baffoons irrelevant with sixteen bars of music. They changed the value system of rock.

My God, I wanted to know how.

That's the purpose of this book. I am well aware that this is, by no means, the first book about Nirvana. Nor the second, or third, or tenth. It's probably not even the hundredth. I know – I've read most of them. I've collected them over the years, trying to piece the story together. Trying to understand how Kurt and Krist and Dave (and Chad, let's not forget Chad. And Pat.) *did it.* Where did they come from? How did they get from point A to point X? Sublime and ridiculous and glorious and tragic and sparkling and grubby all at once? Almost none of those books agree with one another. They muddy up the dates and argue over the facts. There's thousands of articles out there, many of them building myths on unsubstantiated stories spun out of whole cloth (often by Kurt himself) and repeated with no source, and lots of them contradict the books. And each other. There's documentaries and interviews. There's archives and photographs and films, and there's the music, and it's hard to weave a line between it all. Kurt Cobain, impish as he is, wanted to obfuscate and distract.

I realised the only way to find the truth is to untangle that line and stretch it taut and straight. To connect, not just A-Z but A to B and C first. That's my intention here. To tell the story, in chronological order, based on what we *actually know.* To assemble all the evidence and line it up to see where the gaps and contradictions are, and then dive back into the sources and try to make sense of them.

I also wanted this, more than anything, to be about a band. Not a singer. Not a junkie. Not a scandal. Not a suicide. A band. I wanted this book to be about *Nirvana.* That's something a lot of writing about the era struggles to do. I wanted to trim out the tabloid bullshit, the gossip and the rot. I wanted to try and separate out Kurt Cobain's marriage and drug problems and try to put them to one side, to concentrate on the music (maaaaan). To be clear eyed about it. Facts, and then context. And that's all.

Of course, I underestimated how hard that would be. Once you start to dig into Nirvana's story, you realise that Kurt's problems are wound around his art, tightly. You can't discuss Nirvana without discussing addiction. And you can't discuss Kurt Cobain without discussing Courtney Love, the frustratingly mad genius that she is. She makes her self indelible to the tale. Her personality is so powerful that she can't but help warp reality around her. So there is some of that here. But only where it's strictly relevant.

Finally, a note on 'Punk Rock', because that's going to come up a lot. To Kurt Cobain, 'Punk Rock' wasn't simply a fast, aggressive music genre characterised by simple beats played at speed with basic, deconstructed rock and roll riffs.

Although obviously it was that too. That might be what the music genre known as *punk* is. But *Punk Rock*, two words, capitalised, is distinct from that. When Nirvana discuss Punk Rock, they're discussing a frame of mind. They're discussing a value system. They discussing an underground sensibility, even if the money you're making from it is neither underground nor sensible. 'Punk Rock is freedom', Kurt once wrote in his journals, and he'd repeat that statement for much of his life. Punk Rock is a doctrine. It means everything from being true to your own value system to making fun of the pompous. It's rebellion, yes, but it's also irreverence. It's not selling out, and also arriving at your own definition of what 'selling out' means.

In other words, it's tricky to put your finger on. But you'll know it when you see it.

Notes on this timeline

For the purposes of the text, all participants are referred to by the name with which they most commonly identify, thus 'Krist' Noveselic rather than 'Chris' and 'Kurt Cobain' rather than 'Kurdt', 'Curdt', 'Kobain' or any other variation he might have used in the band's early days.

This timeline doesn't list *every* engagement, gig, interview or event the band attended (although I think I've included all of the important ones), and is concerned with telling the wider story as opposed to chronicling every single movement. The shows and appearances listed and discussed are those that tell us something about the band in that particular era: events where something notable happened and important firsts. For a full chronology of Nirvana live gigs and sessions there are plenty of online and published sources, many of which are listed in the bibliography of this book. The best of them is the excellent *LiveNirvana.com.*

Note for US readers

This book is written in British English, in which bands are referred to using collective rather than singular nouns, thus Nirvana are always 'are', 'they' and 'their', not 'is', 'it' and 'its'. It's always 'Nirvana *are* brilliant', not 'Nirvana *is* brilliant', and 'Extreme *suck*' instead of 'Extreme *sucks*'. Which they do.

Cast List

Nirvana

Kurt Cobain – Lead singer, songwriter, guitarist, petulant genius, addict, alleged voice of a generation.

Krist Novoselic – Genial bass player (and occasionally accordion and guitar). Extremely funny. Extremely clever. Frequently drunk.

Bob McFadden – Nirvana's first drummer, 1987. Classic rock fan.

Aaron Burckhard – Moustachiod drummer in Nirvana 1987–1988. Also managed a Burger King.

Dale Crover – Occasional drummer in Nirvana (1988, 1990), drummer in the Melvins, 1984–present. Does not appreciate his kit being messed with.

Dave Foster – Moustachiod drummer in Nirvana, 1988. Has anger management issues.

Chad Channing – Drummer in Nirvana, 1988–1990. Also a singer/songwriter in his own right. Tiny, likeable hippy.

Dan Peters – Drummer in Nirvana,1990, and in Mudhoney 1988–present.

Dave Grohl – Drummer in Nirvana, 1990–1994 (and subsequent occasional reunions). Punk Rock road warrior. Later, leader of solidly reliable stadium rock band Foo Fighters.

Jason Everman – Financial benefactor and hard rock orientated guitarist in Nirvana, 1989, later bass player in Soundgarden (1989–1990). Became a decorated special forces soldier.

Pat Smear – Guitarist in Nirvana, 1993–1994 (and subsequent reunions), previously guitarist in The Germs, and later in the Foo Fighters. A hoot.

Punk Rockers

Buzz Osborne (Melvins) – Influential and opinionated frontman of sludge punk band Melvins and longtime friend of Nirvana.

Mark Arm (Mudhoney) – Lead singer and guitarist of grunge pioneers Mudhoney and Green River.

Steve Turner (Mudhoney) – Guitarist for Mudhoney and Green River

Matt Lukin (Mudhoney, Melvins) – Frequently drunk bass player and one time roomate of Kurt Cobain. There was once a fanzine named after his legs.

Tad Doyle (H-Hour, TAD) – Heavy frontman of the heavy grunge band TAD, who toured extensively with Nirvana. Once played jazz drums for President Nixon at the White House.

Kim Gordon (Sonic Youth) – Bassist and vocalist for influential noise pop band Sonic Youth, who championed Nirvana. Coolest person in this book.

Thurston Moore (Sonic Youth) – Guitarist and vocalist of Sonic Youth, and great champion of Nirvana

Chris Cornell (Soundgarden) – Lead vocalist of Soundgarden with the voice of God.

Courtney Love (Hole) – Lead singer of Hole and Kurt Cobain's wife.

Eric Erlandson (Hole) – Guitarist in Hole, ex-boyfriend of Courtney Love and friend of Kurt and Courtney.

J Mascis (Dinosaur Jr.) – Guitarist and vocalist of alt rock path-finders Dinosaur Jr.

Mark Lanegan (Screaming Trees) – Lead singer of Screaming Trees and solo artist. Kurt considered him his favourite singer.

Calvin Johnson (Beat Happening, The Go Team) – Founder of K Records and member of Beat Happening, Go Team and other bands, an influential figure in the Olympia music scene.

Kathleen Hanna (Bikini Kill) – Lead singer of riot grrrl pioneers Bikini Kill. Friend of Kurt Cobain and sharpie-wielding coiner of iconic song titles.

Tobi Vail (Bikini Kill, The Go Team) – Drummer in Bikini Kill, Olympia pop pioneer, girlfriend and occasional muse of Kurt Cobain.

Dylan Carlson (Earth) – Kurt's close friend and founder of drone metal band Earth.

Slim Moon (Nisqually Delta Podunk Nightmare, Lush, Earth, Witchipoo) – Olympia-based musician, promoter, and founder of the kill rock stars label. Later found God.

Eugene Kelly (The Vaselines, Captain America/Euginius) – Pop genius singer/sonwriter with Kurt's favourite band.

Curt Kirkwood (Meat Puppets) – Guitarist in seminal Arizona band Meat Puppets, performed at Nirvana's 1993 *Unplugged* show and resulting album.

Cris Kirkwood (Meat Puppets) – Guitarist in seminal Arizona band Meat Puppets, performed at Nirvana's 1993 *Unplugged* show and resulting album.

'Big' John Duncan – Nirvana guitar tech and one-time second guitarist. Previously of punk legends The Exploited.

Susan Silver – Soundgarden's manager.

Ryan Aigner – Nirvana's first manager and booker of their first gig.

Tam Orhmund – A friend of the band who briefly acted as their manager.

Alex MacLed – Nirvana's tour manager during the peak of their popularity.

Ernie Bailey – Nirvana guitar tech.

Recording engineers and producers

Jack Endino – Seattle-based producer and engineer who recorded almost all of Nirvana's Sub Pop-era music. Also of the band Skin Yard.

Butch Vig – Producer of *Nevermind*, which turned him into the go-to name for alt rock. Drummer in Garbage.

Steve Albini – Renowned engineer (NEVER a producer) who recorded *In Utero*. Also of the bands Big Black, Rapeman and Shellac.

Scott Litt – Producer best known for working with REM, who remixed 'Heart-Shaped Box' and 'All Apologies' for *In Utero*. He also mixed *Unplugged In New York*.

Andy Wallace – Much-demonised mix engineer who punched up *Nevermind* to make it more commercial.

Craig Montgomery – Nirvana's longtime live sound engineer who also recorded some of their demos and live tracks, including the b-sides 'Anuerysm' and 'Even In His Youth'.

Steve Fisk – Producer who worked with Nirvana on the *Blew* EP.

Bob Ludwig – Veteran mastering engineer who worked on *In Utero*.

Barrett Jones – Dave Grohl's friend and drum tech, and owner of Laundry Room Studios, where Nirvana recorded demos and b-sides.

Adam Kasper – In-house engineer at Robert Lang Studios who worked on Nirvana's final recording session.

The Grown Ups

Jonathan Poneman – Co-founder of Sub Pop Records who signed Nirvana and championed their early career. Inspiration for early b-side 'Big Cheese'.

Bruce Pavitt – Co-founder of Sub Pop Records alongside Poneman, who helped launch Nirvana's career.

Danny Goldberg – One of Nirvana's managers at Gold Mountain Entertainment, who played a crucial role in their major label success. Author of the memoir *Serving The Servants* about his time working with Kurt and Courtney.

John Silva – Another key manager at Gold Mountain Entertainment who worked closely with Nirvana.

Gary Gersh – A&R executive at Geffen Records who signed Nirvana to subsidiary label DGC.

David Geffen – Founder of Geffen Records and DGC.

Susie Tennant – DGC Records' Northwest representative who worked closely with the band.

Alan Mintz – Music industry lawyer who helped Nirvana negotiate their major label deal.

Rosemary Carroll – Nirvana's lawyer and Danny Goldberg's partner.

Janet Billig – Co-manager of Nirvana and part of Gold Mountain Entertainment. Previously signed Hole and Smashing Pumpkins to Caroline records.

The Writers

Everett True – Author of *Nirvana: The True Story*. British music journalist writing mostly for *Melody Maker* who championed Nirvana in their early career and became a friend and confidente.

Michael Azerrad – Author of *Come As You Are: The Story of Nirvana* and later, *The Amplified Come As You Are*. American music journalist who wrote mostly for *Rolling Stone* during this era. His book on the American 80s underground, *Our Band Could Be Your Life* is a must-read classic.

Charles R. Cross – Author of the definitive Kurt Cobain biography *Heavier Than Heaven* and one-time editor of Seattle music paper *The Rocket*.

Lynn Hirschberg – Journalist who wrote a controversial *Vanity Fair* article about Courtney Love that deeply upset Kurt and Courtney.

Gillian G. Gaar – Author of several Nirvana books, notably *Entertain Us* and the *In Utero* entry in the 33⅓ series. Seattle-based music journalist and author who wrote extensively about the Seattle music scene. She's also written several definitive articles on Nirvana's recording history.

John Robb – British music journalist who conducted early interviews with Nirvana for *Sounds* magazine.

Dawn Anderson – Writer for Seattle fanzine *Backlash* who wrote one of Nirvana's first press features.

Keith Cameron – *Sounds* and *NME* journalist who interviewed Nirvana during their rise to fame. Author of *Mudhoney: The Sound an the Fury from Seattle.*

Andy Bollen – Drummer in Captain America and author of *Nirvana: A Tour Diary*, documenting his time opening for the band on the UK leg of the *Nevermind* tour in 1991.

Mark Yarm – Author of the excellent oral history of grunge *Everybody Loves Our Town.*

Nick Soulsby – Author of Nirvana oral history *I Found My Friends*, the excellent *Shards of Incesticide* and the very useful *Nirvana-Legacy* website.

Part One

Load Up

1986

March

- Kurt Cobain, an 18-year-old Punk Rock fan from Grays Harbor, a small town near Aberdeen, Washington, and his friend Dale Crover, the drummer in local sludge punks the Melvins, record a demo tape at the Seattle home of Kurt's aunt, Mari Earl Fradenburg. Mari, thirteen years older than Kurt and a musician herself, has been instrumental in his early musical education; she introduced him to the guitar when he was just two years old, though he didn't learn to play until very much later.[1] When Kurt was given a guitar of his own, a second hand Lindell and a tiny, ten-watt amplifier, gifted by his uncle Chuck for his 14th birthday,[2] it was Mari who taught him how to tune the strings. Later she describes these home demo sessions to biographer Gillian G. Gaar in her book *Entertain Us*, as 'loud', saying 'they would put down the music tracks first, then he'd put the headphones on and all you could hear was Kurt Cobain's voice screaming through the house!' The session takes place over the course of a few days, and results in seven completed songs, among them 'Spank Thru' and an early version of 'Downer'[3]. Kurt calls this proto-band 'Fecal Matter' and titles

1. Kurt's aunt Mari, his mother's sister, is a Washington-based musician known professionally as Mari Earl or Mari Karolyn Earl, who has had a low-key but consistent musical career in her own right since the early 80s, performing in clubs and writing mostly Christian music, released on local labels. Her early 80s album, *Something Bigger Than Me* showcases a lovely voice and a nice turn of phrase, although the disco-flavoured title track has as much of a whiff of cheeses about it as it does a whiff of Jesus. She's also credited as a songwriter on a couple of low-key 7″ releases by the likes of New Orleans based jazz singers the Pfister Sisters and a country singer called Jodie Sinclair. While "Christian-themed singer-songwriter" conjures images that are *anything* but cool, Mari's love of rock music was sincere and deep. Her Beatles records were a constant source of education for young Kurt, and she once gifted him a copy of the Led Zeppelin biography *Hammer of the Gods*, a thoroughly scurrilous and decidedly un-happy-clappy tale of rock 'n'roll excess and debauchery. Mari might love Jesus, but she's no square. In the year's following Kurt's death she has toured local schools talking about the dangers of drug addiction and performing sweet and well-meaning folk songs. She seems to be a good soul, and probably the only person in this story likely to survive the Rapture.
2. Chuck Fradenburg, Kurt's uncle on his mother's side, had briefly been a member of the relatively successful 60s garage rock band The Beachcombers, alongside Dave Reed, the father of one of Kurt's friends. Though Chuck doesn't seem to have played with the band for very long, he did appear on their 1963 local hit, 'Purple Peanuts'.
3. New recordings of both songs would be released officially by Nirvana in later years. 'Downer' appeared on *Incesticide* and some versions of *Bleach*, with Dale Crover again on drums, while a re-recorded version of 'Spank Thru' was released on the *Sub Pop 200* compilation in 1988. The latter remained in the band's setlist right into 1992, including that year's legendary Reading Festival headline performance, and is one

his demo *Illiteracy Will Prevail.* He makes copies of the tape to hand out to anyone who will listen.[4]

- At some point in the following months, another local Melvins fan with Punk Rocker aspirations, Krist Novoselic[5], hears the Fecal Matter tape and is particularly taken with 'Spank Thru'. Kurt and Krist had been at Aberdeen High School at the same time, though since Krist is two years Kurt's senior, they hadn't really been in one another's circle. Later they would connect through Krist's girlfriend Shelli Dilly (who knew Kurt from class,) his younger brother Rob and a shared love of the Melvins; a band they both orbited as sort of friends/hangers-on-cum-roadies, hanging out at the band's shows and rehearsal space.[6] It was Krist that recommended drummer Dale Crover to Melvin's frontman Buzz Osborne. Kurt and Krist start jamming, initially both playing guitar, and form several short-lived bands together, of various degrees of seriousness, including a Creedence Clearwater covers band called The Sellouts, which features Kurt on drums and Krist on vocals alongside a rotating line up mostly composed of members of the Melvins. During 1986, Kurt – whose turbulent home life meant he had couch-surfed his way through the previous year – would crash in Krist's tiger-striped VW van, parked behind the home he shared with Shelli.
- Krist and Shelli leave the extremely poor, working class Aberdeen for a six-month stint looking for better jobs and lives in Phoenix, Arizona. As it turns out, things aren't that much better there, and they eventually come home.

---

of the few songs to be played by all of Nirvana's gigging drummers. In the liner notes to the live collection *From The Muddy Banks of the Wishkah,* bass player Krist Novoselic describes 'Spank Thru' as 'the first Nirvana song'. We can make a pretty strong case that this recording marks the beginning of the band that would become 'Nirvana'. That's why we're starting here.

4. There's some suggestions that Fecal Matter played a live show, opening for the Melvins, around this time, which would have been Kurt's first ever performance – however details that could prove that gig ever happened are sketchy and no reliable sources have ever confirmed it.
5. At this point Krist was going by 'Chris', the anglicised version of his Croatian birth name. He would revert to 'Krist' in 1993 as a show of solidarity with his countrymen in the war-torn former-Yugoslavia.
6. You cannot underestimate the importance of the Melvins in Nirvana's early story. They were originally a classic rock covers band, formed at school in Montesano in 1983, a stones throw from Kurt and Krist's native Aberdeen by singer Buzz Osborne and bass player Matt Lurkin. By the mid 80s they'd discovered hardcore punk via West Coast bands like Black Flag and Flipper, blending their energy and aggression with the heavier and more groove-based feel of rock legends Black Sabbath. When Kurt saw them live for the first time, in 1983, he described them in his journals as playing 'faster than I could ever imagine', though once drummer Dale Crover joined they seemed to take an almost sadistic pleasure in playing as slowly as possible. It's at that point they moved their rehearsal room HQ to Aberdeen, where Crover lived, bringing them into the orbit of the local misfits and high school dropouts that would eventually coalesce into Nirvana. Melvins merged punk and heavy metal in a way none of the hipper hardcore punk bands were doing, and played everything sludgier and weirder than anything anyone had really heard before. Often, they sounded like someone playing a Black Sabbath 7″ at the wrong speed – but in a good way. Melvins, as much as anyone, were the template for the first wave of what would become known as grunge, and their influence is all over Kurt's earliest songs found on *Bleach* and *Incesticide.* As the only band in the Grey's Harbor area that anyone was really paying attention to, they became the focus of the local scene and Buzz Osborne was a mentor and ringleader for the city's weirdo punk kids. It was Osborne that would wax forth about the ethics of hardcore Punk Rock as an outsider movement, a way of life that was more than a music genre. Kurt and Krist lapped it up. As Buzz himself once told Nirvana biographer Jeff Burlingame, 'Remember: No Melvins, no Nirvana'. Everything starts with the Melvins.

- Kurt has continued to write songs and hang out with the Melvins throughout the year. He also roadies for them as they play shows across the state. Matthew 'Slim' Moon, a musician and promoter based in the college town of Olympia, quoted in Carrie Borzillo's *Nirvana: The day by day eyewitness chronicle*, describes the Melvin's entourage as 'four or five really backwards kind of guys. Very much *Deliverance*-like[7]. They would just sort of follow them around'. At first, Slim absolutely includes Krist and Kurt in this bracket.[8] The scene around the Melvins is fun, party-heavy and fuelled by booze and drugs. Around this time, Kurt is busted for vandalism and fined $180 for spray-painting 'Homo Sex Rules' and 'God Is Gay' on people's cars.

April 16

- The Melvins' Buzz Osborne writes to Krist Novoselic in Arizona to tell him that he has heard Kurt and Dale's demo. 'Some of his songs are *real* killer!' he later quoted to Gillian G. Gaar, '... I think he could have some sort of future in music if he keeps at it'. Somewhere around this time Krist and Shelli return to Aberdeen. Kurt and Krist start messing around in semi-serious and completely non-serious side-project bands with friends (again, usually members of the Melvins). Krist was the singer in a Melvins spin-off called The Meltors, exclusively covering songs by the tongue-in-cheek Seattle metal band The Mentors[9], while Kurt sings in a short-term project called (probably) Brown Cow, in which he apparently recites poetry over Osborne and Crover's 'Minutemen-style tunes'.[10]

---

7. A reference to the 1972 John Boorman movie about poor, apparently inbred rednecks in the deep South of the US.
8. Slim Moon is a hugely influential figure in the indie music scene of the Pacific NorthWest, though to begin with he was seen as one of the Melvins' hillbilly hangers on himself. Moving to Olympia to be closer to the city's artsy college scene, he would go on to promote shows and play in several bands, including Earth, alongside another local musician, Dylan Carlson. Both would become close friends with Kurt and Nirvana. In 1991, he founded the kill rock stars [sic] label, eventually signing Bikini Kill, Sleater Kinney, Elliot Smith and Gossip. In the late 2000s, after a brief stint in major label A&R and then management, he quit music completely to work as a minister at a Unitarian Church in Portland, Orgegan. Rock 'n' roll can do that to a man.
9. During a 1985 US Senate committee hearing, discussing obscene themes and language in music, the OTT lyrics to the Mentors' 'Golden Shower' were recited as evidence of the sort of filth America's young was exposed to (those opposing censorship, including Frank Zappa, claimed the song was so ridiculous it actually proved the opposite). After Kurt's death, Mentors' singer and professional wind-up merchant El Duce went on *The Jerry Springer Show* to claim he'd been offered money to kill Kurt himself, also selling his story to the *National Enquirer*. Appearances in such robustly reliable media outlets led the documentary maker Nick Broomfield to, astonishingly, take the claims seriously in his film *Kurt & Courtney*. The band later admitted that the whole thing was a publicity stunt, to the surprise of precisely no-one (except possibly Nick Broomfield). El Duce himself, rather horribly, was decapitated in a train accident in 1997. Mentors bass player Steve Broy eventually published a memoir about the band called *Truth Is Funnier Than Fiction*. Which says it all, really.
10. This is according to an interview conducted for the Melvin's Fanzine *Matt Lukin's Legs* two years later. Minutemen were the super-sharp California punk band known for their short, punchy and incredibly eclectic material.

May 3 (approx)

- Brown Cow perform their first and, as far as we know, only show at Olympia's GESSCO Hall, a college space used by the city's music community to put on all-ages gigs.[11] The space is co-ran by Brett Lunsford of Olympia indie pop legends Beat Happening, who become one of Kurt's favourite bands.[12] The short-lived band opens for the Melvins, and due to a miscommunication (and much to the band's delight) are billed as 'Brown Towel'. No-one is especially blown away by the performance, but the show is notable as Kurt Cobain's official stage debut and is enough to convince Slim Moon, among others, that Kurt is more than just a redneck Melvin hanger-on.[13]
- Kurt and Krist start to treat their musical career more seriously and work harder on Kurt's songs, of which he has now amassed several. Krist decides to move from guitar to bass ('in order to speed things up', as he will later write in his memoir *Of Grunge And Government – Let's Fix This Broken Democracy*[14]). The duo hook up with a local drummer, Bob McFadden, who had been playing in a covers band with Krist's brother, Rob, performing at parties and weddings. The new trio starts to rehearse two or three times a week at a room in Krist's mother's hair salon. Bob isn't especially interested in the band's direction, particularly as they're playing some original songs and he is accustomed to the more lucrative covers band market. 'I just didn't get it,' he would later say. 'I didn't get what they were trying to do'.[15] He later departs the band of his own accord, deciding to focus

11. According to Slim Moon GESCCO stood for Greater Evergreen State College Community Organization, and (as he told Everett True) was 'just a dumb acronym to impress the college into giving us some funding'.
12. Beat Happening are, in their own way, every bit as important in the story of Nirvana, and certainly in the musical development of Kurt Cobain, as the Melvins. The trio, completed by Heather Lewis and Calvin Johnson, founder of local independent record label K Records, formed in 1982 and have proven hugely influential. As Michael Azerrad says in his excellent *Our Band Could Be Your Life*, 'they were resolutely unmacho and played melodic, downright quaint-sounding music. They could barely play or sing. Implicit in Beat Happening's music was a dare: If you saw them and said, "even I could do better than that", then the burden was on you to prove it.' This was the quintessential lofi indiepop band; cute, cultish and wilfully kind-of-rubbish – superficially childish lyrics with a sharp sense of humour, rudimentary musicianship and no bass player. Beneath the tweecore shambles, however, their songs were remarkably robust pop, as a 1986 review in the influential 'Sub Pop' (this name is going to come up again, by the way) column in Seattle's *The Rocket* music paper said, 'they … sing about love, affection, and intimacy without sounding like wimps … this totally rockin acoustic folk LP has more character, more genuine personality, than anything I've heard all month.' Kurt adored them, and would become a paid-up devotee of Calvin Johnson's K Records cult, even getting their logo tattooed on his arm. You could argue that Beat Happening and the Melvins represented the two sides of his songwriting personality (equally, you could argue it was The Beatles and Black Sabbath) and that the tension between the two poles, and between Olympia's indier-than-thou ethos and Seattle and Aberdeen's thuggish belligerence was the motor that drove his creativity.
13. Asked about the show later, by the *Matt Lukin's Legs* fanzine, Kurt said 'I had a splendid time'.
14. Nirvana scholars be warned – Novoselic's memoir is a slim volume, just 89 pages, and is more political manifesto than autobiography. It makes for interesting reading, certainly – just not a great deal of it. Hopefully he'll write a more detailed book at some point.
15. In an interview with Nick Soulsby's *Nirvana-Legacy* website, McFadden confirmed that as well as Cobain originals, the short-lived line-up jammed on Cream's 'Sunshine of your Love', Black Sabbath songs and, rather brilliantly, Wilson Pickett's 'Mustang Sally', a favourite of Krist's. According to McFadden, tapes of the rehearsals have been acquired by the Cobain estate, which raises the prospect of Nirvana's 'Mustang Sally' one day being made available; a sentence I never dreamed I'd get to type.

on his career and family rather than throw himself into the life of a committed punk road warrior.

- The band recruits Aaron Burckhard to play drums, a friend of Dale Crovers and another regular at the Melvins practice space.[16] They go through various names over the coming year, including Pen Cap Chew, Ted Ed Fred, Throat Oyster, Windowpane, Ying Yang Valvestem[17] and Bliss, and are probably most notably known at the time as Skid Row.[18]

1987

Early 1987

- Ryan Aigner of another local band, Psychlodds, who would hang out at Nirvana rehearsals in the same way Nirvana would hang out at the Melvins', becomes the band's first manager, a job he holds for a couple of months.

March

- The band plays their first ever show, at a house party in Raymond, Washington, thrown by Tony Poukkula of local band Black Ice, a mutual friend of Aigner who apparently arranged the booking without Kurt's approval.[19] The set includes 'Downer', 'Aero Zeppelin', 'Spank Thru', 'Mexican Seafood' and 'Hairspray Queen',

16. In a 1991 interview with the magazine *Option*, Kurt would describe Burckhard as 'this stoner guy, but he had a drum kit'. Which isn't actually true; Aaron didn't have a kit of his own at the time and the band had to cobble one together for him.
17. I have only found references to 'Ying Yang Valvesten' once, in a 1989 interview with the Melvins fanzine *Matt Lukin's Legs*. It doesn't crop up in any biographies of the band. It's possible Kurt is just throwing out random names to make the interviewer and his bandmates laugh, although it's hardly a more absurd phrase than any of the others.
18. Absolutely not to be confused with the *other* Skid Row, the sleaze rock band formed in New Jersey, also in 1986 (though singer Sebastian Bach – probably their most recognisable member – didn't join until the following year.) On the harder end of hair metal, the *other* Skid Row were seen very much as part of the excessive and misogynistic rock that Nirvana and their peers were reacting against. Guitarist Dave Sabo had even, briefly, been a member of Bon Jovi and the band were the support band of choice for Guns N' Roses, Mötley Crüe, Mr Big and Aerosmith. The difference between the two Skid Rows is pretty stark – Kurt Cobain wore dresses, was once arrested for spray painting 'Homo Sex Rules' on cars and made out with his bandmates on live TV. Sebastian Bach once went on stage wearing a bluntly homophobic t-shirt that said 'AIDS kills Fags Dead', for which he had to do a lot of grovelling in the press. In August of 1994, Bach wrote to *Rolling Stone* magazine to complain about comparisons made between Kurt's death and John Lennon's, saying 'suicide is the ultimate act of selfishness. Megalomania. Cowardice' and criticising Nivana for singing about 'apathy [and] lithium', claiming that Kurt 'just may have inspired a generation that suicide is the only way out'. Still ... 'Youth Gone Wild' remains a banger. *This* Skid Row shouldn't be confused with *another* Skid Row, an Irish blues rock band from the sixties which gave Thin Lizzy's Phil Lynott and Gary Moore their first professional breaks. There was a lot of this around in a time before Google: Slim Moon would later form a band called Lush, unaware of the British shoegazers of the same name, and of course Nirvana themselves would face a similar issue. More of which later.
19. Krist would later talk about the gig in the liner notes to the Nirvana box set *With the Lights Out*, saying 'we were just snotty and jumped around. We rocked though'. This was actually the band's second attempt to play a show. The first, which was yet another house party, was shut down before it began when a neighbour called the cops.

all of which will be recorded and released during the band's lifetime. Someone (possibly Krist) requests Led Zeppelin's 'Heartbreaker' which the band jam on, segueing into Zep's 'How Many More Times'.[20] Krist is so busy investigating the fridge for signs of beer he misses the start of the gig. At one point he performs standing on a coffee table, and at another balancing on a television set with duct tape over his nipples and fake blood dripping down his chest. Later he urinates on a car from the roof of the band's van. The trio consider the show a success.[21]

April 18

- Skid Row (the west coast punks, not the east coast rockers) perform in a venue that actually has a stage for the first time, at Tacoma's Community World Theatre, opening for local band Soylent Green. Also on the bill are Olympia's Nisqually Delta Podunk Nightmare and Yellow Snow. Entry is $3.50. According to Nisqually's Slim Moon, Kurt performs in a 'glam' outfit with platform shoes.[22] The band debuts their cover of Shocking Blue's 'Love Buzz', which goes over particularly well.[23] In place of a guitar solo, Kurt crouches over his effects pedals changing the settings to create weird sounds and textures.[24] The band will play the Community World Theatre another three times in 1987 under the names Skid Row, Pen Cap Chew and Bliss.

---

20. Remarkably, the whole show was taped, presumably on a boom box. The impromptu cover of 'Heartbreaker' was later released on 2004's *With The Lights Out* rarities box set, and the rest of the set is available online if you poke around a little. It's raucous, feedback strewn and unpolished, no-one claps after the opening 'Downer' (which is weird as it's basically great) and the vocal is drowned out, but the band are undeniably tight and punchy. Even at this very early stage Nirvana sound like Nirvana. They play 'Spank Thru' here, to an audience of 20 or so, in much the same form it would be played to an audience of 60,000 at the Reading Festival five years later. The recording also tells us a lot about the average American rock fan growing up in the 80s – the Led Zep riff book was hard-coded into their DNA.
21. Kurt would completely fabricate the story of this first show, telling *Option* magazine that they had played [San Francisco punk band] Flipper's 'Sex Bomb' for 'an hour', while their girlfriends grabbed at their legs like obsessed groupies and made out with each other, vibing off the hate they generated from the 'redneck' audience. In fact the audience wasn't 'redneck' at all – they were practically upstanding citizens in comparison to the torn jeans, thrift store rescues and ratty shirts worn by the band and its entourage. As Ryan Aignor told Gillian G. Garr, it was like 'one of those situations where you walk into a room and you go: hey, no-one told me it wasn't a costume party!'. Aignor was rather embarrassed by his friend's antics, though the band themselves felt that annoying and offending the uptight 'cool' kids was a win.
22. Photos from this show, taken by Kurt's girlfriend Tracy, can be found online. Kurt, it has to be said, doesn't look notably glam, wearing patched up jeans and a grey or pale blue sweater. We do know that the platforms existed though, as he's asked about them in an interview a few years later in a fanzine called *Snipehunt*, explaining that he bought them 'at an Aberdeen pawnshop which is run by sweaty-incest-rednecks' called 'DILLS SECOND HAND'. Unfortunately, we can't see whether he's wearing platforms at this show, though he does seem suspiciously tall. Kurt appears to be wearing satin trousers at a later Tacoma gig, however.
23. Shocking Blue were a Dutch band formed in 1967, purveying psychedelic-tinged rock. Krist was a big fan of their second album, which alongside the hypnotic 'Love Buzz' included 'Venus' (later covered to great effect by Bananarama). The original version of 'Love Buzz' would be sampled by the Prodigy on their song 'Phoenix'.
24. As neither Shocking Blue nor 'Love Buzz' were especially well known, most audience members assumed this impressive new tune was a Nirvana original. Apparently even drummer Aaron Burckhard didn't know the song was a cover.

May

- Kurt moves to Olympia to live with his girlfriend, Tracy Marander, in a studio apartment on Pear Street. He becomes more involved in Olympia's college arts community.[25]

May 1

- The band, as Skid Row, play the closing night of the GESCCO, which has had its funding cut. Promotor Slim Moon headlines with his own Nisqually Delta Podunk Nightmare. Also on the bill are Landslat Blister and, according to the flyer, 'possibly Dangermouse?', which is a question rather than the full name of a band. The gig is open to all ages and is a snip at $2.50.

May 6

- Skid Row play a session for KAOS FM, the radio station of Evergreen State College[26] in Olympia, on a show hosted by Donna Dresch and John Goodmanson, whose band Dangermouse had indeed, despite ambiguous billing, shared a stage with the trio the previous week at GESCCO.[27] The songs are all tracked live across 30 minutes and a cassette of the resulting session becomes the group's first demo

25. As with his interest in K Records, Calvin Johnson and Beat Happening, Kurt very much fell for the swooning and cutesy hipster scene in Olympia. Gary Lee Conner of Screaming Trees describes the city's music scene in Mark Yarm's oral history of grunge, *Everybody Loves Our Town*, as like 'that scene in *A Charlie Brown Christmas*, where they're all dancing and Schroeber's playing the Piano … it was really innocent.' Future Nirvana drummer Dave Grohl once described the Olympia set to biographer Michael Azerrad as 'hot chocolate party Hello Kitty people'.
26. Evergreen itself played an important role in shaping the music scene of the NorthWest. An 'alternative' college founded in the sixties as part of an experiment in different forms of education, Evergreen allowed students to design their own curriculum, encouraging creativity and entrepreneurship and doing away with grades in favour of in-depth evaluations. The widely-available radio station, student publication, parties and shows by and for Evergreen students meant that the non-traditional vibe had a knock-on effect on Olympia's wider music scene. The campus even had a 24-track recording facility and a fully functional TV studio.
27. Kurt was not a fan of the Olympia act. In a letter to Dale Crover the following year he describes the Alchemy record label as being in a 'pretty sorry state … they must be hard up, they just signed Danger Mouse [sic] JESUSFUCKINGCHRISTALMIGHTY'. Later, while trying to convince J Mascis to join Nirvana on second guitar, he advised him against Dangermouse's Donna Dresch being drafted in to replace Lou Barlow in Dinosaur Jr. Dresch was also, very briefly, in Screaming Trees.

tape.[28] The session includes the band's only known recording of a song called 'Anorexicist'[29] and a cover of Thunder and Roses' 'White Lace and Strange'.[30]

Late 1987

- The trio rename themselves 'Bliss', however, having played a handful of shows across the first half of the year, they start to wind down to the point they effectively cease to function as a band anymore. Krist is living in Tacoma and holding down two jobs, Aaron is still in Aberdeen managing the local Burger King and Kurt is living in Olympia. The trio is spread out across nearly 130 miles, and it's only Kurt, whose girlfriend supports him, that seems to have time to take the band seriously.
- Eventually Kurt writes to Krist asking him to 'come join the band [again], no obligation (well, some).' which Krist happily agrees to. They set up a rehearsal space in Krist's Tacoma house to make life easier for him, although he's also tasked with the two-hour round trip of picking up his bandmates.
- Aaron Burkhard parts company with Bliss[31]. Partly, this is because he still lives in Aberdeen and has a demanding job, meaning he can't commit to the nightly rehearsal Kurt is pushing for. However, occasional manager Ryan Aigner also feels that Aaron was simply not dedicated to the cause. 'He had an interest in girls and drinking that at times superseded the interests of the band' he told Nicholas Soulsby for his oral history *I Found My Friends*. 'He was one of these guys who

---

28. Writing in the era of social media, Bandcamp and Spotify it's hard to get a handle on the importance of college radio in the US throughout the 80s and 90s. What we'd now consider as 'alternative rock'; indie bands, Punk Rock, goth and British imports like The Smiths, The Cure, The Fall, Joy Division and Echo & The Bunnymen, was completely absent from mainstream American radio. The country had no real John Peel figure on national radio, as the UK did, exposing audiences to underground sounds, and it was college radio stations, manned by student music fans, that filled the gap and gave exposure to independent artists. Without college radio, the American indie underground, from Black Flag to REM to Butthole Surfers to Fugazi and on to Nirvana and Smashing Pumpkins would have struggled to have any meaningful national impact, especially as the US didn't have the same dedicated nation-wide music press enjoyed by the UK in the form of *NME*, *Melody Maker* and *Sounds*. Evergreen's campus station, KAOS, was particularly good, having 'the most comprehensive collection of independent music of any radio station in the United States,' according to Sub Pop founder Bruce Pavitt, who moved to Olympia in the late 70s. In an interview with Everett True for his book *Nirvana: The True Story*, he explained 'the music director specifically pushed for a priority system for independent record labels. That meant, if you were putting out your own record, you were guaranteed to get airplay on KAOS.'
29. 'Anorexicist' is a fairly typical Nirvana song of the era – it has a great, heavy groove but no real focus and meanders a little. It's cut from the same cloth as 'Beeswax' and 'Hairspray Queen' but lacks the super-pop chorus of the former or the gonzo spirit of the latter. You can see why it was dropped. It's one of a handful of Nirvana tunes that never got past the rehearsal/early gig stage (along with a much better song called 'Mrs Butterworth', which has a killer riff and a chorus so catchy it could be used to market velcro, and was baffingly never recorded properly. Aaron Burckhard would later say it was his favourite song from the era).
30. The version of 'Love Buzz' recorded here has Kurt's 'effects solo' described by people who saw the band around this time, in which he would let his guitar ring while he twisted the dials of his distortion and delay pedals.
31. Formerly known as Skid Row, also known as Pen Cap Chew, eventually known as Nirvana.

didn't feel the need to go get the Black Flag tattoo.[32] What Kurt and Krist were looking for was one hundred percent dedication'

October

- Kurt places an ad in *The Rocket*, the Seattle music paper that carries the 'Sub Pop' column, which reads 'SERIOUS DRUMMER WANTED. Underground attitude, Black Flag, Melvins, Zeppelin, Scratch Acid, Ethel Merman. Versatile as heck. Kurdt 352–0992'.[33] No-one responds. Instead the band approaches Dale Crover, the drummer on Kurt's Fecal Matter demo, currently on Melvin-hiatus, and asks if he would consider filling the vacant Skid Row/Bliss/proto-Nirvana drum stool on a temporary basis. Crover agrees.
- Kurt books a day's recording at Seattle's Reciprocal studios with engineer Jack Endino, and the trio embark on three weeks of intensive rehearsals ahead of the session. Endino is a Melvins fan, so the presence of Dale Crover peaks his interest. ('well it's not going to be some shitty band if Dale's playing with them.')

32. Formed in 1976 in Hermosa Beach, California, Black Flag are often considered a year zero in US Punk Rock, and a byword for authenticity and undiluted, DIY punk lifestyle. The group was 'more than … the flagship band for American hardcore itself' according to Michael Azerrad's *Our Band Could Be Your Life*, 'they were required listening for anyone who was interested in underground music … by virtue of their relentless touring, the band did more than any other to blaze a trail through America that all kinds of bands could follow.' To have a Black Flag tattoo was to signal your commitment to punk as an ethic, not just a music genre. A few years later, Nirvana were still using the band as the yard stick of underground credibility: 'You can knock on every door within a 20-mile radius of here…' Krist told Keith Cameron in a 1990 interview in *Sounds*, the sentence is completed by Kurt: 'and you won't find a single Black Flag record.' Singer Henry Rollins' 1980s tour diary, *Get In The Van*, is a compelling look at how gruelling that legitimacy can be. Selling out seems much more comfortable. Like the Melvins, they went from blisteringly fast nosebleed Punk Rock to grindingly slow dirges without losing any of their aggression. Where Black Flag went, the US underground followed.
33. A lot of Kurt and Krist's attitudes and aspirations are coded into this short message. 'Serious' is self-explanatory; as Ryan Aigner points out, Aaron hadn't taken the band seriously enough on either a time-commitment or ideological level. Neither had Bob McFadden. The next drummer had to be different. 'Underground attitude' followed immediately by 'Black Flag, Melvins' planted a flag about the importance of DIY values – Nirvana never sounded especially like Black Flag. Not really. Their presence at the head of the list is more a statement about punk purism. To an extent that's true of the Melvins as well, though there's a lot more musical crossover there. The mention of Led Zeppelin is especially interesting, sandwiched between the ultra-sludge Melvins and similarly uncompromising Texas noise-rock pioneers Scratch Acid, both messy, confrontationally tuneless, definitively underground acts. Led Zeppelin are the absolute opposite of the other three bands listed here – maximalist virtuosos who were part of the corporate, stadium rock world. It makes sense, though. By the 80s Zeppelin, despite being British, existed at the heart of American rock fandom; a band simultaneously complex and accessible, straightforward but mystical, hard-rocking but other-worldly. Their ubiquity in 70s and 80s US rock circles, especially of their untitled fourth album and its epic centrepiece, 'Stairway To Heaven', is pretty unique. They're probably the most out-there band ever to be considered mainstream. Their original fanbase, in the US at least, was very blue collar, everyman and extremely young – which probably accounts for their longevity as *the* canon band of rock. They crossed the rock 'n' roll tribes. Their presence in Kurt's list is a signal that Nirvana, while part of the underground, were still connected to the idea of accessible, mainstream rock. Kurt had been gifted the classic Led Zep biography *The Hammer of the Gods* by his Aunt Mari as a teenager – to him they were part of the fabric and romance of rock 'n' roll itself, just as Black Flag were part of the purist ethos of Punk Rock. The final name on the list is Ethel Merman, a vaudeville and Broadway star. In its own way, this inclusion is as important as the others – Nirvana's sense of humour, sense of camp and sense of outsider weirdness was key to the character of the band. Given all of this, the final line, 'versatile as heck', is almost unnecessary. Kurt never wanted his band to be just one thing.

Struggling to hear Kurt properly over the phone, he marks down a session with 'Kurt Covain', set for January 23.[34]

1988

January 23

- Kurt and Krist, along with temp drummer Dale Crover, spend six hours working with Endino at Reciprocal, recording versions of 'If You Must', 'Downer', 'Floyd The Barber', 'Paper Cuts', 'Spank Thru', 'Hairspray Queen', 'Aero Zeppelin', 'Beeswax', 'Mexican Seafood' and most of 'Pen Cap Chew' – the tape reel runs out during the latter and Endino fades it mid-song since the band couldn't afford to buy another reel. A rough mix is created on the fly by Endino and mixed down to a cassette for the band. The producer is impressed by the trio's professionalism, rattling through solid takes of ten tunes in less than a day's work, as well as by Kurt's unique and emotive voice. Most of the songs are recorded in a single take and the session is over by 6pm. Endino charges the group $152.44 (charging for only five hours as the band don't have $30 for a new reel of tape to continue the session[35]). He is impressed enough by the recording to stay in the studio after the band departs to finesse the mixes and create a tape for himself. Kurt funds the session himself with money he makes from a part-time janitor job in Olympia.[36]
- Happy with the results of their day's work, the band head to Tacoma to play a show at the Community Theatre, this time billed as Ted Ed Fred, supporting local agit-punks Moral Crux. The trio play all ten songs they had recorded earlier, plus the two they hadn't had the time or money to get down on tape. Also on the bill that night is Happy Dead Juans Showtime, another local act whose drummer, Dave Foster, is impressed by the band and especially Dale's powerhouse playing. After the show Kurt refuses to take money for the performance but is talked

34. At $20 an hour, Reciprocal was one of the cheapest studios available in Seattle, but there was more to the choice than that. Endino, a member of the Seattle band Skin Yard, had recorded both Green River's *Dry As a Bone* EP and Soundgarden's *Screaming Life*, both released in 1987 on a local label, Sub Pop, started by fanzine-writer and underground music critic Bruce Pavitt and his business partner, Jonathan Poneman, who were trying to forge a tangible identity for the city's sound. The two records were seminal in the perception of Seattle's rock scene, and the emerging sludgey punk/metal hybrid genre becoming known as 'grunge'. Kurt had loved *Screaming Life* in particular and hoped Endino would be able to capture some of the primitive thump and excitement of the record.
35. It's worth noting here that some reports list the tape cost as $40 per reel. It doesn't sound like a huge difference, but for a DIY punk band in 1988, ten dollars was ten dollars.
36. This was arguably the most important, and certainly the most profitable session Nirvana would ever do. Of the ten tracks they put down that day, three were included on their debut, *Bleach*, the following year, and a further four would feature on the 1992 rarities collection *Incesticide*. Since *Bleach* has sold over 2.3 million copies, and *Incesticide* a further 2 million, not to mention various box sets and compilations that feature these songs ... that's a hell of a return on $152 plus taxes and $30 for the tape. In retrospect, it would probably have been worth Endino springing them the cash for another roll so they could finish the session – they'd planned to track another two songs, 'Anorexorcist' and 'Raunchola', neither of which are ever properly recorded. When the band came to compile *Incesticide* nearly five years later, they used the rough mixes from their own cassette copy, rather than the more finessed mixes done after they had departed the studio. This has bugged Jack Endino ever since.

into it by a perplexed Dale Crover, who warns his friend not to let promoters take advantage of him.[37]

January 24

- The band shoots a video at a Radio Shack store in Aberdeen, miming to the previous day's recordings of 'If You Must' and 'Paper Cuts'. Krist plays a child's three-quarter size bass, making him appear even more comically oversized compared to his bandmates. 'If You Must' begins with a tight close up on Dale, before the shot widens to show Krist playing his bass part. When the guitar kicks in, Kurt jumps comically into the frame, launching himself from something high just out of the shot. The results are deemed too amateurish and cheesy and are never used.

Early 1988

- Dale Crover moves to San Francisco to put the Melvins back together with Buzz Osborne, leaving proto-Nirvana once again drummer-less.[38]
- Kurt begins making copies of the Reciprocal recordings, which come to be known as 'The Dale Demo'[39] and passes them around to his friends, also sending copies to local indie labels in Seattle, Olympia and further afield, including Touch 'N' Go, SST, Homestead, Dischord and K, with a covering letter talking up the ethos of his band.[40] A note in Kurt's journal reads 'we are willing to pay for the majority

37. Up to this point, Kurt had felt that the band would get more shows if they played for free, which was more or less true. Tacoma Community Theatre promoter Jim May remembers Skid Row/Bliss/Ted Ed Fred being available at the drop of a hat and always refusing payment. It was Crover that convinced Kurt that punk principles didn't have to be at odds with being paid fairly for your work. It's a lesson he took to heart.
38. The most recent line up of the Melvins had fallen apart the previous year, though there are few different versions of why. According to Everett True's *Nirvana: The True Story,* Buzz Osborne had decided to give up drinking and wanted his bandmates to do the same, aligning them with the notoriously 'straight edge' punk bands like Minor Threat. Hellraising bass player (and former Kurt Cobain roommate) Matt Lukin, however, was having absolutely none of it and the band disintegrated, with Osborne decamping to California. Eventually Crover joined him and they kick-started Melvins all over again with Osborne's girlfriend, Lori Black (incidentally the daughter of 30s child star Shirley Temple) on bass. However, according to interviews conducted for Mark Yarm's oral history of grunge, *Everybody Loves Our Town,* and published on his website, Osborne had already met Black in California and simply wanted to get out of the North West for a fresh start, telling Lukin he was leaving town and the band was breaking up. Lukin believed it was a ruse to ditch him and bring Black in on bass, which, in fairness, is exactly what happened. The new Melvins lineup would survive into the 90s. Meanwhile, Matt Lukin remained in the North West and joined the newly formed Mudhoney, along with Green River's Mark Arm and Steve Turner (the other members of Green River reformed themselves as Mother Lover Bone, then Temple of the Dog with Soundgarden's Chris Cornell and, eventually, Pearl Jam). Mudhoney had been at Reciprocal just days before Nirvana, recording their debut Sub Pop single, 'Touch Me I'm Sick'; probably the first genuinely brilliant record to come out of the emerging grunge scene. It was a tangled web in the Pacific NorthWest in those days.
39. Kurt's title for it was, apparently, *Safer Than Heaven,* though this never appears to have been formally used.
40. His clear target was Chicago's Touch 'N' Go Records – the home of Steve Albini's utterly uncompromising Big Black and weirdo, acid-drenched noise pop slingers Butthole Surfers. The label was one of the touchstones of the 1980s underground. Kurt even refers to the 'Dale Demo' as the 'Touch 'N' Go Demo' in his journals. He was also eyeing SST records, the home of Black Flag, whose founding (and only consistent) member Greg Ginn was one of the label's owners. Friend-of-the-band Mark Lanegan, singer

of pressing of 1,000 copies of our LP, and all of the recording costs, we basically just want to be on your label. Do you think you could PLEASE! send a reply or Fuck off, or not interested so we don't have to waste more money sending more tapes?' Friends like Slim Moon are impressed by the quality of his songwriting, and having Dale Crover on the demo sparks a lot of local interest.[41]

- Local college radio station KCMU starts playing 'Paper Cuts' from the 'Dale demo'.

February 20

- Kurt Cobain's 21st birthday.

March

- With Dale having departed for California, and the band in need of a drummer yet again, Kurt places another ad in *The Rocket*, this time being less specific about the band's punk ethics and influences. It reads 'DRUMMER WANTED: Play hard, sometimes light, underground, versatile, fast, medium, slow, serious, heavy, versatile, dorky, nirvana, hungry. Kurdt. 352 0992'.[42]
- With no response to the drummer ad (again), Dale Crover recommends another Aberdeen local, Dave Foster, a heavy-hitting player who had shared a bill with Ted Ed Fred in his band Happy Dead Juans Showtime on the day the 'Dale Demo' was recorded.[43]

---

of SST-signings Screaming Trees, says in his autobiography that he pushed several Nirvana tapes the label's way and was always baffled at the lack of interest. Ginn remembers receiving a demo but being unimpressed by it, feeling they were 'by-the-numbers-alternative'. Fortunately, this feedback from a man who was practically the pope of the Punk Rock underground doesn't seem to have made it back to Pear Street, Olympia.

41. It's interesting that Kurt was so keen to put his band's album out on an established label – a lot of his peers were content to go down the true DIY route and self-release their music, or create their *own* indie labels. Suffused as he was in Olympia's college pop community, Kurt would have seen this in action. According to Krists' *Of Grunge and Government* the band simply didn't feel they had the business skills to pull off a DIY release. Other friends, like Slim Moon, have said that Kurt had ambitions to get an album released by a label that knew what they were doing from the very start. Kurt's main ambition for his songs, above punk credibility, critical praise and even being paid, was for people to *hear* them. Later he would make compromises with his records to ensure they could be stocked in Kmart and WalMart, because he knew that kids in small towns often had nowhere else to buy music. His whole career is defined by the moments he chose a path that would put his songs in front of as many people as possible.
42. This contrasts with the ad placed a few months earlier in a few interesting ways. Most notably, of course, in that it doesn't mention the name of any other bands. Perhaps Kurt felt the lack of previous interest had been down to his odd mishmash of noisy punk, classic rock and Ethel Merman … as spot on as that was for the tone of his group. This time the emphasis is on versatility; painting a picture of a band with musical ambition. However, there's a lot of contradictions here that make perfect sense in retrospect, but might have been too muddled to attract interest at the time – 'underground' (which we can read as 'credible') contrasts with 'hungry' (read: ambitious, commercial) and again with 'dorky', which rather undoes 'hungry' and 'underground'. Lastly there's 'nirvana', which is either a nod to real spirituality, or just a word Kurt happened to like the sound of. It's repeated over and over in his song 'Paper Cuts', which the band clearly thought was a key track since they'd attempted to make a video for it. 'Nirvana' was obviously on Kurt's mind.
43. There are contrasting opinions on Dave Foster's abilities and contributions to the band. Some remember Nirvana gigs in early 88 specifically because of the hard hitting drummer with a huge drum kit (Kurt and Krist had actually got him to pair his kit down from its original 12-pieces), while others were put off by Foster's moustache and very un-punk style. According to Charles R. Cross's Cobain biography *Heavier*

- Around this time Kurt's girlfriend, Tracy, complains that he never writes songs about her. In response he writes 'About A Girl', a Beatlesy pop song that references their humdrum domesticity and the lists of chores she leaves for him to do everyday while she goes to work. He arrives at the song after obsessive listening to *With The Beatles*. Kurt never actually tells Tracy that the song is about her, and its name comes from future drummer Chad Channing asking him what the song was about – 'it's about a girl'. Other songs composed around this time include early versions of 'Polly' and 'Sappy', both of which would go through numerous transformations before reaching their final form, and 'Clean Up Before She Comes', a melodic sister to 'About A Girl' that never makes it past the demo stage.[44]
- Jack Endino passes a copy of the 'Dale Demo' to Sub Pop records' Jonathan Poneman, who has asked to be kept abreast of anything good that comes through the studio.[45] Poneman is smitten the minute he hears the roar of Kurt's voice on

Than Heaven, someone at the band's first show with Foster grabbed the mic to say 'drummers from Aberdeen sure look weird', which was mortifying to Kurt. Among the indier-than-thou Olympia crowd Foster gained the nickname 'Anger Problem Dave' because of his tendency to blow up when provoked.

44. While the 'Dale Demo' songs and others that would end up on the following year's *Bleach*, like the forthcoming 'Blew', 'Big Cheese', 'Negative Creep' and 'Scoff', all fit the 'grunge' template of Mudhoney, Melvins et al, Kurt's residence in Olympia was feeding into an already well-honed predilection for pop melodies and sweetness as he discovered bands like Scotland's The Vaselines, Japan's Shonen Knife, British feminist indie bands like The Raincoats and weird sixties cult groups like The Shaggs: lo-fi, oddball cultish bands that contrasted with the fuzz-pedal screamers that were becoming the focus of the Seattle scene. He was also a huge fan of The Beatles and Queen, two of the most melodic rock bands of all time. Those that saw the noisy, heavy-as-anything early Nirvana shows were often surprised later when they realised how great a songwriter Kurt Cobain was. 'About A Girl' was probably the first song that really showed off his talents as a melodist.
45. We should spend some time discussing Sub Pop, because it's absolutely crucial in understanding how one city in the Pacific NorthWest became *the* capital of alternative rock in the late 80s and early 90s, with Nirvana as the jewel in its crown. Sub Pop as a record label had grown out of Bruce Pavitt's column of the same name in *The Rocket*, which in turn had grown out of Pavitt's fanzine, *Subterranean Pop*. Pavitt, an underground music fanatic from Park Forest, Illinois, a couple of hours south of Chicago, had started his fanzine while studying at Olympia's Evergreen College in May of 1980, doing it partly for extra credits (Beat Happening and K Records' Calvin Johnson also contributed and the two had a radio show at KAOS) and with the primary aim of championing underground music – the sort of bands that were being played on college radio and basically nowhere else. By his fifth issue, published in 1982, he'd shortened the name to *Sub/Pop* and was also putting out cassette compilations of bands hand picked from regional scenes across the US (*specifically* the US: destroying British indie music's stranglehold on what was considered to be cool and credible was part of his manifesto) with the fanzine printed to fit into the cassette case. 'I always maintained', he later wrote in his book *Sub Pop USA*, 'that culture starts at home, in local communities, through creative interaction. Revolutions always come up from the grass roots, not top-down through corporate hierarchies.' *Sub Pop*'s coverage was highly regionalised, concentrating on each area's local scene. The music industry operated out of LA and New York, so Pavitt mostly ignored the coasts, considering them well served, and focussed on the MidWest, the Pacific NorthWest and the South. A contact address was printed for each featured artist. The *Sub/Pop #5* cassette-zine sold over 2,000 copies – Pavitt claims the proceeds covered his rent for the next year and a half. The Zine was having a genuine impact; major record labels would write to request the latest edition ('I really got a kick out of this one', noted the director of talent acquisition at Columbia Records' East Coast office.) 'SUB/POP IS AMERICAN. WE ALTERNATE BETWEEN A C-60 CASSETTE AND A PUBLICATION' proclaimed the cover of *Sub/Pop #6*. 'WE ARE INTERESTED IN A DECENTRALIZED NETWORK OF REGIONAL AND LOCAL BUMS WHO REFUSE TO GET AN HONEST JOB. SEND US YOUR INDEPENDENT RECORDS, TAPES AND MAGAZINES. WRITE SUB/POP C/O LOST MUSIC NETWORK, BOX 2391, OLYMPIA, WA 98507.'

    Pavitt eventually left Olympia for Seattle, and from April 1983 *Sub/Pop* was upgraded from a fanzine to a column on underground music in the city's music paper, *The Rocket*. The column ran until July 1988, when Pavitt retired from journalism with a very good reason – by now he was running a record label, also called Sub Pop. Writing about his own artists (the last edition features Mudhoney heavily) was becoming something of a conflict of interests.

Seattle's music scene had not been especially exciting during the 80s; only soft-rock megastars Heart had really broken into any kind of mainstream success. As *Rocket* editor and future Kurt Cobain biographer Charles R Cross, writes, 'most clubs were taverns … bands could make their living only by playing covers. A few outlying punk clubs opened up, but they'd usually be shut down within weeks … many people got the idea that Nirvana, Mudhoney and Soundgarden were typical representatives of a healthy music mecca. They were not'. What eventually caused Seattle's now-legendary 'grunge' scene to coalesce was a combination of dire need – zero support and terrible gigs meant bands clung together to release their own DIY records – and soft drugs; by the mid 80s MDMA was running through Seattle like turpentine through a donkey. It created a sense of togetherness and empathy. In the industrial cities of Chicago, Detroit, Manchester and London the popularity of ecstasy and MDMA was accompanied by a boom in mesmeric and repetitive dance music. In Seattle, everyone played super-heavy, dirge-like, slowed-down Punk Rock. A small, local label called C/Z crystalised the scene when it put out the *Deep Six* compilation in 1986, featuring Green River, Malfunkshun, the Melvins, Skin Yard, Soundgarden and the U-Men. The groups all turned up to see each other play, and were bound together not so much by musical similarity but by their difference to everyone else: neither hard rock, nor hardcore punk nor college rock, nor English-influence post punk and indie. These were *odd* sounding bands. (Only Soundgarden had a singer with a conventionally 'rock' voice – Chris Cornell, who was eyed with suspicion by peers lest he accidentally became a rock star. Originally he was their drummer.) It created a sense of community in the city. Olympia had its tweecore underground, with its crushes on cute, obscure pop acts and weird prejudice against bass players, while Seattle had … whatever *that* music was. Bruce Pavitt was paying attention. 'It's slow SLOW and heavy HEAVY' he wrote of *Deep Six* in the April 1986 'Sub Pop' column in *The Rocket*, 'and it's *the* predominant sound of underground Seattle in '86 … proving that you don't have to live in the suburbs and have a low IQ to do some *serious* headbanging'. At roughly the same time as *Deep Six* was released (and sold very slowly, mostly because the primary audience for the record were all featured on it), Pavitt put out his first vinyl compilation, *Sub Pop 100*, with the same ethos as his fanzine cassettes and his column: celebrating regional, underground music from across the USA. It featured Scratch Acid, The Wipers, Naked Ragan and Big Black's Steve Albini delivering a spoken word monologue. 5,000 copies were pressed and they sold out in a few months. A defining moment for Pavitt was realising that he could apply the savvy and contacts he'd used for *Sub Pop 100* to the unique scene showcased on *Deep Six*. It took him another year to manifest Sub Pop as a record label proper, eventually releasing Green River's *Dry As A Bone* EP. With that release he combined three elements that would give an audio, visual and snappy media-soundbyte identity to the new scene. Firstly it was recorded by Jack Endino at Reciprocal, who had an astonishing ability to harness the sludge and chaos and bring out the soul beneath without compromising the sound. Secondly the cover art was a black and white still by local photographer Charles Peterson, who had been covering gigs in the city. Peterson is an incredible documentary photographer who used wide angle lenses to capture the energy of Seattle's live scene, with sparsely attended but completely devoted crowds and chaotic performances. According to Pavitt it was seeing Peterson's photography that convinced him that the city's scene had an identity and energy all of its own, calling the pictures a 'visual unification' that 'totally captured the essence of the music'. Finally, in the marketing Pavitt described the EP as 'ultra-loose GRUNGE that destroyed the morals of a generation'. It was a perfect word to describe the music. To ram the point home, it had been written in capital letters. The scene and the genre now had its name. And from the very beginning, 'grunge' had Sub Pop's soon-to-be-iconic black and white logo attached to it.

Meanwhile another local music critic and DJ, Jonathan Poneman, was falling in love with the city's rock scene. More specifically he was falling in love with Soundgarden, the most conventionally hard rock of the grunge gang. The band had formed in 1984 and were fronted by full-throated, rock dreamboat Cornell, whose rich vocals echoed around half-empty clubs like the voice of God. Catching a Soundgarden show in 85 was enough to make Poneman give up any aspirations he mght have as a performer – he had seen greatness and didn't see the point in competing with it. Instead, he decided to amplify it. Poneman was nother underground fanatic hailing from off the beaten tracks (Toledo, Ohio) who had drifted into Seattle's melting pot of outsiders and weirdos. With $15,000 in savings bonds burning a hole in his bank account (not chump change in the mid 80s) he decided to release a Soundgarden record himself. There was, however, a problem: Soundgarden were already discussing a release with Bruce Pavitt's Sub Pop. It was guitarist Kim Thayil, who had known Pavitt since they were children, that suggested the two pool their resources: Pavitt's brand, Poneman's money. In 1987 the two worked together on the debut Soundgarden single, 'Hunted Down', and the following EP, *Screaming Life*, again featuring Endino behind the mixing desk and Peterson behind the camera for the cover shot. The record was successful, with the band making the cover of both *CMJ New Music Report* and *Rockpool*, two of the biggest magazines

UNAVOIDABLE WIDOW LINE AT TOP OF PAGE TO KEEP NOTE WITH TEXT.

the chorus of the first track, 'If You Must'.[46]

- The band plays their first show with Dave Foster[47] (and their last under the name Ted Ed Fred) at an Olympia college party held at a student house known as the Caddyshack, alongside Slim Moon's new band, Lush. There are around 30 people in attendance.
- Jonathan Poneman calls Kurt at home to tell him he has heard his demo and offers to book the band at one of the 'Sub Pop Sundays', a monthly night curated by the label and held at Seattle club, The Vogue. His Sub Pop partner, Bruce Pavitt, is less excited about the demo but is happy to go along with the recommendation.[48]
- At some point in early March, Kurt renames the band for the final time. Dave Foster finds out when he spots a flyer at Kurt's apartment advertising a show by 'Nirvana' and asks who that is. Kurt replies 'That's us. It means attainment of perfection'.[49]

---

covering underground music. The two men realised they had something incredible on their hands – a thriving local scene with baked in stars and the platform to showcase it. Between them they had the smarts, contacts and funds to run a record label (to an extent – money would always be a problem for the label and its tagline, proudly displayed on its website even at the time of writing, would come to be 'going out of business since 1988'). Sub Pop became a fifty-fifty partnership. By the following spring both Poneman and Pavitt had quit their day jobs and rented an office. It was time to look for some more bands.

46. According to a story in Michael Azerrad's authorised biography *Come As You Are*, Poneman played the tape in the offices of Muzak, a company specialising (appropriately enough) in stock background music for elevators, hotel lobbies and hold music, where Bruce Pavitt and about half of Sub Pop's future roster worked, saying 'If anyone wants to get rich, this band is looking for a drummer'. No-one was particularly fussed. Nirvana, to a greater or lesser extent and sometimes very indirectly, would make a few people in that room rich all the same.
47. Who, in the spirit of Punk Rock purity over heavy metal maximalism, has been asked to strip his drum kit down from 12 pieces to six.
48. This will prove a financially astute move for Bruce Pavitt.
49. Why 'Nirvana'? As previously mentioned, it was a word that Kurt had obviously been rolling around for a while. It's a repeated phrase on 'Paper Cuts' (Kurt sings the word fourteen times) and included in the drummer advert placed in *The Rocket*. The state of 'nirvana' is central to Buddishm, and its meaning is a little less straightforward than Kurt led Dave Foster to believe, though 'attainment of perfection' is along the right lines. It's more true to say that a state of nirvana was one of harmony, in which one has no feelings of greed, hate or ignorance. After that it gets complicated, and religious scholars have been involved in a centuries-long bun fight about what attaining a state of nirvana actually means and how to achieve it. Though it's a bit of a left turn from Ted Ed Fred and Skid Row, and a complete about face from Throat Oyster, the seeds had obviously already been sown: the band had played a few shows under the name of Bliss, a state not a million miles away from the Buddhist idea of nirvana. And you could argue that Kurt would indeed spend his life, one way or another, chasing an ideal of harmony and peace, through music, through love and through drugs. In that sense it fits. Of course musically, Nirvana were rarely perfect or harmonious. Being rough around the edges was part of their charm. They'd be a relatively inconsistent live band through their entire existence, sometimes astonishing, sometimes going through the motions, sometimes barely holding it together. Sonic perfection was never an aim for the band on record either; as it was for contemporaries like, say, Smashing Pumpkins. Kurt always kept a raw edge on his music; cosmic harmony be hanged. Even their closest friends felt that the word 'nirvana' didn't really fit the band. But then, maybe that was the point? Later, Kurt would say that he chose the name because he was looking for a word that was elegant and beautiful, contrasting with the aggressive or absurd names common in the punk world (think of Melvins, Angry Samoans, Minor Threat, Bad Brainz, Big Black, Scratch Acid or, of course, Butthole Surfers.) That's interesting in itself, however – everything else about Nirvana's early days suggests a desire to align themselves with the more uncompromising end of the underground. None of the band was especially religious (they all attended church into their early teens, but with no more enthusiasm than Bart Simpson does), though Kurt and Krist did both explore buddhism, separately attending a local temple group (Krist says he wrote the riff to the song 'Dive' immediately after his visit and speculated that it might have been inspired by the chanting he

March 13

- The band plays their first show under the name Nirvana (the flyer reads 'Nirvana, also known as Skid Row, Ted Ed Fred, Pen Cap Chew and Bliss) at the Tacoma Community Theatre, alongside Slim Moon's Lush. Two new songs, an early version of what would become 'Big Cheese' and 'Blew' are added to the set.[50] Future Nirvana drummer Chad Channing is in attendance.

April

- At some point in early April, Nirvana make their Seattle debut, at the Central Tavern. Sub Pop's Bruce Pavitt and Jonathan Poneman both attend, though hardly anyone else does (some estimates have put the audience size at three, if you include the bartender).[51] Bruce Pavitt isn't particularly impressed, disliking all of the band's original songs and finding Dave Foster's moustache 'problematic'.[52] However he likes their cover of 'Love Buzz', and is impressed enough by Kurt's Olympia connections to consider putting out a single.

April 1

- Sub Pop opens its first office on the top floor of Seattle's Terminal Sales Building, on 1st Avenue, and begins trading as an official LLC Corporation. Bruce Pavitt marks this as the beginning of the company as a real label.[53]

---

heard there). Both decided the spiritual life wasn't for them, but in Kurt's case the terminology, at least, clearly stuck. In all honesty, there's probably no more to it than a word the band liked the sound of. In a letter to Dale Crover published in Kurt's journals, he informs his friend that 'our last and final name is Nirvana', with a note scribbled next to it – 'ooh eerie mystical doom'. Ultimately it was just a pleasing, exotic sounding word that, thanks to timing, remained frozen in place for the rest of the band's career. As Slim Moon told Everett True in *The True Story*, 'if Sub Pop hadn't offered them a 7″, they'd have been called something else a week later'.

50. 'Blew' is the only Nirvana song from this era to remain in the band's set for the rest of their career. It was first performed on 13 March 1988 and was still in the setlist for Kurt's final ever performance on 1 March, 1994 in Munich, Germany. It's a super heavy, but super catchy push-and-pull monster and probably the best distillation you'll find of first-wave grunge, with the bass, guitar and vocal all following one another throughout the song, giving it a grinding power.
51. This gig has rather been airbrushed from the band's history, though the two Sub Pop execs swear it happened. Still, does a gig to two people actually count? According to the punk handbook (which is, obviously, Henry Rollins' *Get In The Van*,) absolutely, yes. Doubly so if the only two audience members run a record label. Krist Novoselic says he doesn't remember even playing: 'Nobody came. Nobody. So we didn't even play,' he told Gillian G. Greer for her book *Entertain Us*. 'We bought a 12-pack of beer and sat underneath the viaduct and drank it'.
52. Poneman and Pavitt both swear that this gig featured Aaron Bukhard on drums, who did return to the drum stool temporarily at some point in 1988, but the timeline doesn't match up. Since both Aaron and Dave had moustaches, it's likely the Sub Pop guys are just getting their wires crossed.
53. When pictures of the office exterior were printed in the packaging of the *Sub Pop 200* compilation that year, listed as the label's 'world headquarters', many assumed that the company used the entire building, leading to the impression that Sub Pop was a much bigger deal financially than it actually was – the label was perpetually broke, especially in its early years, and inhabited only a small office at the very top of the building, not even accessible by the elevator. In the same booklet Poneman was listed as 'Executive Chairman of Supervisory Management' and Pavitt as 'Supervisory Chairman of Executive Management'.

April 24

- Nirvana make what is considered to be their *official* Seattle debut at The Vogue, a former gay biker bar that still has the chemical-vanilla aroma of poppers lingering in the air, owned by a cross-dressing bartender called Monty. The band open with 'Love Buzz' and close with a shambolic jam of Led Zeppelin's 'Moby Dick'. No-one, on or off stage, particularly enjoys the show. Local writer Dawn Anderson of *Backlash* (a Seattle fanzine with a readership of around 10,000) who had been a big fan of the 'Dale Demo', is underwhelmed by the band live but interviews them for her magazine all the same. The audience is composed of the band's girlfriends, some local rock fans and a chunk of the Seattle music family: eg. members of other bands[54] and the Sub Pop usual suspects; Jonathan Poneman, Bruce Pavitt, Charles Peterson, Jack Endino. Kurt struggles to play and sing at the same time on the more challenging songs, something which both Dawn Anderson notes in her write up, published months later, and is also remembered by Jack Endino. Sup Pop photographer Charles Peterson doesn't bother to break out his camera, finding the band un-energised and depressing, and he asks Jonathan Poneman if he's sure about signing them. Kurt himself feels wrongfooted by what he thinks to be a judgey, hipster audience. He later writes to Dale Crover complaining of the 'amount of people who came to **judge** us [Kurt's emphasis]. Not be at a bar, get drunk, watch some bands and have fun. There was a representative from every Seattle band just watching. We felt like they should have score cards'.[55] Oddly, Kurt never posts this letter.

Late April/Early May

- Dave Foster discovers that his girlfriend, Lani, is cheating on him and beats the hell out of her new partner, the son of a local town official. He is arrested and charged, and is eventually sentenced to a year in prison. He serves only two weeks of the sentence and is released, though has his driving licence revoked meaning he can't get to rehearsals with the band.
- Unknown to their current drummer, Kurt and Krist ask Aaron Burckhard to rejoin, He rehearses with them several times, using Dave's drum kit. Meanwhile, Dave continually phones his bandmates to inquire about rehearsals and gigs – Kurt tells him that they have paused active duty to write new songs. They rehearse with Aaron behind his back.

54. Mudhoney's Mark Arm was certainly there.
55. Though Kurt felt other musicians had come to judge his band based on hype generated by the demo, it's more true to say that the close-knit grunge gang would generally turn up to Sup Pop Sundays whoever was playing: the main audience for Seattle grunge bands was members of other Seattle grunge bands. Kevin Whitworth of Seattle's Love Battery told Nick Soulsby that 'there was exactly one crowd [in town], and they (we) went to all the shows. We all knew each other, slept on each other's couches, borrowed equipment, and traded band members.'

- Aaron borrows Kurt's car and is pulled over for drink-driving. The car is impounded. Aaron calls an embarrassed Krist to pick him up from the police station.[56] The following day, Aaron is too hungover to rehearse. The band don't ask him to play again.
- Jonathan Poneman meets with Kurt and his girlfriend, Tracy, in a Seattle cafe. Krist turns up a little later, absolutely sozzled. Poneman offers the band a one-single deal, and insists that the A-side should be 'Love Buzz'. It bothers Kurt that his debut single will be a cover, and he's disappointed that the deal on the table is so limited, though Poneman insists more releases will be forthcoming if the single does well enough. Outwardly, Kurt is quiet and polite and Poneman assumes him to be in awe at the prospect of getting his own record out at last. Krist, meanwhile, yells at the other customers and generally larks about.[57]
- Kurt places an ad in *The Rocket* for a third time, once again looking for a drummer. It reads 'Heavy, light punk rock band: Aerosmith, Led Zeppelin, Black Sabbath, Black Flag, Scratch Acid, Butthole Surfers. Seeks drummer.'[58][59] There are some responses but none are promising. The band consider asking Tad Doyle (aka Thomas Anthony Doyle), drummer with the band H-Hour, to join.

May 6

- Kurt and Krist catch Malfunkshun's final show, at the Tacoma Community Centre.[60] Also playing are Lush (featuring Slim Moon) and Skin Yard (featuring Jack Endino). The duo are introduced to drummer Chad Channing by a mutual friend, and remember sharing a bill with him the previous year when, as Bliss, they played with his short-lived band The Magnet Men. They both recall appreciating his skills and his unusual and extremely loud fibreglass drum set. They invite Chad to check out their next show, hinting that they might need a drummer soon.

56. Burkhard apparently called the Black cop that pulled him over a racial slur. The rest of the band were mortified.
57. At this point in Nirvana's history it is Krist, gregarious, gigantic and usually drunk, that draws the most attention. It's his charisma and sense of humour, rather than Kurt, whose intensity could come off as awkwardness and whose sense of humour, which was sharp and occasionally vicious, was dry and often understated, that people tended to connect with and remember. There were also the songs, of course, but those were often sacrificed on the altar of terrible PA systems in the dive clubs of Seattle, Tacoma, Olympia and the other grubby pits of Washington State.
58. Quite why he bothered is anyone's guess. Neither of the previous two ads had actually yielded a result, and the band had so-far found their drummers through friends (well ... *friend.* Both Aaron and Dave were recommended by Dale Crover). Unlike the previous two ads, which listed carefully chosen influences and intentions, this one could describe half of the punk rock bands in the Pacific NorthWest. You get the sense that Kurt was going through the motions a little with this.
59. A fourth ad for a drummer also appeared that month, this time reading 'Hard, heavy, to hell with your "looks and hair a must" Soundgarden, Zep, Scratch Acid.' This one is a little more interesting, as it's Kurt's first full throated public rejection of the shallow world of hair metal. The inclusion of Soundgarden is also a nod to Seattle solidarity rather than his usual distancing.
60. Malfunkshun were one of the band's featured on the *Deep Six* compilation, and can be considered among grunge's founding fathers. Singer/bass player Andrew Wood went on to form Mother Lover Bone with former-Green River and future Pearl Jam members Stone Gossard and Jeff Ament. Wood was widely expected to become a star and Mother Love Bone predicted to be the first of the Seattle underground bands to get mainstream success. He died from a heroin overdose in 1990.

May 21

- Nirvana, with Dave Foster, now out of jail and unaware his band have been courting and playing with other drummers, play an all-day show at Evergreen College, Olympia. Chad Channing takes them up on their invitation and hangs out with Kurt and Krist. They invite him to come and jam with them in their rehearsal space in Krist's basement in Tacoma. Chad begins rehearsing with Krist and Kurt regularly.[61]
- The rehearsals are some of Nirvana's most intense and intoxicating and the new trio gels quickly, with Kurt's writing and the band's chemistry constantly evolving. Both the finessed version of 'Big Cheese' and 'School' come out of these sessions.[62] 'We'd have the most intense jams,' Krist wrote later in his memoir. 'We'd orbit inner and outer space. It was so serious, if we felt we sucked at rehearsal we were disappointed and we'd sit around bummed out after.'

May 29

- Kurt writes a letter to Dave Foster telling him that his services are no longer required and that the band has found a new drummer. He praises his skills, is extremely apologetic and blames a combination of Dave's lack of availability due to his driving situation and location[63] ('we believe a band needs to rehearse at least five times a week') and cultural differences ('our hobbies and interests are different and a band can't be a unit unless the members are compatible').[64] Kurt

---

61. Chad represents a departure for Kurt and Krist. His recruitment marks the point where they stop being an 'Aberdeen' band and become something else. All of their previous drummers, Dale Crover, Bob McFadden, Aaron Burckhard and Dave Foster, had been local boys and all were connected to the little outsider clique that had grown up around the Melvins. Unlike Aaron (who was in it for the beers), Dave (who didn't really get the scene) and Dale (who was literally in another band) Chad was as much a dedicated, paid up member of the Punk Rock underground as Kurt and Krist were. He didn't actually have a Black Flag tattoo, but he'd probably have considered getting one at some point. Like Kurt, he also had a fondness for cute, weirdo cult bands (it was Chad that introduced him to his beloved Shonen Knife) and, like Krist, he loved classic rock (he introduced both to David Bowie's *The Man Who Sold The World*). He had one foot in the arty Olympia scene and the other in the heavier Seattle one, and lived on Bainbridge Island, a short hop on a ferry from Seattle but 120 miles from Aberdeen. Punk Rock? Check. Classic rock? Check. Underground ethics? Check. Dedicated? Check. Versatile? More or less. His views on Ethel Merman aren't known. He wasn't quite reliable enough behind the kit to take Nirvana all the way, but he was exactly the drummer they needed in 1988. By all accounts he was (and presumably, at the time of writing, still is) also a lovely guy, to boot.
62. 'School' is a huge breakthrough in Kurt's songwriting. While other songs from this period feel very 'Seattle', all sludgey riffs and grinding tempo, 'School' is far more of an 'Olympia' song – super simple (there are only thirteen words, over three lines, in the whole lyric) and based around a brilliantly nagging riff, which when filtered through the Nirvana sound machine becomes darker and heavier and more of a piece with their other material. The words key off of a line in Kurt's letter to Dale Crover, penned after playing their first Vogue show in Seattle: 'Fuck,' he writes. 'I'm in highschool again!'. 'School' would get its live debut later that year (setlist details for mid 1988 are a little sketchy, so it could have been played much earlier) and would have the distinction of being the song Nirvana played most often – at least 290 times between 1988 and 1994. That minimal lyric and insistent riff meant that, unlike a lot of the band's earlier songs, it always felt fresh. From its debut in 1988 onwards, it was played at almost every Nirvana show.
63. This is a bit of a cheek considering the band were occasionally rehearsing at Krist's mother's hair salon, practically in Dave Foster's back yard.
64. This was the real crux of the issue. It's generally agreed that Dave Foster was a decent musician and the band sounded good, plus unlike Aaron he really did want to take his music seriously … though apparently

also apologises for not 'having the guts to tell you in person', with a note scrawled between the lines of text saying 'but we don't know how mad you would get'.[65] Kurt never sends the letter.

- On the same day that Kurt writes his letter, Nirvana make their first appearance with Chad Channing playing drums, at a Sub Pop Sundays show at the Vogue.[66] The band will play occasional shows at house and dorm parties, clubs and small theatres across Washington for the remainder of the year. Chad is never formally asked to join the band.
- Somewhere around this point Nirvana's habit of destroying their gear onstage begins, usually, but not exclusively, at the end of the show. According to Chad the destruction was never planned out. 'It wasn't like we said, "OK Krist, you jump really high and throw your bass in the air and have it knock you out, and Kurt, you get down on the floor and do the worm"' he told Everett True. 'We were [just] so sick and tired of … arena rock .. [It] wasn't what we were about'.[67]
- In late May, Charles Peterson shoots Nirvana for the first time, near Chad's home on Bainbridge Island. The photoshoot takes place in a meadow, in a field of flowers. 'We were all self-conscious about it,' Peterson said later. 'In the end, because we knew it was stupid, the pictures are quite sweet.'[68]

June 11

- Recording begins on Nirvana's debut single, once again at Reciprocal Studios under the careful ear of Jack Endino. Given the speed in which the band knocked out ten songs back in January, everyone expects a half day to be enough to do 'Love Buzz' and a couple of b-side options. However, progress is slow – Kurt feels that Chad's drum sound isn't heavy enough and the band and Endindo spend

---

not enough to take time off work. The main issue was that he and his bandmates had different outlooks. Both sides talked about how the other's friendship group made them uncomfortable. Punk Rock is every bit as snobby and cliquey as any other scene, and Dave didn't fit the mould, he was too mainstream, too typical, too *Aberdeen*. He was fixing up a race car and beating up the guy who slept with his girlfriend. He was from an unbroken home. He had a moustache. None of which were relatable to Kurt Cobain or Krist Novoselic, at least in 1988 (though in later life Krist would have some rather splendid moustaches). The band's friend and sometime manager Ryan Aigner makes the same observation as he made about Aaron Burckhart: 'he wasn't going to get the Black Flag tattoo'.

65. Given Foster's notorious temper, this is understandable. The letter is later reproduced in *Journals*.
66. There is some speculation that Chad actually played with the band at a house party the previous week, however Chad himself has gone on the record as his first show being at The Vogue. Obviously at over thirty years removed, memories are not always reliable.
67. This obviously put a lot of strain on the band's gear and Kurt especially got into the habit of fixing and frankenstein-ing guitars from spare parts. Krist has said that it took him many years after Kurt's death to stop checking for left-handed guitars every time he passed a music store, since he'd gotten so used to keeping an eye out for replacements.
68. The pictures are atypical for a Sub Pop shoot, or a Peterson shoot at the time. They're way more 'Olympia' than they are 'Seattle' – pastoral, sweet and goofy; which is helped by the fact that together Chad and Kurt, both tiny men with long, blonde hair, are *adorable*, while towering Krist is a stringbean goofball. Within a few months, no band on Sub Pop would be photographed without a self-conscious attempt to look a little squalid and urban.

ages trying to get it right.[69] The day's work begins with a fairly sloppy take of 'Blandest', originally envisioned as the b-side, which the band aren't happy with and doesn't set the greatest mood for the rest of the session. Nirvana would have to return to Reciprocal a further three times between June and September to finish their work, eventually recording versions of 'Love Buzz', 'Blandest', 'Big Cheese' and a re-recording of 'Spank Thru', as well as early versions of 'Blew', 'Mr Moustache' and 'Sifting'.

June 17

- The band headline a show at the Hal Holmes Community Centre, which also houses Ellensberg's public library. Also on the bill are Millions of Dead Lenin (aka MDL), King Krab and Lush. Due to a curfew, Nirvana only get to play a handful of songs. After the show Kurt is greeted by Screaming Trees' singer Mark Lanegan, who is deeply impressed.[70] Kurt is already a fan of Lanegan's music, and the two exchange numbers.[71]

---

69. 'Getting the drum sound right' was something that Kurt spent a long time fretting about in Nirvana's early recordings, always shooting for the big, powerful sound that Big Black's Steve Albini, gaining a reputation as an excellent engineer, seemed to get effortlessly on his recordings. 'It must have been 1989 or 1990', Krist told Conan O'Brien during a 2023 podcast to mark the 30th anniversary of *In Utero*. 'We were cruising in our van listening to [Albini produced Pixie's album] *Surfer Rosa* and Kurt put a hand up with one finger pointed and made a decree – "this shall be our snare sound".' Part of the problem was Chad – Kurt was used to drummers like Dave Foster and Dale Crover that beat the living daylights out of their kits; Chad's touch was much lighter.
70. Though Lanegan would later become, arguably, more famous as a solo artist, Screaming Trees were one of the more interesting forces to come out of the whole grunge Sha-bang. Blending punk, psychobilly, pop, psychedelia and hard rock they definitely had more tonal variety than a lot of their peers. They never scaled the heights of Nirvana, Soundgarden, Pearl Jam and Alice In Chains, though like all of those bands they would make the jump from indie to major labels in the 90s. The band finally split up in 2000, having recorded eight genuinely great albums, the last of which wouldn't see a release until 2011. There was another band called Screaming Trees formed at almost exactly the same time in the UK, which shouldn't be a surprise by this point. Honestly, it happened to almost everyone.
71. Mark Lanegan became very close with Nirvana. Kurt admired the intense, unpredictable noise pop of Screaming Trees, then signed to SST, one of Kurt's dream labels. It's astonishing that the two hadn't met earlier, considering how much crossover they had in their friendship groups. Lanegan, from Ellingsberg, Washington, was an old school friend of Calvin Johnson and knew Kurt's friends Dylan Carlson and Slim Moon amongst many others. Possessing a remarkably similar drawl to Kurt's and the same knack for distilling raw feeling into vocal performances, he was one of the few of Cobain's contemporaries that could match him for intensity and pathos, though unlike Kurt he had a baritone that scraped across the bar room floor, with more in common with gravelly outsider genius Tom Waits, than Punk Rock. His life and career are fascinating, and it's arguable that the shape of his work, alternating art forms and switching styles, always interesting, rarely commercial, is a window into how Nirvana and Kurt Cobain's career could have panned out had they never pursued the more accessible direction that made them one of the biggest bands in the world. That said, such spitballing doesn't really get us anywhere – Kurt was Kurt, Mark was Mark. Lanegan had no interest in cultivating mainstream appeal, whereas Kurt was genuinely ambitious and wanted his songs to be heard by *everyone*. And Kurt knew he was good. Though he could be self-deprecating, he often went to bat for how good his own band, songs and albums were (at least until after the fact – both *Bleach* and *Nevermind* were deemed sub-par once their creator had moved on. It would likely have happened with *In Utero* too). Lanegan, on the other hand, struggled with musical self-esteem. He considered Kurt to be a genius with a talent 'genuinely not of this place and time', as he wrote in *Sing Backwards and Weep*, his 2020 memoir. It baffled him that someone with a talent so special would also be a fan of *his* work and band, as Kurt absolutely was.

June

- A few days following the HHCC show, Krist calls Mark Lanegan to ask if Screaming Trees are looking for a bass player, claiming that Kurt's controlling attitude to the band was getting too much for him. Lanegan talks him into continuing with Nirvana, saying 'you guys got something really special there'. [72]

July

- At some point in July, Dave Foster browses the latest edition of *The Rocket* and sees a listing for a Nirvana show at a club called Squid Row in Seattle. It is the first indication that he is no longer a member of the band, who by this point have done several gigs, signed a record deal[73] and started work on their first single, all with Chad Channing on drums. He is livid.

August

- The August edition of *Backlash* is published featuring Dawn Armstrong's interview with Krist and 'Kurdt Kobain'. It's Nirvana's first ever press. The piece features pictures taken before the band's first Vogue show – with Dave Foster cropped out. It's titled 'It may be the devil and it may be the lord, but it sure as hell ain't human'. In the interview, Kurt says that his biggest worry is that the band will be seen 'as a Melvins rip off'. Armstrong doesn't exactly help the cause by referring to the band at one point as 'the Melvins fan club', though she does graciously admit that 'with enough practice Nirvana could become … better than the Melvins'. Elsewhere in the short write-up Kurt admits the band 'weren't ready' for their debut at The Vogue and repeats his line about how 'everyone should have had score cards'. Anderson praises the band's progress ('they can turn an entire audience into pod people') and refers to them as 'the great white hope of grunge'.[74]
- Local photographer Alice Wheeler shoots the band near Krist's home in Tacoma for the cover of the 'Love Buzz' single. Sub Pop's go-to photographer Charles

72. This is a curious detail, revealed in Lanegan's autobiography, *Sing Backwards and Weep*. Krist has never really delved into this side of Kurt in public, and has always painted the band as collaborative, with Kurt as the driving force. He's certainly never openly said he was ever unhappy with that arrangement. Kurt, however, could absolutely be particular and determined about his music – every band has to have someone like that. Unfortunately, that person's drive and vision, while usually the very thing that pushes a band forward, is usually the thing that causes the most friction. It's not at all surprising that a personality as strong as Krist's would occasionally chafe against this – it's something both Chad Channing and future Nirvana guitarist Jason Everman, both songwriters in their own right, would struggle to deal with. Fortunately Krist is, by nature, both easygoing and collaborative, and seems to have been able to keep a handle on his frustrations as the band's career progressed.
73. Figuratively at least. The agreement for 'Love Buzz' was done on a handshake rather than a contract. No-one on Sub Pop's books actually had a contract in place at this point.
74. She also uses 'pain-rock' and 'lead-belly music' to describe the sludgey sounds of Seattle. Creating microgenres is one of the great and timeless traditions of the music press.

Peterson, despite having shot the band once already, is still ambivalent about the trio. 'I usually got the jobs Charles Peterson didn't want', Wheeler would say later tell Mark Yarm.

- Bruce Pavitt and Jonathan Poneman hit upon a money spinning idea for their forthcoming releases – the Sub Pop 'singles club'. This would be a subscription service, charged at $35 a year with members sent a 7″ single every month. Each release, at least at first, would be limited to 1,000 copies.[75] Kurt is disappointed that his debut single isn't going to be given what he considers to be a proper release, but accepts that the idea itself is sound, and that he doesn't really have much choice. 'We were really bummed about that', Krist would later tell his biographer, Michael Azerrad. 'We put a single out and nobody could buy it'.

August 20

- The band is interviewed for a publication called *Nothing*.[76] They complain about being pigeon-holed as a 'real heavy Seattle grunge band'. 'We're gonna break away from that soon', say Kurt. 'We've been working on about 15 songs of mellow type stuff'.[77]

75. The singles club was a massive success with 2,000 subscribers at its peak. Pavitt and Poneman were working hard to create an identity for the label that, like England's Factory, the home of Joy Division, New Order, Orchestral Manoeuvres In The Dark and Cabaret Voltaire, extended beyond the bands it hosted. They wanted the label itself to be a selling point and for people to buy records not just because of the artist but *because they were on Sub Pop*. Both men were music obsessives that understood fandom; the idea of making their releases instant collectibles was a stroke of genius. It helped cement the label as the home of Seattle's exploding grunge scene in the perception of music fans, synonymous with the city and the genre in the same way as Motown was synonymous with Detroit and soul music. The impression was so successful that people often didn't notice that the city's biggest artists, like Soundgarden (after their initial releases), Screaming Trees, Mother Love Bone (and eventually Pearl Jam) and Alice In Chains, were all on different labels. Bands would find themselves advertised across the US and Europe as a 'Sub Pop artist' or 'Seattle grunge' despite only the vaguest association with the label or city. Many of the bands who released 7″s for the Singles Club would never actually record for the label again. Singles Club alumni included Mudhoney, Sonic Youth, Soundgarden, Afghan Whigs, Flaming Lips, Babes In Toyland, L7, Rollins Band and Smashing Pumpkins. 'Sub Pop', like Motown and Factory, came to represent something beyond the records the label actually released.
76. A name that can only have existed pre-Google, because it is absolutely impossible to search for. From context I think this is an Olympia-based fanzine, but I could be wrong. The interview is listed at *livenirvana.com*, which is an excellent resource for early Nirvana press.
77. Which isn't strictly true. Kurt had some mellower songs in his back pocket, but they hadn't made it into the band's set yet. The interview ends with the trio being asked their favourite drink. 'Mrs. Brown's Coffee' says Chad, 'root beer' say Krist and Kurt, with Krist – frequently the drunkest man in the Pacific NorthWest – adding 'alcohol? fuck that.'

September 27

- The band return to Reciprocal to mix their recent recording of 'Spank Thru' with Jack Endino, who also features on backing vocals at Kurt's request, intended for the forthcoming *Sub Pop 200* compilation[78], due for release the following December.[79]

October 28

- Nirvana play their first ever support with a 'big' band, opening for the Butthole Surfers at Seattle's Union Station.[80] The sound onstage is terrible and at one point Kurt slams his guitar into the stage in frustration.

October 30

- Nirvana play a Halloween dorm party at Evergreen, Olympia, with both Kurt and Krist stripped to the waist with fake blood running down their chests. At the end of the set the band indulge in an orgy of destruction, with Kurt properly smashing a guitar to pieces for apparently the first time. The show is great, although friend-of-the-band Slim Moon is livid: his band, Lush, had played one of the best sets of their career earlier that evening and he felt Nirvana's descent into destructive chaos was an attempt to upstage him.

---

78. This would be the only official studio release of 'Spank Thru', though Kurt's Fecal Matter demo version would appear on a posthumous rarities collection in 2004. The song had been recorded once already on the 'Dale Demo' (as well as, more primitively, on the Fecal Matter tape in 1986 and the KAOS radio session the previous year) and attempted again with Chad on drums during the 'Love Buzz' sessions, with the latter considered to be the superior take by the band. It's an important song in Kurt's development, though at this point it was already nearly three years old and his songwriting had long eclipsed it in sophistication. The template for a lot of what Nirvana would become is here – unlike the rest of the band's early recordings it features both clean and heavy parts, a trademark of *Nevermind* but not really featured on *Bleach* at all, and there's both a slamming riff and, that old chestnut, a real pop sensibility, as well as a sense of dynamics. No producer had to tell Kurt to add in those stops in the chorus; that was all him. The theme is kind of goofy and stupid, as befits the teenager who wrote it (it's essentially a paeon to masturbation), but it's solidly catchy and show's that Kurt's melodic instincts were in place long before the songs that made him famous. The band were obviously fond of it, it would remain in their set right to the end of the *Nevermind* era (1992's festival season) when other early songs that were arguably stronger ('Downer', 'Hairspray Queen', 'Floyd The Barber') would fall by the wayside.
79. The previous year's *Sub Pop 100* had been a continuation of the ethos of Bruce Pavitt's fanzine cassettes, now upgraded to vinyl – a collection of underground artists from across the US. *Sub Pop 200*, meanwhile, was more of a manifesto for the label, showcasing only bands local to the Pacific NorthWest and, especially, Seattle. Pavitt and Poneman were deliberately overplaying their hand and writing their own myth. 'We parodied corporate culture through grotesque overstatement', Poneman later said. 'Instead of making *Sub Pop 200* a cheap vinyl record, let's make it an overstated, bloated box set!'. The compilation featured 19 bands, was limited to 5,000 copies and included a 14-page booklet of Charles Peterson's black and white photography capturing the grimy, sweaty excitement of Seattle's scene. It helped underline the sense that 'there's something happening here'.
80. This was a doubly big deal due to the scarcity of touring bands coming through the city – there were few large clubs for them to play, and promoters who did dip their toe into the murky waters of underground music often hastily withdrew it.

November

- 'Love Buzz', the debut single by Nirvana, is released on Sub Pop records, backed with 'Big Cheese'.[81] On the run-in groove are etched the words 'why don't you trade those guitars for shovels', something Krist's dad, a construction worker, was known to yell at his lazy, punk rocker sons. Interest in the Sub Pop singles club means the limited pressing quickly sells out. KCMU, the college radio station based in Seattle, adds 'Love Buzz' to its playlist and the song starts to generate genuine word-of-mouth excitement.
- On a drive home from Seattle to Olympia, Kurt is so impatient to hear 'Love Buzz' on the radio he insists his girlfriend pull over at a gas station so he can call KCMU from the payphone and request his own song. The two couldn't complete their journey until Kurt heard his single played over the airwaves.
- Local writer Grant Alden reviews 'Love Buzz' in the November issue of *The Rocket*. 'Serious traces of musicianship leak through', he says. 'Nirvana sits sort of at the edge of the current NorthWest sound. Too clean for thrash, too pure for metal, too good to ignore'. Elsewhere the review calls the record 'one hell of a first effort'.[82]
- The success of 'Love Buzz' is enough to convince Poneman and Pavitt to plan a Nirvana album, though it comes with the caveat that at present the label doesn't

81. Kurt's lyrics at this point (and to be honest for most of his writing career) are fairly oblique, mostly composed of snatches and fragments he'd collected, although there's often a discernable theme. 'Big Cheese', which has the distinction of being the first original Nirvana song pressed to vinyl and released properly, is actually a broadside at Jonathan Poneman and the pressure Kurt felt from being answerable to a record exec. It's just a little petulant. In a way, it shows Poneman and Pavitt's desire to be seen as a far bigger deal than they actually were was working, even among their own artists – neither could really be considered to be 'big cheeses' in the music industry. The original plan was to back 'Love Buzz' with another song, 'Blandest', but Jack Endino was unimpressed by a lacklustre recording of a tune he considered already to be pretty aptly named. The intention had always been to have another stab at 'Blandest', which Chad had only just learned how to play, but the band never got around to it and eventually the sole take was wiped to free up space on the tape. 'Big Cheese' was, correctly, judged the stronger song anyway. 'Blandest' survives only because the band kept a cassette of their work-in-progress, mixed at 3am on the day of the recording and complete with tape wibbles and hiss. It eventually surfaced on the *Sliver: Best of the Box* compilation. Do you know what? It's honestly not that bad.
82. 'Love Buzz' caused a genuine sea-change for Nirvana, particularly among the Seattle crowd. While they'd been a decent, if haphazard, live band (and were admittedly getting better as they, and particularly Kurt, got more confident on stage) the noisy shows in shitty clubs with dreadful PA systems didn't exactly do their songs any favours. 'They were super loud and sloppy', James Burdyshaw of the band Cat Butt Told Nicholas Soulsby of one of their mid-88 shows. 'They fell on the stage and screamed a lot. Kurt seemed very drunk.' Nirvana were just another solid, noisy punk band in a town that was increasingly full of them, though their sheer heaviness meant they stood out in the more indiepop-oriented Olympia. 'Love Buzz', though, was undeniably good: mesmeric, groovy, dynamic, heavy and melodic. Sure it was a cover, but the original was hardly a well known standard. Besides which, the whole thing is just so very *Nirvana* and you can hear the chemistry in the band, especially in the solo where Krist breaks out of Shocking Blue's mesmeric groove into a super-melodic jam over Kurt's noise-rock solo. Then there's Kurt's scream over the final 'BUZZ!' of each verse. No-one else screamed like Kurt Cobain. Not since John Lennon's gut-punching 'momma don't go!' on the outro of 'Mother' on the *Plastic Ono Band* album. It's a howl that would, within a few years, take over the world. 'I think a lot of people would *like* to say they were blown away by one of those early shows' local record store owner and future Sub Pop staffer Nils Bernstein told Carrie Borzillo, 'but for most people it took the single for them to pay any real attention'.

have the available cash to fund the recording.[83] Nirvana, frustrated by Sub Pop's lack of money and what they perceive to be favouritism toward other bands (notably Mudhoney[84]), keep shopping demos around to other labels, again offering to pay recording and pressing costs for an LP themselves. No-one is interested.

- Kurt asks his friend Tam Orhmund to be the band's new manager, on the grounds that she has great taste in music and lives in Seattle. She's instructed to put together a press kit using existing clippings and send a copy of the 'Love Buzz' 7″ to Touch 'N' Go and the other usual indie label names. No-one bites. Eventually Orhmund's role simply fades away.

December 1

- The band open for punk legends D.O.A at Seattle's Underground club. The headline band miss them completely.[85]

December 7

- *The Rocket* publishes its annual *Rocket Music Directory.* Nirvana's entry reads 'Nirvana: Gunka, gunka, clank, ahh, plunk, deedle, deedle, wah, eeak, unk' and lists the band's contact address as 1502 E. Olive Way, 509, Seattle, WA 98102

December 24

- Nirvana head to Reciprocal to work with Jack Endino on their debut album. This will be the first of several sessions, continuing sporadically until the end of January, clocking in at around 30 hours of studio time. Though this marks the *official* start of recording, technically work on the album had begun almost a year before and continued in the summer: the band attempt to re-record 'Floyd The Barber', 'Paper Cuts' and 'Downer' but ultimately feel they can't surpass the versions done back in January with Dale Crover.[86] The sessions for the 'Love Buzz' single in June also contributed as the band had already cut early versions of 'Blew' and 'Sifting' that are now reworked for the album. They are even using the same tape, saving money by recording over ropier takes from earlier in the year. Recording goes smoothly, with the band well-drilled, as they had been on

83. Being completely broke continued to be Sub Pop's biggest issue. Jack Endino once said that on days the label issued its payment cheques there would be a rush to cash them as quickly as possible as everyone knew that if they waited too long (sometimes even later that same day) the label would be broke again and the cheques would bounce. A lot of the cash the label *did* have was going into finishing Green River's debut album *Rehab Doll* – something of a sunk cost fallacy, since the band had already splintered off to form the diametrically opposed Mudhoney and Mother Love Bone. With no band to promote the album the chances of it recouping were pretty slim.
84. Kurt's journals contain several examples of him complaining about the label focusing on Mudhoney at the expense of other bands.
85. My band opened for D.O.A in a tiny club in Indianapolis during a US tour in 2018. It is literally the only bit of crossover I have with Nirvana, and I will cling to it. They didn't watch us, either.
86. Partly this is down to Chad Channing, who is great on the songs he helped arrange and write drum parts for, but less effective when replicating parts originated by Crover or even Dave Foster.

their first recordings, and the sessions are efficient with everyone happy with the results. The only part of the process that isn't well prepared is Kurt's lyrics, with him often finishing them at the very last minute.[87] Musically, there is little in the way of overdubbing and studio trickery, and the band is relying on Jack Endino's knack for capturing their raw energy cleanly. For reference, they bring in a copy of AC/DC's *For Those About To Rock*, telling Endino it's the sort of sound they're looking for.

At one point, Kurt and Krist tune all of their strings down a step for the song 'Swap Meet'[88], giving it a looser feel. They then move on to record 'Blew', which is written in drop-D[89]. Everyone has by now forgotten that their guitars are in a lower tuning already, so when Krist and Kurt tune their bottom strings down further they're actually playing in the absurdly low key of drop-C. It sounds grindingly cool and heavy, though no-one realises exactly why until after the song is complete. The band offer to record it again in the proper tuning, but Jack Endino insists the new version sounds great – a true happy accident. [90] The super-low bass riff will eventually open the album.

With Krist living once again in Aberdeen, having temporally split with his girlfriend, a day's recording now involves him driving to Olympia to pick up Kurt, then the Bainbridge Island ferry near Seattle to pick up Chad, and on into the city to the studio, doing the whole thing in reverse after the session

87. Kurt's lyrics were often cut and paste combinations of cool sounding lines and slogans with a central theme hovering somewhere amongst it all. The emphasis was on scanning melodically rather than poetic depth – though as his career continued his abilities as a poet and lyricist improved dramatically; his words on *In Utero* are stunning. But that, of course, is in the future. Everett True, probably the journalist most associated with the band, argues that the meaning in Kurt's lyrics has always been secondary. 'Nirvana were always more about the intonation, the energy, the emphasis Kurt placed on certain syllables and guitar riffs than actual words' he says in his memoir *Nirvana: The True Story*. 'And don't trust anyone who tells you any different.'

Around the time Kurt was writing and recording *Bleach* there was definitely a sense of 'good enough', and he would go on record later as saying he didn't 'hold any of those lyrics dear to me'. There are some jewels amid the muck, however – 'About A Girl' has a brilliant lyric, domestic and dispassionate, sarcastic and oddly warm. Even its title, which was casually tossed out when Chad asked Kurt what the song was about, has a kind of primitive poignancy. This is also true of the lean, minimalist but brutally effective 'School'. Kurt had notebooks filled with snatches of poetry and lyrics, and it was often a case of flicking through it to find a line that scanned with the melody.

88. As any guitar nerd will tell you, this means the strings are now tuned (low to high) D, G, C, F, A, D.

89. In which the top five strings of the guitar and top three of the bass are in 'standard' tuning (low-to-high, A, D, G, B, E and A, D, G respectively) but the lowest string is tuned down a whole step to D, giving a much heavier, sludgier sound, where barred power chords that can be played with a single finger, meaning it's easier to play faster, heavier riffs. You can also write some gorgeously melodic stuff in drop-D: Foo Fighters' 1996 hit 'Everlong', written by future Nirvana members Dave Grohl and Pat Smear, does this beautifully.

90. Nirvana were, if only by serendipity, ahead of their time here. Super-low tunings would become fairly common in heavy music fifteen years later when nu-metal bands ruled the roost. Korn's guitarists Munky and Head (not the names their parents gave them) played 7-string guitars, fitted with an additional lower string on top of the usual six, tuned down as low as A. It creates an exceptionally heavy sound that slams through the speakers, with basslines that rattle so much they're practically percussion. The best use of drop-C itself in heavy metal, aside from 'Blew', remains System of a Down's 'Chop Suey', and I'll fight anyone that disagrees.

finishes. He is driving around 244 miles for every recording day or rehearsal. In the thick of winter, always brutal in the NorthWest, the band all have colds and work is done while jacked up on codeine-heavy prescription cough mixture, which adds to the grinding and woozy tone of songs like 'Sifting' and 'Blew'.

Total costs for recording the album come in at $606.17[91], with the band deciding to pay the bill due to Sub Pop's lack of funds.[92] No-one in Nirvana has this sort of cash, so the money is loaned to them by Jason Everman, an old school friend of Chad's.[93]

December 28

- Nirvana open the *Sub Pop 200* release party, alongside Blood Circus, Throw Ups, Swallow and TAD, which takes place across two nights at Seattle's Underground club. By all accounts the band are great, and many of their peers, who had seen them on and off in Seattle and Olympia across the last year, are taken aback by their growth. 'I did not see that craft in the same guy who just a few months earlier was doing nothing but screaming in Squid Row' James Burdyman of Cat Butt, who played the next night, later told Everett True. 'The rest of the night I couldn't give a fuck about any of the other bands, all I could think about was how good Nirvana was.' John Troutman, a friend of band benefactor Jason Everman, and a local record store employee, describes them in Carrie Borzillo's

91. The tiny budget for *Bleach* became part of Nirvana's legend far quicker than you might think – journalists were bringing it up in interviews as early as the winter of 1989; a neat bit of typical myth making from Sub Pop, who included the figure in press blurbs. Poneman and Pavitt instinctively knew how to play the PR game. The claim, however, isn't actually accurate – $606.17 was the cost of the studio time across December '88 and January '89, true, and that was officially the sessions for the album … but Endino and the band had made extensive use of the 'Dale Demo' and 'Love Buzz' recording sessions earlier in the year, which had already been paid for. The true costs of recording was actually closer to $1,000. Still peanuts, frankly, but almost twice the budget that was claimed. For all of that, *Bleach* is still an astonishingly cheap record when you consider it has racked up sales in the millions.
92. This is, obviously, a terrible deal for any band on any record label. The *whole point* of a label is to cover the recording, distribution, marketing and manufacture of your record, and Sub Pop had fallen at the first hurdle. By offering to pay for the recording themselves, however, Nirvana held an ace up their sleeve – for a little while at least, they would be free to take their album elsewhere if an offer arrived. Even Jack Endino was in on it, 'they weren't sure they wanted to put it out on Sub Pop' he told Mark Yarm. 'They were still thinking, maybe we can get on Touch and Go or SST or some other label'. In an undated and unsent letter to an old school friend, Jesse Reed, written somewhere in the latter half of 1988 and included in *Journals*, Kurt says that the band had 'refused to do anything else with Sub Pop, even though they want to put out an EP. We've decided to put out our own LP'. The letter even details back-of-a-cigarette-packet maths for a DIY vinyl release. The label's willingness to commit to an album obviously changed that – the band were desperate to do a real record, capitalising on the buzz (and, indeed, the love) they'd generated with their single and getting something out into stores that wasn't a limited edition, subscriber's only 7". With no offers forthcoming, you can see why they seized the opportunity in front of them, but you also can't blame them for keeping their options open. Another of Kurt's unsent/undated letters, this one to his friend Mark Lanegan of Screaming Trees and penned at some point that Autumn, complains that 'Sub Pop is always broke so we're openly looking for another offer'.
93. Everman had an unusually solid work ethic for one of the so-called slacker generation. For the previous few years he had been spending the summers working on a fishing boat with his father in Alaska, and had saved up something in the region of $20,000. The loan was never paid back. We'll meet Everman again shortly.

book *Nirvana: The day by day Eyewitness Chronicle* as 'unquestionably the best' band on the bill.[94]

December 31

- Having now agreed to let Sub Pop release their album, the band is still distrustful of music industry 'big cheeses' and decide they need a formal contract with their label[95]. A drunk Krist Novoselic turns up on Bruce Pavitt's doorstep that night. Pavitt himself is at a New Year's party at a neighbours house and it's only by chance that he pops home and is able to receive his visitor, who is apparently yelling 'you fuckers! We want a contract!'[96]. 'He is intimidating' Pavitt will later tell Everett True. 'He is drunk, he is big, he is aggressive.' A slightly shaken Bruce tells Krist that a contract will not be a problem and calls Jonathan Poneman. The pair agree to officialise their relationship with Nirvana.[97]

94. This is testimony to how much the trio had gelled through six months or so of extensive jams and rehearsals, sharpened to a diamond point by the preparation for the album recording. Until now, Nirvana would have been lucky to be considered the best band on *any* bill, let alone one as strong as this was.
95. Recording on the album had begun only a week earlier, at which point Jack Endino still felt that the band were keeping their options open, so presumably it was in that final week of 1988 that Nirvana decided it was worth putting all of their eggs in Sub Pop's basket. That month Kurt had taken a book out from the library – *All You Need To Know About The Music Industry* by Donald Passman. It evidently impressed upon him the need for a legally binding agreement when dealing with the record biz, something Sub Pop had rarely entered into. Within a few months Kurt was publically dedicated, or at least resigned, to the Sub Pop cause, saying in an interview with college newspaper *Current* that they had 'definite plans for staying' on the label.
96. As quoted in Charles R Cross's *Heavier Than Heaven.*
97. Sub Pop, as we have seen, preferred to operate on handshake agreements and on a release-by-release basis, rather than extended, formalised deals. Nirvana weren't the first of their artists to insist on a contract: apparently underground poet and performance artist Jesse Bernstein had already demanded a real agreement with the label, and Poneman and Pavitt were negotiating a contract with Soundgarden as well, who had rather complicated things by also signing to SST (no doubt to Kurt Cobain's lasting jealousy). However, Nirvana's, by common consent, appears to be the first contract the label actually signed.

Part Two

It's Fun to Lose

1989

January 1

- Nirvana's new, three-album deal with Sub Pop records comes into force. It promises the band an advance of $6,000 in their first year with the label, with options for $12,000 for their second and $24,000 for their third. According to the terms of the contract the band must deliver an album's worth of material to the label for each year they are signed.[1] 'Three LPs and three long years', Kurt will later say in a note to a journalist at *Current*, the student newspaper at Green River College. 'I feel like I just signed my life away'.

January 2

- A Nirvana song is played on British radio for the first time. Influential DJ John Peel, whose late-night show on BBC Radio One is a must-listen for UK music fans, discovered Sub Pop via Mudhoney's 'Touch Me, I'm Sick' and has just received the *Sub Pop 200* album, from which he is enthusiastically playing cuts. Despite this, it isn't 'Spank Thru' that debuts on Peel's show that night, nor is it even 'Love Buzz'. Instead, Peel opts to flip the band's debut single and Nirvana make their international radio debut with 'Big Cheese', introduced as from 'a new band on Sub Pop records'. After the song ends Peel mentions that 'older viewers will know there was an earlier Nirvana … and back in 1967, when I used to do a programme called *Top Gear* on Radio One, pre-FM of course, this used to get played a great deal'[2], before playing 'Pentecost Hotel', a 1967 folk-rock song by an Anglo-Irish-Greek duo also called Nirvana.[3]

---

1. Though the contract is dated for January 1, 1989, it's very likely that it is backdated. Poneman and Pavitt, neither of whom were exactly experts in contract law, and who certainly couldn't afford a lawyer, assembled the document by photocopying examples out of library books. It's also made out in the names of all *four* members of the band – which we'll come to shortly. A decision to recruit a fourth member wasn't taken until February of 1989. The label certainly couldn't afford to give Nirvana their $6,000 advance yet. In fact, shortly afterwards Bruce Pavitt would attempt to borrow $5,000 from Kurt in order to get *Bleach* produced. Kurt Cobain, living off his girlfriend and money he was earning from a part time job as a janitor, hung up on him. The fact Pavitt thought that Kurt might have that kind of money, especially given the state of his guitars and amps, is a little surprising. In the end, Sub Pop borrowed the cash from someone else.
2. If you're old enough to have listened to John Peel you almost certainly read this in his voice.
3. It's not known at which point Kurt and Krist became aware that a previous band had shared their name, but it obviously didn't trouble them too much. In a draft press release found in Kurt's journals, which dates

January 6

- Nirvana open for Mudhoney at the Satyricon club in Portland, Oregon[4], both their first gig outside of their home state and their first show with their more high-profile labelmates.[56]

January 24

- The final day recording and mixing on the album that would become *Bleach.*

January 30

- John Peel gives 'Spank Thru' its UK radio debut.

---

from early 1989, he writes 'we realise that there was once a 60s band called NIRVANA but don't get us confused with them because they totally suck Big Fucking Dick'. In a 1990 interview filmed at a show in Cambridge, MA, they're described by Kurt as 'this dick-head prog rock band'. Which is a bit harsh, because the original Nirvana were actually pretty good. Their debut album, *The Story of Simon Simopath*, released on Island records in 1967, is one of the first true concept records to come out of the London psych pop scene, and had been released to reasonable acclaim (not least from John Peel). Nirvana #1 disbanded in 1971 after the failure of their third album, though founding member Patrick Cambell-Lyons continued to record under the name into 1972. The original Nirvana reformed in 1985 to tour Europe, releasing a best-of compilation in 1987, thus their reunion shadows the emergence of their nascent namesakes across the Atlantic, neither presumably aware of the other just yet. It's rather satisfying that John Peel had a hand in popularising both bands. Nirvana (UK) eventually attempted to sue Nirvana (US) over rights to the name, which is sort-of fair enough, as they certainly got there first. The matter was settled out of court in 1992, with a behind-the-scenes deal done to allow both bands to continue to release records and tour under the name 'Nirvana'; which is itself a little unusual – usually one or the other would have to change their name, at least in the other's native territory (hence British indie band Suede are known as The London Suede in the US and American power pop band The Beat go by Paul Collins' Beat in Europe.) According to Everett True, the original Nirvana were paid $100,000 for the use of their name.

4. Nirvana would play Portland so often that they were practically counted as a local band. Only Olympia and Seattle accrued more Nirvana shows.
5. Mudhoney, at this point, were the revolting jewel in the Sup Pop crown. The quartet had formed from the ashes of Green River, singer Mark Arm's sleaze-rock-tinged previous group. Commercial ambition had driven a wedge straight through the heart of the band, with Arm and guitarist Steve Turner drawn to the ethos of the underground scene, while guitarist Stone Gossard and bass player Jeff Ament wanted commercial success on a major label. It was an ideological split that couldn't be resolved. Gossard and Ament, along with guitarist Bruce Fairweather who had replaced Turner after he jumped first, would go on to form Mother Love Bone with Andrew Wood, a band with clear rock star ambition (after Wood's death in 1990, they would go on to form Pearl Jam), while Turner and Arm hooked up with Bundle of Hiss drummer Dan Peters and former Melvins bass player Matt Lukin to form the willfully grimier and much less commercial Mudhoney. The band recorded their debut EP *Superfuzz BigMuff* with Jack Endino in 1988 and its lead single, 'Touch Me, I'm Sick', became Sup Pop's signature release, helping gain exposure for the Seattle scene. It perfectly encapsulates the label and the first wave of grunge – noisy and uncompromising but with a belting pop heart, folding in The Stooges, Sex Pistols, underground Punk Rock like Black Flag and classic rock like Aerosmith and Black Sabbath, with guitars played through fuzz pedals (favoured brands of which lend their name to the group's debut EP). It was the first Sup Pop record to really get noticed by the influential British music press, leading to a *Melody Maker* cover for the band in early 1989 and a European tour (and a split 7" via the Sub Pop Singles Club) with Sonic Youth. Kurt Cobain put *Superfuzz Bigmuff* in a 1993 list of the best albums of all time. Courtney Love (more of whom later) says she was inspired to start her own band after hearing 'Touch Me, I'm Sick'. Later, she sent records by Mudhoney and Nirvana to her friend Jennifer Finch, who would go on to form L7. According to Everett True, Finch says she played both and her first reaction was 'wow, Mudhoney could really make some money'.
6. There is some suggestion that Courtney Love was at this show as an audience member.

February

- Nirvana decide to expand their line up with an additional guitarist, mainly to take the pressure off of Kurt, who is self-conscious about having to sing and play at the same time. At Chad's suggestion the job is offered to Jason Everman, the friend who had recently helped out with the loan that funded the recording sessions for the album.
- At the suggestion of Anton Brookes, who handled PR for Sup Pop's UK distributors, Poneman and Pavitt pay for a *Melody Maker* journalist, Everett True, to fly to Seattle with a photographer to experience the city's scene, get exposed to some of the bands on the label and interview Mudhoney[7]. They send him *Sub Pop 200* and a stack of 7″s – he is completely smitten and develops a close relationship with the Sub Pop team and many of the label's acts.[8]

February 7

- Jason Everman makes his debut with Nirvana at a dorm party at Evergreen in Olympia; later that night he is formally invited to join the band.

February 10

- Nirvana play their first California show, opening for the Melvins at the Covered Wagon in San Francisco. While looking for a pharmacy for flu medicine in the city's Haight Ashbury district, they spot an AIDS awareness poster advising heroin users to 'Bleach your works'. Kurt is fascinated that a substance as common as household bleach might become a valuable, life-saving resource. Bruce Pavitt, who is along for the ride, suggests they name their forthcoming album, originally to be called *Too Many Humans,* simply *Bleach.*

February 11

- The band open for Mudhoney in San Jose. Despite everyone being sick and the show being poorly attended, Mudhoney's Steve Turner rates this as his all-time favourite Nirvana performance. At one point Kurt plays guitar standing on his head.

---

7. It's difficult for modern audiences to understand how vastly different the music press was in the UK and US in the 80s and early 90s. The only really mainstream, national US music magazine was *Rolling Stone*, which certainly didn't cater to the underground (its alternative rival, *Spin,* had only gotten a few years under its belt at this point and wasn't a major player). Smaller, regional and specialist magazines like Chicago's *Maximumrocknroll* and Seattle's *Rocket*, fanzines like *Suburban Punk* or college-focussed publications like *CMJ New Music Report* and *Rockpool* didn't have huge, national footprints. The UK was blessed with a truly national music press that was focussed on cooler, independent bands – the big three were *NME*, *Melody Maker* and *Sounds*, and its rock-focussed weekly spin-off, *Kerrang!* These magazines, of which only *NME* and *Kerrang!* now survive, and in reduced form, were genuine tastemakers that wielded real clout. The music press in the US actually took its cues from the UK, so a good tactic was to break US bands in Britain first and let the American press pick up the scent from across the pond.
8. True is probably the journalist most associated with Nirvana and his memoir, *Nirvana: The True Story*, despite its punny title and some factual inconsistencies (which True fesses up to) is, for my money, the most evocative book on the band yet written.

February 18

- *Melody Maker*'s Everett True gives Nirvana their first mention in the British press, reviewing 'Love Buzz' alongside two other singles, U-Men's 'Solid Action' and Some Velvet Sidewalk's 'I Know', all underground Seattle and Olympia bands. His write up of 'Love Buzz' is delirious. 'Nirvana are beauty incarnate' he writes, describing the song as 'a relentless two-chord garage beat which lays down some serious foundations for a sheer monster of a guitar force to howl over. The volume control ain't been built yet which can do justice to this three-piece!' True, who is completely smitten with the sounds emerging from the Pacific NorthWest, concludes his piece by asking 'WHAT IS GOING DOWN OVER THERE?'

February 25

- Nirvana play with Jack Endino's band, Skin Yard, alongside The Fluid and Girl Trouble at Seattle's University of Washington HUB Ballroom[9]. It's the biggest show the band have yet played, with an estimated audience of around 600, testimony to the growing excitement around the city's rock scene. The crowd's enthusiastic slam dancing and crowd surfing, alongside Nirvana's now familiar orgy of destruction, leads the venue's management to cancel future live gigs. Everett True, in the middle of his Seattle sojourn on Sub Pop's dime and being outrageously indulged by his hosts, performs a short set himself in his oddball pop guise of The Legend! before the headliners. [10]
- After the show the band hang out at Jason's place and Kurt and Krist rib him relentlessly about his heavy metal record collection. One friend told Carrie Borzillo that walking into Jason's metal-themed bedroom was 'like walking into *Hellraiser*'.

---

9. Nirvana, The Fluid and Girl Trouble all appeared on *Sub Pop 200*, however despite Jack Endino's close association with the label, Sub Pop were not especially interested in Skin Yard, who they considered too trad metal. The band did put out a 7″ through the Singles Club later that year though, which given everything Endino did for them is the least they could do.
10. Reports vary on this night. Several fans in attendance are on record as saying that Nirvana were incredible, and it's the first time that the sceptical photographer Charles Peterson was genuinely impressed by them. Charles R Cross, former editor of *The Rocket*, claims the apex of the night's slam dancing and stage-diving occurred during Nirvana's set, saying that they were the perfect soundtrack to such violent expressions because they 'never slowed down and rarely even paused between numbers'. Everett True, meanwhile, found the band *under*whelming, and remembers a lot of faffing and tuning between songs which, in fairness, sounds a lot more like Nirvana than the slick machine Cross describes. He also remembers an indifferent audience response, with The Fluid getting the lion's share of the slam dancing and crowd surfing. It's possible that True's disappointment comes because he was seeing them after weeks of hyping (Jonathan Poneman had been selling them to him hard for the duration of his visit), so while Seattle's gig regulars and Sub Pop's extended family were seeing a band with a fairly ropey live history being much improved with a beefed up guitar sound (and playing through a decent PA on a larger stage for once), True was approaching the show from the other side – a much-touted band whose single he had loved, who to him ended up being a let-down when he found them to be 'another formless compendium of noise for noise's sake, no pop tunes or spark or anything.'

March 18

- Everett True's *Melody Maker* piece on Sub Pop is published in the UK.[11] Alongside a full feature on Mudhoney is a double-page rundown of the best of the Pacific NorthWest's rock scene. Working to a tight deadline and with no band bios available, True has simply phoned Sub Pop's office and spoken to Jonathon Poneman, who dictated descriptions for his acts which were written down verbatim. Nirvana's reads 'No rock star contrivance, no intellectual perspective, no master plan ... You're talking about four guys in their early twenties from rural Washington who want to rock. You're talking about four guys who, if they weren't doing this, would be working in a supermarket or lumber yard, or fixing cars.' [12] An accompanying interview snippet, taken from a much longer conversation True had with the band the previous month, sees Krist doubling down on this 'real scary; redneck hometown backwoods' version of the band's origins.

April 7

- Nirvana play a headline show at the Annex Theatre, Seattle, supported by Love Battery. Kurt dives into the audience during 'Blew' and is carried aloft by the crowd, something which Jonathan Poneman can only remember happening to Mudhoney's Mark Arm prior to this.

April 21

- Kurt records a one-off single with The Go Team, a side project of Calvin Johnson also featuring drummer Tobi Vail, which has been an ongoing concern since 1985, releasing occasional cassettes and 7″s featuring various guests.[13] Kurt works on a song called 'Scratch It Out', due for release later in the year.

April 22

- An interview with Nirvana runs in the UK music magazine *Sounds*, conducted over the phone earlier in the year by journalist John Robb, in which they are described

11. Though the piece in *Melody Maker* was Nirvana's first UK press, Everett True wasn't the first British music journalist they spoke to – John Robb of *Sounds* had already conducted a telephone interview, though his piece wouldn't be published until after True's.
12. True is constantly plagued by the fact that the most quoted piece of writing of his entire career was actually dictated by Jonathan Poneman.
13. In many ways The Go Team (not to be confused with The Go! Team, the noughties English indie-dance outfit of nearly the same name) were the soul of Olympia's twee scene – more of an idea than actual band with a shifting membership in which everyone would change instruments. One of their earliest releases was completely instrumental with a note inviting the listener to write their own words. In 1989 they were attempting to release monthly 7″s on Johnson's K Records with various collaborators, including Everett True in his occasional indiepunk singer guise of The Legend! (Under which name he recorded '73 in 83', the first single put out by Alan McGee's Creation Records). The project appealed to Kurt, who despite playing in a very loud punk rock band, was kicking against the narrow, meathead mentality that was part of most rock scenes. Johnson and Vail's rejection of virtuosity and foregrounding of art-for-arts-sake was the antithesis of bands like Mother Love Bone and Soundgarden.

as 'the potential trump card in Sup Pop's pack'. It is their second interview to be published in the UK music press.[14]

May

- Around this point the band starts using their 'Elvis Cooper' backdrop – a large picture of Elvis Presley with Alice Cooper's trademark make-up daubed in magic marker.[15]

June

- At an unspecified date, Nirvana record a session at Evergreen State College, produced by Greg Barbior of Lush. Ostensibly the band are there to record a cover of the Kiss song 'Do You Love Me' for a tribute album being issued by C/Z records. The quartet learned the song in the van on the way to the session and, tanked up on red wine, deliver a fairly straight-forward but not-exactly respectful, rather half-assed version, complete with a lot of goofing around at the end of the song, pastiching the macho posturing that crops up on the original record. The band also do a few takes of a new song, 'Dive'.[16]

June 9

- The first of Sub Pop's 'Lame Fest' shows takes place at the 1,400-capacity Moore Theatre in Seattle[17] – a substantially bigger venue than any of the bands are used

14. Though, as discussed, the first to be conducted.
15. If you're looking for a working definition of the band's sense-of-humour and outlook, then this is it. Elvis was the ultimate symbol of the musical establishment and comfortably the most beloved and revered figure in American musical history. Hitching his image to the cartoon debauchery of Alice Cooper was a joyous slaughtering of sacred cows.
16. 'Do You Love Me' is a pretty obsolete footnote in the output of the band. It's badly recorded and totally goofy, with a rare vocal performance from Krist Novoselic that is somewhere between hilarious and unlistenable ('oh god, that was a disaster', Krist would later tell Conan O'Brien on a 2023 podcast). You get the sense that the parody is affectionate rather than vicious, though. Kiss was rarely one of those bands Nirvana took aim at, and you'll be hard pushed to find any American rock fan raised in the 70s who didn't have a soft spot for the band. Rather than the product itself, the session is notable for two reasons: Firstly, this is the only time Nirvana ever recorded in the studio with Jason Everman on guitar. Everman had carefully maintained the party line that he'd played on *Bleach* in several interviews (for example, 'we went out on a limb and recorded five new songs' he told *Flipside* that Spring) but hadn't made it onto a Nirvana record until this point. Nor would he again. More notable than Jason, however, is the earliest known airing of 'Dive', one of Kurt's first truly great songs (I would argue that 'About A Girl' was the other) and a huge leap forward in his songwriting. The band ripped through the song instrumentally several times (including a pretty out-of-place, slightly awkward Jason Everman guitar solo), with Kurt apparently working on the lyrics as they listened to the playback.
17. 'Lame Fest' was, of course, a genius title for the label's annual 'big gig'. It played wholesale to the mythology of what would become known as 'Generation X' (although that nickname wouldn't crop up until after Douglas Copeland's book of that name had been published in 1991) or the 'slacker generation'. Sub Pop made disaffection and miserablist self-deprecation part of its brand. Around this time the label started printing t-shirts that simply said 'LOSER' in giant letters – they sold incredibly well. It's the same thinking that was behind the quote Jonathan Poneman fed Everett True about how Nirvana would be chopping wood, fixing cars or stacking shelves if they weren't playing music, or how Tad Doyle was portrayed as a hulking, barely literate brute rather than, as was actually the case, a whip-smart polymath who had once played jazz drums at the White House for President Nixon. Like the English punks of the 70s,

to. On the bill are Nirvana, TAD and Mudhoney[18], billed as 'Seattle's lamest bands in a one-night orgy of sweat and insanity'. The event doubles as a release party for *Bleach*, which is available to buy for the first time at the merch table. Expectations are low, with TAD's Tad Doyle and Mark Arm, of headliners Mudhoney, both feeling that the label has bitten off more than it could chew with such a large venue. Promoters at the Moore Theatre itself feel very much the same, and book less security than they habitually would have. The show sells out.[19]

June 10

- Contrasting the previous evening's successes, Nirvana play a last minute show opening for Cat Butt in Portland. The gig is virtually empty, and the band spend the show taking requests.

June 15

- *Bleach* is officially released, with a 1,000 copies pressed on white vinyl and a further 2,000 on more traditional black vinyl with a free poster.[20] The press blurb,

Sub Pop learned to celebrate anti-intellectualism, boredom and anti-fashion as branding. As an added bonus, if you were already calling your gigs 'lame' and your fans 'losers', you were stopping anyone else from getting those insults in first. Pavitt and Poneman would later say that these marketing ticks were all instinctive rather than thought-through. Nevertheless, they were effective.

18. One account also lists another Sub Pop band, Blood Circus, but I can't find any evidence of that from any other source.
19. Bruce Pavitt would later tell Mark Yarm that Lame Fest was 'the moment that grunge blew up'. As with everything the Sub Pop bosses throw around it's a sentiment that should be taken with far more than a pinch of salt – Lame Fest wasn't a catalyst in itself, but it *was* a very public example of how popular the local scene had become. A lot of people needed to see that to believe it – including many of the bands themselves. As Mudhoney's Steve Turner comments in his memoir, 'wow! Who are all these people and where were they a year ago?'. A review in the *Seattle Times* read 'The whole point of this show seems to be based on the perverse, reverse idea that grungy, foul-mouthed, self-despising meatheads who grind out undifferentiated noise and awing [sic] around their long hair are good – and "honest" – by virtue of their not being "rock stars." How confounded this primitivism is, which defines bands in the reverse image of someone else's market position, instead of music… If this is the future of rock n' roll, I hope I die before I get much older.' As bad reviews go, Sub Pop couldn't have asked for a better one.
20. Nirvana's *Bleach* is the best selling album Sub Pop has released in its (at the time of writing) nearly-forty year history. Obviously that has a lot to do with how famous Nirvana would become. Kurt Cobain was a globally recognised household name in the way that Mark Arm of Mudhoney or even someone like bone-fide rockstar Chris Cornell of Soundgarden never would be. He transcended the idea of a 'rock star'. And that was before his death elevated him to rock-icon hood. It was more than just the celebrity and major label success, however (I'm assuming you know that's what's coming, right?) *Bleach* is a genuinely great record, though it took a while for people to notice it – one story goes that when the band played an in-store at LA's Rhino Records while on tour, the shop only had five copies in stock. Whether or not they sold them all that day, history does not record. Anyone that *did* buy a copy would find themselves in possession of an unpolished gem. Jack Endino managed to capture something honest and primitive and inject it with a lot of space and clarity without compromising the punk assault. There are *incredible* riffs on here as well – 'Blew', 'School' and 'Negative Creep' especially. There's 'About A Girl', the shiny sixpence in the chimney sweep's ear, instantly disproving anyone who dismissed the record, and the band in general, with the usual adjectives that plagued the grunge groups: 'dirge', 'lumpen', 'tuneless' ect. There's pop hooks all over the place, too; even something super heavy like 'Floyd The Barber' sparkles in the choruses. There's obvious musical chemistry, especially on the breakouts and solos (which notably, and presumably to Jason Everman's discomfort, often feature no overdubbed rhythm guitar at all – Endino captures a three piece band *sounding* like a three piece band, who then went on tour pretending they'd made their album as a quartet). 'Love Buzz' is a great example. Even the tracks recorded with Dale

written by Poneman and Pavitt, reads 'hypnotic and righteous heaviness from these Olympia pop stars.[21] They're young, they own their own van and they're going to make us rich.'[22]

June 16

- Kurt and Krist open for Lush, the band featuring their friends Slim Moon and Greg Barbior, at a show in Olympia promoted by local noisemaker Kathleen Hanna. Billed as 'Industrial Nirvana', the two-piece version of the band improvises (badly) over a drum machine. At one point they are joined by The Go Team's Tobi Vail for a 'noise jam'[23]

June 21

- Kurt, Krist, Chad and Jason return to The Vogue in Seattle to play a warm up for their upcoming tour. They debut two new songs, 'Dive' (as demoed at Evergreen State earlier that month) and 'Polly'.[24]

Crover back at the start of 1988, predating the name 'Nirvana' itself, still sound great. And there's that voice. No-one, honestly no-one, sounds like Kurt Cobain. There's all sorts of cliches and superlatives that you can hurl at that howl, and many have; it has a quality that's hard to nail down. The other Seattle screamers didn't sound like this. There is something utterly and uniquely captivating about that voice. Nirvana would make better records than *Bleach* with more mature songwriting, better fidelity recording and more finessed performances, but there's an argument that it captures the band in an unspoilt, pure form that they would never quite find again. There's a purist hardcore of Nirvana fans for whom it remains their best album. When Sonic Youth's Thurston Moore took his band's new album, *Goo*, to be mastered, it was *Bleach* he took with him as an example of a 'perfect record' (as he says in his memoir) for the mastering engineer to use as a reference point.

21. Categorising the band as 'Olympia pop stars' is an odd choice, as it intentionally goes against Sub Pop's usual mythologising of *Seattle* as a Punk Rock mecca with a tight scene. In truth Nirvana were as much of an Olympia band as they were a Seattle one (neither is completely accurate), but the term 'Olympia pop band' conjures very different vibes to 'Seattle punks'. The band and label were already trying to distance themselves from a pigeonhole that was unarguably doing them some favours.
22. It is extremely unlikely that anyone believed this at the time. It turned out to be more or less true, though.
23. According to witnesses, this never-to-be-repeated version of Nirvana was absolutely awful, which was fine as they weren't taking it in the least bit seriously. Kathleen Hanna and Toby Vail would, of course, go on to form the genre-defining Riot Grrrl band, Bikini Kill.
24. It's worth noting here that, just a week after the release of *Bleach*, Nirvana debuted a song from *Nevermind* for the first time. Kurt claims in several interviews, both around this time and around the release of *Nevermind* two years later, that the band had several more melodic songs in the mould of 'About A Girl' which they had opted to leave off of *Bleach* in order to give that record a specific sonic identity. Aside from maybe 'Clean Up Before She Comes', which never appears to have been in serious consideration for release, 'Polly' and the as-yet-unaired 'Sappy' (which both date back to 1988) are the only possible examples that we know of, suggesting this is probably exaggerated myth-making from Kurt regarding his own band's depth; distancing himself from the grunge crowd. Neither song was attempted in the studio by the band until well after *Bleach* was put to bed. That said, across the second half of 1989 Nirvana would accrue a stack of extremely hummable tunes, notably 'Dive', 'Stain', 'Even In His Youth' and 'Been A Son', so they could have theoretically rehearsed some of these earlier in the year. It does beg the question 'if you have songs that good, why not perform them?'

June 22–July 17

- Nirvana's extensive tour in support of *Bleach* (their first ever tour) begins at The Covered Wagon in San Francisco, a venue they'd played earlier in the year with the Melvins. Despite this nominally being Nirvana's tour, they will actually be the opening act for a local band at many of these gigs – in San Francisco it's the improbably named punk-funk crossover band Bad Mutha Goose. The tour is planned to run for 26 shows and will take Nirvana from the West Coast to Arizona and Texas, through the midwest, on to Philadelphia and New Jersey and across to Boston before finishing in New York City. The quartet will do the whole thing with no road crew or tour manager, taking it in turns to drive their white Dodge van across the vast stretches of highway that criss-cross the United States.[25] The aim for most shows will be to make enough money for motels, food and gas through ticket and t-shirt sales.[26] Across the tour the relationship between Jason Everman and the other three members of Nirvana starts to fray.[27]

---

25. The 'official' Nirvana biography, *Come As You Are,* by *Rolling Stone*'s Michael Azerrad, states that this van was 'soon nicknamed "The Van"'. Which is a fairly preposterous thing to say. Literally all vans are nicknamed 'The Van'.
26. Nirvana's sole shirt on this tour has become something of a classic. Known as the 'Vestibule' shirt, it featured a diagram of the upper circles of hell as depicted in Dante Aligheri's 14th-century poem *Divine Comedy*, which Kurt had found in a book. Recently, the grand-daughter of British artist C.W Scott-Giles attempted to sue Nirvana and their representatives over the image, which she claimed was identical to the *Dante's Inferno* artwork Scott-Giles had created back in the 1940s. The case was thrown out of a California court by a judge who told the plaintiff to try again in the UK, where the image is actually copyrighted. It's all a lot of fuss over nothing, really. Most people buying that shirt in 1989 weren't doing so because of Dante's Inferno. They were buying it because the back of the shirt bore the legend 'Fudge Packin' Crack Smokin' Satan Worshippin' Motherfuckers'. Kurt would later tell *NME* that each member of the band was represented by one of the four statements, though in truth it was just something Krist Novoselic had graffitied on a wall once.
27. Nirvana's first tour was pretty successful, all things considered. Obviously they weren't selling out every night and playing to fanatical crowds and obsessive fans – that would come soon enough. But they were on the road, doing it properly. They were doing what rock bands were supposed to do. Crashing with friends. Playing shows. Eating up the miles. 'God, we were seeing the United States for the first time,' Kurt told Michael Azerrad. 'And we were in a band and we were making enough money to survive. It was awesome. It was just great.' By the time the tour hit the midwest the album had started to get some traction on college radio and word of mouth was starting to spread to the point that audiences were picking up. The band were, more or less, on form. Most nights ended with an orgy of destruction on stage, especially if the gig had been very good or very bad, which meant a lot of the limited funds available went on instrument repairs. Later, after Chad's departure, Kurt would claim that the guitar and drum trashing was often an expression of frustration at his drummer's playing, though given his propensity to be spiteful about former members in interviews, this may or may not be in the case. In Boston, Kurt failed to get his guitar fixed in time and let Jason Everman take sole duties for the night, with Kurt just handling the vocals – the only gig he ever performed as solely a singer. There were adventures and scrapes galore: the time Krist smashed into a dresser full of crockery belonging to Lori Barbero from Babes in Toyland. The time they ended up using their van to help someone move house in New York City. The time they slept in the van (sorry, 'The Van'), clutching baseball bats in case of alligators. They were very young men on the road for the first time, with a record to sell. Life was good – or at least it was for three quarters of the band …

July 13

- The band plays Maxwell's in Hobokon, New Jersey. In attendance are Sonic Youth's Kim Gordon and Thurston Moore[28] and J. Mascis of Dinosaur Jr[29], all of whom are blown away. Kurt hangs out with Mascis and Moore after the show, during which, half joking and half serious, he asks Mascis if he'd be interested in replacing Jason on guitar.[30]

---

28. Sonic Youth were, by this point, the definition of a successful underground band. They were as big as anyone thought a noisy, alternative rock band could get. The previous year they'd released *Daydream Nation*, a bonafide art rock classic that had punched through to the acceptable world of *Rolling Stone* magazine, who judged it the fourth-best alternative rock album of the year (behind Pixies, Soul Asylum and Janes Addiction, but ahead of REM's *Green*). Lead single 'Teen Age Riot' had even made it out of the sheltered bay of college radio and into the rarified and choppy waters of FM rock stations. Whenever Kurt made lists of his favourite albums (a particular pastime of his), *Daydream Nation* was usually there. Sonic Youth themselves had been in the game for a while at this point – *Daydream* was their fifth album, and they had built a nationwide following while remaining uncompromisingly noisy and unassailably cool. The band had emerged from New York's artsy No-Wave scene of the late 70s and early 80s, a discordant, often tuneless and avante-garde response to the overground success of the CBGBs set (Blondie, Television, B-52s, Ramones). Artists like Lydia Lunch and The Contortions took the lessons of the Velvet Undergrond and Yoko Ono and brought them into the 80s, dancing on the bleeding edge where sculpted sound might be considered music or might be considered an art statement. Sonic Youth guitarists Thurston Moore and Lee Ronaldo had been involved in pioneering composer Glenn Branca's discordant 'Guitar Orchestra' (which also featured members of Swans and Helmet in its alumni) and took those lessons in dissonance and discord with them when they hooked up with cool-as-all-hell Californian bassplayer, visual artist and fashionista Kim Gordon, with whom Moore would form the alternative nation's first true power couple. Gordon says that naming their project 'Sonic Youth' crystallised the sort of music they wanted to make – the energised sound of young America's most creative hearts. They'd wound their way through the 80s blending just enough pop sweetness into their gloriously artsy noise to make them, probably, the hippest rock band in America. By 1989 they were ready to take the next step and were in the process of securing proper management and a deal with a major after feeling their recent masterpiece had been handled pretty horribly by their label, Enigma Records. Since Enigma, though an indie, had major label distribution anyway (through EMI and Capitol), they figured they may as well cut out the middle man and sign to a big player themselves. It was an important statement – if Sonic Youth, the most independent and alternative of bands, could deal with the mainstream music biz, then there was no shame in it.
29. Dinosaur Jr had formed from the ashes of first-wave Massachusetts hardcore band Deep Wound, in which Mascis played drums. After the band split in 1984, he and guitarist Lou Barlow re-formed under the name Dinosaur, with Mascis moving to guitar and Barlow to bass, sharing vocals. They were an exciting, hooky, hodgepodge of influences: you could hear classic-sounding songwriting, but also in the mix was a mess of hardcore punk, folk, college rock, fuzzy no-wave art rock (Barlow and Mascis were huge fans of Sonic Youth) and, though Mascis isn't fond of the comparison, the gnarlier end of Neil Young. A messy, self-titled debut album released on Homestead records was largely ignored by almost everyone … except for a San Francisco supergroup called the Dinosaurs, comprised of members of a bunch of acid frazzled 60s hippy bands like Jefferson Airplane and Country Joe and the Fish, who promptly filed a lawsuit (pretty unfairly, since 'Dinosaur' and 'Dinosaurs' are different words). Unable to take on such behomoths, the trio added the 'Jr' onto their name (arguably it's a better name, anyway) forcing a recall and re-release of their second album, *You're Living All Over Me*, which had come out on SST. It was that record, which has become an alt rock classic, that put Dinosaur Jr on the map, focusing their influences into the kind of melodic fuzz that was catnip to college radio and the British music press. By the time they enter the Nirvana story, in the summer of 1989, they had released *Bug*, one of the templates of melodic alternative rock, featuring their classic single 'Freak Scene'. Kurt was a fan, certainly, but considered them contemporaries rather than a direct influence – it's telling that in the exhaustive lists of his favourite albums and songs in his published journals he never lists anything by Dinosaur Jr, although 'Losercore', the debut single by Sentridoh, Lou Barlow's lo-fi side-project, does crop up (though he misatributes it to Barlow's main non-Dinosaur band, Sebadoh). However Dinosaur Jr do make it to a draft of the 'thank you' list for *Nevermind*. Though not the final version. Make of that what you will.
30. He says no. It's unknown how seriously the offer to Mascis was taken – it's unlikely such a strong-willed figure and such a great songwriter in his own right would have survived the dictatorial Cobain, and

July 18

- Nirvana play the Pyramid Club in New York City as part of the city wide festival called 'New Music Seminar'. Though some friends and fans enjoy the show, the band and others in their circle think it's a disaster.[31]

Late July

- During their stay in New York, Kurt and Krist decide that Jason isn't working out as a guitarist. Jason, meanwhile, frustrated by a lack of creative input and less interested in the melodic direction of the new songs, is also unsure Nirvana is the band for him – though he is unaware that the decision has already been made on his behalf. The band decides to cancel the rest of the tour, which was due to continue into Canada, and head back across the country via as direct a route as possible. It's an uncomfortable journey in more ways than one.[32] Kurt and Krist want to leave Jason at the apartment of the band's friend, Janet Billig, with whom they had all been staying during their time in the city, but she talks him out of it. Though he is technically never sacked, after returning to Seattle no-one in Nirvana contacts Jason Everman ever again.[33]

---

with Dinosaur now an established Big Deal, it's not like he needed the job. The following year, rumours spread that he might join Nirvana on drums, replacing Chad. Mascis would eventually get to play with Nirvana in 2014, fronting a reunion of the band in a tiny club in Brooklyn for a gig that followed their Rock 'N' Roll Hall of Fame induction.

31. 'They were awful', as their live booker Danny Bland tells Everett True. Sonic Youth's Kim Gordon, however, notes in her memoir *Girl In A Band* that the show was 'amazing'.
32. Several accounts of this trip, based on interviews with the band, have versions of 'they barely spoke on the way home'. This is probably a slight exaggeration – it takes almost two days to drive from New York City to Seattle. It's unlikely Krist Novoselic has been quiet for that long in his entire life.
33. There's a few different versions of why Jason departed Nirvana. Later, when the band were feeling generous they would tell interviewers that it was a matter of musical differences, though when they were in a more spiteful mood things took a nastier turn. Kurt, for example, told his biographer Michael Azerrad, that Jason was the only fly in the ointment on that first tour – 'if Jason wasn't such a prick, it would have been much better'.

Everman turned up in the Nirvana story at the exact point he was needed. The band had been toying with the idea of another guitarist to take the pressure off Kurt, he was a friend of Chad's, who vouched for him, he seemed cool, more or less ... and he had *pots* of money. Jason had spent his summers working on commercial fishing boats in Alaska and had saved something like $20,000 by the time he came into the band's orbit. He often ended up bankrolling them, which was handy when neither band nor label had two cents to rub together. It wasn't just paying for the *Bleach* sessions – Jason also had the t-shirts the band were selling printed, and stumped up a lot of the cash needed to keep the tour on the road; including getting the guitars that Kurt delighted in smashing to pieces replaced or repaired. He'd even been responsible for setting up the mail box for Nirvana's mailing list, the address of which was advertised on the rear cover of *Bleach*. All of this made him useful. Unfortunately, he just wasn't a great *fit* for Nirvana. His heavy metal style chafed against the band's more low-key Punk Rock outlook. Onstage he was a headbanger, taking full advantage of his glorious mane of strawberry-blonde curls. Kurt felt his performances were contrived, posey and overly sexual. He was *too rock-star*. He even brought girls back after shows, something no-one else in Nirvana was doing at that point, and Kurt and Krist felt it was tacky. Jason was into metal and hard rock while Kurt was getting into weird, cutesy pop from Scotland and Japan. Kurt had designs to take Nirvana in a more pop direction, while Jason was pushing for them to play the heavier numbers on *Bleach* where he could flex onstage. The difference in approach is exemplified on the version of 'Dive' recorded at Evergreen earlier in the year, which contains a rockist Everman solo that is horribly out of place and, it has to be said, pretty poorly played. People who saw Nirvana at the time have remarked often that the guitarist just didn't seem to fit ('when Jason was in the

Summer

- Nirvana audition guitarists to replace Jason, who still doesn't know he's been fired. Among those who try out are Robert Roth of the band Storybook Crooks (and, later, Sub Pop signing Truly), who rehearses with the trio for an afternoon and feels pretty good about the experience. He's told they'll make a decision after their upcoming tour, which they're planning to play as a trio. Hanging out after practice, Kurt implies heavily to Roth that he's thinking of sacking Chad Channing. The band also rehearses with a friend of Chad's, Ben Shepherd.[34]
- Jason Everman is offered the newly-vacant post of bass player in Soundgarden.[35]

August 12

- *Bleach* is released in the UK on the Tupelo Recording Company label, which had also handled the UK release of Mudhoney's *Boiled Beef & Rotting Teeth* EP

band it stood out because he sucked', Candice Pearson told Everett True for *Nirvana: The True Story*). A recording of the show in Boston where Kurt doesn't play guitar at all, is an absolute mess. Jason's guitar style, alone in the spotlight for once, has entirely the wrong feel. As Craig Montgomery, who did sound for the band sometimes, tells Mark Yarm – 'all the guitar sounds that sounded like Nirvana were coming from Kurt'.

On the other hand, you have to feel for Jason. Nirvana was Kurt's show, through and through. Everman had joined the band under the impression he'd be able to make a musical contribution. He was a songwriter himself, and found Kurt had absolutely no interest in playing his stuff. His role was essentially to just double the guitar parts onstage and do what he was told. He was promoting an album he hadn't played on, in a band now going in a direction he wasn't especially comfortable with or suited to. As the US tour progressed, he became more withdrawn and visibly unhappy. He prided himself on his professionalism, and every night had to watch his bandmates treat their instruments appallingly ... and expect him to help get them fixed and bail them out when they needed something. As he told Gillian G Gaar, 'If you do not have the necessary equipment, it creates a challenging situation in regard to the next performance'. Jason, in many respects, was acting as the tour manager the band didn't have: the responsible, boring one. What's more, he didn't drink or do drugs, making him very much the outsider of this already 'outsider' band. As the tour drew on, Jason felt more and more like a square peg. In New York, Kurt and Krist went to see Mudhoney and Sonic Youth play The Ritz. Jason went to see metalheads Prong at CBGB. Not only would Jason probably not get 'The Black Flag tattoo'; he'd probably get a Judas Priest one instead. When the band headed home, Jason was privately intending to quit, while Kurt and Krist were privately planning to fire him. Neither party bothered to inform the other of their decision, and both simply got on with their lives, though apparently Jason was still saying he was in Nirvana while hanging out at Sub Pop's offices a few weeks later. He worked it out, eventually. The schism wasn't really anyone's fault.

34. Rehearsing with two guitarists who don't know about each other to replace a guitarist who doesn't know he's been sacked ... and never telling any of the three that they're in or out of the band, is a very Nirvana mood. They treated drummers pretty much the same way.
35. Jason played with Soundgarden for six months or so before being fired and replaced by ... would-be Nirvana guitarist Ben Shepherd, who had been the band's first choice anyway. Shepherd had held them off since he thought he was joining Nirvana. It was musical chairs in Seattle that summer. Though he played with a few more bands, Soundgarden was Jason's final foray into music on a professional level. A few years later he joined the US Army and eventually, after a period studying Buddhism in Tibet, became a Special Forces green beret, serving in Afghanistan and Iraq in the 2000s, earning several medals and an honourable discharge. Since then, he's formed a band with other veterans and taken up sailing around the world. It has been, unarguably, a hell of a life. At the band's invitation, he attended Nirvana's inauguration to the Rock N' Roll Hall of Fame – though didn't perform at either the glitzy ceremony, nor the sweaty club gig the surviving members played later that same night.

and the *Sub Pop 200* compilation. The tracklist is slightly re-ordered, curiously dropping 'Love Buzz' in favour of 'Big Cheese'.[36]

August 20

- United by a love of vintage blues music, specifically Huddie 'Lead Belly' Ledbetter, Kurt and Krist form a Seattle supergroup of sorts with Screaming Trees' Mark Lanegan and Mark Pickerel and are booked for a day's recording with Jack Endino at Reciprocal.[37] Four Lead Belly tracks are attempted – 'They Hung Him On A Cross', 'Ain't It A Shame[38]' (both sang by Kurt), 'Where Did You Sleep Last Night'[39] (sang by Mark) and an instrumental, 'Grey Goose'. Only 'Ain't It A Shame' and 'Where Did You Sleep …' are completed to a releasable standard. The group is never officially given a name. Mark Pickerel suggests 'The Jury', Kurt suggests 'Lithium', though no-one is hugely excited by either. Endino marks the tape as 'The Jury'.[40]

---

36. The album had already been given an 8/10 write-up in the UK's *NME*, the best selling of the weekly music papers, with Edwin Pouncey reviewing the Sub Pop version as an import the previous month. *Melody Maker's* review coincided with the UK release and was just as enthusiastic – 'tanked up and over the straight edge. Full throttle into oblivion. Yeah, bleached. Gone.' said the magazine's mono-named reviewer, Push. They liked it, if that isn't clear.
37. Lead Belly is another off-the-beaten-track choice in Kurt's arsenal of influences. He'd been introduced to the singer by Slim Moon, after reading an article on him by William S Burroughs (another Cobain favourite). Though not quite a household name, except in very savvy muso households, Lead Belly is arguably one of the most influential musicians of all time: part of the base-stock of which Rock N' Roll was originally comprised. He is to rock music what Victorian music hall is to modern stand up comedy. You might not always spot the similarities, but one could never have existed without the other. Born in either 1888 or 1889 (accounts vary), Huddie Leadbetter would spend his early life in and out of prison, including serving time for murder. On one occasion he escaped and went on the run, on another he successfully begged for clemency by writing a song; or so he claimed (his prison warder denied this). He's credited with writing dozens of songs, and had a repertoire of even more. Like many folk singers he was a sponge for old tunes, and in those days, when records weren't widely available, folk memory was often the only way such music was passed on. You can see the appeal for an artist like Kurt – much like the Punk Rock he had fallen in love with as a teenager, Lead Belly's career was about authenticity. He lived the life that he sang about. He was the real deal. His songs had real depth, and real pain.
38. 'Ain't It A Shame', a rattling rockabilly number in which Kurt's voice raises from a low register to a raspy screech is a great match for Nirvana's sardonic sense of humour, its references to fishing, drinking and wife-beating sketching the same sort of thuggish characters Kurt himself wrote about on 'In Bloom', 'Swap Meet' and 'Mr Moustache'.
39. The haunting track is based on a song Lead Belly recorded as 'In The Pines', an old folk standard that had been knocking around in a couple of different versions since, at the very least, the 1870s. There's hundreds of recordings, but Lead Belly's stands out – threatening, maudlin and plaintive all at once. Lanegan does a great job of capturing it, as indeed did Kurt a few years later.
40. Kurt and the rest of Nirvana collaborated with their peers surprisingly rarely considering just how cross-pollinated the Seattle scene was at the time. You only have to look at the tangled Rock Family Tree that takes in Green River, Mudhoney, Melvins, Nirvana, Malfunkshun, Mother Love Bone, Temple of the Dog, Soundgarden and Pearl Jam to see that. The Jury, as we may as well refer to them in absence of anything better, is the only serious example we have of Kurt collaborating with one of his direct peers after the Nirvana bandwagon was rolling (patchy projects with Dylan Carlson in Earth and Tobi Vail are slightly different, in that neither were true peers at that point – Nirvana were streets ahead of them). Partly this is because Kurt was very much used to running his own show. We know that both of Kurt's bandmates and his recently-departed guitarist occasionally struggled with how controlling he could be about his music. In the case of The Jury, Kurt seemed to be very much behaving himself, not wanting to tread on Mark Lanegan's toes, since he was a writer and performer he held in huge esteem. Occasionally he'd been known to refer to him as 'my favourite singer'. For his part, Lanegan, who was in

August 21

- A second day of recording for the band that may or may not be called The Jury has been booked ... but all four band members fail to show up.[41]

August 26

- Nirvana play the Centre of Contemporary Arts in Seattle, alongside labelmates Mudhoney, Cat Butt and Black Supersucker. It's their first show as a three piece since the departure of Jason and they will remain a trio until 1993. They debut a super-poppy new song, the new-wavey 'Stain'.[42]

August 30

- The band's first full interview in influential British weekly *New Musical Express (NME)* is published.[43] Writer Edwin Pouncy confidently proclaims that 'by the time they tour Europe this coming October, Nirvana's future as the next big thing will be in the bag'.[44]

September

- Sub Pop decides that a new Nirvana EP is needed to support the upcoming European tour.[45] The band are booked into Music Source Studios in Seattle, a 24-track studio usually used for corporate work and commercials, with producer Steve Fisk.[46] Over the course of two evenings they finish versions of 'Stain' and 'Been A Son[47]', two of Kurt's catchiest songs yet, and lay down incomplete versions

---

awe of Kurt's Cobain's songwriting, was doing exactly the same thing – Screaming Trees were a chaotic band, and he was used to having to make his voice heard to get anything done. Both were keeping their dictatorial instincts in check out of respect for a friend and peer. Of course, the problem with that is that you *need* someone in a band to be the point of the spear and take the lead. The Jury likely staggered to a halt because neither frontman was willing to be the asshole every band requires to push it forwards.

41. Endino did manage to muster the group's attention for a few hours, a few days later, when 'Ain't It A Shame' and 'Where Did You Sleep Last Night' were mixed, which the group intended as a double a-side Sub Pop 7"; the two vocalists taking a song each. Like so many great ideas that came out of this particular group of musicians, the concept was abandoned. This recording of 'Where Did You Sleep ...' would eventually be included on Lanegan's wonderful 1990 solo album *The Winding Sheet*, while 'Ain't It a Shame', alongside the other two tracks from the session, would finally emerge on Nirvana's 2004 rarities box set *With The Lights Out*.
42. With 'Stain' we can see Kurt pursuing the super-economic songwriting he'd begun with 'School'. It contains one verse, repeated three times, a four-note riff, a three-chord chorus and one of those brilliantly noisy Cobain solos that always felt so right in their simplicity. There's no bridge, no key change and the middle-eight is just Krist playing the riff from the verse with a solo over it. 'Stain' is just over two and a half minutes of deliciously poppy self-deprecation, and there's a great bit where Kurt shouts 'urgh!'. In its own way, it's pretty perfect.
43. Note, the issue is actually dated September 2, as UK weekly magazines always carry the date of the following Saturday. *NME* was actually published on a Wednesday, however. And Tuesdays in London.
44. He was out by around 18 months.
45. With typical Sub Pop efficiency, the *Blew* EP, as it will be titled, won't be ready in time for the tour it was supposed to help promote.
46. The exact date of this session is unknown, though Fisk believes it was in the first week of September.
47. This version includes an excruciatingly loud bass solo that swamps the rest of the track. Partly, the song is a victim of the abuse Krist put his gear through on tour – his speakers were blown and distorting. Lest

of 'Polly',[48] 'Even In His Youth'[49] and a track known only as 'Token Eastern Song' due to its droney, Led Zepish riff.[50]

September 26 – October 12

- Nirvana return to The Vogue in Seattle to once again kick off a US tour. The band wind their way through the Midwest, playing shows that had been cancelled earlier in the year prior to Jason's exit. The gigs are a combination of well-received support slots with local and nationally-touring bands, notably including Oklahoman psychedeliacs Flaming Lips, fellow Sub Poppers The Fluid and Bronx-based funk/rock fusionists 24–7 Spyz, with occasional Nirvana headline shows. The support slots are often triumphs, with the band holding their own in front of audiences in the hundreds, by some accounts blowing the headliners off stage – though, despite the underground success of *Bleach*, their own headline shows usually pull in an audience between 20 and 40 people. At this point 'underground success' was almost a contradiction in terms.[51]

October 18

- TAD and Nirvana share the front cover of UK music weekly *Sounds*, with a feature written by John Robb.[52] It's Nirvana's first magazine cover anywhere in

anyone should think the presence of the bass solo was at Krist Novoselic's insistence, its actually specified on Kurt's original home demo of the song, on which he literally can be heard saying 'now the bass solo' at the right section. Though this version of 'Been A Son' would be used on the *Blew* EP, the band opted for a much punchier take recorded for a BBC radio session when it came to putting together the *Incesticide* compilation. Curiously, the 2002 *Nirvana* best-of collection would return to the original recording.

48. This version of 'Polly' is the biggest indication so far of the sonic direction the band would go in on *Nevermind*. It has a quiet intro and first verse, then roars into life on the chorus, a trick they would arguably overuse on later records but had yet to commit to at this point outside of 'About A Girl', which rather pulls its punches. The irony, of course, is that the final version of 'Polly' would be one of the few tracks on *Nevermind* that didn't use the quiet/loud trick at all.
49. This version has a brilliantly noisy intro that would later be re-recorded as 'Endless, Nameless', the 'hidden' track on *Nevermind*.
50. 'Token Eastern Song' aside, these tracks show a huge leap in Kurt's lyrics. He is more obviously inward-looking and more focused on tracks like 'Been A Son' (about his younger sister being a disappointment to their father), 'Even In His Youth' (about *Kurt* being a disappointment to his father) and 'Stain' (about the way his own shortcomings are perceived by others), and brutally economic on 'Polly', inspired by the rape and kidnap of a 14-year old Tacoma girl in 1987. Kurt opts to tell the story from the rapist's perspective; an extraordinary decision which he handles with real poetic skill. It's a remarkable piece of writing, possibly his first truly great lyric, and certainly a contender for his best. As his music became deceptively simple and deliberately punchy, with more double-tracking and harmony parts to bring out the sweetness, Kurt's lyrics were becoming more layered and interesting *and* more economically written. He was learning to say more with less. He was leaps and bounds ahead of the Kurt Cobain that wrote 'Downer' and 'Spank Thru' just three years earlier.
51. Accounts of this tour are of a band frustrated by the low-turnout for their headline shows, completely exhausted and struggling with poor health – colds, bronchitis and Kurt's ever-present stomach pains, the latter of which leads to a smattering of cancelled gigs. The shows are energetic, but often messy – pretty characteristic of this era of the band.
52. *Sounds* completed the inkie-indie holy trinity of the British music press, alongside *Melody Maker* and *NME*, though it sold less well than either and was even outsold by its own Heavy Metal offshoot, *Kerrang!* The paper tended to have a less London-centric view of music than its competitors, and was also more likely to champion the sonically weird and unpalatable – always a good thing. *Sounds'* John Robb was probably the first UK music journalist to really catch on to Nirvana, though of course it was *MMs* Everett

the world. That same day, *Melody Maker* runs a feature by Everett True titled 'Bleached Wails', promoting the tour.

October 20

- Nirvana and label-mates TAD fly to London to begin a European co-headline tour that will see them on the road until 3 December. The four members of TAD, three members of Nirvana, plus a road manager, Edwin Heath, and Sub Pop resident sound engineer Craig Montgomery are crammed into a single splitter van, with hired gear shared by both acts[53], plus merch and luggage. The two bands, alternating as headliners, will play a gruelling 37 shows across the next 42 days, visiting nine different countries: the UK, the Netherlands, West Germany, Hungary, Austria, Switzerland, Italy, France and Belgium. Also on the tour, though travelling separately, are Edinburgh punks The Cateran, who will open the UK shows. The touring party is picked up at the airport by booking agent Russell Warby and, after a chinese meal, goes out to explore London, a city none of them has visited before. Kurt, suffering from bronchitis as well as his ever-present stomach problems and having given up drinking for the present as a result, decides not to join his bandmates on a brief site-seeing pub-crawl, save to have his photo taken outside the British Museum.

October 23–25

- The tour begins in Newcastle-Upon-Tyne, with a show at a club called Riverside. TAD headline, as they will for many of the UK dates, given that they've had more British press and radio than Nirvana at this point. The three bands will then wind their way through the north of England, playing in Manchester and Leeds.[54] Audiences hover around the 100–150 mark, packing out the small venues and a marked improvement from the crowds either band (or both together) could attract out in the sticks on a US tour.[55]

True that became their great champion. None of the UK's weekly music papers exist in their original form anymore. *Sounds*, sadly, was the first to go, closing its doors in 1991. *Melody Maker* lasted another decade. *NME* managed to push on to 2018, though it was much reduced when the weekly print mag was finally stopped. *NME*, at least, still exists as a pretty comprehensive (if occasionally click baity) website with occasional special edition print issues, as does *Kerrang!*. Alas, *Sounds* and *Melody Maker* long went the way of 60s & 70s titles like *Record Mirror* and *Disc & Music Echo*, remembered only by music fans of a certain age. Britain's music scene is much diminished by their absence.

53. Well, okay, first they got on a plane to London. *Then* they squeezed into a splitter van. And it really would have been a squeeze. Kurt and Chad might have been tiny and pixie-like, but Krist and Tad Doyle, one astonishingly tall, one hugely overweight at 300 pounds (21 stone), rather countered this. Standing together they presumably looked like the number ten (this joke, by the way, borrowed from the great Terry Pratchett.)
54. The touring party has to take a 400-mile-round-trip detour between the Manchester and Newcastle gigs, to London, to replace equipment trashed at the first show of the tour – Krist, it turned out, was not pleased with the piddling Trace Elliot bass amp with which he'd been provided and, hopped up on cheap cider, had made his feelings known through his usual poetry of blunt force trauma.
55. Newcastle, Manchester and Leeds are, of course, all pretty major population centres with great music scenes, but then so are Chicago, Cincinnati and Boston and at this point, Nirvana would struggle to pull 100 people in those cities. Thanks to the buzz around Sub Pop in the British music press the UK shows were, across the board, well attended with energised crowds of moshing kids.

October 25

- The new issue of *Melody Maker* carries a review of the forthcoming *Blew* EP, in which writer Simon Reynolds tears the release to shreds. 'Dismal, muddy, thuggish trad-rock that adds further weight to the notion that Sub Pop is the hype of '89,' says Reynolds. 'These warhorse riffs are only fit for the knackers yard.'[56]

October 26

- Nirvana record a session for John Peel at BBC Radio One's Maida Vale studios,[57] tracking versions of 'Spank Thru'[58], 'About A Girl', 'Love Buzz' and 'Polly'.[59] The tracks are produced by Dale Griffin.[60]

---

56. Ouch.
57. Peel Sessions were something of a beautification for underground bands in the UK. Recognition by John Peel on his late-night show meant credibility and exposure ... or at least it did sometimes – plenty of bands had recorded tracks for the show and then subsequently never been heard from again. Those that *did* become hugely famous were often pretty-much banished by Peel after a certain point in their growth (most notoriously Marc Bolan and T.Rex ... though there were exceptions – Blur, The White Stripes, Belle & Sebastian and Pulp spring to mind) with the DJ preferring to keep his programme focused on new bands. Peel had joined Radio One, the BBC's station dedicated to current pop music, when it launched in 1967. Initially he was one of the rotating hosts on a show called *Top Gear* (not the TV one with the cars, obviously) which dealt with more underground music. He'd come from the pirate station Radio London, where his show *The Perfumed Garden* had been a hippie freak out must-listen. Peel eventually became the main host of *Top Gear* which was quickly moulded around his own tastes, and he'd regularly host live sessions by bands, including an early, career-making appearance by Marc Bolan's Tyrannosaurus Rex. While other Radio One DJs aged out of the station and went off to cosier careers playing oldies, Peel stayed at the cutting edge and was still hosting a show consisting of underground, unknown and sometimes unpalatable music right up to his untimely death in 2004. He was there for punk, he was there for acid house, he was there for grunge, britpop, drum n bass and more. A 'Peel Session' became a rite of passage for up-and-coming bands, with everyone from The Smiths to Napalm Death passing through Maida Vale. Some bands only came once, others were regular visitors. The Fall, for example, recorded over 24 separate sessions over 25 years. The sessions were rarely truly 'live', and were instead recorded during business hours, working fast with minimal overdubs, much as bands would have recorded in the early sixties, which led to more exciting, and rawer takes than polished official releases. John Peel himself was usually not present which, as Smashing Pumpkins' Billy Corgan writes in the liner notes to his b-sides collection *Pisces Iscariot*, was often disappointing to visiting US bands wanting to meet one of the UK music scene's most influential figures. Instead he'd turn up at Radio 1's Great Titchfield Street studios much later to host his late-night show, sometimes only hearing the sessions for the first time at that point. Many of the sessions captured bands in classic form, often surpassing their official releases in energy. The Smiths' early sessions, for example, are usually considered superior to the band's first album by fans. They were subsequently collected on *Hatful of Hollow*. Many groups considered their Peel sessions a goldmine for b-sides and bonus tracks, Nirvana included, and Peel's show often yielded definitive takes of classic songs. That's not strictly true of Nirvana, though the version of 'Spank Thru' recorded here might have the edge on the *Sub Pop 200* take and, as previously noted, a later BBC recording of 'Been A Son' is miles better than the EP version. The 1989 session definitely captures the *Bleach*-era band on their best form, particularly on a sharp and muscular 'Love Buzz'. The tracks have never been officially released, though it's pretty easy to track them down online.
58. Incorrectly labelled as 'Spanx Thru' on the record of the session, meaning that's also what Peel announced the song as when the session was broadcast.
59. Here Nirvana abandon the loud/quiet dynamic of the version they demoed just a few months earlier – though a 'full band' recording and more muscular than the version that will appear on *Nevermind*, this has clean guitars throughout. Live recordings from the tour, however, show them playing the heavier version. This is different again to the 'New Wave' version that would appear on *Incesticide*. The trio were still feeling their way through how they wanted the song to sound.
60. Originally the drummer with Mott the Hoople, whose definitive recording of David Bowie's 'All The Young Dudes' is one of the peaks of early 70s British rock. Nirvana, of course, would later cover Bowie themselves.

October 27

- TAD and Nirvana make their London debut, a big moment for any US rock band, at SOAS (the School for African and Oriental Studies), part of the University of London. The venue has been cobbled together by student promotors, with a PA and makeshift stage set up in a refectory rather than a bespoke gig venue, such as the nearby ULU – whose 'social secretary'[61] apparently wanted nothing to do with this grimy American punk stuff. The show is a sweaty, loud and chaotic triumph, converting journalists and fans alike to the Nirvana cause. Kurt caps off the encore by setting off a fire extinguisher.[62]

October 28–30

- The tour does a quick criss-cross of England: south to Portsmouth, back north to Birmingham, and east to Norwich. Crowds and shows are consistently good. Both bands are surprised and delighted by how popular they appear to be in the UK.

November

- Nirvana contribute 'Mexican Seafood', one of the unreleased tracks recorded with Dale Crover back in January of 1988, to a four-track 7″ EP released by Seattle label C/Z records[63]. Also featured are tracks by Hellos Creed, Yeast and Coffin Break. It's Nirvana's first non-Sub Pop release.

November 1

- Krist and TAD's Kurt Danielson get blind drunk on the ferry across the North Sea to the Netherlands. Upon arrival at the hotel that's been booked for them, Krist falls to the floor of the lobby, refuses to move and then innocently calls the owners a homophobic slur, not realising that they are actually gay. The touring party is thrown out of the hotel and forced to find alternative accommodation.[64]

November 2–5

- Nirvana make their Dutch radio debut, recording 'About A Girl', 'Dive' and 'Love Buzz' for the national VPRO station in front of a live audience, before playing a show in Rotterdam, then heading on to Groningen, Utrecht, Apeldoorn and

---

61. British student unions are usually governed by a team of (often clueless) elected students. I should know. I was one.
62. *Sounds* reviewer Roy Wilkinson is unimpressed by Nirvana, calling them a 'shadow of the teen thug combo' they had been as a four piece, and reckons TAD is the band with the most longevity. *Melody Maker*'s Neil Perry, meanwhile, is far more receptive, noting that Nirvana 'colour their darkness with splashes of stark beauty' and 'reach some sort of crazy peak, bursting hearts and brains alike'.
63. The label's *Deep Six* LP, released back in 1986, was arguably the album that lit the touch paper for the Seattle grunge boom.
64. Given how vocal Nirvana were about gay rights, one can only imagine that Krist was mortified by this once he'd sobered up.

Amsterdam. On the final night of the Netherlands leg, in Melkweg, Kurt screams so loudly into the poor quality PA, which the band are already overdriving, that he blows out the monitor speaker servicing the drums and permanently damages Chad Channing's hearing.[65] Conditions are rough, money is scarce, audiences small and morale is low. What little food is available is pretty awful. Kurt and Tad Doyle are both ill, Kurt with his usual ongoing stomach issue, Tad with explosive diarrhoea, both with Bronchitis.[66]

November 8

- After a day off for travelling, the tour hits West Germany, starting with the B-52 club in Mönchengladbach. According to witnesses, there are 20 people in attendance. The tour will continue to wind its way across West Germany.

November 9

- The fall of the Berlin wall marks the symbolic unravelling of communism in East Germany and opens the way for German unification. Nirvana and TAD are miles away, playing a show in Hannover. In a later interview with Seattle's *The Rocket* Krist will later claim that none of the touring party were aware of the historic events happening around them.

November 11

- Two days after the fall of the wall, the bands arrive in Berlin itself for a show at a club called Ecstasy. The traffic going into the city is astonishing, the journey

65. The venues the tour had hit in the UK were fairly decent, at least as far as the top rung of the toilet circuit goes. They had strong audiences and proper club PA systems that were used for touring bands all the time. This wasn't the case when TAD and Nirvana arrived in mainland Europe, where the way hadn't been smoothed, as it had in the UK, by national music press and radio. These were mostly small clubs and pubs at the grottier end of the spectrum, whose beleaguered monitors had been gummed up with one too many spilled cans of cheap beer, and whose speakers had long since blown out. For many of the shows in the Netherlands and Germany the bands pulled the same tiny audiences they did in the Midwest or South of the US. Because Nirvana would, within a very short time, be one of the most buzz-grabbing bands on the planet, it's easy to forget that outside of their local scene, the hipster music centres of LA and New York and the rarified pages of the British music press, Nirvana were nobodies at this point. In fact, for many of the shows it was the name 'Sub Pop' that brought the audience in. Local music fans might not have heard of the individual bands, but those with their ear to the ground knew the label's reputation, at least through Mudhoney. Both bands spent much of the tour bitching about the lack of support they'd gotten from Pavitt and Poneman back in Seattle, how long the tour was, and how harsh their conditions were, but the truth was that, without the Sub Pop name, neither band would have attracted much interest outside of the Pacific NorthWest. Meanwhile, poor Chad Channing's hearing never fully recovered.
66. Lots of the tales of this tour involve Tad Doyle becoming something of muse for Kurt. Every night he would hack and cough so much that he would inevitably vomit, and Kurt relished his daily job of holding a bucket for his friend to void his stomach into. The two would then rate and review that day's sputum. Tad was also taking the diarrhoea medicine Imodium for the bug he'd picked up in the UK (blamed on late night kebab joints and a tuna and sweetcorn pizza, a combo which the visiting Americans thought verged on unholy.) Kurt would use a misspelling of 'Immodium' as the name of the fierce, buzzing power-pop song debuted shortly before this tour, which would later be retitled 'Breed'.

takes substantially longer than expected and the little touring party are baffled by the miles and miles of Trabants, the tiny state-issued and notoriously bad East German cars, streaming out of the city.[67] The groups arrive at the venue exhausted and in terrible spirits and it's only when they're told about the momentous events happening in the city, with their promoters informing them that they are 'witnessing history', that things start to make sense.[68] The 600-capacity club had been expected to sell out, but the unprecedented events in the city mean just 227 people are in attendance. The gig is beset with technical issues and Kurt ends the show prematurely, smashing his guitar, a white Univox Hi-flier, beyond repair.[69]

November 13

- Following a show in Oldenburg the previous night, in which Nirvana debuted a new song, 'Sappy', the tour heads to Hamburg. Though tempers are fraying and energy among the group is low, some time is still found to visit the Reeperbahn, the street of bars, strip clubs and sex shops that was famously the site of the amphetamine-fuelled late-night residencies in which a pre-fame Beatles honed their craft in the early 60s. The band are delighted to note that the area is swarming with East German visitors keen to blow off the steam of Soviet oppression with strippers, beer and rock 'n' roll.[70]

November 14–24

- The tour winds its way through Germany, Austria and Hungary. Audiences are tiny, dipping into single figures in the more remote areas, though a show in a rock club in Budapest, another city in the process of parting the Iron Curtain, was packed to the rafters with metal fans delighted that American rockers had arrived in their country at last.[71] The two bands are exhausted and demoralised. Kurt is at a particularly low ebb – in constant discomfort, run down and home

---

67. Known in the UK as a Lada. British readers of a certain age will remember the endless playground jokes at the car's expense. Owning one made you a pitiable curiosity.
68. This according to interviews conducted by Everett True for *Nirvana: The True Story*.
69. Berlin should have been one of the jewels in the crown of the European tour. Other shows in Germany may have been attended by the tiniest of audiences, but West Berlin, one of continental Europe's artsiest and hippest cities, with an incredible Punk Rock scene, had the potential to be extraordinary. Unfortunately, the fall of the wall, just two days earlier, had thrown everything up in the air. Impromptu street parties and celebrations had erupted across the city and most people's plans had gone out of the window. The venue wasn't even half-full. The flipside of this is that the show was attended by both East and West Germans alike. Just not many of them.
70. The area's reputation for vice is well founded. That night the two bands came into possession of scatalogical pornography so revolting it even turned the iron stomach of Krist Novoselic.
71. Accounts of this tour are often contradictory. The comprehensive *LiveNirvana* website claims that the band's set in Budapest was truncated and lacklustre, dragging on for just over half an hour, though Chad Channing, talking to Gillian G. Gaar for her book *Entertain Us*, remembers a powder-keg audience just happy to see them.

sick. On 17 November, at a show in Gammelsdorf, Germany, Nirvana debut their cover of The Vaselines' 'Molly's Lips'.[72]

November 15

- It's *NME*'s turn to review the *Blew* EP. The magazine's Ian McCann is slightly more positive than *Melody Maker*, though his compliments are decidedly back-handed. 'If I was 15, hated black music and lived a frustrated Nuneaton life,' he says 'then I'd buy this without hesitation'.[73]

---

72. Kurt was absolutely obsessed with The Vaselines, and they were comfortably his favourite band. The Vaselines, at their core, were a duo from Glasgow, Scotland (not Edinburgh, as Kurt erroneously described them onstage several times) – Eugene Kelly and Frances McKee. They'd originally intended to make a fanzine together, but accidentally became a couple and formed a pop group instead. Influenced by The Velvet Underground, the legendary weirdo crooner partnership of Lee Hazelwood and Nancy Sinatra, the pneumatic pop of Orange Juice and the artschool oddity of Yoko Ono, the duo (later expanded to a quartet) knocked out a couple of EPs and an album, Dum Dum, between 1986 and 1989, when they split up. Their lyrics were witty and managed an odd combination of child-like and filthy, their structures were economic and their storytelling pretty magnificent, and while they weren't especially well known, what fans they *did* have were absolutely smitten. It was a short lifespan, but an influential one – they walked so later Scottish indie royalty like Teenage Fanclub, Arab Strap and Belle & Sebastian (and less royal but no-less awesome bands like Bis) could run. What no-one, least of all the band themselves, saw coming was that their biggest influence was on a punk rocker from Aberdeen, Washington who would one day become the most important rock star in the world.

    Kurt discovered The Vaselines in Olympia, where Scottish tweecore groups with filthy lyrics and no bass player were the highest currency a music fan could have. If you loved Beat Happening and The Go Team, you'd certainly love The Vaselines. The Olympian vibe had absolutely influenced Kurt's musical pallet, as he wrote in an undated letter to Dale Crover, reproduced in his *Journals*, 'I've not lost my soulful, embeded roots as a punk rock, hard, heavy, gunka gunka gunka music slut ... but I *have* learned to appreciate some of the Calvin [Johnson]/simplistic stuff enough to do my own rendition, which is actually something I've been planning on doing for years'. Kurt was, by his nature, a contrarian. Nirvana's initial music had been heavy, even lumpen, and of a piece with the other sounds coming out of the Seattle area. They were absolutely, definitively a Sub Pop band in terms of their style, and Jack Endino had ensured they sounded like one, too. *Bleach* had been full of big rock sounds, and Kurt had been happy to channel the sonic sludge of Black Flag and the Melvins that had inspired hum. Being pigeonholed, however, was the absolute antithesis of Kurt's outlook. Almost as soon as his band started to be spoken about in the same breath as the super-heavy TAD and the metal-tinged Soundgarden, he immediately switched tack. In interviews he talked constantly about twee pop – the Sarah Records label, Shonen Knife, The Pastels, Pixies, The Smithereens, Marine Girls and The Vaselines. This last would be the band he'd trumpet more than any other, and the band Nirvana covered most often. Covering the Vaselines was a statement – 'we're not a metal band. We're not a typical "Sub Pop" band. We're something else'. The economic storytelling of the Vaselines fed into the pop-orientated simplicity that infected Kurt's newest songs, a conscious attempt to create space between Nirvana and the bands they were always lumped in with. This wasn't just about indie semantics, though. Kurt's fandom was absolutely genuine – Nirvana covered two Vaselines songs for their 1990 Peel Sesson, he begged Eugene Kelly to join him onstage at the 1991 Reading Festival, both Peel covers turned up on the 1992 *Incesticide* collection and he insisted on covering the band again during their 1993 *MTV Unplugged* performance. Perhaps most tellingly, Kurt would name his only daughter, Frances, after The Vaselines' Frances McKee. In a drafted and undated letter to Eugene Kelly, reproduced in *Journals,* he writes 'I have to say the songs you and Frances have written are some of the most beautiful songs ever and I just feel like everyone should hear them.'
73. That 'hated black music' comment will have stung the staunchly anti-racist band, though once someone pointed out to them that Nuneaton in the West Midlands is basically England's answer to Aberdeen, Washington they might have gotten the writer's point about their appeal to disaffected youths from crap towns. For what it's worth, this author discovered Nirvana while growing up a mere nine miles from that particular crap town.

November 20

- The *Blew* EP is finally released as a 12" vinyl on the Tupelo label in the UK, having handily missed all but one date of the UK tour. The tracklisting is 'Blew' (from *Bleach*), 'Love Buzz' (the *Bleach* mix of the song – as yet unreleased in the UK), and 'Been a Son' and 'Stain' from the sessions with Steve Fisk back in October.[74]

November 22

- Nirvana's Peel Session is broadcast on BBC Radio One.

November 25

- A heavy cold means that Kurt is too ill to perform at a show in Fribourg, Switzerland. TAD perform a full set, with the other slot on the bill taken up by an impromptu band comprised of Tad Doyle (drums[75]), Krist Novoselic (bass) and tour manager Edwin Heath (guitar) who entertained the audience with an impromptu, 15-minute jam. It's a shame – after playing to tiny audiences for days, the club is rammed with 400 punters.[76]

November 26

- This time it's Tad Doyle who is too ill to perform, almost passing out from the intense heat onstage in a tiny and rammed club in Mezzago, Italy. Returning a favour from the previous night, Kurt steps up to sing TAD's 'High On The Hog', 'Sex God Missy', 'Wood Goblins' and 'Ritual Device'.[77]

November 27

- Arriving for their show in Rome, the bands find Sub Pop's Bruce Pavitt and Jonathan Poneman waiting to meet them.[78] Nirvana's set that night is a disaster.

---

74. Despite the stinky reviews, the *Blew* EP would go to number one in the UK Independent charts in January of 1990.
75. Tad was briefly considered as a drummer for Nirvana. This would be the closest he ever got.
76. A review in the Swiss newspaper *Freiburger Nachrichten* praises Tad's drumming and wishes that the short-lived jam band had played for longer.
77. In a later interview with Italian publication *Patasgnafa*, Nirvana would claim that Tad had to be airlifted to a hospital for three days of bed rest. The most unlikely part of this outlandish claim is the bed rest bit. No-one got three days off on this tour.
78. Pavitt and Poneman had come to Europe ahead of the upcoming Lame Fest UK, to be held at London's Astoria, in which the Nirvana/TAD tour would come to a screaming conclusion as the opening acts for Mudhoney, just begnning their own European run – a huge deal for the label. They'd decided to meet the bands a few days earlier in Italy in order to provide some moral support, having had reports from the road that Kurt, especially, was homesick, exhausted and at the end of his rope. According to *Experiencing Nirvana*, Pavitt's tour memoir, 'the artists were tired but glad to see us'. His one-time partner, Jonathan Poneman, had a more realistic view. Interviewed in 1992 by Michael Azerrad, Poneman admitted 'from their perspective I can see them thinking "these arrogant sons of bitches … we don't have any money, we're barely eating, we're riding around in this cramped van … and here come the moguls"'. Poneman was bang on. As sound engineer Craig Montgomery told Gillian G. Gaar, 'everybody was mad at the

Breaking a string during 'Big Cheese'[79], Kurt vanishes backstage to fit a new one[80], leaving Krist and Chad to keep the audience entertained with a lengthy jam.[81] After returning for 'About A Girl', 'Breed' and part of 'Spank Thru', Kurt brutally smashes his last remaining guitar, a cherry red Hagstrom II F-200. He then climbs the PA stack, a reported 35 ft above the venue floor, and threatens to jump, egged on by the crowd – a fall onto concrete that would probably kill him or at least lead to multiple broken bones plus injuries to fans. Eventually, he is cajoled down by venue security. He then clambers onto the balcony and starts threatening to throw a chair down into the crowd, until someone relieves him of it. His bandmates and label bosses are visibly shaken.[82] After the show, a member of staff argues with Edwin Heath about an apparently broken microphone, which Heath maintains is fine. Hearing this, Kurt takes the microphone and smashes it on the floor, declaring 'now it's broken'.[83] Backstage, realising that Kurt is seriously struggling, Krist and Chad agree to break up Nirvana, though they later change their minds and decide to continue the tour. Poneman and Pavitt offer to take Kurt by train to the next show in Switzerland and buy him a new guitar to replace those he'd destroyed on the road.[84]

Sub Pop guys for putting them through this gruelling tour ... there was a little bit of: oh, here's these guys, living high on the hog, and they haven't even paid us the money they owe us yet.'"

79. Which, given that it was about Jonathan Poneman, was delivered with particular venom.
80. Replacing the string was a necessity – he'd smashed his back-up guitar beyond repair in Berlin the previous week.
81. According to Everett True, Kurt and tour manager Edwin Heath got into a screaming match with both declaring that they were quitting the tour that night. It's likely this happened during this break, in the several minutes Kurt is offstage. Kurt, by this point, is wound up as tightly as he could go, and was frustrated with the sound problems onstage. It's worth noting that recordings of the gig showcase a bracingly punkish, characteristically loose Nirvana set that sounds great.
82. Kurt did this tour straight and sober – this wasn't behaviour prompted by booze or drugs. Krist would later say that he believed that the fact Kurt had nothing harder than cigarettes to cushion reality contributed to his stress levels.
83. This incident features in almost every book about Nirvana, and almost sounds too perfect an anecdote to be true, however it's backed up by accounts from Poneman and Pavitt, who witnessed it.
84. There's, obviously, a lot going on with this incident. How serious was Kurt about throwing himself off those speakers? It's unclear. Later he told *The Observer*'s Jon Savage that he was 'ready to die' on that tour, though he doesn't refer specifically to the Rome incident, and threatening to jump could have been misjudged bravado or plain old petulance, which Kurt was more than capable of. What had most affected him, aside from the poor sound and iffy equipment, was looking into the audience and seeing, as Pavitt quotes, 'the kind of guys who used to beat me up at school'. Earlier that day Kurt had given an interview to Italian music magazine *Mucchio Selvaggio* in which he'd underlined the idea that he wasn't comfortable with being associated with the type of audience that had a 'sexist macho attitude'. After the show Kurt had asked his bandmates 'are you guys having fun anymore'? Affable Chad actually *was* having fun, though he kept that opinion to himself, since the other two were in crisis mode. Krist and Kurt agreed it was time to call it a day, with Chad left with little choice but to agree with them, for Kurt's sake. It was Jonathan Poneman who took Kurt aside, calmed him down and convinced him to continue the tour, although, according to Cobain himself, only after he'd offered to sign him as a solo artist.

November 28

- After buying Kurt a new guitar (a black Washburn Force 31[85], costing around $150[86]) and seeing the rest of the touring party on their way, the two Sub Pop bosses, alongside TAD drummer Steve Wied, take Kurt sightseeing around Rome, including the Coliseum, Vatican City and the Sistine Chapel. As evening descends, the two musicians and two execs board an overnight sleeper train to Geneva. Kurt places his wallet and passport into his sneakers, which he leaves beside his reclining chair, and goes to sleep. During the night someone steals them.

November 29

- Discovering that Kurt's passport is missing, Pavitt and Poneman have to swing into action to get him a temporary visa to perform in Geneva that evening. Nirvana debut their cover of Lead Belly's 'Where Did You Sleep Last Night'.[87]

November 30

- While the rest of the party head for the next show, Kurt accompanies his label bosses to the city of Berne, where the US consulate is based, to go through the tedious process of replacing his passport before heading to that night's gig in Zürich.[88]

December 1

- Nirvana make two debuts – in Europe they play their first French show, at Issy-Les-Moulineaux near Paris, while back home in Seattle they're awarded their first US magazine cover, gracing the front page of *The Rocket*. The Paris gig is broadcast on the radio show *Planet Claire*, on Aligre FM.

December 3

- Following the previous night's gig in Belgium, the touring party board a ferry back to the UK and head to London for the final show of the tour, Lame Fest

---

85. Rome was obviously short on left-handed guitars. Pictures from the tour show Kurt playing the Washburn strung upsidedown, with the cable plugging in just under his ribcage and the strap gaffa-taped to the opposite side of the body from where it should be.
86. Interviewed for Mark Yarm's oral history of Grunge, *Everybody Loves Our Town*, Pavitt claims that despite their appearance as 'big cheeses' living 'high on the hog', he and Poneman could barely afford the $150 Kurt needed to buy a new guitar.
87. Chad Channing remembers this as one of the best shows on the tour. Nirvana had never performed the Lead Belly song as a full band before, though of course Krist and Kurt had recorded a version with Mark Lanegan and Mike Pickerall that would eventually be found on Lanegan's debut solo album. The song was unrehearsed, and Chad improvised the whole thing.
88. The long wait to sort out his passport doesn't help Kurt's mood much. It takes six hours, which he mostly spent nursing a hot chocolate with his hood up. What *does* lift his spirits, however, is the fact that the bands were well looked after in Switzerland – the hotels, food, venues and gear were all of a much better standard than they had experienced elsewhere.

UK[89] at the 2,000-capacity Astoria[90], with TAD and Nirvana playing as opening acts for Sub Pop's biggest band, Mudhoney, currently playing a European tour of their own. It would be the biggest show any of the three acts had played. Arriving with just 20 minutes to spare before showtime, and with no time for a soundcheck (despite the start of the show being pushed back), Nirvana and TAD toss a coin to see who will play first and who will be main support to Mudhoney. It's a big deal, because the opening act will have to play to a half-full room as the crowd enters. TAD win the toss, and Nirvana open the show with Kurt declaring 'Hello, we're one of the three official representatives of the Seattle Sub Pop scene from Washington State!'.[91] The set is plagued by sound problems. At its close, Kurt tosses his newly acquired Washburn guitar at Krist, who wields his bass like a baseball bat, with the two instruments crashing together. Krist's bass narrowly misses hitting Mudhoney's Dan Peters in the head. Kurt proceeds to smash his final guitar of the tour into matchwood.[92]

---

89. Though this show has commonly been referred to as 'Lame Fest UK' in lots of subsequent literature, it doesn't seem to have been marketed as such before hand, or at least not very much. The tickets themselves say, simply 'Mudhoney + Support', while music press listings have 'Mudhoney/TAD/Nirvana'. The marquee board outside of the Astoria lists only Mudhoney. 'Lame Fest' is, however, mentioned in the *NME* review of the show (though not the *Melody Maker* one) so Pavitt and Poneman must have gotten at least some people to buy into the concept. Mudhoney actually played two shows at the Astoria that week: Lame Fest was the Sunday night, while the following night's support came from Cosmic Psychos. You'd be pretty gutted if you'd opted to go to the Monday night show, wouldn't you?
90. Like most of Soho's iconic gig spaces, the Astoria, located where Oxford Street met Charing Cross Road, has long since vanished. The club was a mainstay of the capital's music scene from its opening in 1976 to its closure in 2009, sacrificed at the alter of London's ravenous need for rail infrastructure. The venue, which had hosted gigs from everyone from Smashing Pumpkins and Blur to Bowie to Eminem closed its doors in January 2009 after holding a charity 'Demolition Ball'. Within six months it was a hole in the ground waiting for an overpriced railway line. Those of us with long enough memories still mourn the loss of one of the UK's best sticky-floored rock clubs. See also the LA2, Metro club, the 12 Bar and the Borderline; smaller venues within a stone's throw of the same spot.
91. Which just goes to show that Kurt could be a team player when required. In many interviews around the time he would state in no uncertain terms that Nirvana were *not* representative of the 'Sub Pop' scene, nor were they actually from Seattle. Here, though, it was important to show a united front.
92. This particular Nirvana show holds legendary status as the gig where the UK music press really stood up and listened – causing a ripple effect that spread across the Atlantic to the US and beyond. That said, memories of the performance vary massively. Krist Novoselic himself said that the gig 'stunk … a zero out of ten', and Kurt too expressed massive disappointment with technical problems and broken strings, though appreciated the 'intensity of the crowd', according to Bruce Pavitt. Both felt that they'd blown their shot at the biggest show on the tour, and both were resentful of TAD taking the later slot they felt should have been theirs. Mudhoney's Dan Peters has described Nirvana's set as 'fucking horrible'. Similarly *Melody Maker* reviewer Simon Price hated the show, being particularly scathing of Krist Novoselic ('the lanky, rubber-legged frog-like bassist starts making a real jerk of himself … he'll *have* to go'). Others, though, remember a set of transcendent punk fury. *NME's* Edwin Pouncy lauds Nirvana as 'Sub Pop's answer to The Beatles' with a 'non-stop, high voltage performance', *Sounds'* Keith Cameron waxed lyrical about the 'genuine tension in the air', calling them a 'potent proposition.' 'It was the most amazing band I've ever seen', he told Michael Azerred a few years later. 'This is the night,' wrote Everett True in his memoir, 'that I first really connected with the power and rage and frustration and sheer devilment of Kurt Cobain.' Sub Pop's Bruce Pavitt said of the show, 'that night, everything shifted … Mark Arm from Mudhoney looked on, speechless, at the the band that was about to dethrone his own … it was a turning point for Nirvana, for Sub Pop records and for rock history'. Without a TARDIS we can't experience the atmosphere in the room, however we *can* at least listen to the show. Craig Montgomery, Nirvana's sound man, had the foresight to record the gig on cassette, and the whole thing can be tracked down online (the very start of the performance, plus versions of 'Polly' and 'Spank Thru' ended up on Nirvana's 1995 live album *From The Muddy Banks of the Wishkah.* In those halcyon

December 4

- The three Sub Pop bands accompany their label bosses to the Rough Trade record store in Covent Garden to do a little shopping and sign some record sleeves, including Nirvana's *Blew*. Shortly afterwards, TAD and Nirvana, exhausted, return to the US, though in Krist's case he does so via the country known at the time as Yugoslavia, where he visits his father.[93]

Mid December

- Kurt contributes guest vocals on 'Down in the Dark' on Mark Lanegan's debut solo album, *The Winding Sheet*. The record will also feature Kurt's guitar and Krist's bass on 'Where Did You Sleep Last Night'.

December 30

- Krist Novoselic marries his girlfriend, Shelli, at a ceremony in his Tacoma apartment. Matt Lurkin of Mudhoney/Melvins is best man.

---

days of the music industry's last great hurrah, those two tracks paid for Montgomery's new house). It's a messy show, sure, but then what Nirvana gig isn't? There's not another band in history that spent so much of any given performance checking they were in tune. That was as true in 1989 as it was in 1994. Krist and Chad's jam through Black Sabbath's 'Hand of Doom' and The Stooges' 'Now I Wanna Be Your Dog' gets a little self indulgent, but there's not much else they can do while Kurt changes a string. There's a crackling vibe here though; after three months on the road, the trio are tight as a drum. The energy is off the scale, as proved by a constant stream of stage diving, equipment trashing and wild abandon. 'Kurt threw himself around the stage like a man possessed', Anton Brookes, Sub Pop's UK press officer told Mark Yarm, 'it was obviously one of the key points in Nirvana's history.' He later told Gillian G. Gaar that he remembered thinking 'that's the future of rock 'n' roll'. He wasn't wrong.

93. This was a formative tour for Nirvana. On the one hand, gigging continuously had sharpened their live set to a razor's edge. Sure, Nirvana shows were still messy affairs, full of broken strings, smashed guitars and constant checking they were in tune – if ever there was a band in need of an electronic tuner pedal it was Nirvana – but once the songs kicked in, they sounded monstrous. Kurt had long gotten over his problems singing and playing at the same time and his performances were assured and confident, but with a sense that chaos could explode at any moment that gave his gigs an especially compelling edge. They could be an astonishing live proposition. On the other hand, the touring itself had been hell. Kurt never forgave Sub Pop for the conditions they put them through, the tiny budgets and lack of food (he would later claim they only had the budget for one meal a day), the gruelling schedule and the shoddy equipment. What was worse, is that after almost three months of hard work, they had almost nothing concrete to show for it – money for the performances never seemed to materialise. The tour left the band bitter, shattered and resentful and determined to find a more financially secure way of working in the future … one that may very well involve ditching the label that had given them their break.

Part Three

Bring Your Friends

1990

January 2–3

- Nirvana reconvene at Reciprocal to record a new song with Jack Endino. The song, 'Sappy', had been debuted on the recent European tour. Kurt pushes Endino to create a more 'Steve Albini' style sound, especially to the drums[1]. Kurt's insistence on micing the room in the way Albini would and getting an 'Albini' drum sound means that most of the session is spent on mic placement and set-up.[2] No-one is 100% happy with the recording, and since there is no planned upcoming Nirvana release, the track is shelved.[3] The session for this

1. Steve Albini had obviously been hovering in the back of Kurt's head for a few years at this point. Albini, who claimed his full name is technically 'Steven None Albini', since his father refused to leave the 'middle name' section of his birth certificate blank, was one of the most respected studio engineers in alternative music, with impeccable Punk Rock credibility. Born in 1961, he spent his childhood roaming the country, since his father researched wildfires for a living. Eventually he settled in Illinois, close to Chicago, and became besotted with the more sonically unpalatable end of Punk Rock. He formed Big Black, the band that made his name, in 1981, creating an uncompromising and jagged post punk noise based around a drum machine and Albini's slashing, discordant guitars. Their 1987 masterpiece, *Songs About Fucking*, remains one of the 80s US underground's touchstone recordings. It was so definitive, in fact, that the band split up as soon as they'd done touring it, having pretty much achieved what they'd set out to do. Kurt was also a fan of Albini's next band, the probably-wouldn't-be-called-that-these-days Rapeman ('god damn, they were fucking cool live', as he wrote in his journal), formed with members of another Cobain-touchstone, Scratch Acid. In 1992 Albini would form the post-rock outfit Shellac, with whom he was still playing with at the time of his death in 2024. He's best known, though, as a recording engineer (never a 'producer', since to his mind all he's doing is recording a band to the best of his, and their, abilities). Shortly before Nirvana went into Reciprocal to record *Bleach,* the Pixies' Albini-recorded *Surfer Rosa* had been released and quickly became one of Kurt's favourite albums of all time. He was completely obsessed with the production, particularly the wallop and pound of David Lovering's snare and kick drum – a sound he was chasing for the rest of Nirvana's career, ultimately leading to Albini recording *In Utero*. Albini's philosophy, as summed up in the liner notes to Big Black's *Pigpile* live album, could have been a playbook for Nirvana themselves: 'Treat everyone with as much respect as he deserves (and no more), avoid people who appeal to our vanity (they always have an angle), operate as much as possible apart from the "music scene" (which was never our stomping ground), and take no shit from anyone in the process.' Albini died of a heart attack during the writing of this book, aged just 61. I'd like to think that quote is as good an epitaph as he could have wanted.
2. Endino, interviewed for Gillian G. Gaar's book on *In Utero*, suggests that Reciprocal studios was just the wrong size and shape for the sounds Kurt was trying to get.
3. Jack Endino was a little baffled as to why the session ever took place, since Sub Pop hadn't fired the starting pistol on a new Nirvana album yet. He was also less than impressed with the song, which he felt fell below the band's usual standards. Listening to that recording now, that seems a little harsh. There's something melonchly at the heart at its heart that gives it a nagging and compulsive charm, also present on Kurt's achingly simple home demo recorded the previous year. Chad's propulsive drums certainly help. This recording would eventually see release on the 2004 compilation *Sliver: The Best of the Box*, but

one single song, which has no release plan, costs around $500 – almost as much as the main sessions for *Bleach*.[4]

January 6

- Nirvana and TAD reunite to play their first show of the year, at the Husky Union Building (HUB) Ballroom at the University of Washington, playing a 'four bands for four bucks' night, with The Gits and Crunchbird filling out the bill[5]. This time there is no questions of who would headline – Kurt and Krist quietly but definitively inform the members of TAD that Nirvana would close the show and, what's more, be the closing act on the forthcoming West Coast tour, which the two bands were due to undertake the following month.[6] Following a ferocious performance, Nirvana are given a lifetime ban from the venue for engaging in an orgy of destruction at the close of their set.[7]

Nirvana would attempt another version of 'Sappy' almost every time they were in a studio between 1990 and 1993. It was clearly a track they believed in. 'Something just drove Kurt to keep busting it out', as Krist told Gillian G. Gaar. 'Maybe he thought he was going to put that song over the top. He had some kind of unattainable expectations for it. I don't know.' As for why the January recording? Having just come back from a tour where he was asked constantly in interviews about the next Nirvana album (he would usually promise it was coming in 1990), and having written (in 'Imodium'/'Breed', 'Polly', 'Sappy' and 'Dive') some of the best songs of his life, with a clear pop-orientated direction, he was obviously itching for some forward momentum.

4. It's unclear who paid for this recording, since it seems unlikely that the perpetually broke Sub Pop would finance a session ad-hoc. The band certainly couldn't afford it and Endino wasn't in the habit of giving out freebies.
5. The Gits were a mid-western band, playing bluesy, Clash-influenced punk, who had relocated to Seattle the previous year and quickly found a following among the city's waifs and strays. By the early 1990s they would be teetering on the edge of real success, and having released two great records through C/Z, were poised to follow Nirvana, Soundgarden, Alice In Chains and Pearl Jam and sign to a major (Atlantic in this case). They had the world at their feet. Tragically it would never happen – firebrand singer Mia Zapata was raped and murdered on her way home in July 1993. It took nine years to bring her killer to justice, with the case having grown cold until new DNA evidence came to light. Following Mia's murder, a non-profit organisation called Home Alive was set up in Seattle in her name, with a brief to give women affordable self-defence lessons. The group was formally wound down in 2010, after 17 years, but survives as a volunteer collective.
6. Losing the coin-toss in London hadn't sat right with Nirvana. For all of their Punk Rock ethics and local-scene camaraderie, they (and especially Kurt) were also hugely ambitious. Despite the great reviews, it was felt that Lame Fest UK had been a missed opportunity and Kurt wasn't about to let fate rob him of his chance again. It was also clear to a lot of people that Kurt was right – Something was *happening* with Nirvana. 'Tad was not happy', the band's Kurt Danielson told Gillian G. Gaar, 'but I could see the writing on the wall.'
7. The venue management should have known what they were getting themselves into. A preview of the show ran in the local press, stating that 'Tad will collapse the stage about 10:00 p.m. and Nirvana will destroy the rest of the Ballroom about 11:00 p.m ... Slam-dance neophytes curious to try the favorite sport of the Sub Pop showcases can call The Daily Slam Dance Hotline, 543–2702, for instructional consultation and protective gear tips.' The unhinged spirit was captured by photographer Charles Peterson, who snapped the majestic sight of an uninhibited stage diver, soaring overhead. In 2024 he told *The Guardian* that he spotted the man atop an amp before he jumped and told him 'Dude! Don't do it!'. Thankfully for Peterson, who has sold that particular photograph many times over in the ensuing thirty years, his advice was ignored. And thankfully for the airborn fan, the crowd caught him.The shot can be found on the rear cover of the 1996 Nirvana live album, *From The Muddy Banks of the Wishkah*.

January 12

- Nirvana join the Melvins for the first of three NorthWest shows, starting at Satyricon in Portland. Kurt and Krist insist on headlining, claiming that 'things were really taking off' for them, and implying they were now the bigger band.[8]

January 19

- It's back to business as usual as Nirvana drop down to main support and the Melvins headline at a gig in Olympia. Calvin Johnson's Beat Happening open the show.[9] Making good on the plot he had hatched with TAD's Kurt Danielson back in Europe, Kurt plays the show with mock needlemarks on his arms, drawn on with fake costume blood, jokingly implying that he was doing heroin. Some in the crowd believe him.[10]

January 20

- Nirvana are back at the top of the bill for their show with the Melvins at Legends in Tacoma.[11]

---

8. They were also, apparently, 'really weird about splitting up the money', according to the Melvin's Buzz Osborne, talking in Mark Yarm's *Everybody Loves Our Town*. 'That was when I knew that things were not the same with these guys. They had become exactly what I had always tried to avoid'.
9. Nirvana being the meat in a Melvins/Beat Happening Sandwich is absolutely appropriate. They were the centre of the Venn diagram. The two bands were among Kurt's primary influences, and his ability to meld the sludgey volume of Melvins and the catchy, messy pop of Beat Happening was pretty much his super power.
10. Kurt, by this point had already done heroin at least once, in 1986 or 87 (his story changed depending on the telling), though he hadn't yet made any sort of habit of it. In his journals he wrote that he'd tried the drug ten times between 1987 and 1990. Seattle had a reputation for heroin, especially amongst its musician community, that went back to the early 80s ('[we] thought Seattle bands were drunks and heroin addicts without any convictions or creativity', as Olympia musician Slim Moon told Nicholas Soulsby). It was a reputation that had some basis in fact. 'In Seattle, heroin was fast becoming a staple in pretty much everyones's diet … I watched it take over the city', wrote Seattle native and Guns N' Roses bassplayer Duff McKagen in his memoir *It's So Easy and other Lies*. 'I witnessed my first overdose when I was 18 …By the time I was 23, two of my best friends had died from heroin overdoses.' Smack was easy to get hold of – Seattle was a port city and an international trading hub, so the drug came in cheap from the Far East, and could be a deeply attractive escape in a city characterised by rising poverty and miserable weather. By 1992, *Entertainment Weekly* would be reporting that Seattle was the fastest growing capital city for heroin overdoses in the entire United States, with a 225% increase in 'heroin-related emergency room visits'. For the young punks it also held a dark glamour with its associations with Iggy Pop, Lou Reed, Sid Vicious and seedy decadence. Kurt's name would shortly be added to that list. The two Kurts, Cobain and Danielson, had been making fun of the idea of becoming junkies on tour in Europe, treating them as tragic figures of fun. Both would become addicts. Heroin would impact the careers of pretty much every one of the key, first wave grunge bands. Often fatally. It was everywhere. Kurt's reaction, as ever, was to make light of it.
11. It's unknown why the Melvins switched back as headliners for the Olympia show. Maybe Buzz Osborne had put his foot down? Nirvana's re-appearance at the top of the bill the next night in Tacoma suggests the audience reaction had proven Kurt right – Nirvana had overtaken and outpaced their mentors. Possibly, of course, they were just taking it in turns, though Osborne's rather shirty response to the idea he play main support suggests a less cordial arrangement. A breathlessly enthusiastic review of the Tacoma gig, appearing in local paper *The Current*, is a pretty clear indication that Kurt, Krist and Chad were absolutely accepted as headliners.

February 9

- TAD and Nirvana's west-coast US tour begins at the 1,000+ capacity Pine Street Theatre, Portland, where both bands are the opening acts for Screaming Trees.[12] The tour then winds its way down the coast through California, into Mexico, back up through Phoenix and then up through Califnornia on the way home, via Chica. It's a more successful and *much* more fun tour than the 1989 dates.

March 12

- Nirvana and TAD head north for a one-off date in Canada, at The Town Pump in Vancouver, British Columbia.

March 20

- A Nirvana video shoot takes place at Evergreen College, Olympia, using borrowed gear and student filmmakers, working on the sly during Spring Break with the intention of creating a VHS that could be sold at shows. The band are shot on multiple cameras at once, edited on the fly in the control room, as they perform versions of 'School', 'Big Cheese', 'Floyd The Barber' and a new song, 'Lithium'[13], against a blue screen, onto which is inserted footage Kurt has taped from the TV, including cheesy disco dancing, body builders, commercials and an out-of-

12. According to Eric Moore of local openers Rawhead Rex the venue was oversold and packed to the rafters, and there was a genuine buzz in the air. A recording of Nirvana's set (Jack Endino was on hand to record the three bands that night) was later released as the bonus disc for the 20th anniversary edition of *Bleach*. It's a corking show … messily energetic, and ear-splittingly loud. There's always an element of chaos to Nirvana performances, especially during this era, but at their core Nirvana are sharp as a tack and tight as a drum as that chaos roars around them. It's a definitive post-*Bleach*, post-Jason, pre-Grohl performance. Also on the bill was a short spot by The Legend!, aka *Melody Maker*'s Everett True, who performed his forthcoming, Syd-Barretish novelty single 'Do Nuts', which he had (somehow) convinced Sub Pop to release. True even managed to vaguely review himself in his write-up without giving away who 'The Legend!' actually was.
13. With the addition of 'Lithium' the pieces of what would become Nirvana's breakthrough record are starting to fall into place. Arguably, 'Lithium' is the first of *Nevermind*'s real cornerstones to be written. It's one of those songs that changes things. This early, scratchy take has slightly different and occasionally inaudible lyrics, but the structure is almost identical to the performance that prompted the biggest singalong of the band's career at the 1992 Reading Festival. In many ways it follows exactly the same format as the version of 'Polly' debuted the previous year – Kurt begins with clean guitar played with a slightly scattery rhythm while Chad keeps the beat with rim shots and the ride cymbal, before everyone launches into a monster, distorted chorus. Where 'Lithium' differs is that Kurt's vocal is every bit a part of the heaviness, with his screamed, goosebump raising 'yeaaaaah yeaaaaaaah'. The original versions of 'Polly' *stayed* heavy once they'd gone heavy, while 'Lithium' drops back to muted and gentle in the verses. Nirvana's switching between heavy and loud and back again was the trick that put them over the top – and one they quite happily admitted to stealing from The Pixies. Krist plays a big part too; his bass's descending counter-melody on the verses contributes hugely to the sweetness. He then adds root notes, anchoring the guitar in the chorus, the whole band switching back and forth between brutal and melodic. On 'Blew' Nirvana had learned that locking everything together, bass, guitar, vocals, into a grinding riff added real power. On 'Lithium' they learned a better trick: of containtaining that power, unleashing it and pulling it back again. It's arguably the purest and most effective use of the technique in the whole Nirvana canon. According to Chad, the track was thrown in almost as a warm up on the day of filming. Those in attendance were absolutely floored by it. 'It was like they did a whole change', cameraman Alex Kostelnik told Gillian G. Gaar. 'They'd already impressed everyone and then they did this song, and you thought: they're doing it again! They're upping the ante!'.

copyright silent horror movie, *Häxan*, aka *Witchcraft Through the Ages*. Also in the mix is home movie footage shot by Kurt on Super-8 film, including melting wax, burning toys and stop-motion animations of dolls.[14]

Late March

- Sub Pop greenlight Nirvana's second album, which Kurt tentatively has titled 'Sheep', and the band start two weeks of rehearsing and writing at The Dutchman, a south Seattle rehearsal space they share with Mudhoney among others. A letter sent out to Nirvana mailing list members confirms that they expect their new album to be released 'in September on Sub Pop records'. Jack Endino is committed to working with legendary 60s/70s psychedelic rockers Blue Cheer, so Sub Pop opt to record the album at Smart Studios, in Madison, Wisconsin with local producer and musician Butch Vig, whose work with nuttso Wisconsin noiseniks Killdozer on their latest record, *Twelve Point Buck,* has impressed Jonathan Poneman.[15] Poneman also contracts Vig to work on The Fluid's new EP, *Glue,* Smashing Pumpkins' 'Tristessa' single and TAD's forthcoming *8-Way Santa*.[16] [17] The Nirvana album sessions will be folded into the Midwest/East Coast leg of the seemingly-unending *Bleach* tour, due to start on 1 April.

14. Kurt and the band lost interest in this project and the tapes were never formally released. It's possible they were unhappy with the footage, which looks amateurish and sounds pretty bad, though even through that you can see that the performance is great – in spite of Chad Channings 'rock star' sunglasses. Kurt had originally wanted the additional material projected behind the band, but the student filmmakers instead opted for a 'chroma key' blue-screen. It looks very 1986. The recursive, 'Bohemian Rhapsody' effects on 'Floyd The Barber' look especially bad.
15. Butch Vig had been twiddling nobs in the underground for most of the 80s. Born Bryan David Vig in 1955 in Viroqua, WI, he had a penchant for sound that was nurtured in a musically savvy household and honed through a film studies major at the University of Wisconsin; great training in marshalling disparate elements into a cohesive piece of storytelling – the role of a producer. The 1980s saw Vig and bandmate Steve Marker founding Smart Studios in Madison, a sanctuary for indie bands and a lab for Vig's production experiments. His approach was simple: keep it real but make it shine. His early career was a masterclass in making the underground accessible, setting the stage for the grunge explosion with a drum sound that could cut through the flannel. For a while, he became as much Sub Pop's go-to guy as Jack Endino, and he helmed several entries in the Sub Pop singles club, including Smashing Pumpkins' 1990 debut 'Tristessa' – establishing another relationship that would further his legend as *the* go-to alternative rock producer. He bounced between sessions with Nirvana (the Sub Pop sessions at Smart and the later recording of *Nevermind*) and Smashing Pumpkins (cutting the 'Tristessa' single for Sub Pop and then doing their *Gish* and *Siamese Dream* albums) across the next few years, and changed the face of alternative music in the process. Vig completes the three wise men of alt-rock production, alongside side Jack Endino and Steve Albini. Between the three of them they redefined the template for recording rock music, and did so across a range of budgets and styles and with faultless punk ethics. It's no coincidence that they each helmed one of Nirvana's three albums.
16. Though probably not at the same time.
17. *8-Way Santa* is one of the more storied albums of the early grunge era. A huge step up in terms of songwriting and performance, captured brilliantly by Vig, it was hoped the record would be a breakthrough for the band. Unfortunately they based the album's cover around a picture of an anoymous young couple found in a photo album in a thrift store. Shortly after the record's release in early 1991, the couple in question came across it and sued Sub Pop, leading to the withdrawing and pulping of the first pressing. Shortly afterwards the song 'Pepsi Jack' was released as a single, with Poneman and Pavitt using Pepsi's logo on the cover and essentially daring one of the world's biggest brands to sue them over it. Which, of course, it promptly did. To this day, Tad Doyle refuses to utter the word 'Pepsi'. The two law suits, between them, tanked any possibility of the album being profitable. It's Sub Pop's business model in microcosm.

April 1

- The tour begins at Chicago's Cabaret Metro. Nirvana had played here in 1989, opening for Eleventh Dream Day, local stars celebrating their graduation to the big leagues after signing with Atlantic. Nirvana had blown them off the stage. They return now as headliners in their own right. They debut a new song, marked on the setlist simply as 'New Song'.[18] After the show, the band drives through the night to Madison to begin work on what they believe will be their new album.[19]

---

18. This was the first performance of 'In Bloom' (briefly titled 'Knows Not What It Means', or on this very first outing, simply 'New Song') another of the key building blocks of *Nevermind.* Though the lyrics weren't yet finalised, as is almost universally the case for any new Kurt Cobain song, the version of 'In Bloom' Nirvana play in Chicago is astonishingly close to the one that would be released as a single in 1992, and it's another huge turning point in the band's development. Like 'Lithium', 'Sappy' and the early incarnation of 'Polly', this was midpaced rock – not the none-more-grunge, Sabbath-indepted slow plod of *Bleach* tracks like 'Blew' and 'Sifting', where the dragging pace adds to the brutality and heaviness, but a tempo that emphasised the melody and the vibe. This was 'power pop', a term Kurt had been throwing around a lot in recent months. Power pop is fairly nebulous as music genres go, and the name has been used to describe everyone from The Who to early 2000's pretend-punk boyband, Busted. The usual use, and certainly the one Kurt intended, was of a punk rock that swapped speed for melody, kept things deceptively simple and used big, big chords. It's what you get when you supercharge the cutie bands so beloved of Kurt and his Olympia chums, or when you put metal on a tight leash. It's about melody and power. It can be heavy or lightweight, but it *has* to be punchy. The transitionary era of Nirvana that stretches between the release of *Bleach* and the recording of *Nevermind* is as instinctive a demonstration of the term as you'll find. 'Dive' was probably Kurt's first foray into power pop, but it's with 'In Bloom' that he perfected it. Everything about the song is contributing to the melody; Kurt's huge chords and blasts of fuzz pedal, Krist's fluid bassline, even the drums – Chad's *blat-blat-ba-ba-ba* fill at the start of the song is as much a riff as anything the guitar is doing and as much a hook as any of the singing. And it's *all there* in that first performance. Some mumbled lyrics and a sloppy solo aside, Kurt had written his first song that immediately and unarguably sounded like a bonafide hit single. As TAD's Kurt Danielson would tell Gillian G. Gaar, 'that song was a quantum leap … it just took my breath away'. Lyrically, while the verses were still clearly in flux, the chorus was very much locked. In it, Kurt bemoans the same gun-toting, shit-kicking school bullies he complained about so much on *Bleach*, only now they were turning up for his shows and singing along to his songs. The experience in Rome, especially, had left its scars. Kurt still believed in the purity of underground music as something outside of the establishment and certainly outside of fashion, and the blurring of those lines was starting to niggle. It would only get worse. That's also the thinking behind the proposed album title of *Sheep*, with Kurt mocking the faceless masses that would follow the herd to the record store to buy his new album – an idea that simultaneously amused, excited and revolted him. 'In Bloom' is the first indication of Kurt's reluctance to be adored by the wrong people and his suspicion that it might actually happen. That he'd done so with the most accessible song he'd ever written, a song that would ultimately contribute to making that problem exponentially worse, is something of an unfortunate cosmic irony. You'd hope that, later, Kurt would, at the very least, have got some kind of bitter kick out of the worst parts of his audience singing about themselves as they joined in on the choruses.
19. Curiously, the 14-song setlist Nirvana played that night lists just three of the new pieces they were intending to record in the coming week – 'Dive' and 'Imodium' (aka 'Breed'), which were both well bedded in by now, and 'New Song' (aka 'In Bloom'). Since we know 'Polly', 'Lithium' and 'Sappy' were pretty well formed by this point, and we can assume 'Pay To Play' (later retitled 'Stay Away') must have been in reasonable shape (Butch Vig claimed in later interviews that nothing was substantially rearrange or rewritten in the studio, at least musically) it feels odd that the band would shy away from trying them out live, particularly as 'Pay To Play' and 'Lithium' had never been performed publicly before. Maybe they were just prioritising 'the show' and sticking to their more well honed songs? After all, they now had an audience familiar with their output, it does make a certain amount of sense to give those people songs they knew. Metro, one of Chigago's most respected venues, was a relatively big show for them too. It's not that surprising that they'd choose to lead on their best foot, and then go into the studio energised.

    Both 'Pay to Play' and 'Lithium' were kept out of the regular setlist on the April/May US tour. While the former was eventually debuted later in the Spring – though it was only played once on that tour – audiences would have to wait until August to finally hear 'Lithium'. Considering how incredibly strong a song that is, it's interesting that it was kept back.

April 2–6

- Recording begins at Smart Studios for Nirvana's next Sub Pop release, with Butch Vig at the mixing desk.[20] Eight songs are completed[21]: 'Imodium', 'Dive'[22], 'In

20. Aside from 'About A Girl', Vig hadn't been particularly blown away by *Bleach*, and had viewed Jonathan Poneman's claim that this band could be 'as big as the Beatles' with understandable scepticism. However, he was deeply impressed by Kurt's new songs and Krist's mercurial bass playing, which he smartly identifies as a melodic counterpoint to the vocals.
21. The sessions go pretty well, with the band telling Vig that they want him to make them sound as heavy as possible in order to contrast the melodic sweetness of Kurt's latest batch of songs. To that end, Vig puts plywood under the drums to create a more 'live' feel and offers Chad use of his own 'Terminator' snare drum (the same drum that Jimmy Chamberlin would use to remarkable effect on Smashing Pumpkins' *Gish*). Most of the instrumental tracks are recorded as a band, with Kurt punching in some minimal overdubs. Vig has to talk him into doubling up his vocal parts (which creates a thicker and more impactful sound) by reminding him that it's something John Lennon did a lot. Though Kurt's voice is pushed to its limits during the sessions, requiring periods of rest, and despite some tension over Chad's drumming, which Kurt seemed unhappy with, the recordings turn out extremely well, and the band, producer and label are all happy with the results. As it turns out, only two of the songs from this session would actually be issued by Sub Pop in the end – 'Dive', on the b-side of Nirvana's next single, and 'In Bloom', which was included on a VHS compilation of the label's acts. At the time of recording, however, the band sincerely believed they were making their new album.
22. Which feels slinky and powerful and has an excellent groove to it. Later, Courtney Love, Kurt's future wife, would cite this recording of 'Dive' as the song that finally made Nirvana 'click' for her. You can totally see why.

Bloom', 'Lithium'[23], 'Polly'[24 25], 'Pay To Play'[26], 'Sappy'[27] and a cover of The Velvet Underground's 'Here She Comes Now'.[28]

---

23. This is very close to the version that ends up on *Nevermind*, though there are a few subtle differences. Most notably the sceams of 'yeeaaaaaaaah' in the chorus are actually 'heeeeeeeey' here, and secondly the verses are played on the same acousic guitar Kurt uses on 'Polly', which is interesting and a little disconcerting when you've been listening to that exact guitar sound on 'Polly' for nearly 30 years only for it to appear in another song you're already deeply familiar with.
24. Unlike the earlier live and radio session versions performed in the eight months since the song had been debuted, Vig and the band opted to record the song softly and base it around Kurt's battered Stella acoustic guitar, which was his choice instrument for songwriting and noodling on the road and which only had five strings – Kurt rejected Vig's offer of a more pristine, better quality acoustic, preferring the darker sound of his own. The bass and Kurt's Stella were tracked together, with the lightest of cymbal percussion overdubbed afterwards, and Kurt adding vocals and harmonising with himself. The skeletal arrangement is perfect for the song, far more so than the power pop versions the band had been playing in Europe, and will become the definitive take. The spooky, minimalistic recording, apt for the stark and horrible subject matter, and indeed the dispassionate way Kurt wrote about it, is completely different to anything Nirvana had recorded before. Gentler, more subdued and somehow more harrowing because of it. It was a masterpiece. So much so, in fact, that when the band came to record *Nevermind* in LA the following year they realised they were unlikely to better the version tracked back at Smart. It's this recording that can be heard closing side one of the album, which of course means that, though his days on the drum stool were numbered at this point, Chad Channing technically does play on *Nevermind*, albeit only through softly hitting cymbals. In much the same way that recording of *Bleach* technically started with the 'Dale Demo' in January of 1988, despite the official sessions not taking place until the following December, the inclusion of this version of 'Polly' means that the April 1990 recordings at Smart, which would ultimately be considered demos themselves, are the true beginning of the recording of *Nevermind.*
25. Though it's widely believed that the '*Polly says ...*' false start on the third verse was a mistake on the day, Kurt had actually been singing it exactly like that for months. Presumably there *had* once been a false start, or at the very least an ad-lib, either at a show or in rehearsal, and the band had liked it and kept it in.
26. Later retitled 'Stay Away', this was a punkier take on power pop, led by Krist's crisply melodic bassline snaking over a snare roll before a satisfyingly noisy punk guitar crashes in. Along with 'Imodium' it shows us that, despite the forays into super pop, heavy metal, hard rock and artsy outsider music, Nirvana would always be a punk band at heart. This version of the lyric showcases Kurt's sincerely-held punk ethics, railing against 'pay-to-play' gigs, where venues either charge bands to perform or make them sell their own tickets rather than paying them a fee or a cut of the door. As a theme, it was ultimately a little too provincial for the band's major label debut, and the version that makes it onto *Nevermind*, though musically very similar, has substantially rewritten lyrics.
27. This second attempt to nail Kurt's most elusive song is more subdued than the version cut with Jack Endino back in Seattle. This time it has an eight-bar intro before the vocal comes in and a more meandering guitar solo. There's no slam of distortion here – possibly, with 'Lithium' and, to a lesser extent, 'In Bloom' pulling the same loud/quiet trick, the band felt this was an opportunity for some textual variety (the same is likely true of 'Polly'). Unfortunately, it renders the song a little dull. For my money, Endino's version has the edge at this point, though there'd be a couple more attempts before the song finally made it to market.
28. Butch Vig remembers Kurt strumming Velvet Underground covers on his acoustic guitar between takes during the session. They're not a band he mentioned often, though their 1968 classic *White Light/White Heat* does make it onto one of his innumerable 'best albums of all time' lists in *Journals..* The Velvet's combination of rock n' roll, cutesy pop and weirdo art jams put their DNA very much in the Cobain ballpark, and Lou Reed's low-key drawl is a close fit for Kurt's softer singing side. 'Here She Comes Now' is the cutest (and most Vaselinesy) track on *White Light/White Heat,* and Nirvana's version sticks relatively close to the vibe of the original, though the trio push it further and allow it grow in intensity until Kurt hits his fuzz pedal and then pitches his voice into his screamy register. It's a decent rendition, recorded apparently as-live with minimal overdubs, and worked out pretty much on the spot (Chad Channing had never even heard the song until the day they tracked it). It's a slight performance of a relatively slight song, but it's not without a charm of its own. You can hear the band enjoying themselves as they jam through a largely improvised ending. This cover was a commission from Gary Held of Tupelo records, the indie label that distributed Sub Pop in the UK, who was working on a Velvet Underground tribute compilation with Manchester-based Imaginary Records called *Heaven and Hell,* that would be released later that year. Also onboard were some of the most interesting bands in the British underground at the time, including Chapterhouse, James, the Wedding Present and Ride, plus Nirvana's Washington colleagues, Screaming Trees. 'Here She Comes' would also be released in the US the following year as a double A-side 7", twinned with the Melvins' cover of 'Venus in Furs'.

April 6

- After finishing recording for the day, the band are joined by TAD for a show at the tiny Underground club. Butch Vig, who has never seen Nirvana play in front of an audience, is blown away by the energy of the show, and by how overstuffed the venue is with excited fans. Following five days of intense recording, and with crummy sound in the venue meaning he's having to scream to hear himself, Kurt blows his voice after ten songs, smashes a guitar and stalks off stage.

April 7

- There are still some songs left to work on, but with Kurt's voice in tatters following the previous night's show, Vig and the band call time on the recording sessions.[29]

April 8

- The tour resumes in Milwaukee, WI. The band will be on the road until 14 May, and will play 21 shows across 35 days in the US and Canada.

April 25

- While in New York City for a show, Nirvana shoot their first ever music video, with director Steve Brown, for the recently-recorded 'In Bloom'. The day's shooting involves footage of the band miming to the song in Brown's studio and larking around on the streets, including playing their instruments on Wall Street and eating hot dogs while wearing creepy masks.[30]

April 26

- The band returns to New York's Pyramid Club for a headline show. The set is beset with sound problems[31] and the jaded New York audience continually heckle.[32]

---

29. It's suggested that either Vig will go to Seattle later in the year to complete the record or the band will head back out to Madison at some point. Ultimately, neither happens. When Nirvana enter a studio with Butch Vig again, over a year later and on a completely different label, they will ('Polly' aside) start from scratch. The album that may, or may not, have been called *Sheep* is never completed.
30. The 'In Bloom' video would be released the following year on the *Sub Pop Video Network Volume 1* VHS compilation, alongside tracks by Mark Lanegan, Mudhoney, The Fluid, The Dwarves, TAD and Beat Happening among others. It's a solid enough video, and something of a time capsule of Nirvana during this period, especially as very little pro-shot footage of the *Bleach* era exists. It also includes footage shot at a show in New York the following day, and in Amherst a few days later – you can tell them apart because Krist's haircut has changed rather dramatically in the latter. Director Brown makes good use of the band's puckish charisma on the streets, combining it with Kurt's natural intensity against the sheets in his studio, where he mimes his vocals with the shadows of Krist and Chad performing behind him. Links to the *Bleach* artwork are created by occasional shifts into negative. It's not the sort of music video that will propel any band to the top, but it's a decent promo for an underground band in 1990.
31. Nirvana were touring without regular sound man Craig Montgomery and relied on the in-house sound engineers at each venue. Jonathan Poneman, who was in town for the big New York show, tried on the day to fly Montgomery out, but to no avail. He would eventually join the band in time for the last week or so of the tour.
32. As Krist tries to keep things light while he asks for sound adjustments, someone shouts 'SHUT UP YOU DORK!' Krist's response is brilliant: 'What, were you a jock in high school? Were you a letterman

In the audience are members of alternative rock elite Sonic Youth, who have also dragged along representatives from their label, DGC, as well as punk legend Iggy Pop, who pogoes throughout and is delighted to note that Kurt is wearing a Stooges t-shirt (Kurt is actually horrified by this coincidence). The band are mortified by how badly they feel the show goes. Later that night Krist shaves his head as an act of personal penance, while Kurt briefly decides to quit the band.[33]

April 27

- The tour continues at an Amnesty International benefit concert at Hampshire College in Amhurst. Kurt wears a dress and Krist debuts his shaved-head-of-shame. The show is way, way better than the previous night's New York performance.[34]

May 1

- Sub Pop release *The Winding Sheet*, the debut solo album by Mark Lanegan, featuring the cut of 'Where Did You Sleep Last Night' from 1989's Jury sessions, with Krist on bass and Kurt on guitar. Kurt also contributes vocals to 'Down In The Dark'.[35]

---

in high school or something? [high voice] "Oh look there's a dork walking down the hall", well you can take your girlfriend Mandy or Buffy and screw her in the back seat of your muscle car for all I give a shit.' That heckler? Bob Nastanovich from New York indie band Pavement. A little later someone can be heard screaming 'The singer deserves overtime! He's carrying the band!'. This is Pavement's Stephen Malkmus.

33. Again we ask the question, 'was the show really that bad'? Listening to a recording now, over thirty years later – no. Absolutely not. It's fine, at least for the most part. For the majority of the set, the band are tight and loud and the songs feel like waves, smashing into the audience who occasionally refuse to be budged by them. Throughout the show Kurt and Krist ask for fixes to the sound, and it's worth remembering that what the audience can hear is *not* what the band can hear – onstage, things can sound very different. By the end of the show the band start to get to sloppy and there are mistakes – a result of not being able to hear each other properly combined with a certain belligerence generated by the vibe in the room. 'Been A Son' has a false start and 'Negative Creep' descends into absolute chaos as the band start trashing their gear. It's telling that 'Blew', their traditional set-closer at the time, goes unplayed. Cynical New York crowds are hard won, and the show wasn't well received, in truth. Singer Victor Poison-Tete, of support band Rat At Rat R, called the set a 'ten minute temper tantrum' by the 'FM Jesus', and told Nick Soursby that he found the whole thing contrived and left early, while Page Hamilton of Helmet told Carrie Borzillo that 'they were just kind of sloppy'. The guys from Pavement were clearly equally unimpressed. A review in *Sounds* calls the show 'a sorry, unimpressive collection of ground down, dead-beat AmeriSloth rock … far removed from the wrenching euphoria of their last UK tour'. Ouch. The jaded, hipster audience didn't help things. 'Every time we play New York we love to come to the Pyramid Club', Krist announces in a faux-cheesy voice at the end, 'you guys have been spectacular'. It's genuinely unclear if he's being sarcastic. Others, though, are full of praise. Janet Billig, the band's friend, told Everett True that this was the night Nirvana 'came out and took over NYC. They were amazing.' Another contemporary UK review, available at the *LiveNirvana* website but frustratingly unsourced, raves about the performance under the headline 'Grunge For The Conneiseur' calling it a 'full blown, sonic guerilla assault'. It just goes to show that a gig is rarely as bad as the band thinks it is. Iggy Pop, by all accounts, enjoyed himself enormously.
34. An understatement. The same *Sounds* review that gave the New York gig a full-on kicking also followed the band across the next two shows, which get rave write-ups.
35. Lanegan's day job with Screaming Trees would dominate his reputation, especially at the time, but *The Winding Sheet* really is an absolutely gorgeous record, and for me it's his solo stuff where he really shines. Many people will tell you, more or less correctly, that he would write better albums, both as a solo artist and as a serial collaborator, especially working with Josh Homme or Isobel Campbell, but this first has an atmosphere and a sort of curiously weary innocence that feels special. At least to me. Dave Grohl would

May 14

- The tour draws to a close at The Garage in Denver, Colorado[36] and the band head back home to the NorthWest.[37]

May

- Worried that Nirvana might shop around for a new label, Sub Pop issue the band with a brand new, 30 page contract – Pavitt and Poneman are in talks with major labels about partnership deals that would have greatly improved distribution while keeping their independence. Such a move wasn't covered in their existing contract, so Nirvana were being issued with a new deal that accounted for any change in

---

later rate this as one of his favourite albums of all time, and listened to it obsessively after he moved to Seattle. Which we'll come to shortly. Sub Pop, by the way, invoked Lanegan's absolute fury when they shipped the record with a cover photo he had expressly asked them not to use.

36. There are listings showing a gig in Boise, Idaho on 17 May which is often mentioned in biographies, but that show appears to have been cancelled.

37. This had been a patchier tour for Nirvana, compared to the breezy run down the West Coast they'd played with TAD earlier in the year. While audiences were generally much healthier than the last time the band had slogged across to the East Coast, there were still underattended shows and venues with terrible sound, and the absence of Craig Montgomery for many of the shows was felt. However, interviews throughout the tour show a band in good spirits, and what recordings are in circulation generally capture great performances, but for the ever present sound and tuning problems. Reports of the gigs are massively conflicting when you read the various accounts and reviews: the band might think they sucked at one particular show, but someone in the audience will remember being awed. A friend of theirs might think a show was incredible, while a review of the same night would be lukewarm. It might depend on what you're looking for from a band, and what your expectations were. If you'd heard the hype from the UK music press and the myth-making Sub Pop had deployed across the media, and had you heard and loved *Bleach*, you might show up expecting to see a slick heavy metal band, like Soundgarden for example. In which case you might find Nirvana's cheeky amateurishness off putting. They were a *messy* band. To an extent, they always would be. Sonically perfect rock shows were never the intent. If, however, you were a punk rock fan or if you went with an open mind, you'd find a loud, fast, poppy band that razorbladed your face with fuzz guitar and then bathed it in the antiseptic cream of melody. A band that was both intense and *fun*. Either you found the gear-trashing hijinks cool and cathartic, or you found it petulant and wasteful, and maybe even performative. Either Krist was hilarious or a loudmouth drunk. It's all about perspective. The pre-*Nevermind* Nirvana were never pristine and they could lean into their messiness, especially between songs. When a song kicked in, though, they were usually a powerful, tight and well-drilled unit. They might spend a lot of the show tuning up and complaining about vocal levels, or trashing their gear, but when they start to play all of that chaos is controlled and channelled into the performance. It all depends which elements you want to highlight – when they slam into the song it's almost always amazing.

There were certainly problems on the tour though – Kurt was getting increasingly frustrated with Chad's playing, and could be mean-spirited. He'd often take his bad moods out on his drummer. Chad was usually the recipient of the chaotic destruction on stage, too; Kurt diving into the drums, or pulling them down. At one show he dumped a pitcher of water over him, and it's hard to tell if it's in frustration or fun. In turn, Chad's spirits were pretty low and his heart wasn't quite in it anymore. It was now clear to him that he wasn't going to be making a songwriting contribution, drum parts aside (and even those were often dictated by Kurt), and that Kurt wasn't interested in his compositions and wanted to micromanage his playing, which was frustrating him and reflected in his performances.

By the end of the tour everyone was exhausted. Between 28 September 1989 and 14 May 1990 Nirvana had played 90 shows, usually several in a row, with gruelling amounts of travelling for a band that were still touring in a van with a couch in the back and a trailer. Everyone was burnt out. A bigger problem for Kurt, however, was the growing realisation that his band was appealing to the sort of people he hated. During an interview with the journalist Bob Gulla during the tour, Kurt had said 'we've actually had some jocks at a few of our recent shows and they liked it a lot. Which is scary.' It was promoting some existential dread. Kurt was making a conscious effort to write melodic pop music, but hadn't considered the downside of being so accessible. And he still had some gems to write.

circumstance the label might undergo. Krist and Kurt, who had indeed been privately considering a move to bigger label, take the contract to Soundgarden's manager, Susan Silver, and ask her advice. Kurt, especially, is adamant that he wants to get off Sub Pop. She tells them that they need a lawyer and, encouraging them to meet her in LA later that week, introduces them to a music industry lawyer, Alan Mintz, who specialises in working with new bands.[38] Mintz is impressed

38. Why were Nirvana so keen to find a new label? Sub Pop, after all, had signed them when no-one else was giving a second glance, had put out their debut single in a desirable format that meant it had sold out immediately, had put them infront of the influential British music press and created links with journalists who were falling over themselves in praise. They had booked them proper tours and provided a van to drive while on them, released and distributed their debut album and hitched them to an increasingly hyped brand that had given them context and generated interest. What was good for one Sub Pop band, after all, was often good for all of them and Nirvana had benefited from interest in Mudhoney and TAD, and vice-versa. What's more, they'd sent them to Europe, personally helped them out when things were falling apart in Italy, generally accommodated Kurt's whims and, just recently, had hooked them up with an amazing production partner in Butch Vig. It's not a bad track record, all told. It's not like Kurt and Krist weren't aware of that and didn't appreciate it. Publicly they were always complimentary and positive about their label. There are several interviews given by the band during the 1989 European tour and the two US jaunts they had undertaken in 1990 where they whole-heartedly praise Sub Pop and seem enthusiastic about staying on the label ('we don't have any interest in being on a major label,' Kurt told *Dirt* in 1990. 'It would be nice to have better distribution, but everything else that goes on at major labels is just a bunch of shit.')

There were, however, some considerable drawbacks. Sub Pop was perpetually broke – Bruce Pavitt had twice asked the equally broke Kurt, of all people, for a loan in order to fund a Nirvana release, failing at a fundamental purpose of a record label: to pay for the release of records. Bills went unpaid. Checks bounced. The band felt they were becoming relatively successful, and *Bleach* was selling reasonably well for an underground release, but there was barely any money to show for it. They were full time musicians who weren't actually making a living wage from their job. What's more, the gruelling tour through Europe had severely eroded the band's good will. There had been barely any money for food and places to stay, and for every well attended show in London, Rome or Paris, they had played tiny and distant venues to ever tinier audiences, all while crammed uncomfortably into a van with another band. It had been exhausting and miserable, and the resentment had been exacerbated when Poneman and Pavitt had waited for one of the more glamorous and touristy cities on the agenda, Rome, to fly themselves over and join in the fun.

In a purely practical sense, it was felt that *Bleach* hadn't been especially well promoted or distributed. More than once the band had met fans on the road who told them that they were desperate to buy a Nirvana record but hadn't been able to find one in stores. The *Blew* EP, intended to promote the UK tour, had been released with only one UK show left to play. Kurt constantly complained about the lack of decent promotion and PR. 'We haven't been promoted with our shit', he told British fanzine *Sleep* later that year. 'We went on two seven week tours and got two interviews'. It's not the first time Kurt had complained about the lack of interviews his label had arranged to help sell their records, though on this front he was being pretty unfair: this quote was taken from the *34th* interview Nirvana had given in 1990. On tour that spring, he had often whined about the lack of interviews arranged by Sub Pop *during* an interview Sub Pop had arranged. He wasn't exactly being disingenuous – it's more that his take on events was being coloured by his disillusionment. Kurt was always looking for someone to blame for his frustrations. There was a general feeling that using a major label would mean a better funded, better distributed and better promoted album, that would come with an advance they could actually live off.

For his part, Jonathan Poneman has always felt that Kurt's attitude was unfair. 'He said many times with regard to *Bleach*, "This record should be selling millions of copies"' he told Mark Yarm, 'and I'm explaining to him … that the idea of a band like Nirvana selling between 30,000 and 50,000 records then was amazing'. He admits that, with the benefit of hindsight, that this sounds 'foolish and condescending on my part', especially as *Bleach* did indeed go on to sell 2 million copies, but at the time few people would have argued with him. The biggest alternative rock bands in the country, Sonic Youth, Pixies, Dinosaur Jr, Jane's Addiction, wouldn't dream of their albums selling 'millions'. REM were really the only indie-orientated college rock band to break into the big sales leagues, and sonically 'The One I Love' and 'Orange Crush' were a long way from 'Negative Creep' and 'Blew'. Looking back from an era where Green Day, Pearl Jam and, not least, Foo Fighters sell out stadiums Poneman's attitude seems short sighted, but it's worth remembering that it's *Bleach* we're talking about here. *Nevermind* absolutely

by a cassette of the Smart sessions, recorded earlier in the year[39], and agrees to represent them and help them find a deal.

June

- After much soul-searching, Krist and Kurt finally decide that Chad isn't working out anymore. They drive out to Chad's home on Bainbridge Island to deliver the news in person.[40] With no drummer, another UK/European tour planned for the summer is cancelled.

---

sounds like a multi-platinum album, but *Bleach* is far less palatable. Kurt's pop heart is there, absolutely, but it's naive to think an album that sludgey, uncompromising and occasionally brutal would make Nirvana into household names, even with the muscle of a huge label behind it. The real issue wasn't any perceived under-performance of *Bleach* – that album had absolutely done its job. It was Nirvana's *next* album that was preoccupying both label and band. Even then, before 'Smells Like Teen Spirit', 'Come As You Are', 'On A Plain' and 'Drain You' had even been written, it was clear that this was going to be an accessible album with mainstream potential, and the band wanted to give it the best possible shot they could.

The other big problem with Sup Pop was one of image. Read or listen to almost any interview Nirvana give in 1989 and 1990 and they are inevitably asked about their label and the 'Sub Pop phenomenon'. Sub Pop was a powerful brand, one that punched above its weight in terms of notoriety, and its reputation went before it. Nirvana weren't just a 'NorthWest band', they were a 'Sub Pop band', lumped in automatically with label mates Mudhoney, TAD, Afghan Whigs, The Walkabouts and The Fluid, and by extension with other associated Seattle artists; Screaming Trees, Soundgarden, Mother Love Bone, Alice In Chains, Skin Yard, the Melvins. To Kurt, the band were being defined by something they *weren't*. Though there was some shared DNA there, Kurt's interests and influences were brighter and poppier. He liked Punk Rock and cute, lo-fi guitar pop, while Sub Pop's reputation was for hard rock and metal. Nirvana were an Olympia and Tacoma band far more than they were a Seattle one. Being on the label often defined bands as far as the general public saw them, and Sub Pop's extremely successful self-hyping was beginning to overshadow the music. During an interview with Swedish radio station P3, in 1989, Krist and Kurt notably bristle at being defined as a 'Sup Pop band' ('we were a band before we were a record label', snaps Krist). 'It just scares me,' Kurt told *Dirt* magazine in 1990. 'I wonder whether [fans] like us because we're a Sub Pop band or because we're ourselves.'

Poneman and Pavitt's myth-building also made the band uncomfortable. Speaking via the medium of Everett True in a March 1989 issue of *Melody Maker*, Poneman had branded the band 'guys in their early 20s from rural Washington who wanna rock, who, if they weren't doing this would be working in a supermarket or lumber yard, or fixing cars'. Perhaps most insultingly the snippet had claimed that they had, literally, 'no intellectual perspective'. You can understand why people as smart as Kurt Cobain and Krist Novoselic would be narked by this. 'I feel like we've been tagged as illiterate redneck cousin-fucking kids who haven't got a clue what's going on,' he told *The Rocket* the previous December. 'That's completely untrue.' While it's understandable that this would annoy or upset the band, it should also be remembered that Kurt had played into that myth himself, contributing details to early bios about living under a bridge in Aberdeen (which never happened), or meeting Krist in a woodwork class (which he didn't).

When word reached Sub Pop's top brass that one of their biggest names was looking to jump ship (the news coming via local scene scuttlebutt. Kurt was never one for talking things through when he was planning on ditching), Poneman and Pavitt were gutted, feeling that the move was pretty ungrateful. 'Literally a year and half after he was sleeping under bridges he was on the front cover of *Melody Maker* in England. I'd say that was pretty effective promotion,' Bruce Pavitt told Mark Yarm. And while the 'living under the bridge bit' wasn't quite true, you can absolutely see where he's coming from.

39. It isn't just Mintz who is impressed. The band have been frantically dubbing copies of the tape, which is now their calling card for finding a new label (they also include 'About A Girl' and 'Love Buzz' from *Bleach*) and passing them out to anyone they can think of, often accompanied with a sheepish 'don't tell Jonathan.'
40. This didn't surprise Chad. Like Jason Everman before him, he had realised that he was never going to get his songs on a Nirvana record. To him, this was because of Kurt's bulletproof creative vision and control-freakery, though Kurt would tell his biographer, Michael Azerrad, that it was simply a matter of Chad's songs not being good enough: 'And there's nothing else to be said about it'. For Chad, a songwriter who played guitar, piano and violin as well as drums, sitting behind the kit and playing what he was told was

July 4

- A gossipy piece in the new issue of *Sounds* speculates that J. Mascis of Dinosaur Jr. could replace Chad Channing as the drummer in Nirvana.[41]

July 11

- Enlisting Mudhoney's Dan Peters on drums, Nirvana record their new single, 'Sliver'.[42] Sub Pop has decided that it is time for a new Nirvana release and Kurt

---

never going to be enough. Chad Channing's contribution to Nirvana, however, can not be overlooked. Nirvana's fourth drummer (discounting regular temp Dale Crover) was the first that really gelled and stuck the course. He played on most of *Bleach* and toured all of it, enduring the gruelling slogs and crummy venues, which far outweighed the good ones. Listen to any show with Chad on drums (there's an excellent one included as a bonus disc on the 20th anniversary re-issue of *Bleach*), and you can hear the chemistry. Occasionally patchy, Chad may be, but he was a crucial part of the band at the point they first made waves, and his drumming style (possibly in spite of Kurt's direction) was a part of their character. Everett True quotes Mudhoney's Steve Turner: 'I liked Chad's drumming for Nirvana' he says in *The True Story*. 'A little sloppier and a little looser. It swung more ... Chad could be really *shitty*. But so could Kurt, so could Krist'.

At the time, Chad's sacking was considered a risk. It broke up what was, undoubtably, a good thing, and many in the band's circle were really unsure about the move. 'After the tour, Kurt called me and told me they were thinking of kicking Chad out and asked my opinion about it', Craig Montgomery said during a Reddit Q&A in 2017. 'I was against it because I still thought the three of them had a great chemistry together.' 'Krist pulled me aside and told they were booting Chad out of the band', Soundgarden's Ben Shepherd told Everett True, 'and I go "Damn. I don't know, man"'. For Kurt and Krist, though, losing Chad was a levelling up exercise. During the speedy recording of *Bleach*, Kurt had left Chad to do his own thing, since there hadn't been time to be finickity. But on the sessions for the new album at Smart, with Butch Vig, he'd really started to push him to play what was in his – Kurt's – head. And Chad wasn't always up to the job. Vig himself picked up on it at the time ('I noticed tension between Kurt and Chad,' he told *Uncut* in 2021. 'Kurt would sometimes go behind the drums and show Chad how to play.') Interviewed for an official interview disc (remember those?) distributed by their label to accompany the release of *Nevermind* in 1992, Krist would say that Chad had 'really compromised his style to suit the band ... it was a good departure'.

The last six months had been eye-opening for Nirvana. Kurt and Krist had started to see the potential of their career; that they could make a living out of their band, but to do that they needed to shift things up a gear. That meant a new drummer – one that could keep up with them. For their part, though, it still wasn't an easy decision. Kurt and Krist *liked* Chad Channing. Most everyone did. He was a likeable, slightly odd little guy that suited a band of likeable, odd guys. They had travelled the world together, sleeping in vans and under stars, playing heroic and shambolic gigs alike, and they had made a great album and written some new songs that everyone believed in. That the two founder members of Nirvana made the long trip to Bainbridge Island to deliver the news themselves, feeling absolutely horrible about it, says everything. No-one else in the band's history had ever been sacked in person. In fact, most of them had never officially been told they had been sacked at all. Chad himself was relieved, telling Azerrad that it was 'a big weight off my shoulders'. Kurt could be blunt about the incident publically ('we just kicked Chad out', he told *Offbeat* magazine the following year. 'We needed a heavier and technically better drummer.') or else simply lie about it completely ('Chad Channing just wanted to leave', he told Singapore's *BigO* in 1992, 'although I'm not sure why.') while Krist put a more positive spin on things ('He simply had too many commitments to fulfill,' he said in Germany's *No Trend Press*. 'He's happier now.') but in truth, both men felt bad about what happened. *The Independent* later quoted Kurt on Chad's sacking: 'I felt like I'd just killed someone'.

41. This was never on the cards, though Krist and Kurt had sounded him out about playing on their new single as a one-off.
42. Dan Peters, himself a phenomenal drummer, believed he was permanently joining Nirvana, a band he knew well and whose music he loved. His belief was well founded – Kurt and Krist had told him the job was his. Though Mudhoney had a busy summer of European festivals and an Australian tour planned, guitarist Steve Turner was mulling over the possibility of going back to school and had enrolled at a local community college, and while Mudhoney weren't specifically planning to 'break up', it did seem that things were winding down for a while. Bass player Matt Lukin even went back to his day job as a

is keen to record a new song with a new drummer, and since the track is so short, it has been decided that the quickest way of getting it down on tape is to drop Nirvana into a TAD recording session at Reciprocal and have Jack Endino cut the song quickly while the other band were on lunch, using their gear. TAD take some convincing, feeling they were having their session hijacked, but ultimately agree. Kurt, Krist and Dan nail the basic track in an hour.[43]

July 25

- The new issue of *The Rocket* carries an article titled '*Sub Plop? Is the price of world domination too high?*'. In it, writer Grant Alden outlines the financial woes facing the label, speculating that they might be in debt to the tune of $20,000 – $30,000.[44] Alden also argues that things aren't as bleak as they seem, since forthcoming albums by Mudhoney and Nirvana are likely to be decent sellers and would likely turn the label's fortunes around. The problem, however, is that the article doesn't exactly fill Mudhoney and Nirvana with confidence in their label. Both are now considering moving on.

---

carpenter. While mulling this news over, Peters had bumped into Krist's wife, Shelli, at Seattle's Vogue club one night, who dropped hints that, should he be interested in occupying Chad Channing's drum stool, the opportunity might be there. Between Mudhoney tours, he joined Nirvana in local practice space The Dutchman where they jammed the set and worked on new songs, including 'Sliver'. Kurt and Krist had bought him a much bigger drum set, assuming that his lighter kit wouldn't punch through the volumes they played at – something Peters was a little miffed about. He had, after all, been playing in a loud punk band for years. He didn't use it. He also noticed immediately that Nivana rehearsals were much more business-like and pressured affairs that contrasted with the laid-back, have-a-few-beers-and-enjoy-ourselves vibe of his other band. Still, it was clear that Nirvana were going places and with Mudhoney possibly slowing down, a sideways move to Sub Pop's *other* big proposition (or at least other, *other* big proposition – Afghan Whigs were also doing well at that point) might be a sensible career move. After recording the single, Peters set off on a European tour with Mudhoney, assuming it would be his last with the group, and fully intending to settle into a new role in Nirvana in the autumn. He didn't break the news to his bandmates until they returned from the tour in September.

43. 'Sliver' is perhaps the Nirvana record that most encapsulates Kurt's love of twee pop, and it's as straightforward a song as he would ever write, both narratively and musically. The song tells the tale of a little boy freaking out after he's left with his grandfather while his parents go out to a show. Eventually he has dinner (mashed potatoes and, ya know, 'stuff like that'), with ice cream for afters, falls asleep infront of the TV and wakes up safe in his mother's embrace. For someone who had recently penned an incredibly stark and nuanced first-person song about rape, it's something of a departure; though a charming one. The song swings along on a bouncing Novoselic bassline in the verses, until the cranky protagonist has a temper tantrum in the choruses and demands to be taken home, at which point Kurt hits his fuzz pedal, Peters starts throwing in machine-gun snare rolls and everything turns into The Buzzcocks. There's no solo, no middle eight, no bridge. It goes quiet-LOUD-quiet-LOUD-quiet-LOUD and ends. Kurt would later say that 'Sliver' was an experiment in simplicity, an 'attempt to write a real pop song' and, as he told Michael Azerrad, a way 'to prepare people for the next album.' The band would proudly talk up how it was knocked out in an hour, which suits the narrative of this tiny, perfect, bubblegum pop gem. It's not quite true. A second session was held for Kurt to finesse the vocals, and *that* session took almost ten hours – an absolute age in Nirvana terms. Still, 'Sliver' is undeniably a great single, as instant and likeable as you could possibly find. It's also a great showcase for Kurt Cobain's ability to tell emotional stories with his voice. On paper, the lyrics are free of drama and tension, but Kurt sings them as if his character is experiencing the most traumatic night of his life. Which makes sense, of course: if you're four years old, being jilted by your parents for the night is pretty scary. It also makes sense that Kurt could channel that feeling so authentically – like many children of divorce (his parents had split up when he was nine years old), a sense or fear of abandonment was never far below the surface.
44. It's not a coincidence that one of the local businesses awaiting payment for work undertaken for Sub Pop was ... *The Rocket*, who did the type setting for the label's releases.

Summer

- The band sends out their first fan club letter.[45] After giving some advice on how to get high by huffing the fumes from a shaving cream bottle, it goes on to update fans: 'Chad isn't in the band anymore. We'll miss him. We will have a single out real soon. We recorded with Butch Vig in Madison. What a swell guy. We don't know what may lie ahead, maybe we'll sign with Disney. Maybe we'll get a drum machine, maybe we'll get Phil Collins on drums.' The letter is signed 'Robyn Zander' and 'Jethro Bo-Dean'.[46]
- C/Z records finally release their Kiss tribute album *Hard To Believe*, which include's Nirvana's version of 'Do You Love Me', recorded over a year ago when the band were a very different proposition.[47]

August

- Kurt and Kathleen Hanna, a friend of Kurt's sort-of girlfriend, Tobi Vail[48] get drunk on Canadian Club whisky and scrawl graffiti on the wall of a 'teen pregnancy centre' in Olympia, which is actually a right-wing organisation aimed at discouraging young women from getting abortions.[49] Emboldened, they spend the evening getting increasingly smashed and end the night passing out in Kurt's apartment, where Kathleen has graffitied copiously on Kurt's bedroom walls. Amongst the slogans, insults and doodles are the words 'KURT SMELLS LIKE TEEN SPIRIT'.[50]

---

45. This wasn't really, yet, a proper 'fan club', it was more a mailing list, comprised of people who'd written to the band at their official address, 4739 University Way NE Suite, 1606 Seattle WA 98105, printed on the reverse cover of *Bleach*. The mailbox had been set up by Jason Everman, the only person to have ever been in Nirvana that was organised enough to sort out that sort of thing. Previous fan mail had been replied to with a generic letter that began 'Dear _______', with the senders name filled in. Don't bother sending anything to that address, by the way, the branch of Mail Etc that handled the mailbox has moved down the street, and it's unknown whether anyone actually maintains the box associated with that address anymore. It's an empty shop at present.
46. Robyn Zander, or rather *Robin* Zander, is the singer in Chicago power-pop band Cheap Trick. Kurt would later describe Nirvana as 'the 90s version of The Knack or Cheap Trick' in the sleeve notes to *Incesticide*, and in 2013 Cheap Trick's guitarist Rick Neilson performed a set of their songs at London's Kentish Town Forum, with Foo Fighters' drummer Taylor Hawkins on vocals, backed by a suspiciously familiar rhythm section comprised of Dave Grohl (drums), Krist Novoselic (bass) and Pat Smear (guitar). Meanwhile, Jethro Bo-Dean, or rather *Bodine,* was the most dim-witted of the redneck Clampett family from the 60s TV show *The Beverly Hillbillies*.
47. That was a version of Nirvana that included both Jason Everman and Chad Channing, for starters. Even more than that, though, anyone who saw Nirvana touring with Sonic Youth that summer or heard the songs on the *Blew* EP, released at the tail of 1989, or the double-pop whammy of 'Sliver' and 'Dive', which would be out by the end of the year, would scarcely recognise the thin sounding, messy quartet larking around covering Kiss.
48. The two were dating and Kurt was besotted with her, but to Tobi it was never especially serious. They were in love, but Kurt wanted more than the younger, care-free Tobi was willing to give. Eventually he broke up with her over it, smashing his own heart into a million pieces in the process.
49. Kathleen writes 'FAKE ABORTION CLINIC', Kurt falls back on his favourite graffiti slogan. 'GOD IS GAY'.
50. Teen Spirit was a cheap, girl's deodorant. Some Nirvana biographies have said that Tobi Vail used it, and Kathleen was saying that Kurt smelled like his girlfriend – her own version of a 'territorial pissing', I suppose. Kathleen corrected this in her 2024 memoir, *Rebel Girl*. 'Earlier in the day, Tobi and I had

August 13

- The band are in California ahead of a tour with Sonic Youth. Since Dan Peters is in Europe finishing up his Mudhoney duties, Nirvana have drafted in their usual super sub – the Melvins' Dale Crover – and have driven to San Francisco to collect him on the way to the first tour show in Vegas.[51] Since everyone's at a loose end Melvins' singer Buzz Osborne, whose house they're staying at, suggests they head into the city to see Washington DC hardcore band Scream play a local club, the I-Beam. Scream and the Melvins had played shows together and are friends. Kurt had, in fact, seen Scream in Tacoma a few years previously and hated what he remembered as hard rock posturing, and was even less impressed with them when they'd turned up at a party he was attending after a show in Olympia, just a few weeks previously, where they apparently acted like 'rocker dudes' and 'assholes', as he would tell Michael Azerrad.[52] Despite this, he agrees to attend the show at the I-Beam to keep the peace and for something to do. Afterwards Kurt and Krist are introduced to Scream backstage, though they don't get to speak to the band's drummer, who has massively impressed them during the gig – a hyperactive, and hard-hitting 21-year-old punk from Virginia by the name of Dave Grohl.[53]

---

been at the local supermarket looking at deodorants,' she wrote, 'and we both laughed hysterically when we saw one called Teen Spirit. *What the fuck does teen spirit smell like?* Capitalism knew no bounds'. Kurt, apparently, didn't know about the deodorant and assumed it was a cool-sounding statement about youth rebellion. Incidentally, 'not knowing about deodorant' is a criticism Oasis singer Liam Gallagher once levelled at grunge bands in general.

51. An understandable question at this point, is 'why don't Nirvana just hire Crover full time, since they seem to love him so much?' The answer, of course, is that you couldn't pry Dale Crover out of the Melvins with an iron bar. At the time of writing he has been with the band for 40 years, and he has always been deeply invested in the unique and idiosyncratic music that he and Buzz Osborne write together. He liked Nirvana as friends and peers, but he considered their habit of trashing their instruments to be cliched, actually quite tedious since smashing a guitar takes quite a while, and disrespectful. He also struggled with Kurt's dictatorial tendencies. Kurt was always the supreme leader of the band, and had the final say on everything, prodding the others into creating the vision he had for the songs. Dale had known him since he was a teenager, making demos on his aunt Mari's four-track; Kurt and Krist used to be hangers on for *his* band. He was never going to be interested in being, not simply *the* drummer, but *their* drummer. The relationship he had with Buzz Osborne was far more symbiotic and creative. He agreed to do the Sonic Youth tour as a favour, with the proviso that any damage done to his drum kit would result in swift and violent retribution.
52. At this point Kurt was still dating Tobi Vail, who was performing a solo set at the party, which the guys from Scream had been pretty scathing about. With typical tact and characteristic humour, Courtney Love, Kurt's future wife, described Kurt's taste in women at this point to Mark Yarm in *Everybody Loves Our Town*, as 'pudgy chicks pounding on pots and pans and singing about their vaginas'.
53. Dave Grohl was, at this point, living the Punk Rock dream. He'd joined Scream in 1986, aged just 17, after blowing guitarist Franz Stahl away by turning up for a low-key audition knowing how to play the group's entire back catalogue, including unreleased songs he'd heard on bootlegs. Had Stahl known the teenage Grohl at all he wouldn't have been surprised – he had taught himself to play the drums largely by playing along to Scream records. Formed by Franz Stahl and his brother, vocalist Pete Stahl, with bassist Skeeter Thompson, Scream were one of the second wave of true hardcore punk bands who, like the Melvins in Washington, Deep Wound, over in Massachusis, Beastie Boys in New York, Butthole Surfers down in Texas and Scream's DC neighbours Minor Threat, seized the primitive, loud, fast and political gauntlet thrown down by Black Flag, the Bad Brains, Dead Kennedys and Suicidal Tendencies. The young Dave Grohl was completely obsessed with them, sensing that here was a band that were able to widen their scope from the speed-obsessed blunt instrument of thrashy punk and incorporate some

August 16

- Sonic Youth's *Goo*[54] tour starts at the excellently-named club, Calamity Jane's Naville Nevada, in Las Vegas, with Nirvana as the main support.[55] The tour

---

of the classic rock and melodic bands he himself loved: Led Zep. The Beatles. The Stooges. He would play along in his room using pillows instead of actual drums – a technique that would work for literally nobody else, but which helped him develop an instinctive style that involved walloping ten bells out of any real drum kit he got to play. He still plays drums like that now. He'd applied to audition for Scream (lying about his age in the process) purely so he could say he'd played with them and for the thrill of getting to jam with his favourite band. There was absolutely no expectation of actually getting the gig. Which is why he was *so* shocked when they offered him the job. He turned them down, thinking he should finish school, stick with the band he'd formed with friends, Drain Bamage, and not disappoint his mother, an open-minded public school teacher whom he adored. Seeing the band play a show a few months later, he quickly realised he'd nearly missed the opportunity of a lifetime. Luckily, they'd held the drum stool vacant for him.

Born in Warren, Ohio, in 1969, to middle class parents (a teacher and a Republican political journalist, respectively) Grohl had been drawn to music from a young age. His early influences were eclectic, ranging from classic rock staples like The Beatles, Led Zeppelin and Kiss to punk pioneers like Iggy Pop, The Ramones and Black Flag. He'd discovered the raw energy and DIY ethos of hardcore as a 13 year old, visiting his Punk Rocker cousin in Chicago, and after that he had never looked back, teaching himself guitar and then drums, via those cushions, playing in local bands with friends and immersing himself in the music. He became a passionate authority on Scream, the Melvins, Bad Brains, Dead Kennedys and every one else in the Punk Rock canon.

In the four years following his recruitment by Scream, Grohl toured relentlessly. This was a real road-warrior band who, like Blag Flag before them, had the purist view that punk's most immaculate form existed in clubs and infront of audiences, and it was up to bands to put the miles in to find them. Crisscrossing the US (and, later, Europe) in a van and playing shows in dingy clubs, sweat-soaked basements and anarchist squats wasn't for everyone – it was a grueling lifestyle, as Nirvana could attest, but unlike Kurt Cobain, who always tired of the road quickly, Grohl found it paradise.

By August 1990, however, Scream were at a crossroads. The rigours of constant touring and the changing musical landscape were taking their toll. Bassist and founding member Skeeter Thompson had been in and out of the group for the last few months, often leaving them in the lurch, while cancelled gigs and a crummy management contract took slices out of the band's morale. Thompson would quit for good shortly after the show at the I-Beam, vanishing without a word on the day of a gig, and leaving his bandmates stranded in LA trying to work out how to salvage their career. Grohl, sleeping on the floor of Franz and Pete Stahl's LA-based mud-wrestler (no, really) sister, eventually took a job tiling the walls of a local coffee shop in order to be able to afford to eat, all the time wondering what the hell he was going to do next. Luckily, something would present itself fairly soon.

54. In 1989 Sonic Youth had left behind their indie roots and signed to DGC – a subsidiary of Geffen records newly created to work with upcoming artists. The band had been a priority signing for newly recruited label execs Gary Gersh and Mark Kates (who both came from the alternative scene themselves), due to their underground credibility. DGC badly needed a band like Sonic Youth to act as the 'Judas Goat' – a term applied in the livestock industry to a normal goat which lives a healthy, safe and happy life residing in a slaughterhouse in order to show the other animals that it's all cool and groovy and they're definitely, *definitely* not going to be shot between the eyes with a bolt gun, so they're free to stay docile and, incidentally, step right this way. That was Sonic Youth for Geffen. After all, if *Sonic Youth*, the coolest, artsiest, most credible band around were trusting DGC, then it was safe ground for any artist. The band got a pretty sweet deal from their new label, who guaranteed them total creative control and encouraged them to bring in other cool bands as potential signings.

    In the summer of 1990 they had released *Goo*, their first major label offering. It was a masterful, poppy but still extremely and defiantly Sonic-Youthy album that also featured J Mascis from Dinosaur Jr, Chuck D from Public Enemy, and had a cover drawn by underground punk's go-to artist, Raymond Pettibon, who had done Black Flag's early artwork (he was, handily, Greg Ginn's brother), including their iconic logo. That's quite a who's-who of who's cool. *Goo* would go on to sell 200,000 copies in its first year, setting a new benchmark for success for an 'alternative' band. Remarkably, there are those at parent label Geffen who considered this to be pretty poor numbers for a major label act and would probably have dropped them. Fortunately there were cooler heads at DGC, in both senses of the word, that knew keeping Sonic Youth on the label was vital to establishing its reputation and attracting new talent.

55. Having secured their own major label deal, Sonic Youth were now keen to use their platform to highlight bands they thought were cool (which was exactly what their label hoped would happen), and they *loved*

consists of seven shows, including the Hollywood Palladium in LA, Seattle's Moore Theatre and the New York Theatre in Vancouver, Canada.[56]

August 18

- On a night off from the Sonic Youth tour, Nirvana play a headline show at San Diego's The Casbah. They debut both 'Lithium' (although it's abandoned halfway through) and a new song, 'Verse Chorus Verse'.[57]

September 1

- 'Sliver' is released in the US on Sub Pop. 3,000 7″ records are pressed, divided between clear pink, marbled blue and plain-old black vinyl. The B-side is 'Dive', taken from the sessions with Butch Vig back in the spring, with Chad Channing on drums. It is the last 'new' Nirvana song released to feature Channing.[58]

September 6–20

- Scream play their final show with Dave Grohl for three years, at the Cannibal Club in Austin, Texas. Following this, they will drive to LA where bass player

---

Nirvana, correctly seeing the potential in Kurt's songs and the band's sound. Thurston Moore had, after all, brought in *Bleach* to the mastering sessions for *Goo* as an example of the sonic flavour he was after. Moore and Gordon brought Nirvana onto the tour with the specific aim of giving them a hand up to the next level by getting them in front of their own label and big league management, Gold Mountain. Thurston Moore even gave Neil Young a Nirvana tape, hoping he'd consider them as a support act. The two bands, who would tour extensively together in 1991, established a friendship that would last decades – when Nirvana were inducted into the Rock N Roll Hall of Fame in 2014, Kim Gordon took vocals on 'Aneurysm'. Later that night, when the surviving members of the band reconvened to play a tiny, one-off club show in Brooklyn, she performed the whole encore, doing 'Aneurysm', 'Negative Creep' and the final, closing (and first-ever live performance of) the brilliantly discordant *In Utero* b-side, 'Moist Vagina'.

56. This was a successful trip out for Nirvana, who got to fly their flag in front of Sonic Youth's sold-out club audiences, though arguably in Seattle and Portland they were as much of a draw as the headliners were. Recordings show a much slicker set of performances than previous tours, thanks to a combination of proper club venues with decent gear, and the influence of the tight and extremely hard-hitting Dale Crover (playing every set wearing only bikini briefs, according to Thurston Moore) pushing them way faster than they played with Chad. It's a joy to hear Crover playing 'Floyd The Barber', the only one of his *Bleach*-era songs still in the set. This would definitely be the best Sonic Youth's Kim Gordon and Thurston Moore will have seen them play, and good form to impress the various execs they were attempting to parade their friends before. There's still an element of Nirvana chaos, of course, with Kurt throwing himself into the audience (sometimes backwards) and the usual guitar smashing antics. The band, however, respect the sanctity of their temporary drummer's gear.
57. 'Lithium' would drift in and out of the set for the rest of the year before finally taking its rightful place as a setlist mainstay. It's still curious as to why a song this strong isn't wheeled out more often, though considering Nirvana played with four different drummers throughout 1990 it's perhaps not *that* surprising: Crover, Peters and Grohl all had a lot of songs to learn. Meanwhile 'Verse Chorus Verse' gets a rare live outing here. The new song is one of Kurt's less interesting, a Pixies-indepted quiet-loud-quiet-loud mid-pacer that, in comparison with the other new songs, sounds as formulaic as its title. It's not exactly *bad*, but as with other largely-forgotten Nirvana tracks (see also 'Token Eastern Song', 'Old Age', 'Blandest', 'If You Must') it treads through a format that works better elsewhere. The most interesting thing about it is its title (which was also considered as a possible name for both *Nevermind* and *In Utero*); Kurt was already well aware that his song structures were getting a little formulaic. This was his way of cutting any criticism off at the pass.
58. Technically there were two more Channing-era tracks still to be released during the band's lifetime – 'Big Long Now', an off-cut from the *Bleach* sessions, which would eventually surface on the *Incesticide* compilation and, of course, the version of 'Polly' that would end up on *Nevermind*, though since the former is an older song and the latter features only the occasional cymbal hit, it's pretty fair to say that 'Dive' is Chad's final, proper contribution to the band that fans would hear during the group's lifetime.

Skeeter Thompson will abandon the tour, leaving the band stranded. Buzz Osborne, remembering how impressed Krist and Kurt had been with Grohl's playing, and sensing that Dan Peters might not be the best fit for Nirvana, passes Krist's number on to Dave, who puts in the call only to be told, regretfully, that Dan Peters will be taking on the Nirvana drum stool. Later that night, Kurt and Krist call Dave back, having reconsidered. It's decided that Dave should fly up to Seattle and jam with the band.[59]

September 21

- Dave Grohl, his drum kit crammed into a cardboard box, arrives in Seattle to meet Nirvana with a view to becoming their new drummer. He's met at Sea-Tac airport by Kurt and Krist, and will be staying for the time being at Krist and Shelli's place in Tacoma. He's invited to Nirvana's show the next day at the Motor Sports International Garage – the biggest headline show they have ever played.[60]

September 22

- Nirvana, with Dan Peters on drums, headline Seattle's Motor Sports International Garage[61] to an audience of over a thousand. Nirvana headed up a strong line up of The Derelicts[62], The Dwarves[63] and the Melvins[64]. The show is packed and chaotic. Security is pretty poor, so the stage is invaded with a near-endless stream of stage divers. It is clear to many who had been involved in the scene for a few years that Nirvana have not only 'stepped up', but are in a quite astonishing ascendence, with more photographers and reviewers, more sing-a-longs, more stage diving

---

59. Krist initially grills Dave on his favourite bands, before Kurt (who is delighted at the idea of stealing Scream's drummer) shuts him down. 'I thought I should ask,' Krist told Gillian G. Gaar. 'I'm trying to ask him these questions, and Kurt's like: shut up! Why are you asking that shit? Tell him to get up here! So I'm like: OK, just come on up.' As it turned out, Dave was a fan of *Bleach* and was well aware of the buzz growing around the band. Though it was an agonising decision to walk out on the Stahl brothers, effectively ending Scream (and with an unreleased album, *Fumble*, already recorded and unreleased ... it wouldn't come out until 1993), Nirvana was an opportunity that proved too tempting. In the end it was Grohl's mother who told him he should put himself first for a change and ultimately convinced him to take the chance presented to him.
60. Dan Peters, remember, still thinks he's the drummer in Nirvana at this point. It's unclear if Dave, who has yet to so much as set up his drums, was warned about this, although it would have been a risky move to let him blunder into Dan without knowing the lay of the land. Given Kurt's usual passive-aggressive approach to management, it's likely he and Krist were waiting to see if Dave would work out before definitively telling Dan he was no longer needed. It must have been an incredibly awkward few days for poor Dave Grohl.
61. Literally a car garage. A big, echoey space that apparently sounded pretty awful according to Buzz Osborne of the Melvins and Nirvana sound engineer Craig Montgommery – although others remember this show sounding great.
62. A hard drinking, snotty Seattle punk band. Not to be confused with the hard drinking, snotty London punk band active a decade earlier.
63. A hard-drinking, snotty punk band from Chicago.
64. Less punk these days, but still snotty. Moderate drinking. Some posters for the show had Melvins as the headliners, suggesting that, though this is often seen in hindsight as Nirvana's first really big headline show, at the time it was being sold as a great line-up of bands, rather than one star turn and their support acts. It also tells us that the heirarchy between Nirvana and their mentors was still a little fluid.

and generally a bigger buzz than the band (or most Seattle bands) had ever gotten before. At the end of the show, Kurt smashes his Aria Pro II guitar beyond repair, stalks to the back of the stage and, momentarily overcome by the emotion of the show, sits with his back against a wall and bursts into tears.[65] In the audience is not only Dave Grohl,[66] but DGC Records' Mark Kates, alongside other record company execs, who is being urged by his own recent signing, Sonic Youth, to sign Nirvana – the show is enough to convince him to take their suggestion seriously. During the show Kurt reassures Sub Pop's Jonathan Poneman that rumours of the band signing to Capitol Records were untrue.[67,68]

September 23

- Keith Cameron of *Sounds* interviews Nirvana at Krist Novoselic's place in Tacoma, and the band throw a barbeque for the occasion. Initially, they'd told Dan Peters that he didn't need to be there, but he reassures the band that he can borrow his wife's car and make the interview and accompanying photo session. Bobbing around at the same time is Krist's current houseguest. 'This guy called Dave, he's the drummer in Scream, is hanging in the background,' Dan later tells Mark Yarm, 'having hamburgers and wotnot, and nobody says anything.'[69] During the interview the band openly talk about their search for a new label. 'We feel a loyalty to Sub Pop ... and we don't want to start a war', Kurt says, 'or at least lose

---

65. This moment is captured in a now iconic photograph by *Sounds'* Ian Tilton. Given what happens to Kurt in later years, it feels prophetic, though those who saw it happen remember it being a blip – he was smiling again a few minutes later.
66. Dave is one of the few in attendance who *wasn't* blown away by Nirvana – he said later that he was far more excited to see the Melvins. It's possible he was just playing it cool for an interview. He was, however, *incredibly* impressed by how many shirts the band sold.
67. If Kurt and Krist were trying to keep quiet about their search for a new record label, they were doing a pretty poor job of it. Everyone seemed to know that Nirvana were looking to leave Sub Pop, much to the chagrin of Pavitt and Poneman who could clearly see the writing on the wall – Nirvana were the carrot they were dangling to try and get a major label to partner with them. The two execs were deeply hurt that a band they had plucked from obscurity were now trying to walk away, after all, no-one else had been interested in Nirvana at almost any stage before then. The band had even attempted to get *Bleach* released on another label, but no-one had bitten ... you can see why Pavitt and Poneman were upset. It wasn't just Nirvana, either – starting with Soundgarden a couple of years earlier, the bands they'd stuck their necks out for just kept on leaving. Keith Cameron, interviewing Nirvana for *Sounds* that week, went straight out and asked Jonathan Poneman about the the rumours. His response was refreshingly direct and realistic: 'Ethically speaking, I have a signed agreement and I don't want to get fucked over. Having said that, I don't think they want to fuck me over. Those guys are very popular, they're very talented and they want to check things out. That's fine. But sooner or later they're going to have to sit down with us and make a deal'.
68. Kurt later claimed that an exec at Capitol had joked about identifying with the *rapist* in the song 'Polly', (saying 'are you *beatin'* that bitch?', as reported in Michael Azerrad's *Come As You Are*) immediately ruling the label out of the running for ever more.
69. This is a slightly delicate situation. Nirvana absolutely want Dave Grohl to play drums, but they haven't actually played with him yet and for all anyone knew, things might not gel. As a result, Peters has to be kept carefully in the picture in case his services are still required.

our friendship with Jon and Bruce … they're aware of what we're doing right now, and hopefully we can all agree on something'.[70]

September 25

- Nirvana rehearse with Dave Grohl at the Dutchman. Instantly, they know they have found their new drummer.[71]
- Kurt plays an acoustic session for Calvin Johnson's *Boy Meets Girl* radio show on Olympia's KAOS, announcing that Dave Grohl, their fourth drummer of the

70. While they clearly *were* aware, as Kurt well knew, it was only through rumour and hearsay. Kurt and Krist had never actually come out and said it to them directly. As Poneman says in the same interview, 'I get bummed out by the lack of communication'. Danny Peters, sat listening while his replacement is stood mere feet away eating burgers, would probably agree.
71. 'Finally, we found the perfect drummer,' Kurt would tell UK fanzine *Sleep* the following month. 'If he leaves, we quit. It's as simple as that. The drummer dilemma is officially over. Period.' And more or less, it was true. After five drummers (six if we count Dale Crover, which we probably should – though he never considered himself to actually be *in* the band, he played on more Nirvana recordings than Bob McFadden, Aaron Burckhard, Dave Foster, and Dan Peters combined) Dave Grohl was the perfect fit for Nirvana, and once in the mix the writing was on the wall for poor Danny Peters. As Matt Lukin, who played with both Melvins and Mudhoney told Mark Yarm 'Crover kind of spoiled Nirvana … Dan's more *tippy-tappy*, while Dale's more *thunk-thunk-thunk*. Grohl [like Dale] is more of a beater'. A summer of playing shows with Dale Crover had underlined for Kurt and Krist the sort of drummer they wanted – Dan Peters is a great player, absolutely; he's fast and tight and he plays his snare drum like a small, bore drill. But he's a very punk drummer, he's all about pushing forward and nimble rolls. It suits some Nirvana songs, sure – he was arguably the perfect player to record 'Sliver' – but listening back to the Motor Sports gig on 22 September, he does sound out of place on the heavier and slower numbers. 'In Bloom' especially, just doesn't have the punch it has when played by Chad, Dale Crover or Dave Grohl. And the fact the band were worried that he wasn't loud enough to get over their amps speaks, well, volumes. Dave Grohl, on the other hand, is kind of a thug. He hits *hard* and he plays *loud*. He automatically makes everything sound heavier. More than that, though, he's also an incredibly versatile player. As well as his obsession with blindingly fast hardcore punk, Dave's favourite drummer of all time was Led Zeppelin's John Bonham, one of the all-time masters at marrying creativity with heaviness. Dave, like Bonham before him, was a dextrous player with tremendous feel. He could create hooks and vibes, he could batter a listener into submission with sheer volume, walloping his kit and always hitting two cymbals at once. When required he could play *really* fast. He was also a human metronome. While Chad Channing played with a swing that pushed and pulled at the beat, and Crover and Peters both pushed slightly ahead, Dave Grohl sat right in the pocket of the beat. He was rock solid. It meant that Nirvana could go in any direction they needed to, and their drummer could come with them. It helped that another of Dave's favourite ever players was Dale Crover, the closest thing the band had previously had to a 'perfect drummer'. Dave's style was close enough to Dale's that he knew instinctively what Nirvana songs needed. And just to cap it off, Dave Grohl *literally* had a Black Flag tattoo.

year, had joined the band and sheepishly admitting that Dan Peters hasn't yet been informed.[72] He debuts two new songs on the show, 'Opinion'[73] and 'Dumb'.[74]

October 11

- After weeks of constant rehearsing at the band's new practice space in Tacoma, Nirvana play their first show with Dave Grohl, at the 500-capacity North Shore Surf Club in Olympia at a new club night being ran by Calvin Johnson, close to where Kurt (who now has Dave as a permanent couch-based house guest) lives. Support comes from Slim Moon's latest project, Witchipoo. There are some initial sound problems due to the power going out, and Dave putting a stick through his snare drum. The show sells out, with an audience of 500 people queuing round the block before the doors open. Dave Grohl, used to playing hardcore shows to tiny audiences, is so shocked he calls his mother to tell her.[75]

---

72. To his credit, Kurt at least called Dan to tell him personally that he was out, which is more than Aaron Buckhart, Dave Foster or Jason Everman got (though, conversely, he never actually told Dave Grohl he was *in* the band. It was just taken as a given). As is typical of the Seattle merry-go-round, Dan briefly joined Screaming Trees before settling back into Mudhoney where he remains at the time of writing, 34 years later. He has no regrets, has enjoyed a great career, and he harbours no ill-will against Nirvana – even he could see that Grohl was the final ingredient they needed, though he is still, understandably, a little peeved about how things were handled. There was another element in the mix, which Kurt, Krist and Dave have all mentioned at some point: Dan joining Nirvana would probably have broken up Mudhoney, and no-one wanted to be responsible for that, though to claim that was a major factor in their decision is probably giving everyone involved too much credit. Kurt and Krist would have regretted being responsible for Mudhoney's demise, but they were ambitious enough to have done it if they had to.
73. 'Opinion' is something of a lost gem; a punky, super-short, wryly bitter and super-catchy four-chord broadside at Seattle's music scene snobbery. This scrappy acoustic version remains the only available recording of the song (you can find it on the *With The Lights Out* box set), which you could absolutely hear being turbo-charged with distortion and sitting on *Nevermind.*
74. 'Dumb', a rather lovely if sombre treatise on outsiderdom, far more delicate than anything else in the Nirvana canon at that point, would eventually end up on the band's third album, *In Utero*. The fact it was being performed before they'd even recorded their *second* album shows just how prolific Kurt was at this time in his life. The songs were coming thick and fast.
75. Power issues aside, this is an astonishingly assured show, especially for a band breaking in a new drummer. Kicking off with a trio of covers (the Vaselines' 'Son of a Gun' and 'Molly's Lips' and The Wipers' 'D7' – they also end the night with Devo's 'Turnaround') the band are super-tight and there's very little of the between-song messing about of the Chad Channing era. Even when the power issues force a pause in 'Blew' the band blast back into it without missing a beat, a testimony to the five-hours daily practice they'd been putting in to gel as a unit, complete with improvised 'noise jams' in which their chemistry really began to bloom as they moved from loud to quiet, fast to slow, with instinctive telepathy. Listening to the show now, especially in comparison to gigs from earlier in the year, there's a sense that this is a different sort of show: a 'big' band playing to 'fans', rather than a club where a local act is playing to a general crowd. 'Blew', the first Nirvana-original of the night, is greeted with a huge cheer, as are most of the songs from *Bleach*. There's a general sense, again, of a band in the ascendant ('This band inspires poorly dressed record executives to wade through the crowd handing out diamond-studded business cards', reads a review in *USA* magazine). It was the public's first experience of the Nirvana line-up that would conquer the world, and while this is audibly the same band with the same songs that had played Olympia many times before, it was also a different one: ten times more assured, a million times tighter, smashing one song into the next without pause. They sound, absolutely, in every sense, *huge*. Those that knew Nirvana best, who had followed the journey since 87 or 88, immediately noticed the difference. 'Thanks a lot, Nirvana! You guys were great!' announced the club's MC at the end of the show. 'We'll see you on MTV!'

October 19–24

- The band fly to London for their second UK tour, a short, seven-day jaunt (with no mainland Europe dates this time) ostensibly to promote the 'Sliver' single.[76] Support for the whole tour comes from L7.[77] They spend a few days before the tour kicks off properly hanging out in Shepherd's Bush, where they stay at the Dalmacia hotel[78], a small B&B off Shepherd's Bush Green. Despite the fact the band are sharing a room and, predictably, all have heavy colds[79], to Dave Grohl, used to sleeping in anarchist squats or in the van when touring with Scream, it's paradise.[80]

October 21

- Nirvana head to the BBC's Maida Vale studios to record their second John Peel session; their first set of recordings with Dave Grohl as their drummer.[81] Eschewing original material, they record the four covers they had played at Dave's first show: 'Son of A Gun' and 'Molly's Lips' by Kurt's beloved Vaselines, the latter

---

76. Or possibly the 'Sliver' single was being released to promote the tour. It was a moot point ... Sub Pop, with characteristic efficiency, hadn't managed to get the song released in the UK in time for these shows, anyway. You'll remember that the same thing happened with the *Blew* EP exactly a year earlier.
77. Formed in 1985, the hard drinking, all-woman L7 were already a force to be reckoned with at this point, and something of a beautifully blunt instrument as a live band. They're often thrown in with grunge, though since they weren't from Seattle and predated the whole thing, it's more accurate to say that they evolved in parallel to it, imbibing the same influences. Equally, they're usually lumped in with the burgeoning 'Riot Grrrl' scene of super-feminist Punk Rock that emerged in Olympia around the same time, spearheaded by Bikini Kill, but again this is reductive and the band *hated* the comparison. To them, the Riot Grrrls were highlighting their womanhood and making it an important part of their identity as musicians. L7, meanwhile, just wanted to be a great rock n' roll band. The Riot Grrrls wanted 'girls to the front' at their shows. L7 wanted *everyone* to the front, and were happy to let the audience fight it out to see who got there first. Even their name was deliberately chosen so as not to highlight their gender. Their politics, however, were pretty aligned with Bikini Kill et al – pro-abortion rights, anti-discriminatory legislation, anti-commercialism: all the usual causes of the ascendant alt rock in-crowd. They were a fierce live proposition with a reputation for hell-raising, and could drink most anyone under the table. They wrote some incredible tunes too. Thurston Moore of Sonic Youth once jokingly called them 'foxcore', circling them into a made-up-on-the-spot music genre of female-fronted bands that included the Riot Grrrl acts as well as grungier fare like Hole, Lunachicks, Babes In Toyland, Dickless and STP. The name took off ... much to Moore's embarrassment and the frustration of all the bands tarred with the label. At the time, the band's bass player, Jennifer Finch, was dating Dave Grohl. Incidentally, when a British music magazine *Lime Lizard* asked Kurt about 'Foxcore' his response was 'what does that make us, "Zitcore"?' Which, frankly, should have stuck.
78. The Dalmacia was owned by a Croatian couple who had named their establishment after the region of (then) Yugoslavia from which they originated. Since Krist Novoselic is also Dalmatian by heritage, they welcomed the band with open arms.
79. It's not really a Nirvana tour if at least two thirds of the band aren't horribly ill. This was three young men with *terrible* diets, who all drank and did drugs of one sort or another. No-one worked out, no-one ate healthily, everyone smoked like chimneys. They were as likely to take vitamins and exercise as they were to cover a Guns N' Roses song. If they weren't sick, they were hungover, and if they weren't sick *or* hungover they were exhausted, and if they didn't seem to be any of those things, they were either drunk or high.
80. 'Nirvana's west London hotel room looks like a cross between cardboard city and a teenager's homework den ... Dirty laundry sprawls over three beds, empty lager cans sit disconsolately on the table', writes *NME*'s Steve Lamacq. 'To me,' Dave Grohl told a BBC documentary in 2021, 'that was some Four Seasons shit'.
81. Dave's influence is pretty obvious on these tracks, three of which appear on *Incesticide*. His playing audibly lifts the band compared to previous radio sessions, and his harmonies create a new pop dimension.

having been in Nirvana's set since their last European tour a year previous, 'D-7' by Wipers and 'Turnaround' by Devo.[82]

October 23

- The tour kicks off in Birmingham, with the band returning to London after the show.[83]

October 24

- After an interview with *NME*'s Steve Lamacq, the band do a photoshoot around Shepherd's Bush Green with *NME* photographer Martyn Goodacre, and an indoor shoot, to escape the bitter cold, with *Melody Maker*'s Stephen Sweet. At the end of the *NME* shoot, Goodacre is taking solo shots of an increasingly grumpy and uncooperative Kurt. Promised that it would be the last picture of the day, Kurt, sitting on the steps outside the Dalmacia, looks up directly into Goodacre's lens, eyes rimmed with black eyeliner[84], his expression neutral. 'I felt that something

82. Kurt liked to make statements with his choice of covers, and from that point of view, this second Peel session is a doozy. Nirvana hadn't released anything in the UK for almost a year ('Sliver' wouldn't come out there until January), so this was the first indication British fans (and, more crucially, the British music press) would have of the band's new direction, and they used it to go super-pop. The two Vaseline songs are tiny gems, short, punchy and bitter-sweet and there's a direct lineage between both songs and 'Sliver' ('Molly's Lips' is two-chord love-letter to Molly Weir, the Scottish actress who played Hazel McWitch in the British children's show *Rentaghost*. It is pretty unlikely that anyone in Nirvana knew this, but still ... a connection between legendary grunge-era degenerates Nirvana, with their voice-of-a-generation frontman and iconic rock anthems ... and ITV's enjoyably shonky and weird *Rentaghost*, a show aimed at eight-year-olds, is enjoyably surreal.)'. Wipers, meanwhile, were first-generation Seattle 'punks', formed in 1977, and very much a 77-vintage band, whose relationship with punk was more about being around at the same time as it was a genuine influence. They were playing intense rock'n roll, sure, but they never branched into hardcore or super-aggressive Oi!, instead they were doing what Nirvana and Mudhoney were doing ... only twenty-years earlier. In covering them, Kurt was leap-frogging the Sub Pop and Seattle bands with which he was constantly associated and going back to the true source. Ohio weirdos Devo, on the other hand, are proto-New Wave and were punk before punk. Their music is a little artsy, a little fidgety, a little knowing and a lot smart, and they are rarely heavy or especially aggressive. It's an element Kurt hadn't highlighted in his music before. All four songs are *fun*. This was Nirvana shrugging off Black Flag and Black Sabbath (if not Black Francis); shrugging off grunge and Sub Pop. These songs are smart, and knowing and catchy and direct and deceptively simple; largely adjectives you couldn't apply to TAD or Soundgarden, or even to *Bleach*.
83. It's roughly a two hour drive from Birmingham to Shepherd's Bush. British readers might be wondering why the band didn't stay in Birmingham for the night. US readers won't have blinked at this at all. I've toured in both countries, and it's difficult to truly comprehend the distances North Americans are happy to drive until you've done it yourself. That country is *huge*. Many fans in the United States wouldn't blink twice at a ten-hour round trip to see a band play for 45 minutes. In the UK, it's sometimes hard to get someone who lives in South London to make the trip to Stoke Newington. For Nirvana it would have seemed ridiculous to waste money on a hotel when there was a perfectly good one a few hours away. Plus they had an interview with *NME* the next morning.
84. Kurt, here, is smack in the middle of his one-and-only eyeliner phase. He has black-rimmed eyes throughout this tour and into the new year, though loses interest in stage makeup soon after, presumably feeling that it's too much effort. He looks cool as all hell with it, though. Daniel Riddle, of Portland industrial band Hitting Birth, who was around the scene at the time, has a darker theory, however. As he told Nick Soulsby for his book *I Found My Friends*: 'those of us with blue eyes knew that was more about hiding your eyes with pinned-out pupils when you're doing dope.' That's an entirely reasonable conclusion – Kurt had, apparently, started to use more regularly at this point, though the drug was by no means the huge part of his life it would later become. He was, however, already being secretive about

weird had happened when I took the shot', he later told Gillian G. Greer. 'There was sort of a connection. Kurt just opened his soul for a second.'[85]

- That night, Nirvana return to London's Astoria. Just a year earlier they had lost a coin-toss and had to be the opening act of a three-band-bill here – tonight they're playing their own show as undisputed headliners, and if the size of the guestlist (and those trying to convince staff that they're on it) and the queue around the block is any indication, the show is the hottest ticket in town. The band play a triumphant, 19-song set. [86]

October 25–29

- The tour continues through Leeds, Edinburgh, Nottingham and Norwich. In Edinburgh a campaign of letter writing and string pulling by Kurt has resulted in his dream support bill – alongside L7 are Japanese cutsie popsters Shonen Knife and, joy upon joy, a one-off set by a specially-reformed-for-the-occasion Vaselines, reducing Kurt, as he will later tell *Melody Maker*, to an 'hysterical nine-year-old girl at a Beatles concert'.[87] The band fly home to Washington in late October.

---

it. That said, it's unlikely he'd have been using on a UK tour of this size that was over so quickly unless he had some very good contacts. He'd certainly have struggled to hide it from his bandmates. Hiding his more worrying indulgences with a makeup *was* possibly a factor, but looking extremely cool and punk-rock was likely Kurt's main concern here.

85. There are, of course, many, many photographs of Kurt Cobain that have been called 'iconic', but Goodacre's black and white shot from October 1990 is one of the few genuinely worthy of the title. The close up sees Kurt assuming a curiously blank expression. It is soulful, true, but it could also be considered to be bored or even disdainful. He looks miserable, though apparently his true mood that day was closer to 'tetchy'. The shot was overlooked for Lamacq's *NME* article, which appeared the following January, however it would resurface on the cover of the magazine printed the week following Kurt's death in 1994. By this time the photo takes on layers of new meaning. Kurt's expression is neutral enough that the viewer can throw their own interpretation over the top. Instead of boredom, we see despair. There's suddenly depth, where perhaps it hadn't been before. Suddenly he looks utterly weary of the world he's just departed. It's amazing how much the context changes. This, after all, is a picture of the Kurt Cobain of October 1990, writing songs at the top of his game, chased by record labels, on tour in the UK where the shows are always packed and fizzing with fans, having just recruited the drummer that completed the jigsaw of his sound. 'Smells Like Teen Spirit', *Nevermind*, Courtney Love, global fame, *SNL*, addiction, interventions, pressure ... that's all in the future, and he absolutely doesn't know it's coming. Nobody could have. One facet of the picture that remains true in both contexts, however, is that Kurt is beautiful. His hair is newly cut much shorter than it has been in years, he's wearing eyeliner that makes him look like a young Iggy Pop, has the scrappy beginnings of a beard and his eyes are absolutely piercing (especially in a colour version of the image that would be published by *Mojo* magazine in 2023). He looks, as Martyn Goodacre says, like 'the last true rock star'. 34 years on and the shot is still being used for magazine covers.
86. For a second year in a row, *Melody Maker*'s Nirvana review is basically 'meh', which must have annoyed Everett True, the band's great champion at the magazine, no end. 'The mythology of remoteness comes around again', writes Jonathan Selzer, referring to the band's outsider status stoked by the Sub Pop hype, 'but no-one is willing to come round to the fact that Nirvana simply don't live up to it.' Fortunately reviews in *NME*, *Sounds*, *Raw* and *Kerrang!* are far kinder, verging occasionally on orgasmic.
87. This was that rare thing for Nirvana, and arguably a true first – a whole tour in which nothing dramatically went wrong, where every show was well attended and well recieved and everyone had a hoot for the full run. It cemented their UK reputation and their growing confidence in both their abilities and their future. Plus, their stay in London included meetings with a couple of record company execs who were more than happy to get them drunk and keep them well fed, and included a bonus trip to see The Pixies at Brixton Academy – the first time the trio had caught one of their biggest influences live (Dave describes the Pixies as 'our idols' in his memoir). Not bad for less than two weeks on the road.

November

- Nirvana take two huge steps forward in the 'professionalisation' of their career. First of all, Kurt signs a publishing deal with Virgin[88], leading to the first big cheque of his entire life – an advance of $3,000, all in one go.[89] Secondly, and most importantly of all, Nirvana – as a unit – signed with Gold Mountain management, who also handled their friends Sonic Youth.[90] Nirvana, a grotty Punk Rock band from Washington State, now has a lawyer, a publisher and a manager. Everything they need, in fact, to pry them off of Sub Pop and onto a major label.

November 25

- The buzz around Nirvana reaches fever pitch as the band play Seattle's Off-Ramp in front of a rabid audience that includes representatives from several major record labels. The band, who had been rehearsing intensely since their return from the UK, play a quite astonishing 31-song set, throwing everything

88. You know things are getting serious when bands sign publishing deals. A publisher's responsibility is to monetise an artist's work, usually through commercial syncs such as a song being played over a TV clip or used in a movie, or on an advert. Most importantly, they're also responsible for collecting the royalties from those appearances, as well as radio and TV plays and record sales. There's very little point in signing your publishing unless you have music you're expecting to actually sell in the broader market place. It's not a very Punk Rock thing to do. It does, however, say everything about how excited the industry in general was becoming about Nirvana – Virgin Publishing president Kaz Utsunomiya personally flew to Olympia to sign the deal, impressing Kurt with his tales of working with Queen (one of the few bands Kurt loved but rarely admitted to) and The Clash.
89. Kurt immediately spent $1,000 in Toys 'R' Us on BB guns and models he could shoot or destory in his art. He also, apparently, bought a $20 second-hand child's bicycle that he could only ride if he sat with his knees up to his ears. He would ride around on it, like a circus clown, trying to make his friends laugh and weird out the general public. His roommate, Dave Grohl, having gotten his first substantial paycheck from the tour (some $400 – a fortune for the young gutter punk) behaved very much the same way. Both managed to be broke again fairly soon.
90. Gold Mountain Entertainment had been established by former Led Zeppelin publicist Danny Goldberg and fellow 70s mogul Ron Stone, who'd worked with Bob Dylan, Neil Young and Joni Mitchell. By the late 80s they were already handling country music megastar Bonnie Rait and had taken Belinda Carlisle from moderate success as part of all-girl New Wave band The Go-Gos, and made her an international pop megastar, thanks to her 1987 banger 'Heaven is a Place on Earth'. Eyeing the success of Jane's Addiction and REM and looking to find similarly hip talent who could potentially break big, Goldberg hired John Silva in 1990 – Silva was the manager of underground duo House of Freaks (a sort of proto 80s White Stripes) and California second-wave punk band Red Kross. Just to underline his underground credentials, he'd once been Jello Biafra from Dead Kennedys roommate. Within a few months Silva had brought in Sonic Youth, for very much the same reason Geffen records had – they were the ultimate tastemakers and curators of the alt-rock underground. It was Sonic Youth that had pushed Silva to look at Nirvana, and Sonic Youth he returned to again when his boss, Goldberg, was reluctant to sign them – Thurston Moore and Kim Gordon's endorsement proved to be the clincher. Recently, Goldberg had declined to sign Dinosaur Jr and had subsequently watched their career explode, so was now willing to take some chances, lest he became a sort of alternative rock version of Dick Rowe (the man who turned down The Beatles). In early November, Silva had met the band in Olympia, where Kurt took him to see Beat Happening, almost certainly to see how this 'suit' would react to one of his favourite, and also most ramshackle and indier-than-thou bands. Silva gave them the thumbs up (lying through his teeth, as it happens) and thus got the approval he was looking for from Kurt. He then flew the band to LA to meet with Goldberg, who impressed them with stories of Led Zeppelin's heyday and promised, emphatically, that he could get them off Sup Pop and onto a major. It was enough for the band to agree to sign with Gold Mountain there and then, with Silva operating as their day-to-day manager and Goldberg available when the big guns were needed.

in their arsenal at the show: nine songs from *Bleach*, including one, 'Swap Meet', they'd somehow never gotten round to playing before, 'Spank Thru' from the *Sub Pop 200* compilation, 'Stain' and 'Been a Son' from *Blew*, all of the songs they'd recorded with Butch Vig, including a truly show-stopping version of 'Lithium', ('that's a top 40 hit right there!' Soundgarden's Ben Shepherd screams, excitedly, to his guitarist, Kim Thayil) 'Sliver'[91], their now-established double punch of Vaselines songs, 'Son of a Gun' and 'Molly's Lips', plus the Wipers' 'D-7' and a jam on 'Where Did You Sleep Last Night'. It's a triumphant encapsulation of Nirvana's entire career, thus far. Five new songs are also debuted, including the delicate 'Dumb', which Kurt had already played on Calvin Johnson's radio show, another delicate and sombre piece called 'Something in the Way'[92], and a sludgey, pounding and brittle piece called 'Oh, the Guilt'. The show is topped and tailed with two incredibly strong new numbers, 'Anuerysm' and 'Radio Friendly Unit Shifter'.[93] Due to local licensing laws the venue has to cut the power on the show during 'Dive'. Remarkably, organisers allow the gig to continue so long as the crowd moves outside while the room is reset, the bar closed and the alcohol locked down, at which point the show begins again. That night, Charisma records, who have long been courting the band, offers Nirvana a $200,000 deal. Kurt, Krist and Dave are keen to accept, Gold Mountain, however, have other ideas.

December

- After a couple of months of being wined and dined by the music industry, with all-expenses-paid trips to LA and nice dinners in London, Nirvana and their

91. 'Thanks Danny' says Krist from the stage after 'Sliver'. Dan Peters was in the audience, grudgingly realising that Dave Grohl was the perfect drummer for Nirvana after all.
92. The version they performed at this show is almost identical in structure and tone to the recording on *Nevermind*. It must have absolutely floored those in attendance.
93. Both of these, especially 'Anuerysm', which is one of only a handful of songs credited to all three members of Nirvana, showcase the chemistry and and dynamics the trio was developing. 'Anuerysm' has everything that's great about this version of the group, and you can practically hear the jam session that inspired it; the band moving from quiet to loud, slow-building and exploding, changing gear and tempo throughout. It has extended instrumental sections but never feels indulgent, it's so *noisy* but also incredibly poppy, it's full of barbed hooks and stings in both the lyrics and the vocal melodies, it's heavy but it's also somehow slinky. It's a song that only the Cobain/Novoselic/Grohl line up of Nirvana could have pulled off. 'Radio Friendly Unit Shifter' (then titled 'What Is What I Need') – which, like 'Dumb', wouldn't appear on a record until *In Utero*, three years away at this point – is another excercise in tension and release, bulldozed along and, in some ways, held together by a pounding hardcore snare beat that constantly pushes against the tempo of the song; never quite an off-beat but always threatening to wobble the piece into something far more awkward, with the trio hitting the bubblegum-pop switch whenever they get too close to the math-rock precipice, while fighting the instinct to relax into a four-to-the-floor Motown groove. It sits on a knife edge, and balances there, sharp and clean.

    The two songs are a huge leap forward in the band's songwriting. Kurt had entered the most prolific period of his entire life, spurred on by his excitement at the band's progress on the one hand and his painful break-up with Tobi Vail on the other. 'Drain You', 'On A Plain', 'All Apologies' and 'Pennyroyal Tea' also date from this period and 'Smells Like Teen Spirit' may already have been written at this point, too – Paul Branningan's Dave Grohl biography, *This Is A Call*, quotes Minor Threat/Fugazi's Ian Mackaye as hearing an early recording of the song that Christmas while Dave was home in Washington for the holidays, though it's possible he's misremembering this as other sources put '...Teen Spirit' as emerging a few months later. Still, it's clear Kurt was writing at quite an astonishing rate. Tobi herself told Everett True, 'he was in the process of writing the whole next two albums of songs'.

management agree to sign with DGC, the subsidery of Geffen that Sonic Youth had signed to the previous year.[94] The deal is for $278,000, with the band opting for a slightly lower advance in favour of an increased royalty – that said, it's still the most a label has ever offered a band from the Seattle underground. As part of the deal, Sub Pop recieves $75,000 and a small royalty on upcoming Nirvana releases, which will also carry the Sub Pop logo, and permission to release one more limited Nirvana single in the new year.[95]

- While negotiations and fine print are worked out with DGC (which will take until the following April), Gold Mountain put the three members of Nirvana on a $1,000 monthly retainer each. It's comfortably the best money any of them have ever made, and means they can dedicate themselves to writing and rehearsing without the pressure of making rent and putting food on the table.

---

94. Why DGC and not Charisma? Obviously DGC's advance was higher, though Charisma would likely have negotiated had that been a real factor. Ultimately though, DGC had a team the band felt more comfortable with. A&R Gary Gersh had signed Sonic Youth, marketing exec Ray Farrell had come from underground label SST and thus was a direct link to Black Flag, whose halo of punk authenticity was unimpeachable, and had also worked with Mission of Burma and Flipper, one of both Kurt and Dave's favourite bands, while promo man Mark Kates had worked with Beggars Banquet records, the home of uncompromising UK art-rock noiseniks The Fall, of whom Kurt was a fan. The label were prepared to accept the band's underground ethos as part of their identity (if we were to be cynical, they probably realised that Nirvana's perceived authenticity was part of their appeal and were smart enough to keep it intact) and, as they had with Sonic Youth, allow them creative freedom. Crucially, however, in the background, would be parent-label Geffen, and Geffen had Guns N' Roses, the biggest rock band in the world. Kurt had a stated aim – 'All my life I have dreamed of being a rock star', as he had told *Sounds* just a few months previously. When the band had met Columbia records' boss Don Lenner, earlier in the year, he had asked Kurt what his ideal career plan was. Kurt's response, according to Dave Grohl anyway, who has told this story many times over the years, was 'We want to be the biggest rock band in the world' (Krist and Dave thought he was joking at the time; in his 2013 keynote speech at the SXSW festival in Austin, TX, Grohl admitted 'I laughed. I thought he was fucking kidding. He wasn't.') Geffen had made a star of Axl Rose and his band – its subsidiary, DGC, could do the same for Kurt. Crucially, they could do so while giving the band some semblance of punk sensibility and the aura of the underground. It was the best of all worlds. As Dave says in his memoir, *The Storyteller*: 'It was a no-brainer'.
95. Though Nirvana did feel guilty about ditching the label that had first taken a chance on them, and though Poneman and Pavitt would always harbour a little bitterness toward them because of it, the deal with DGC actually saved Sub Pop. It was a badly, badly needed injection of cash. 'I don't doubt for a minute,' Poneman told Michael Azerrad in 1992, '[that] had we not had that agreement, Bruce and I would probably be washing dishes at this moment'. Thanks to the absolutely unprecedented sales of *Nevermind* and, later, *Incesticide* and *In Utero*, both of which Sub Pop received royalties for, and the knock-on effect it had on sales of *Bleach* (including reissues marketed far more heavily and available far more widely than ever before), plus the halo of success Nirvana were able to throw around some of their peers like TAD and Mudhoney, the deal Nirvana made with Geffen effectively ensured Sub Pop's survival. As bitter as its founders might occasionally admit to being about the whole thing, the label's existence as a going concern thirty-plus years later is in large part thanks to Kurt & Co's abandonment of it in 1990. Of course, you can also argue that Nirvana could have saved Sub Pop by staying with the label and allowing it to release their next record. Kurt and his managers were well aware, however, that Pavitt and Poneman had neither the capital nor the industry muscle, and perhaps not the stomach, to give the band the exposure they felt the new songs deserved. The irony is that, had Nirvana stayed with Sub Pop, they would likely have remained a top-end underground band rather than global mainstream stars, and Kurt might well have been much happier. Then again, perhaps not.

December 23

- Dave Grohl, who has returned to his family home in Virginia for the Christmas holidays, spends a day recording at his friend Barrett Jones' Laundry Room studio in DC, working on some of his own songs.[96]

December 31

- After a tumultuous 1990, a year in which they had burned through four drummers, recorded some of the best music of their career but released barely any of it, played over 60 shows and seen their popularity surge to the point that they're now fighting off major labels with a stick, Nirvana blow off steam by playing a New Year's show at Portland's Satyricon, with free bottles of champagne given to attendees.[97] The show is notable for how few songs from *Bleach* are performed.[98] Nirvana have evolved past it. Within a year, their lives will be utterly unrecognisable.

---

96. Though a multi-instrumentalist, a singer and a song-writer, Dave had kept his broader musical ambitions quiet in Scream and Nirvana. Partly this was because he was happy to play the drums and enjoy the ride, partly it was modesty – in Nirvana, especially, he was working with a songwriter coming into his own and at the top of his game: if Kurt Cobain had just played you 'Pennyroyal Tea' and 'All Apologies', are you really going to feel confident about venturing your own stuff? Lastly, it's possible that Dave sensed, as Jason and Chad had, that Kurt simply wasn't interested in sharing the creative limelight. Still, over the years he had amassed a clutch of material, some riffy and punk, some more introspective and stummed, and he spent his downtime documenting them with friends in DC. These would later emerge on a cassette-only album called *Pocketwatch*, combined with later recordings and released under the name LATE! on the Simple Machines label, as part of its' mail-order 'Tool Cassette Series'.
97. Predictably the stage is a mess of broken glass by the time Nirvana step up, leading to the typically-barefoot Krist to do a quick sweep before kick-off.
98. There is some indication that either 'On A Plain' or 'All Apologies' was debuted at this show, but no recording has ever emerged – a hand-written setlist merely lists 'new song' toward the end of the set.

Part Four

Here We Are Now

1991

January

- Sub Pop releases its last Nirvana single – a split double A-side with The Fluid, featuring a live cut of 'Molly's Lips', recorded the previous February in Portland, with Chad on drums, backed with The Fluid's 'Candy'. It's restricted to 7,500 7″ singles, the first 4,000 of which are on 'swirled green' vinyl.[1] The word 'Later' is etched into the runout groove on the Nirvana side, a final goodbye from their label.
- 'Sliver' is released in the UK by Tupelo. The 7″, as with the US version, is backed with the Butch Vig-recorded 'Dive'. An expanded 12" edition adds a live take of 'About A Girl', recorded in Portland the previous February, while the CD is rounded up to four tracks with 'Spank Thru', recorded at the same gig.[2] Omitted on all versions, however, is the answering machine conversation between Krist and Jonathan Poneman found at the end of the title track on the US release. Differing from the Sub Pop original, the UK version uses a Charles Peterson shot of the band on the cover, flipped into negative to echo the sleeve of *Bleach*. Reviews are strong – *NME*'s Edwin Pouncey calls it 'the best record this label has put out since Mudhoney's 'Touch Me, I'm Sick", while in *Melody Maker* Everett True uses his review to take a potshot at the 'lesser writers' who don't get the band, presumably still stung on their behalf by Simon Price and Jonathan Selzer's recent eviserations of Nirvana live shows. The single peaks at 90 on the official UK singles chart, but manages to make top five in *NME* and *Melody Maker*'s respective indie charts.

---

1. Kurt wasn't happy with this version and actively pushed back against its release, though not especially hard. By this point he was so desperate to get off the label and get his career on track that a limited vinyl-only release of a live cover version wasn't really worth going to war over. Besides which, anything that spread the good word of The Vaselines was okay by him. His preferred idea for the next Nirvana record had been to put out the Peel Session recorded the previous year at the BBC, with the Smart Studios version of 'In Bloom', under the title *Nirvana sings the songs of… Devo, Wipers, Vaselines & Nirvana*. He'd even drafted a letter (which he never sent) to Eugene Kelly of The Vaselines to ask permission to use his songs and sketched an idea for the sleeve design in his journals, which would have featured Krist, Dave and Kurt dressed as choir boys. Though the plan was abandoned in 1991, it would eventually became the Australia/Japan-only *Hormoaning* EP, released in 1992 to coincide with a Pacific and Oceania tour. It did indeed feature the full Peel Session (plus 'Even In His Youth') but alas did not have a Nirvana-as-choristers on the sleeve.
2. These two tracks come from the same show later included as a bonus disc for the 20th anniversary edition of *Bleach*.

January 1

- Having gone into song-writing overdrive since Dave joined the band, Nirvana record their first studio session, heading into Music Source in Seattle, where the extra tracks for the Blew EP had been recorded. The plan is to record a new EP and demo some of their latest compositions. Production duties are handled by the band's live sound engineer, Craig Montgomery.[3] Seven songs are recorded, 'Aneurysm', 'Oh, The Guilt', 'Radio Friendly Unit Shifter', 'On A Plain', 'All Apologies' and new versions of 'Even In His Youth' and 'Token Eastern Song' (both previously demoed at the same studio back in September 1989). No-one is especially pleased with the results.[4]

January 18

- The band play their first show of the year, an anti-war benefit at Evergreen, protesting the US military intervention against Iraq in the Gulf.[5] They debut

3. 'Craig, our sound man, wanted a shot at doing the record and we thought we'd give him a chance,' Krist told the *Blacklash* fanzine a few week later, 'but it worked out kind of screwy'. Montgomery had been bugging the band to let him record them for quite some time. 'Being young and naive, I thought that if this session went fantastically that I might get a chance to work on the record,' he said during a Reddit Q&A in 2017. 'Instead, our gear was in crappy shape, it was hard to get good sounds, and most of the songs were not even complete so we couldn't really get good results.' It probably *was* naive of him to think that he could be trusted with Nirvana's major label debut – having just forked out the best part of $300,000 on the band, DGC were going to want a safer pair of hands. If the hope was to get something useable for an upcoming album, they'd definitely picked the wrong studio. As Kurt would tell *Backlash*, 'it didn't go well … the place is [only] good for Nordstrom commercials'.
4. In the end, only two of the seven songs tracked that day were completed – 'Aneurysm' and 'Even In His Youth', the latter of which had been knocking around for a while. Of the new songs only 'Anueurysm' was in any kind of finished shape, and it's easily the jewel of the session, capturing the trio's powerful dynamics. Nirvana would later re-record the song for a BBC radio session, and it's that version that is included on *Incesticide*, but for me, Montgomery's more muscular recording has the edge. The versions of 'Aneurysm' and 'Even In His Youth' recorded at Music Source would end up as b-sides on the 'Smells Like Teen Spirit' CD single later in the year. Montgomery can be pleased that, though he never got to work on a Nirvana album, he did at least contribute two of the three songs to appear on their best-selling and most well-known single.

   The other new numbers recorded that day are certainly embryonic (none of 'On A Plain', 'Radio Friendly Unit Shifter' and 'All Apologies' have proper lyrics), but, again, we can see the levelling-up happening in Kurt's compositions. 'On A Plain', even in this state, sounds huge. Another of Kurt's flirtations with power pop, it's deliciously catchy. 'All Apologies', meanwhile, is the most embryonic of all here. In this version, with its' definitive recording for *In Utero* still three years away, it sounds far more indiepop and ramshackle, channeling the Kurt's beloved Raincoats, the Velvet Underground and Olympia's Velvets-indebted Beat Happening, with a tambourine and a scrappy, lo-fi rhythm guitar counter-pointing the familiar riff and, if we're honest, rather spoiling it. Beneath the none-more-twee trappings, however, are the bones of a beautiful and powerful piece that's arguably the most sophisticated thing Kurt had yet written. Put next to 'Something In The Way', debuted at the end of 1990, 'In Bloom' and 'Lithium', you can hear clearly why major labels were clamouring for Nirvana. These songs are *extraordinary*. Alas, that cannot be said of the final track attempted that day – a new version of 'Token Eastern Song' that, though more dynamic and heavier than the take recorded with Chad over a year previously in the same studio, doesn't really improve on the first version. It's a wee bit more robust, sure, but it doesn't sound like anyone's heart is in it. Kurt doesn't get around to doing vocals, and 'Token Eastern Song' would be doomed never to make it onto a Nirvana record.
5. Krist delivers a speech saying 'Wasn't World War One supposed to be the war to end all wars?', though this was marred by someone in the audience shouting to 'Shut up and play' ('That was one of the things I thought was sad about watching a cool band like Nirvana get bigger;' Fitz of Depression's Ryan von Bargen told Nick Soulsby. 'More brain-dead assholes. Good for business, bad for subcuture.' Krist,

two new songs, the raw, punky 'Territorial Pissings' and a super heavy art-rock jam called 'Endless, Nameless'.[6] Also on the bill is Helltrout, featuring one-time Nirvana drummer Dave Foster, who appears to have mellowed since his passive-aggressive sacking back in 1988, and completely fails to punch either Krist or Kurt in the face. He even lends the band his drums.

March 2–8

- Nirvana embark on a short Canadian tour. It's largely uneventful and an opportunity for the band to bed in some new songs. Interviews done on the road show an evolution from previous themes – 'Tell us about Sub Pop' has been replaced with 'why Geffen?'

April 17

- Kurt begins Nirvana's set at Seattle's OK Hotel by saying 'Hi, we're major label corporate rock sell-outs'.[7] The band are headlining a bill that also features Bikini Kill and Fitz of Depression[8] and during the show, which is being filmed for a

---

especially, had been vocal about his feelings about war in the Gulf (British and American forces were deployed in the area after Iraq invaded neighbouring Kuwait), though he could be characteristically flippant about it – he'd told *Sounds* the previous year that the war was 'gonna be so great. And I want it to happen, I really do, cos it's going to throw a wrench in the works'. Nirvana's support of an anti-George HW Bush, anti-Gulf War movement suggests that, on balance, Krist had decided that causing chaos for the Republican party wasn't worth the lives a war would cost.

6. Kurt had been very open about his embracing of melody and and power pop on his new songs, 'Territorial Pissings' however is *pure* punk – a three-chord thrash pushed along by Grohl's blasting drums. Only snippets survive from recordings of this show, but 'Territorial Pissings' sounds pretty close to the version recorded for *Nevermind* later in the year, though Kurt does throw in one of this trademark noisy guitar solos. Despite being at the noisier end of the spectrum, the song is another indicator of how much distance there was between Kurt's earliest and most recent songs – musically 'Territorial Pissings' is far, far more straightforward than something like 'Floyd The Barber' or 'Hairspray Queen', and yet is also more brutal. Kurt was getting very, very good at the 'less is more' technique. 'Endless, Nameless', meanwhile, was based around a jam the band had been kicking around for two years – it can be heard at the start of the version of 'Even In His Youth' recorded at Music Source in 1989. The loose, heavy freak out was a perfect example of how the trio was shaping its chemistry and dynamics. As Dave Grohl describes in his memoir, *The Storyteller*: 'Every rehearsal began with a "noise jam," which became a sort of improvisational exercise in dynamics, ultimately honing our collective instinct and making it so that song structure didn't necessarily need to be verbally arranged; it would just happen.' He goes on to compare the band's unspoken chemistry to how murmurations of birds move as one across winter fields. 'Endless, Nameless' is a perfect demonstration of this.
7. Actually, this isn't *technically* true. First he played a solo version of 'Pennyroyal Tea', before being joined by Dave for 'Polly'. *Then* he said 'Hi, we're major label corporate rock sell-outs'. Appropriately enough, the band then slam into 'Big Cheese'. The statement itself was also premature – they hadn't actually signed their deal yet, but since it was just a matter of working out the fine print, while preparations were being made by DGC for the band's upcoming album, including booking a studio and producer, it's basically true.
8. A rumour had gone around that the gig was supposed to be a benefit to help Fitz of Depression singer Mikey Dees pay off a traffic fine, but Dees himself denies this – though Kurt did throw the band an extra $250 to help get their van sorted for an upcoming tour with the Melvins and pay off some tickets. That doesn't quite make it a benefit however. Fitz of Depression themselves were a decent Olympia punk trio, whom Dave Grohl had befriended after moving to the city, finding them one of the few bands around he thought as scummy as he was. Bikini Kill, meanwhile, had recently formed around singer Kathleen Hanna and drummer Tobi Vail (notable local figures for many, many reasons who also happened to be the ex sort-of-girlfriends of Dave and Kurt). Their overtly feminist punk was as catchy as it was socially

documentary on the Sub Pop and grunge phenomen called *Hype!*, debut two brand new songs. The first, 'Pennyroyal Tea', is ghostly quiet and unfathomably intense, and Kurt plays it solo to start the show. The second is a monstrous rock number called 'Smells Like Teen Spirit' which sends the mosh pit into overdrive and causes dropped jaws amongst many of the band's friends.[9]

---

aware, and their self-released demo tape *Revolution Girl Style, Now* was, alongside Hanna's *Bikini Kill* fanzine, defining the feminist Riot Grrrl movement.

9. It's not an understatement to say that 'Smells Like Teen Spirit' stopped people in their tracks that night. 'The reaction was instantaneous,' Jonathan Poneman told Everett True. 'The crowd went absolutely crazy. The first part of the song was so good, and then it goes into the chorus and the chorus left the verse in the dust .. it was like time stood still.' Seattle journalist (and future operator of the Nirvana fan club) Nils Bernstein was also there, telling Carrie Borzillo that 'after the song was over, I could swear there was a two-second pause before everyone just freaked out'. Footage of the audience during the song confirms the immediate spell it cast – the moshpit goes *nuts*.

As odd as it may seem now, there was a time before 'Smells Like Teen Spirit'. A time before that intro. A time before the distortion kicked in and then faded out for the verses. A time before all of those hello, hellos and the screaming that followed. A time before Kurt Cobain told us, ya know, whatever, never mind. A time before that video. Like 'Hey Jude' or 'Tutti Frutti' or 'Jingle Bells', 'Smells Like Teen Spirit' is woven into the fabric of our culture. A lot of people won't even remember the first time they heard it; it's just one of those songs that's always *been there*. Its opening bars, those four chords divided by a little staccato chug and referencing the rock 101 of 'Louis Louis' and 'Wild Thing' (which Nirvana jammed onstage that night, not entirely coincidentally) and, by extension rather than design, Boston's 'More Than A Feeling', is in the canon of Great Rock Riffs, shoulder to shoulder with 'Smoke On The Water', 'Day Tripper', 'Voodoo Chile (Slight Return)', 'Sweet Child O'Mine' and 'You Really Got Me'. When you pick up a guitar for the first time, it's one of the first things you want to learn (handily it's also very easy to play. You'll nail it years before you get to Guns N' Roses and Hendrix). 'Smells Like Teen Spirit' changed *everything* – for rock. For youth culture. For Nirvana. *Especially* for Nirvana. That was all in the future, though.

'Teen Spirit' had come out of those 'noise jams' that Kurt, Krist and Dave always opened their rehearsals with. By now they were experts in each other's ticks, developing that peculiar musical telepathy that anyone whose been in a really good band, one that gels and stays together for a couple of years will be very familiar with. It's a hard thing to describe if you've never been a part of it. You learn to anticipate when your band mates are going to shift into something else, a different mood or a different key, and you shift naturally with them. At its most effective, it's all done on a subconscious level and it feels like magic, though it probably just comes from muscle memory and a close working relationship. By early 1991, Nirvana had gotten to that point. They were also really enjoying playing with the quiet/loud trick they'd borrowed from the Pixies, breaking their jams down to minimal hush and then exploding simultaneously into these huge, heavy crescendos; Kurt hitting his fuzz box, Dave anticipating with a snare roll and then slamming into both crash cymbals at once, Krist moving from melodic noodling to heavy-as-hell root notes. It was deeply satisfying. The riff from 'Smells Like Teen Spirit' was just another cycle they'd been playing with, though one they were returning to more and more. They'd been recording their rehearsals on a boom box and taking the tapes home to listen to; unfortunately the stinking pit of clutter and bad habits that was Kurt and Dave's apartment often swallowed those tapes and never returned them, and several musical ideas were lost. The direct, nagging, gnawing riff of 'Teen Spirit', however, was too simple to be forgotten, and the band found themselves returning to it again and again. Later, Kurt would tell *Rolling Stone* that he 'made the band play it for an hour and a half'. It was Krist that suggested slowing the song down and letting the rolling groove of the verses change the mood, giving the choruses punch and impact. Dave responded by lifting the drum intro from The Gap Band's 1980 disco classic 'Burn Rubber On Me', and playing a funk groove over the riff. No previous Nirvana drummer would have thought to do that. It's not for nothing that 'Smells Like Teen Spirit', like 'Aneurysm', is one of the few Nirvana songs to be credited to all three members – it would take the combination of Krist Novoselic, Kurt Cobain and Dave Grohl, at that exact point in their lives, to write it.

It was shaped, more and more, into something with extraordinary impact and deceptive simplicity, though all three band members claim they didn't think it was anything special. Kurt thought 'Drain You', written at the same time, was far better. He wouldn't finish the lyrics until shortly before it was recorded – Kurt very rarely did. What lyrics he did have were all soundbites and snapshots, and even when it was finished it wasn't exactly a song with a clear and compelling narrative. There's little broadsides and needles presumably at the expense of Tobi Vail, and some sloganeering on the theme of generational

April 18–24

- The band set off on the long 16-hour drive to LA where they are to record their new album at Sound City studios. Krist and his wife, Shelli, go ahead in a van with the band's equipment, with Dave and Kurt following behind in Kurt's 'trusty' Datsun B210. Unfortunately Kurt's car, a battered blue wreck from the 70s, whose wheels have a habit of falling off, is not quite up to the 1,000 plus-mile drive across two states. Ten hours into the journey, with the car over heating and its water tank having to be topped up every 90 minutes, having barely scratched the surface of the trip, the duo give up and return to Tacoma ... which takes another ten hours. They abandon the car in a local quarry and relieve some of their frustration by throwing rocks at it until the windows are obliterated, then head to Krist's place in Tacoma to pick up the trusty Dodge van with the couch in the back that they use for touring. They set off again for California, making a stop in San Francisco to hang out with Dale Crover and his girlfriend, Debbi Shane of SF punks Dumbhead, and catch the recently re-formed Flipper, a band they both adored, at the Covered Wagon.[10] During the brief stay, Dave, Kurt, Dale and Debbi head to Dumbhead's rehearsal space and form a brief jam band that they christen 'The Retards', playing songs by all four friends, just for the hell of it. Dale contributes a drum part to a song Kurt had been working on, but hadn't yet been able to nail – it will shortly be worked into 'Drain You'. When they eventually arrive in LA, one of the first things Dave and Kurt do is get tickets to the Universal Studios theme park.[11]

---

malaise. For a chorus Kurt recycles a catchphrase he was fond of using when arriving at parties. 'Here we are,' he would announce sarcastically to the room, 'entertain us.'

It didn't matter that lyrically, 'Smells Like Teen Spirit' was mostly about bitterness and boredom: no-one could understand the words anyway. The important thing, was how the song made you *feel*. The title was in place fairly early on, and if it didn't tell you much about what the piece was actually about, it certainly summed up how it *felt* to listen to it. Kurt had originally wanted to call it 'Anthem', at least according to Tobi Vail, but since her band, Bikini Kill, also had a song of that name she bullied him out of using it. Instead, Kurt reached for the graffiti another member of Bikini Kill, Kathleen Hanna, had left on his wall one drunken night the previous year, phoning her to check she was okay with him using it ('And I was like, as long as I can get out of this conversation and not think about [that night] anymore, you can use whatever you want', she told Mark Yarm. 'So I hung up and thought, How the fuck is he gonna use "Kurt smells like teen spirit" as a lyric?').

Later, many people, including management, label execs and even Dave Grohl said that they didn't expect 'Teen Spirit' to be the big hit on the record, with the smart money being on 'In Bloom' or 'Come As You Are' being the song that broke through. I've always suspected, though, that Kurt knew what he was doing. You don't call a song 'Smells Like Teen Spirit' unless it can justify the promise of that title (or at least the promise Kurt *assumed* it had, since he didn't know he was actually referencing a deodorant at this point.) As the song grew tighter and tighter he must have known that what he was writing summed something up. A feeling. A spirit. He'd wanted to call it 'Anthem', for heaven's sake. Later, looking back with 20/20 hindsight, he told *Rolling Stone* that he was trying to write 'the ultimate pop song'. Something the Pixies could have played. And just like that, he did.

10. Another of the Bay Area's first-wave punk bands, and a big influence on Kurt, Dave and the Melvins. If getting a Black Flag tattoo was a way of marking your body with the spirit of pure punk, spray painting 'FLIPPER RULES!' on a wall was how you marked your territory. Krist would briefly join Flipper during another reunion in the mid 2000s.
11. There are many moments in Nirvana history I would love to visit if I had a time machine – the shows at the Off Ramp or the OK Hotel, or the London Astoria for example, but I think observing Kurt and Dave having a day out at Universal Studios might be quite near the top of the list.

April 29

- Final rehearsals for what would become *Nevermind* begin at Burbank, near LA. Producer Butch Vig is present to listen to how the new songs are coming along[12] and is blown away by the band, particuarly Dave's drumming. When they get to 'Smells Like Teen Spirit' he immediately makes them play it again.[13]

April 30

- The deal with DGC is finalised. Nirvana are now major label recording artists.[14]

---

12. While everyone had loved working with Butch Vig the previous spring, and while his work on the songs spoke for itself, it wasn't a given that he would be producing the whole of *Nevermind.* Kurt had said in interviews as recently as February that the plan was to return to Smart with Butch to do some of the noisier tracks, but that a more established producer would be brought in for the big pop singles. Don Dixon's name had been thrown around, since he'd produced two of Kurt's biggest influences for the more melodic and accessible side of the album: REM and The Smithereens. Also in the mix was Scott Litt, who had been behind the desk for REM's more recent hits and David Briggs who had worked with Neil Young and Crazy Horse. Kurt's journals go on to mention more names, though they're more of a fantasy wishlist: Bill Price, who had produced the Sex Pistols' *Nevermind The Bollocks* (one of Kurt's favourite albums of all time, though curiously the note in the journal entry has 'Guns N' Roses' written next to it first, as Price had recently done a full mix of the *Use Your Illusion* albums, making him, presumably, a choice Geffen would have been keen on.) There's also Gil Norton, who'd produced the Pixies' *Doolittle*, Alan Moulder, who had engineered My Bloody Valentine's seminal *Loveless* and mixed Jesus and Mary Chain's *Automatic,* and Ron St Germain, who worked on Sonic Youth's *Goo* (Kurt refers to them simply as 'the Youth'.) It's a fascinating list that's very revealing of the band's intentions for their forthcoming album: these are names that specialise in accessible, poppy radio hits, with a handful of cooler-than-thou English indie producers in for good measure. The view that Kurt and the band were gunning for a mainstream sound is underlined by the names absent from their wishlist – Steve Albini and Jack Endino, for starters.

    Vig, meanwhile, was to stay on as engineer, working with whatever big name was brought in. It's not quite the great sell-out betrayal that it seems on paper – Vig had never helmed a major label album before, and the stakes and budgets were considerably more than he was used to. What's more, the easy-going Vig was fine with it, and was looking forward to watching from the sidelines to see how a big name producer worked, wondering what he could learn from them. Nirvana met with several producers, and quickly realised none of them were right for the album they had in mind. Scott Litt and Don Dixon would have softened their edges too much (and, more to the point, Litt was in the middle of getting married and thus unavailable) and David Briggs was – as Krist would tell Butch Vig later (as relayed in an interview with *Uncut*) – 'a burnt out hippie'. No-one had made them feel as comfortable as Butch Vig did, and no-one else seemed to grasp what they were trying to do quite as instinctively. Krist called Butch at Smart that March, while he was working on Smashing Pumpkins' debut, *Gish*, to ask him if he would be available for a month or so's recording any time soon. Thus it was that no-sooner had Vig wrapped up his work with one seminal 90s artist on the cusp of megastardom, he flew straight down to LA to work with another. Smashing Pumpkins' Billy Corgan would later accuse his producer, tongue only slightly in cheek, of ripping off the guitar tone they had worked up together and using it on Nirvana's album.
13. He had already heard boom box recordings of the new material. The band had sent him a cassette recorded at their Tacoma rehearsal space, a large barn outside town. The tape began with an introduction from Kurt saying 'Hey, Butch, it's Kurt, we're excited to come and rock out with you. We're going to play a couple of new songs, and we've got Dave Grohl, and he's the greatest drummer in the world.' (as Butch relayed to Paul Brannigan.) Even through the poorly recorded, fuzzy quality of the internal microphone on a boom box, Butch heard enough to know that the band were onto something special. A demo of 'Smells Like Teen Spirit' from that cassette, or one very like it, can be found on the *With The Lights Out* box set.
14. The fact that the band were already in LA, in the early stages of making their new album, suggests this really was just a formality – the deal had truly been done back in December, and the contract itself was just so much admin. Alas, this final step did not immediately transform the trio into wealthy major label rock stars; at least not yet. Of the $280,000 advance, $160,000 was earmarked for the recording of the album. Surprisingly the biggest expense wasn't the studio, which was billed at $500 per day – most of the budget was eaten up by the band's month-long residence in an apartment in LA's Oakwood (an area known for putting up actors, models and rockstars to the point Kurt, Krist and Dave nicknamed it 'Cokewood') while they made their record plus a week or so's use of a Burbank rehearsal room. After

May 2 – May 19

- Recording begins on the album that would become *Nevermind* at Sound City studios, located at 15452 Cabrito Road, Van Nuys, just outside LA[15]. According to Butch Vig one of the first songs to be recorded is 'In Bloom'. Principle recording would continue through to 19 May. In that time the band track 17 songs in various states of completion – 'Smells Like Teen Spirit', 'In Bloom'[16], 'Come As You Are'[17], 'Breed' (now officially retitled from 'Imodium'),

---

managers and lawyers had taken their slices of the pie, it left the three members of Nirvana with $30,000 each. It's not peanuts, but it's not exactly a high-end rock star lifestyle, even in 1991. After taxes, you'd make more doing almost any desk job. By summer of 1991 Krist was trying to sell his car to Cat Butt's James Burdyshaw for $500 in an attempt to make ends meet.

15. At this point Sound City had fallen onto hard times. In his documentary about the studio, called simply *Sound City* (2013), Dave Grohl remembers his first reaction being one of disbelief – '*this* is *Sound City*?'. The place was apparently squalid; there's a moment in Grohl's film where a former employee claims someone could have urinated in the corner and no-one would have batted an eye, although others have since come forward to say that the filthier aspects of the studio had been played up for the movie. Regardless of what else they were smeared with, however, the walls of the building were also lined with gold records, momentos of some of the era-defining albums that had been recorded there: Neil Young's *After the Goldrush*, Fleetwood Mac's *Fleetwood Mac* (plus *Rumours* was mixed there), Rick Springfield's *Working Class Dog*. It had been a go-to studio in the 80s, with everyone from Ozzy Osborne to REO Speedwagon to Barry Manilow recording there, though the work had started to dry up in recent years. Since *Nevermind*, the success of which gave Sound City a much needed shot in the arm, the list has only grown – Rage Against The Machine's astonishing self-titled debut was recorded there the following year, soon to be followed by memorable residences from Tool, Kyuss, Rancid, The Black Crowes, Red Hot Chili Peppers, Metallica, Johnny Cash, Weezer, System of a Down, Slipknot, Kings of Leon, Slayer, Nine Inch Nails ... the list goes on and on. Tom Petty practically lived there in the 80s and 90s. Some of those bands were attracted by the studio's reputation for iconic albums, but many came to Sound City because they knew its strengths: its main studio room had an incredible drum sound; the gear was top-spec, the staff were experts and local characters, and the main control room boasted a rare Neve 8028 console; one of only four in the world. When the studio finally closed for business, after a life-time of financial wobbles that made Sub Pop look like a Fortune 500 company, the Neve desk was purchased by Dave Grohl, who installed it in his home studio where it was used to create an accompanying album for the film, featuring several of the studio's alumni including Stevie Nicks, Rick Springfield, Trent Reznor, Josh Homme and, just for good measure, and despite him never having been to Sound City, Paul McCartney. It was Butch Vig that booked Sound City for *Nevermind*, sight unseen, based partly on its great sonic reputation and partly because, having hit leaner times, it was affordable. DGC had plenty of money, sure, but Nirvana were still a relatively unknown quantity, expected to shift 50,000 albums, 100,000 at most, vying with Pixies and Sonic Youth for the title of Kings of the Underground-Overground. They weren't anticipating making megabucks from Nirvana, and the label wasn't going to shell out big money to put them in a state-of-the-art space. Sound City was good, it was cheap, and it was available. It was also, crucially, in LA, meaning recording could take place under the watchful eye of the band's Gold Mountain management team whose offices were based there.
16. Of all the tracks re-recorded for *Nevermind*, 'In Bloom' adheres closest to the demos recorded a year earlier at Smart, and it's a testimony to Chad Channing's playing that his parts are more-or-less replicated by Dave, which is also true of 'Lithium', 'Breed' and 'Stay Away'. Dave's biggest contribution to 'In Bloom' isn't his thundering replication of Chad's drums part – it's his double-tracked vocal harmonies on the chorus.
17. This was one of the last songs written for the album – to the point that it hadn't even been played live prior to the *Nevermind* sessions. It was also, by far, the poppiest song Kurt had ever, and arguably would ever, write. Discarding the two sombre, acoustic pieces that close each half, 'Come As You Are' is the only song on *Nevermind* that isn't driven by pure power. Even when the familiar *huge* distortion kicks in at the middle eight, it doesn't feel like it defines the song, which rests on its melody at every stage. The whole thing revolves around a deliciously bubblegum riff, made woozy and off-kilter by a chorus effect and Krist doubling his part with a six-string octave bass, leading into a chorus that almost cries out to be jangly indie-pop, but which the band probably wisely resisted in favour of a watery, slightly dissonant feel that stops the song turning into Beat Happening or The Velvets in the way their recent demo of 'All Apologies' had.

The riff itself, which is another one of those beginner pieces new guitarists of a certain generation always seem to learn, bears more than a passing resemblance to 'Eighties', an early hit by British post-punks Killing Joke, and though the lift is probably accidental, or at the very least subconscious, it is, unfortunately, also screamingly obvious, to the point that Kurt hesitated to release the song as a single (as usual his more mercenary instincts won through – 'Come As You Are' is so obviously a hit song that *not* releasing it as a single would verge on deranged). For their part, Killing Joke considered suing and took extensive legal advice, entering into a dialogue with Nirvana's publishers who, according to guitarist Geordie Walker, taking to *Guitarist* magazine in 1994, responded by claiming that Nirvana had never heard of Killing Joke. 'The hysterical thing,' he goes on to say, 'is that Nirvana had already sent us a Christmas card!' It's a comment that possibly should be taken with a large pinch of salt. The band dropped the case after Kurt's death, with frontman Jaz Coleman saying 'It's a short fucking life mate, we could have gone fishing or something'. Dave Grohl later returned the favour by playing drums on Killing Joke's 2003 album, T*he Death and Resurrection Show.*

'Come As You Are', in its own way, has a fascinating place in the Nirvana canon, fulfilling very much the same role that 'About A Girl' does on *Bleach*; a way of turning to the audience and saying, 'oh, by the way … did you know we can also do *this*?'. 'Smells Like Teen Spirit' may have been the instant classic and 'Lithium' the sing-a-long' anthem, but 'Come As You Are' is poppier and more commercial sounding than either. It's a song that none of the band's peers could have attempted, not Mudhoney, not Soundgarden, not TAD, not Pearl Jam, not Sonic Youth, Dinosaur Jr or even the Pixies. Of the 90s alt-rock set, only REM and Smashing Pumpkins could be so melodically charming and ambiguously bitter on the same song. In fact, of all of Kurt's influences, the only band that could really come close to a song like 'Come As You Are' is The Beatles, whose thumbprints can be found at its heart. This is a direction the band chose never to revisit, which is unsurprising since they grew noticably embarrassed about how accessible and poppy *Nevermind* was – despite that being the mission brief from the word go. In a way, 'Come As You Are' is a viewport into a different reality, in which Nirvana embraced their poptastic instincts more fully instead of reacting against them as they did on *In Utero*. It marks the logical end-point of Kurt's search for melodic perfection and the final manifestation of his dalliance with the sugary Olympian light touch of the era between *Nevermind* and *Bleach*. Once out of his system, he seemed to have no desire to revisit it.

'Lithium'[18], 'Territorial Pissings'[19], 'Stay Away'[20], 'On A Plain', 'Lounge Act',[21] 'Drain

18. Though it adheres fairly closely to the Smart studios demo, the recording of 'Lithium' was still a frustrating process with Kurt getting increasingly agitated at Dave's habit of speeding up into the choruses, meaning some of the power ebbed away. At one point that frustration manifested in the band abandoning 'Lithium' altogether and launching into a brutal version of 'Endless, Nameless' ('I've never seen so much rage on a person's face, it was *scary*', Vig later told Rick Beato during a 2023 YouTube interview), culminating with Kurt smashing his Mosrite guitar – the first time he'd wrecked one of his instruments in the studio rather than onstage. Vig had the good sense to keep the tape running, and the jam was included warts-and-all as a hidden track on the CD (you can hear Kurt smash the guitar by playing 'Something In The Way' on most CD copies of *Nevermind* and forwarding to 19.32). That pretty much ended the day's season. As they departed, Vig suggested that Dave try playing 'Lithium' to a click-track for the next attempt and lent him a portable drum machine to practice along to that night. Grohl had never played to click before, and immediately resented the idea, feeling it was a slight on his playing. When work resumed the next day (after Butch had scoured LA for a replacement left-handed Mosrite guitar), it turned out that Dave was, in fact, a natural at playing to a click and locked in immediately, giving the song its relentless anthemic power. The song was done in a single take. Looking back on it years later, for the *Nevermind* episode of VH1's *Classic Albums* documentary series, he's still a little aggrieved, noting 'it's okay to speed up a little, isn't it?'
19. The most straightforwardly punk moment on *Nevermind* featured, as the band proudly said in many interviews, Kurt jacking straight into the Neve board to get a raw guitar sound. As with many Nirvana stories that originated with the band themselves, it's not *quite* the whole truth – Butch felt that the guitar sounded a little thin, so he also set up an amp – the final track blends both. The song begins with a rare Krist Novoselic lead vocal after Kurt had asked him to sing 'some hippy crap' at the start of the song. On the spur of the moment he burst out with the chorus of 'Get Together', an old Chet Powers number that had been a forgettable late 60s hit for The Youngbloods. The song is about the most definitive interpretation of 'hippy crap' you can possibly imagine, a paean and plea for universal love and brotherhood that had been used by the National Council of Christians and Jews for a series of faintly nauseating Public Service Announcement TV promos. The juxtaposition with a nihilistic punk song with a name like 'Territorial Pissings' is delicious. 'Territorial Pissings' itself would later become one of Nirvana's go-to set closers.
20. Though musically very close to the original version, there is an obvious difference to the *Nevermind* recording – the lyrics and title are completely different. Kurt actually recorded the song with the 'Pay To Play' lyrics during the *Nevermind* sessions, but had a last minute change of heart and completely rewrote the words. It becomes substantially broader and more relatable, playing into Kurt's favourite themes of outsiderdom and alienation which, let's face it, is a lot more universal than complaining about the ticketing policies of small venues in the Seattle area.
21. One of the more overlooked moments on the album, 'Lounge Act' is another late addition that had never been debuted live. It boasts one of Krist's best ever basslines – an intro no other bass player would write, all loopy and syrupy and crisp before Kurt and Dave slam in. It's absolutely delicious. Lyrically, this is one of the few songs that is *definitely* about Tobi Vail. Kurt admits as much in an unsigned letter found in his journals, saying 'I don't write songs about you, except Lounge Act, which I do not play, except when my wife is not around.' The line about 'wearing a shield' is a nod to Kurt's one and only tattoo: the K-in-a-shield logo of Calvin Johnson's Olympia-based K Records. The tattoo was partly Kurt showing his commitment to underground and independent music, celebrating one of the most DIY record labels operating in the US at the time. He also, as he alludes to in 'Lounge Act', very likely did it to impress Tobi, proving to her that at his heart he would always be Punk Rock. It was important to him. Punk authenticity was everything to Tobi and her friends. Bikini Kill would eventually sign to Slim Moon's kill rock stars label.

You'[22], 'Something In The Way'[23] and 'Endless, Nameless'[24] are all completed. Four more songs are attempted and then abandoned – 'Verse Chorus Verse'[25],

22. A common complaint about *Nevermind* is that it's 'overproduced', a view even Kurt would occasionally lean into when he was feeling particularly petulant, and one that stung Butch Vig, who rightly felt that he'd done his best to capture these fairly stripped back power-pop songs in the spirit in which they had been written. *Nevermind* was *exactly* the album the band had wanted to make. 'Drain You' is one of the few moments on the record that genuinely does have a dense production, with several guitar sounds dipping in and out of the mix, panned widely. The breakdown saw Kurt himself indulging in the studio fun, by adding weird sounds – squeaky ducks, toys, rattles and aerosol cans. You can hear them swimming in and out of the mix. Despite being the only track on the album that even came close to justifying his complaints about the production, 'Drain You' remained one of Kurt's favourite Nirvana songs.
23. 'Something In The Way' was 'definitely the hardest track to record on *Nevermind*', Butch later told VH1's *Classic Albums*. The band already had its sombre arrangement in place, and already played it live, but getting the delicate feel right was proving difficult. In the end, a frustrated Kurt lay on his back in the control room and strummed it on his battered, five-stringed acoustic, singing softly, to demonstrate the mood he wanted. It was the same guitar that had been used to record 'Polly' the previous year. Realising that this was *exactly* the mood the song required, Vig hurriedly set up microphones and turned everything that could possibly make a noise off, capturing Kurt's hushed, sparse performance. The take was perfect. Listening to it now, you can *hear* the silence around him – the quiet hiss of a microphone recording emptiness and space. Unfortunately, this now opened up a new set of problems as the band attempted to play along to the recording. Kurt never tuned that guitar properly, so it was in a mysterious key all of its own and, what's more, without a click track or drums, his tempo had wandered throughout the song. Krist and Dave often had to 'punch in', bar by bar to account for the meandering timing, while the inexact tuning created problems for the bass. The cello part, played by LA musician Kirk Canning (handily available as the partner of L7 drummer Demetra Plakas), was tracked on the last day of recording, the band having completely forgotten to find a cellist until they met one at a party. Canning worked his parts out on the spot, and of course had exactly the same issue as Krist did with odd tuning and timing. All things considered he did a stunning job; that cello adds a mournful lowing that lifts the track. Still, it felt messy, and Vig resorted to using brand new recording software that had to be hired in especially to 'fix' tuning and timing issues on a computer nudging the notes into place. Digital recording is now ubiquitous, of course, and it is now recording on tape that feels like a novelty, but back in 1991 this was cutting edge. After every edit the computer would need to be left to render, taking over an hour – if the adjustment hadn't worked well and needed to re-done, the whole session had to be deleted and uploaded all over again. It was time consuming, though it ultimately did the trick. Everyone agreed that, though the technology was impressive, the level of faffing around meant that digital recording was unlikely to catch on.

According to former Queens of the Stone Age bass player, Nick Oliveri, the song had been co-written with Screaming Trees Mark Lanegan, who'd contributed some lyrics as a quid pro quo for Kurt's work on *The Winding Sheet*, which does make sense as 'Something In The Way' *sounds* like something from a Lanegan solo album, and its themes of sleeping rough under bridges, drinking rain water and boiling grass, feels a lot like something Lead Belly would have written – an artist they both worshipped. Lanegan was happy to help out on the song as a favour and never asked for credit; something he understandably regretted later, when *Nevermind* started to sell. 'I remember him kicking himself in the butt a little bit about that', Oliveri told Lanegan's biographer, Greg Prato, remembering him saying, wistfully, 'If only I had that 'Something In The Way' publishing…'.
24. This absolutely brutal, screaming and feed-back filled take of the song was tagged onto the end of the CD version of the album as a hidden track. Listeners who left their stereo running after 'Something In the Way' would have the bejesus scared out of them 13 minutes and 51 seconds later. It's a trick that was only possible in the CD era, though the inspiration was actually The Beatles – 'Her Majesty' appears 20 seconds after the end of the 'The End' on *Abbey Road*, which was about as much as you could get away with on vinyl. Dave Grohl tells a brilliant story about someone returning their copy of *Nevermind* to a record store because they thought the long silence and then the explosive punk noise at the end of the album was a fault. When told it was intentional he apparently declared 'Well I don't think it's very funny' and demanded his refund. Nirvana started a trend for hidden tracks that persisted on rock albums for a good few years.
25. A full instrumental version of 'Verse Chorus Verse' was completed, but Kurt lost interest in the song and never recorded a proper vocal, though there was a scratch vocal recorded live. It was for the best – the song is generic to the point of Nirvana-by-numbers, and would have stuck out like a sore thumb on an album as concise as *Nevermind*. It's a song that drags its feet, and the band knew it. It never even made it to the mixing stage.

'Old Age'[26], a third attempt at recording 'Sappy'[27] and a jangly, REM-like number known only as 'Song In D'[28]. The band's aim is to make a record that is as poppy as it is heavy, and as dark as it is light. Butch Vig's role, aside from capturing the sounds in the best way possible, is to help shape the songs. For example, he shaves some sections out of 'Smells Like Teen Spirit', shortening the guitar solo and adding the coda after every chorus.[29] Nirvana, well drilled after months of solid rehearsing, try and capture songs in as few takes as possible to keep things fresh sounding, recording live as a trio with Kurt doing scratch vocals. Kurt would then overdub guitars and solos and do lead vocals, often finishing the lyrics at the very last minute,[30] with Dave adding harmonies. Many of the songs on the album are first takes. Everyone is pretty thrilled with the results.[31]

---

26. Another abandoned track, though it has more going for it than 'Verse Chorus Verse'. It's pleasant enough, and certainly catchy but it never goes anywhere – all that was completed was a basic rhythm track (clean guitar, bass, drums) and a scratch vocal. There is a sense that had this been spruced up and made more dynamic, with some sonic light and shade sketched in, it could have at least have made a decent b-side.
27. This is the least successful attempt at capturing 'Sappy' so far. The key is different and there's some other tweaks, but Kurt's heart wasn't in it and the song was abandoned pretty early in the process.
28. This one is probably the biggest mystery of the *Nevermind* sessions, as it was abandoned completely and, unlike 'Verse Chorus Verse', 'Sappy' and 'Old Age' has never surfaced on a bootleg or been included in a rarities compilation. Apparently it had real hit single potential, but Kurt thought it sounded 'too much like REM'. According to the *LiveNirvana* website, who asked Butch Vig specifically about this tune, it was exactly that poppiness that had made Butch want to pursue it. It's telling – Kurt had spent the last few years disowning the more metal elements of *Bleach* and preaching the pop gospel, proudly aiming at pop perfection and wilfully making an album of more accessible, simplified and melodic rocks songs, but was beginning to realise that there was only so far he was willing to go.
29. As has been discussed, many of the figures involved at the band's management, label and even within Nirvana itself didn't expect 'Teen Spirit' to be the break-out hit of the record. Yet, whenever someone visited the studio, be it label bosses or the band's friends like L7, it was 'Smells Like Teen Spirit' they were played first, Vig turning the studio monitors up loud, blasting out a rough desk mix that would inevitably blow the listener to the back wall of the control room.
30. Kurt was extremely resistant to the the album sounding too processed or overproduced, and so had to be gently coaxed by Butch to add overdubs to his rhythm guitar parts. It's fairly standard practice to 'double' guitar tracks, with the guitarist playing the exact part a second time, the two being played back simultaneously. This can 'thicken' the sound, giving it more punch – especially useful with the quiet/loud dynamics so beloved by Nirvana. The two tracks will sometimes use different amps, guitars or effects to create a more interesting sonic texture, and the inevitable tiny differences between takes can make a song sound more live and exciting. The same thing is true of vocals, where double-tracking can make a performance sound much stronger. Kurt was often resistant to the idea, clinging to his purist punk ethos. Butch Vig, however, had an ace up his sleeve. The Beatles had used double-tracking extensively, and Kurt was a *huge* Beatles fan. Whenever he was being difficult Vig would remind him that, if it was good enough for John Lennon, it was good enough for him. If all else failed, he would fall back on simple deception – 'I think I would lie to him,' he told VHI's *Classic Albums*, 'saying there was a problem on the track, it didn't record properly or it was out of tune, so let's just do it again.' Vig had, by now, become an expert at Kurt-wrangling. The irony was that, though Kurt wasn't a fan of the process, he was unusually good at it. 'Usually when a singer doubles his vocals, it's hard to get the phrasing the same', Butch told Charles R Cross and Jim Berkenstadt for their book *Classic Albums: Nevermind*, 'but I put both takes in the monitors and listened to them side by side and it sounded just great.' Every once in a while, Kurt would point-blank refuse to do a double track or play another take, meaning that occasionally Vig would cheat, faking one by copying the guitar over to a new track and putting it slightly out of sync to create an illusion of two guitars.
31. Recording *Nevermind* was one of the most pleasurable times the band would have. They were young, staying in LA, they had enough money to be getting by with, and could afford to treat themselves, they were making a record that obviously sounded great, and the recording process, despite the odd hiccup, felt remarkably easy. Vig would arrive at the studio around 11am to get set up, the band would stroll in around 2pm and they'd work through to 11pm, before heading out to party at the beach or catch a

May 20–28

- Work moves to the nearby Devonshire studios where Vig mixes the album with input from the band. At the end of the sessions it is agreed by everyone that the mixes aren't working, and that a new mix engineer with 'fresh ears' needs to be brought in.[32]

May 29

- Nirvana mark the end of the *Nevermind* recording sessions with a show at LA's tiny Jabberjaw club, helping out their friends in Fitz of Depression, whose own LA

---

show. The only exception to this pattern was the penultimate day of recording, 18 May, when the band didn't show up at all – the previous night they had been celebrating Krist's 26th birthday (which had actually been 16 May) by going to see Butthole Surfers and L7 play the Hollywood Palladium. On the way home, the van, driven by an extremely high-on-mushrooms Krist, had been pulled over by the cops. The inebriated bass player had then quickly downed the remains of a bottle of Jack Daniels before the police could catch him with it. While Kurt and Dave walked back to their apartment, Krist spent much of the next day in a police cell.

It was an eventful evening … that same night, at that same show, *Melody Maker*'s Everett True introduced Kurt to the singer of another band who had put out a Sub Pop single, 'Dicknail', earlier that year and had just recorded their debut album, produced by Sonic Youth's Kim Gordon: Courtney Love of Hole. You're probably familiar with the name. ('I was an English music critic, on the lookout for the Next Big Thing,' wrote Everett in *Nirvana: The True Story*. 'She was a struggling musician/actress, desperate to become that Next Big Thing.') Though Kurt and Courtney later mythologised this first proper meeting and embellished it with all sorts of details, it didn't immediately have the ring of star-crossed lovers meeting across a crowded bar ('I know you,' Courtney apparently said. 'You're Kurt Cobain and you're an asshole'). They teased each other like school children, and left it at that. That night, back at Nirvana's apartment, Kurt decided to annoy the smitten Everett by calling Courtney and asking her out. There's two versions of what happened next – in one, Kurt and Courtney arranged a date for the following day, which Kurt didn't show up for, and in the other Kurt invited Courtney to the apartment to do drugs, and she declined. With 30 years distance, it may be that even Courtney doesn't remember which is true. Either way, and despite contrasting reports that they may or may not have met, briefly, in previous years, this was the true start of the acquaintance, though they wouldn't become a couple until much later in the year. Kurt and Courtney, after all, both spent 1991 being rather busy.

32. There are three stages to making an album: recording, mixing and mastering, and all of them, in their own way, are equally important. The mixing stage is where the album's sound is sculpted. It's not just about 'making the guitar louder and the bass quieter' or 'turning the vocals up', it's about delicate EQing, panning, treating sounds, selecting the best takes, identifying any issues and correcting them and 'riding the levels'. The mixing stage is where the record gains its identity – in the hands of a creative engineer a good mix can rescue an average recording, equally though, a bad one can undo all the good work in the studio. The first mixes of *Nevermind*, apparently, fell between the two stalls.

Despite being a relatively straightforward album that had been performed and recorded well, mixing *Nevermind* was not a straightforward process. Kurt began to second guess himself, and push for the album to sound darker and heavier; deliberately sabotaging his own pop instincts, asking for a less trebley guitar sound or a less prominent vocal ('Turn all the treble off the guitars – I want it to sound like Black Sabbath' as Butch remembers in a 2011 interview with *Izotape*, or 'Take all the high end off the snare' as he told *Mojo*). Left to his own devices, Butch may well have turned out a version of *Nevermind* that would pass muster with the label, but with Kurt and the band (none of whom were especially familiar with the art of record mixing) constantly on his back, micromanaging, he didn't stand a chance. Added to this, the mixing was being done straight after the recording. Tracking at Sound City had gone over schedule, and the usual few days of extremely necessary headspace between recording and mixing were suddenly no longer available as Vig and the band rolled straight from one to the other on consecutive days. Everyone was burned out and over-familiar with the material, making it hard to be objective. In 2016 Vig was the most blunt he's pretty much ever been on the issue, telling *Billboard*, 'It sounded like shit.' Gary Gersh, the band's A&R at DGC, agreed as did their manager, John Silva. The band, too, were in full agreement. No-one was satisfied with the early mixes, and it was decided that someone with a proven record as a mix engineer was needed.

gig had been cancelled. Kurt suggested lending Nirvana's burgeoning popularity to the cause, offering to play if a show could be rearranged. The show sells out at 48hrs notice and the ticket money goes to helping Fitz out of their pickle. Nirvana debut 'Come As You Are' and 'On A Plain'. After the show, a drunk Kurt runs outside and vomits on the sidewalk and comes back to find Iggy Pop waiting to meet him.[33] To the band's astonishment there are people in the audience singing along to songs they had been recording over the past few months – the 1990 Smart sessions had been widely bootlegged.

June

- Communion Records release Nirvana's cover of the Velvet Underground's 'Here She Comes', recorded over a year before at Smart studios, as a double a-side with Melvins live take of 'Venus In Furs'.

June 1–9

- Experienced mix engineer Andy Wallace mixes Nevermind at Scream Studios in the Studio City area of LA, working with Butch Vig and the band.[34] Though the band have a few small concerns about the polish and gloss Wallace has been able to apply to their songs, they also appreciate the punch he has given them and sign off on the mixes.[35]

---

33. Kurt wrote about the show in an unsent letter to Tobi Vail, which can be found in *Journals*, saying it was 'a really fun show' but 'we were really fucked up on booze and drugs, out of tune and rather, uh, sloppy. It took me about fifteen minutes to change my guitar string while people heckled and called me drunk.' Of meeting Iggy Pop he said he was 'a really friendly and cool and nice and interesting person ... it was probably the most flattering moment of my life.' It is indeed a sloppy show, especially for a band who had just finished making an album and should be tight as a drum, but it sounds like everyone is having a ball.
34. Gary Gersh, Nirvana's A&R at DGC, had faxed over a list of potential mix engineers for the band to consider, among them was Ed Stasium (a string of Ramones albums, Cobain-favourites the Smithereens) and Scott Litt, who had also been in the mix to produce *Nevermind*. Litt had produced and mixed REM's *Green* and their latest album, *Out of Time* – meaning he'd been the man behind the sound of 'Orange Crush', 'Stand' and 'The One I Love', and more significantly, 'Losing My Religion' and 'Shiny Happy People'; bone fide radio hits all. Kurt, however, was now in the mood to be petulant. He accepted the need to get a new mix, but that didn't mean he was going to let someone turn his work into ready-made radio fodder. The list had names followed by their major credits, and the last name on the list read 'Andy Wallace, Slayer'. Wallace had mixed two of the thrash pioneers' classic albums – *Seasons In The Abyss* and *Reign In Blood*. He'd also worked on Sepultura's breakthrough, *Arise*. The heavy metal pedigree was enough to meet Kurt's approval – it felt like a neat way to counter any pressure to make the album more radio friendly. What Kurt was overlooking was that Andy Wallace had also mixed Madonna (the *You Can Dance* version of 'Get Into the Groove') and Run DMC's 'Walk This Way'.
35. 'All we wanted to do was record these songs and get a record out', Dave told Michael Azerrad, 'so it was just like, "let's get it over with"' 'We just went along with the game', agreed Krist. Within a few months the band themselves would be pretty down on Wallace's mixes. 'Looking back on the production of *Nevermind*, I'm embarrassed by it now,' Kurt says in *Come As You Are*. 'It's closer to a Mötley Crüe record than it is a Punk Rock record'. He wasn't being entirely fair. It's true that Wallace had made the album a little more immediate and radio-ready – he used digital reverb and mixed in ambient samples to give the drums more of a 'live' feel, since it was felt that Butch had recorded them too dry, he also added more stereo separation and worked on ramping up the dynamics, using compression to make the loud bits louder, and adding occasional effects (the distinctive chorus guitar sound on 'Come As You Are', for example, isn't present on the original mixes.) Wallace

gave the record an immediacy that punched through the speakers of even the cheapest car stereo or transistor radio. His intent was never to make the album sound glossy – he was just trying to present its rawness in the best possible way ('while mixing I did not try to polish it at all,' he told *Sound on Sound* in 2014. 'I was trying to keep the sound in your face and raw, while at the same time providing the dynamics and architecture that I like to hear. And I'm still very happy with the result.'). It's not as if Nirvana had handed him Black Flag's *My War* and watched as he turned it into Phil Collins. *Nevermind* is, for the most part, a power-pop record, not a Punk Rock snarl, and Wallace's mixes never stray far from the blueprint he'd been given.

That said, were they really necessary in the first place? When Butch's original 'Devonshire mixes' were first released, on the 20th anniversary 'Super Deluxe Edition' of the album, there was some trumpeting in the music press about hearing *Nevermind* 'as Kurt had intended it', shorn of its shiny-happy-makeover. Ultimately, though, the first-draft mixes aren't all that different: the songs speak for themselves. If Butch Vig's mix of 'Smells Like Teen Spirit' had been released, would it have still been a game-changing hit? Probably. Wallace gives it a bit more impact on that big drop in the intro, which is arguably the most important part of the whole song, and his mixes are all a little more dynamic and exciting, but Vig's original mix is absolutely fine. The song still leaps out of the speakers at you. It still feels like a monumental release of energy. It's a similar story with 'Come As You Are', 'In Bloom', 'Breed' and 'Lithium'. These are incredible songs, well performed and well recorded. It would take a particularly ham-fisted mix engineer to bungle them, and Vig was far from that. Wallace's mixes are more immediate, sure, especially if you listened to the two versions back to back, but if the Butch Vig mix of 'In Bloom' showed up on the radio, it was still going to be damned effective. Similarly, Wallace had the good sense to leave 'Polly' and 'Something In The Way' well alone – both songs had captured the creepy atmosphere of their subject matter perfectly. Where the new mixes really help is on the record's second tier of songs; the ones that aren't quite the stone-cold classics the singles have become. The Devonshire versions of 'Lounge Act' and 'Stay Away' feel a little flatter than those we ultimately got, they drag just a little. What Wallace does, more or less, is take the base stock and whizz it through a Soda Stream, injecting it with bubbles and fizz. The classics on *Nevermind* would probably still be classics if only the 1990 Smart session versions had come out and 'Smells Like Teen Spirit' had been recorded for a Peel session; Wallace's real achievement was to make the less dynamic parts of the album, 'Stay Away', 'Territorial Pissings', 'Lounge Act', as punchy and immediate as the obvious singles. He made sure the whole album demanded your attention. Vig, who is a fan of Wallace's mixes and appreciated the learning opportunity of watching him work, still did a stand up job. Had he been allowed a week's distance from the material before coming back to it, and had he not had Kurt Cobain looking over his shoulder – a Kurt who was suddenly realising that the pop album he'd been wanting to make for three years was becoming a reality and finding that he may have gone just a little too far – it's very possible he'd have turned in mixes that everyone would have waved through. And maybe that would have been enough to slightly temper a mega-success that was a little beyond what Kurt had wanted.

It's true that Kurt turned on *Nevermind* fairly quickly, especially as it began to hurtle out of his control, arriving in the bedrooms and keg parties of people he would never have thought would be Nirvana fans. The album gathered context its creators had never expected, and the band were forced to distance themselves from its more accessible elements in order to save face and punk credibility. Had *Nevermind* done the numbers most people in the know were expecting ... 50,000, 100,000, maybe 200,000 at the outside, it's likely Kurt would have been less damning in his later assessments. But it sold eight million copies and, to him, nothing *that* popular could be possibly all *that* good. Someone had turned him into something he never intended to be, and since he couldn't blame himself for that, it was Andy Wallace and his can of sonic turtle wax and graded emery cloths that became the sacrificial lamb (though it's worth noting that Kurt also turned on *Bleach* shortly after its release, deriding it as ham fisted and needlessly metal and blaming Sub Pop for making Nirvana sound like the rest of their stable). It's always seemed a little unfair to blame the mixes. After all, it was Kurt who had been saying in interviews just months before that Butch Vig would be doing the punkier songs while bigger names were brought in for the singles. It's Kurt who relentlessly pursued 'the ultimate pop song'. If *Nevermind* came out too shiny, too ready-wrapped for the mainstream, then he brought that on himself, and his regrets coloured how he saw the record. Kurt didn't live long enough to make peace with his most successful album – his colleagues, however, absolutely have. In 2021, *Uncut* magazine asked Dave Grohl if he would change anything on *Nevermind* if he could. The answer is emphatic – 'No. No! No! ... I wanted everyone to say that this album is *killer*. I was very critical of it while we were doing it, but over time it became what it is.' 'Three people made that record,' Krist told VH1's *Classic Albums: Nevermind* in 2002, '[with just] a drum set, a bass and a guitar. And it's undeniably the best thing I ever did in my whole life.'

June 10–20

- Nirvana undertake an eight-show West Coast tour supporting Dinosaur Jr.[36] On 18 June the band debut a new song, 'Rape Me' (Kurt playing it on a whim and taking Krist and Dave, who had only just learned the song, by surprise.)[37]

July

- Kurt is evicted from his apartment on Pear Street, Olympia for not paying his rent. The singer of a rock band signed to a major label who has just recorded a $160,000 album in LA will spend the next few weeks sleeping in his car.[38]

August 2

- *Nevermind* is mastered at Masterdisc studios in New York City by Howie Weinberg, who has mastered albums from everyone from Cheap Trick and Pantera, to LL Cool J, Herbie Hancock, Public Enemy and The Beastie Boys.[39]

---

36. By many accounts, Nirvana were consistently outplaying the headliners at these shows. A review of the first night in *Clot* magazine cites Nirvana as 'tight as a mosquito's ass' while branding Dinosaur Jr 'dull dull dull. So bloody dull.' *Flipside,* reviewing the LA show called Nirvana 'fucking intense ... I was impressed' but went on to say 'we only stayed for two songs of Dinosaur Jr because they were kinda boring'. *Kerrang!'s* review of a show in LA focused on openers Hole ('there's a revulsive chemistry at work here, as delicate as it is enormous') and Nirvana ('a noisy joy') and ignored Dinosaur altogether (full disclosure it's worth noting that the *LA Times* review of the same show raved about Dinosuar and branded Nirvana out of tune and formulaic. That review was an outlier though.) Dinosaur Jr were in the midst of an identity crisis – founding member and co-frontman Lou Barlow had been unceremoniously booted out in 1989, and J. Mascis played almost everything on the band's new album, *Green Mind* and was touring the album with hired hands. Some of the magic had gone. Nirvana, meanwhile, with the confidence of a trio that know they have a great album in the can and buzzing on their new songs, were playing an all-killer set of the most immediate bits of *Bleach* and the unreleased *Nevermind*, and their shorter running time, as the support band, meant that all fat had to be trimmed. Thus poor J. Mascis had to take the stage to an audience who had just heard 'Smells Like Teen Spirit' for the first time and were feeling that their night had probably peaked.
37. If you're keeping track, almost half of *In Utero*, an album that wouldn't be recorded until 1993, had been written by this point – 'Dumb', 'Radio Friendly Unit Shifter', 'Pennyroyal Tea', All Apologies' and 'Rape Me', the latter having been written in LA during the mixing of *Nevermind.* This was the most prolific songwriting period of Kurt's entire life.
38. Dave had moved to Seattle the previous month after getting tired of sleeping on the couch in an increasingly fetid apartment shared with his bandmate's pet turtles and rabbits and keen for a living situation in which he had his own room or, at the very least, a bed.
39. Mastering has, in the past, been described as a 'dark art'. It's the final stage in the sonic process for a piece of music. A mastering engineer uses EQ and compression to make a piece of music sound consistent and polished across various playback systems. In the case of *Nevermind* this involved enhancing the album's loudness while maintaining the raw intensity of the tracks. The mastering process focused on fine-tuning the balance between vocals, guitars, and drums, ensuring clarity and punch that could translate effectively from high-end audio equipment to everyday car radios, and making sure each song sounded like the last. It's perhaps the least intuitive part of the whole process for outsiders, but the results can be extraordinary. In some cases, mastering is when an album suddenly sounds 'proper' – it makes songs sound like *records*, not merely recordings. It can also go too far. Since the late 90s the industry has engaged in what has come to be known as the 'loudness wars', in which mastering engineers attempt to make records sound as 'loud' as possible using compression, regardless of the actual volume of the playback. The idea is to make music that sounds as immediate and exciting as possible on the radio or on a Spotify playlist. The problem is that the 'louder' and more compressed a song, the less dynamic range it has, as the process sheers off the 'unecessary' frequencies. It can leave songs sounding flat and lifeless, stripped of their natural dynamics and energy in subtle ways that the human ear can pick up, although often a listener

August 15

- 'Smells Like Teen Spirit' receives its radio debut at KXLU[40], a small listener-supported but influential alternative rock station connected to LA's Loyola Marymount University. The band are interviewed on air, and announce that they're seeking extras to appear in the video for the song, due to be filmed that weekend.
- That night, Nirvana play a showcase at the Roxy Theatre in West Hollywood.[41] They debut 'Lounge Act'. After the gig, flyers are handed out advertising for extras for a music video shoot at the weekend.[42]

August 16

- Following the radio premier on KXLU, 'Smells Like Teen Spirit' hits college radio and alternative stations across the US and is an immediate hit, with switchboards lighting up to request the song.[43] The song is also added to commercial metal and rock stations.[44] Around this time another Nirvana, a pretty unsuccessful

---

couldn't tell you exactly what's missing. *Nevermind*, fortunately, predated the worst excesses of this trend, though subsequent reissues have not.

40. Boston's WFNX had the honour of being the first commercial station to play the song, having obtained a cassette copy early in the month, though there's no record of which station played the song first. The station's head of music, Kirt St Thomas, who went on the write his own Nirvana biography, *Nirvana: The Chosen Rejects*, says that requests for the song started coming in at an unprecedented rate from the first play.
41. This show, at a 500-capacity club off Sunset Strip, was arranged with a specific aim: to get the staff at Geffen onboard with Nirvana. To many at Geffen, DGC was the 'Dumping Ground Company', a silo of the wider group that took in the acts too weird or niche for mainstream appeal. The execs dealing with Guns N' Roses and Aerosmith weren't considering Sonic Youth and Nirvana a priority. Sensing that there was real commercial appeal to 'Smells Like Teen Spirit' and *Nevermind*, DGC's Mark Kates put together the show as a showcase for what his most recent signings could do. It worked. Nirvana were incredible (in 1997 *Kerrang!* would even rate this show at number one in 'the 100 best gigs of all time'.) and a hundred stuffed-shirt record execs suddenly saw the light. According to Danny Goldberg, Geffen's creative director Robin Sloane told him 'I feel like I just saw The Who in London in 1964'. It was an important turning point for Nirvana's champions at their label – suddenly a Gold Record (500,000 sales) didn't seem out of the question. In fact, that would be a drop in the ocean.
42. The flyer read '*Nirvana needs YOU to appear in their upcoming music video, Smells Like Teen Spirit. You should be 18 to 25 years old and adapt a high-school persona, i.e., preppy, punk, nerd, jock… No clothing with name brands or logos please! You will need to be at GMT Studios, Stage 6 on SATURDAY AUGUST 17 at 11:30 a.m. Be prepared to stay for several hours! Come support Nirvana and have a great time!*'. 'We were still worried about [not enough] people showing up to be extras,' Mark Kates told Gillian G. Gerr. 'That was something we were honestly concerned about.'
43. In radio parlance this is known as 'heavy phones', and it was a feature of 'Smells Like Teen Spirit''s radio introduction across the world. The song detonated a bomb as soon as it hit the airwaves anywhere.
44. Radio in the US, then as now, was highly genre-specific. Unlike the UK's mainstream national stations, the US radio landscape was extremely segmented – College stations played alternative rock and underground music that commercial stations wouldn't touch, while, metal stations focused on bands like Pantera and Ozzy Osbourne but ignored alternative bands like Sonic Youth or the Pixies. Commercial rock stations, such as LA's KROQ or San Diego's 91X, might occasionally play a Mudhoney track during a specialist show, but their main playlist typically featured bands like Metallica and Guns N' Roses, while others would stick to the commercially comfortable ground of hair metal – Skid Row, Mötley Crüe and Whitesnake. Meanwhile, college rock stations steered clear of the heavier major label music. A slim category, 'Alternative Metal' could cross the divide, featuring bands that combined alt-rock credibility with a crossover hit – Jane's Addiction, Faith No More, and Red Hot Chili Peppers managed to sit across a few of these radio ghettos. This is where DGC hoped to position Nirvana. 'Teen Spirit', however, broke further and wider than anyone could expect, smashing conventional broadcast boundaries. By September, it was receiving heavy rotation not only on college stations but also on hard rock/metal stations like LA's KNAC and major commercial rock stations like Seattle's KISW and LA's KROQ.

LA Christian band start sending cease-and-desist letters to local radio stations demanding they stop playing 'Smells Like Teen Spirit' since they had a registered trademark on the name 'Nirvana'. Most stations point-blank refused, since the song was unstoppably popular.[45]

August 17

- The video for 'Smells Like Teen Spirit' is shot at LA's GMT studios, directed by Sam Bayer. The video depicts a high school pep rally, complete with cheerleaders with a Punk Rock 'Anarchy A' on their sweaters,[46] and a crowd of moshing kids recruited from the recent show and radio appearance, overseen by a janitor.[47]

Furthermore, it made significant inroads on traditionally pop and metal-focused stations such as New York's Z100, Los Angeles' KIIS-FM, Chicago's B96, Atlanta's Star 94, and Miami's Y100. Even San Francisco's KMEL, a *hip-hop station* played 'Smells Like Teen Spirit'. No one had managed to capture the entire rock-based radio market like this before. The penetration was such that, according to Gold Mountain's Danny Goldberg in his book *Serving the Servants*, the week after the single was released to radio stations, John Silva was called by an acquaintance who'd attended a Guns N' Roses show in New York City, where 'Teen Spirit' had been played over the PA between acts. Apparently, the intro had been greeted by a huge cheer. While this would indeed be a huge marker of success for an unreleased single that had just been pushed out to radio, it's worth noting that Guns N' Roses' "Use Your Illusion" tour didn't hit New York City until December of that year, by which point 'Smells Like Teen Spirit' would have been a familiar hit to an arena rock audience.

45. If you're curious, they released a self-titled album in 1990 and it's absolutely dreadful. While the UK Nirvana were paid off by Geffen and allowed to continue to use their name, the LA Nirvana, who were apparently influenced by 'Boston and Queen', were actually sued by *our* Nirvana for issuing the cease and desist. According to Michael Azerrad's *Come As You Are,* the LA Nirvana eventually agreed to sell their trademark for $50,000 and curiously, were allowed to continue trading under the name, although doing so would seem an extremely odd decision considering how ubiquitous the name was becoming. A year later their manager was interviewed in *Billboard* about how they were trying to crack the Latin American market under the Nirvana name, but had 'not ruled out changing their moniker'.The LA, Seattle and British Nirvanas were far from the only ones to have used the name. Perhaps unsurprisingly, given that it's a fairly common word, there have been, at best guess, something like 19 bands called Nirvana successful enough to have been pressed to vinyl or featured on a compilation, going from the 60s to the 90s, based in Spain, Germany, Australia, Sweden, Finland, Croatia, Japan, France, Laos and several in the US, including one that featured notorious Michael Jackson lookalike Daimyo Jackson, joined by his brother (a Prince tribute) and sister (who did Sheila-E). Someone should do a Nirvana-only compilation album.
46. This image had been inspired by a picture in Kathleen Hanna and Tobi Vail's *Bikini Kill* fanzine.
47. The concept had been Kurt's, who'd sketched the idea out in his journal and pitched it to DGC with one line: 'pep rally gone wrong'. Originally it was to be more elaborate and loosely based on the Ramones' movie *Rock 'N' Roll High School* and Jonathan Kaplan's 1979 Matt Dillon-starring teen-delinquent drama *Over The Edge,* which features scenes of high schoolers locking their parents in the school while they riot outside. ('That pretty much defined my whole personality' Kurt told Michael Azerrad. 'It was really cool. Total anarchy.' He would later tell *Melody Maker* that he remembered people leaving the movie theatre after seeing it and immediately smashing windows and vandalising stuff.) Kurt's journal features a shopping list of props for the shoot, including 'mercedes benz and a few old old cars', 'access to an abandoned mall', school gym, 'a cast of hundreds', and specifies '1 custodian, students' and '6 black cheerleader outfits with Anarchy A's on chest'. 'That was the genesis of it', Krist told VH1. 'School and youthful rebellion'. Unfortunately DGC had allowed a comparatively modest budget of less than $50,000 and the idea had to be pared down. First-time director Bayer reckons he was given the job because 'my reel was *so* bad ... let's hire this really crappy director' seeing his appointment as an act of self-sabotage and rebellion against their label, as he says in the *Classic Albums: Nevermind* documentary, though Danny Goldberg reckons Bayer's appointment actually came from DGC. Getting real kids (some dressed as high schoolers and some who literally *were* high schoolers) was easy but keeping those kids in line through a tedious shoot was another matter. The extras had been told to prepare for a long day, but since most of them hadn't been in a music video before, they didn't realise just *how* long they would be required to

August 19

wait. As the time dragged on the kids got more and more restless. And not just the kids – Kurt, jacked up on Jim Beam, was himself getting bored of miming along to a song he was already beginning to tire of. Eventually Bayer lost control of both his star and his cast, and the frantic moshing and slam dancing, plus the trashing of the set and the band's gear at the climax of the clip was completely real ... as were Kurt's looks to camera, filled with anger and contempt. 'Kids went crazy at the shoot,' Geffen's Robin Sloane told Danny Goldberg in *Serving the Servant*. 'Sam, to his credit, just kept filming. None of that was really orchestrated'. Poor Sam Bayer, screaming into his megaphone and trying to regain control over the chaos, just had to hang on for real life. It was only when he looked through the eyepiece of his camera as the extras tore the set to shreds, that he realised that what he was capturing was *perfect*. Kurt's instincts, as ever, had been right all along; a lesson Bayer would have double-underlined when his initial edit of the video was rejected. Kurt was flown to LA to go through the edit shot-by-shot, making changes. It was Kurt that wanted to make sure that when the camera focused on his hands playing the guitar they would always be in the wrong place for that part of the song.

A few years ago, Sam Bayer's original video was leaked to YouTube, and sure enough there are some different elements that make the video seem a little more generic, a little more mannered, a little more smugly knowing. There's a stuffed-shirt Principle, more shots of the janitor who has a little story of his own, going from quietly working to enjoying the music, and a dweeby, nerdy character (like Eugene from *Grease*) who seems to be trying to teach a class. While the Principle is completely removed from Kurt's edit, the dweeb does survive in the video's final shot, trussed up with a dunce's cap on. Bayer's version also has sexier and more frequent shots of the cheerleaders, who were local strippers (or as Kurt later told MTV news, 'prostitutes and tattoo artists'), and it makes sense that Kurt, whose most recent girlfriend was *literally* in Bikini Kill, the very template of feminist punk, would tone that down. The following year he would tell Michael Azerrad that he'd originally wanted the cheerleaders to be completely diverse, with lots of body types, genders and skin tones, subverting the idea of cheerleaders as high school aristocracy, and according to Dave Grohl, interviewed by Mark Yarm, they wanted to use L7, while Kathleen Hanna said the band had asked Bikini Kill to fill the role (they declined); but that was all squashed somewhere down the line in favour of fairly typically 'hot' white girls doing sexy dancing. Toning down the 'hot babes', getting rid of the stock characters and being subversive with the shot choices definitely sharpened the video, it made it cooler and it has certainly aged better as a result. However, like Butch Vig's original mix of the song, had the original edit of the video been the final cut, chances are it would have impacted almost as well as Kurt's version – perhaps even exactly as well. The elements that made the video resonate are already in place, from the gritty greys and sepia colours to the intense performance of the band. The slam dancing and set-trashing happened for real, and it's as clear in Bayer's cut as it is in Kurt's, and that's the element that feels most exciting. Kurt's edit is definitely better, no doubt about that, tighter, a little weirder, and a little less cliche, but Bayer's would have worked all the same.

There's one curiosity that's left hanging, however. The story first told in Azerrad's *Come As You Are*, and repeated in numerous Nirvana books and articles, goes that Kurt insisted on a shot right at the end of the video with a close up on his face. It's the only truly clear shot of Kurt's face in the whole video, and he looks both mischievous and handsome. Bayer lobbied to get the shot removed, but the label trusted their artist more than the director. And rightly so – it's a perfect closing moment. However, the original edit that leaked onto YouTube *also* has that shot. In fact, the closing moments of both edits are almost identical. Danny Goldberg, in *Serving The Servant*, says that John Silva also remembers Bayer lobbying to get that shot removed. If it was a piece of typical Cobain myth-making, it's one that has Mandela-affected its way into his managers' memories as well.

The 'Smells Like Teen Spirit' video absolutely sums up the chaotic, energetic, rebellion of the song itself and translates it perfectly to an audience who would find themselves feeling exactly the same. For Nirvana, it would change *everything*. It did its director a favour as well – he'd go on to helm videos for REM, Eminem, Smashing Pumpkins, Garbage, Justin Timberlake, My Chemical Romance, David Bowie, Ozzy Osborne, Metallica and, well, just about everyone. He also directed the remake of *Nightmare On Elm Street*, though that is substantially less fondly remembered. Still, it's a hell of a resume, and it all started with 'Smells Like Teem Spirit'; 'That changed my life,' he said on his Instagram account. 'I was a broke struggling artist when I got this job – like a Hollywood fable – I lived it.'

Shortly afterward when filming was completed, the band published an open letter to everyone involved – 'TO THE EXTRAS: On August 17th we greatly appreciated your enthusiasm and patience during the shooting of our video "Smells Like Teen Spirit". Please be advised, though, that the cancer-causing smoke inhaled by the lot of you during those twelve grueling hours has now been banned from rock vidoes. The black soot in your noses, when utilised propely, does have an array of practical uses: anything from faux hash to a welcome addition to anyone's aluminum foil or rubberband ball obessesibe type

- The band depart for a short tour of European shows, playing festivals and opening for Sonic Youth. The tour, starting on 20 August, will take in Ireland, the UK, Germany, the Netherlands and Belgium. Much of it will be captured by filmmaker Dave Markey, who will later edit the footage, with this assistance of Kim Gordon, into a road movie, *1991: The Year Punk Broke*, featuring Sonic Youth, Nirvana, Dinosaur Jr, Babes in Toyland, Mudhoney, Gumball and the Ramones, with cameos from Courtney Love[48], Iggy Pop and various members of the band's road crew. [49]

August 23

- It is the opening day of the 1991 Reading Festival[50]. Nirvana are halfway up the bill on the main stage, sandwiched between grubby London indie-punks

---

collection ... Ear wax, maybe? Anyhow, thanks a lot!! YOU MADE THE VIDEO!!; just check it out and see- NO SHIT! – Kurt, Chris and Dave'.

48. Kurt and Courtney's relationship hadn't yet begun, and at this point she was dating Smashing Pumpkins' Billy Corgan. There's a delicious quote in Michael Azerrad's *Come As You Are* where he describes a piece of footage in which Courtney, backstage at the Reading Festival, looks into the camera and says 'Kurt Cobain makes my heart stop. But he's a shit.' It's been quoted in several Nirvana/Kurt Cobain books since, including Charles R. Cross's Cobain biography *Heavier Than Heaven* which adds the detail that she was responding to Markey asking her 'if she has anything to say'. Both books are semi-official, with their authors allowed access to private material and interviews with people involved. The interesting thing is that the footage doesn't appear to exist. Markey didn't include it in *1991: The Year Punk Broke* (despite claims in some Nirvana biographies that literally say the quotes comes from the movie), which makes no sense as it's a brilliant line you would jump to include, and later told Azerrad that it wasn't filmed by him. In 2023 Azerrad revisited *Come As You Are* and created a heavily-annotated edition, *The Amplified Come As You Are*, in which he addresses this – 'Sometimes I get things wrong – but I never make things up. But I just can't remember where I saw this footage. One possibility is that Courtney fed the story to me. But then where would I get the visual imagery of "staring straight into the lens" and walking away? I may never know the answer. And that really bothers me.'
49. Kurt would later describe these few weeks on tour as one of the happiest periods of his entire life. And it's no wonder – he was on the road with some of the best bands in the world, he had made an album he was proud of and was being told continually that it was amazing, he'd just filmed a music video, people were responding, there was a sense of momentum but one that came without too much pressure. Nirvana were a band on the rise, but everyone thought they had a handle on how high that rise would take them. They could look at Sonic Youth, the Pixies, Jane's Addiction maybe; bands who could still walk down the street, but whose shows sold out and whose new music was eagerly awaited. Kurt, Krist and Dave were looking forward to joining those ranks, and their exuberance was manifesting in high jinx. The short tour was a glorious montage of moshpits, pranks, food fights, emptied fire extinguishers, trashed gear and good times. It's quite possible no-one has ever had as much fun on the road. They would never again feel so carefree and excited. 'I hate to say it was the calm before the storm because it was pretty fucking intense', Dave Grohl later told the *Irish Independent*, 'but if you can imagine that being calm, try imagining the storm.'
50. Reading is one of the key dates on the British music calendar, evolving out of a 60s jazz festival into one of the UK's biggest rock weekenders – less meatheaded and more progressive than Donnington's Monsters of Rock (now Download) and less hippy-orientated than Glastonbury, though its audience has crossover with both. By 1991, the event was clawing its way out of a late-80s malaise where it leaned into goth (The Mission headlined in both 1987 and 1989) and, unwisely, MOR rock (Bonnie Tyler, who got pelted with clods of turf by an unruly audience, and Meat Loaf both played in 1988 on a bill headlined by shoulder-padded pop rockers Starship). The 90s saw alternative rock gradually become, along with Britpop, the festival's stock in trade (Pixies, Smashing Pumpkins, Foo Fighters, Green Day and Rage Against The Machine have all headlined) and the event would get much bigger throughout the 90s and 2000s, adding a second site at Leeds in 1999, and keeping more or less in lockstep with whatever it is young people are listening to. 1991 was a transitional year, which also featured James, Sisters of Mercy, Carter USM, Kurt favourites The Fall and Teenage Fanclub, and Blur (whose 'There's No Other Way'

Silverfish[51] and shoegaze band Chapterhouse. The night will be headlined by Iggy Pop, and further up the bill are Dinosaur Jr and Sonic Youth. 35,000 people are in attendance, although it's unlikely all of them were watching Nirvana. Still, since this is the main stage on the opening day, it's certainly the biggest audience they have ever played to and by the end of the show the crowd is *huge*. The band are joined through their entire set by 'interpretative dancer' Tony Hodgkinson[52] and during 'Molly's Lips', to Kurt's eternal delight, by the Vaselines' Eugene Kelly, playing the biggest show of his life by quite some distance.[53] During the closing 'Endless, Nameless', Kurt launches himself into the pit, only to be rescued by Thurston Moore, who ushers him back to the stage where he executes a perfect running jump into Dave's drums, dislocating his shoulder in the process. 'Nirvana were mindblowing. Phenomenally good … band of the day and no mistake,' said *Raw* magazine. 'Anti-rock god posturing at its most thrilling,' said *NME*. 'Nirvana? This came close'. [54]

August 27

- 'Smells Like Teen Spirit' is released to UK radio on a white-label 7″, backed with 'Drain You'. Among the first DJs to play it are BBC Radio 1's big daytime radio names Simon Bates and Steve Wright.[55]

---

was, apparently, Kurt's favourite pop song of the year). The festival wasn't quite what it would become, and wasn't quite what it had been. It was still, however, a huge event.

51. Who gleefully get Kurt, Krist and Dave stoned before their set.
52. Antony Hodgkinson, the drummer in Derby-based band Bivouac, was a friend of Nirvana's UK booking agent, Russell Warby. He had originally been charged with collecting the band from the airport, back on their first tour in 1989. As things became more hectic, having familiar faces taking care of business was a genuine comfort, so Tony was also part of the operation when Nirvana returned the following year on Dave Grohl's first tour. While hanging out one day, the band dared Tony to go onstage with them wearing Warby's girlfriend's dress ('not much of a dare!' as he later told *Leeds Live*). He turned up at their next gig stripped to the waist, wearing a skirt and covered in tribal body paint, and proceeded to spend the show doing what could loosely be called 'interpretative dancing' to Nirvana's set, throwing a mixture, as he told the BBC for the documentary *When Nirvana Came to Britain*, of 'Native American tribal dancing and pogoing and just doing something odd, freestyle … people said "that looks crap, I could do that" … well that's the whole point of it, ya know?'. 'He became a dear friend,' Dave says in the same film. 'Kurt loved him, we all loved him.' After that, he had an open invitation to dance onstage at Nirvana shows, and was a feature of both of their Reading Festival performances.
53. Not that he could see that crowd. 'I wasn't wearing my glasses when we went on,' he later told *Uncut*. 'All I could see was this white light and a massive pink blob which was the audience.' Still, he enjoyed himself – 'I was flying for the rest of the day'.
54. Later, Nirvana's UK Publicist would tell Everett True that 'before Reading, the press only grudgingly acknowledged Nirvana. After Reading everyone wanted to know them.'
55. Anyone that knows their British radio history might have done a double take at this. Simon Bates, *the* Simon Bates, he of cosy jumpers, a rich, almost mid-Atlantic radio voice, and the schmaltzy, long-running feature 'Our Tune', in which couples dedicated soppy love songs to each other's memories, and the man who for years appeared at the start of VHS cassettes to explain the age rating … in short, the least likely person in Britain outside of, possibly, Margaret Thatcher, to play a stone-cold anthem of teen rebellion on 'The Nation's Favourite' radio station for the first time … *that* Simon Bates. Production assistant (and future DJ in her own right) Claire Sturgess had already heard the song via a friend who worked at a record plant, so was familiar with it when a plugger from Geffen came in to give the single the hard sell. It was Sturgess that was able to convince Simon Bates who, as it turns out had a rebellious streak, to give the track a spin. 'Which he thoroughly enjoyed,' she tweeted in 2018, 'because it thoroughly pissed off the management.' *However*, lest we get too excited, records show that Bates was actually off

The town sign celebrating Nirvana's origins, visible as you enter Aberdeen, Washington. (*Author's personal collection*)

Kurt's mugshot, taken after his arrest for spray painting 'GOD IS GAY' and 'HOMO SEX RULES' on cars in 1986. (*Greys Harbor Police Department*)

Every effort has been made to locate the copyright holders for these images, obtain relevant permissions and credit appropriately. The author apologises for any omissions or oversights.

Kurt Cobain's hand-drawn poster for the band's first show under the name 'Nirvana'. (*Museum of Popular Culture, Seattle*)

The 1989 four-piece Nirvana line up, L-R: Kurt Cobain, Jason Everman, Chad Channing, Krist Novoselic, taken on tour in New Jersey. (*Ian T Tilton/IMAGO*)

Touring buddies Nirvana and TAD, taken in Hoboken, New Jersey, June 1989. Note Tad Doyle is wearing one of Sub Pop's iconic 'LOSER' shirts. Front, L-R: Gary Thorntenson. Kurt Danielson, Steve Wied, Back L-R: Jason Everman, Tad Doyle, Krist Novoselic, Kurt Cobain, Chad Channing. (*Ian T Tilton/IMAGO/Avalon*)

Jason Everman serving with US Special Forces in 2013. (*Unknown, reproduced under creative commons licence*)

Chad Channing, Krist Novoselic and Kurt Cobain photographed for *NME* in April 1990, New York City. (© *Steve Double / Camera Press*)

Chad Channing, Krist Novoselic and Kurt Cobain photographed for *NME* in April 1990, New York City. (© *Steve Double / Camera Press*)

Dan Peters performing in Manchester, UK, December 1989. He would briefly join Nirvana the following year. (*Paul Blackwood*)

A poster advertising Nirvana's watershed 1990 show at the Motor Sports International Garage, Seattle – the only gig the band would play with drummer Dan Peters. (*Experience Music Project, Seattle*)

Dave Grohl performs with Scream in 1989. (*Tobby Holzinger / Agentur Spirit*)

S›U›B P‹O‹P

SUB POP SINGLES CLUB

☆

Hey loser. Wanna find some action? Tired of being left out? Here at SUB POP we've just started a special club for lonely record collectors like yourself: THE SUB POP SINGLES CLUB. Every month we'll send you a limited edition 45. All you have to do is SEND US YOUR MONEY. $35.00 for a full year, $20.00 for 6 months. Your subscription begins the month we receive your $$$.

☆

OUR RELENTLESS SCHEDULE:

OCT 90 **Poster Children**
NOV 90 **Poison Idea**
DEC 90 **Reverend Horton Heat**
JAN 91 **Nirvana/Fluid**
FEB 91 **Velvet Monkeys**
MAR 91 **Unrest**

Canadian: *$45, **$25 Overseas: *$55, **$30

YES. I am lonely and I want to join your SINGLES CLUB. Here is my money.
☐ $35 Full Year* ☐ $20 6 Months**

NAME ______________________

ADDRESS ______________________

____

SUB POP:
P.O. Box 20645,
Seattle, WA 98102

An order form for the Sub Pop singles club printed in a magazine circa 1990. (*Author's personal collection*)

Nirvana photographed on tour in London, UK, October, 1990. L-R, Kurt Cobain, new drummer Dave Grohl, Krist Novoselic. (*Lorna Van Bel/IMAGO/xFAMOUSx*)

Krist, Kurt and Dave shortly after recording *Nevermind*, photographed at the Warfield Theatre, San Francisco, June 1991. (*Joe Giron/IMAGO*)

DGC's open call for extras for the 'Smells Like Teen Spirit' video. These flyers were handed out at Nirvana's show at the Roxy Theatre, West Hollywood in August 1991 ahead of filming. (*Author's personal collection*)

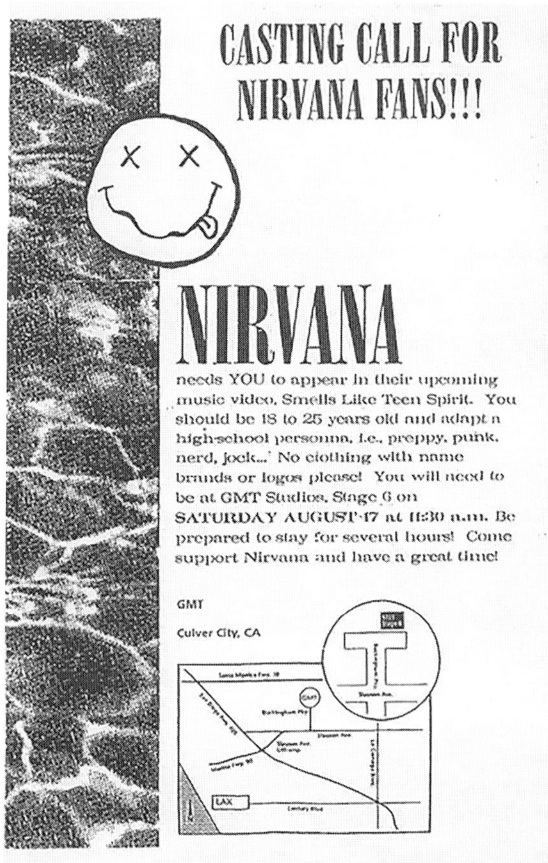

Kurt Cobain and Courtney Love photographed for *Sassy* magazine in New York City, early in 1992. (Montage of Heck *publicity still via moviestilldb.com, original photograph by Dora Handel*)

Kurt's Mosrite Marc IV Gospel guitar, on display at the Experience Music Project, Seattle. (*Francisco_Antunes*)

Nirvana shot for *NME* in Madrid, July, 1992. This picture would accompany an article by Keith Cameron that caused Kurt to name a gun after him. (© *Steve Double / Camera Press*)

Krist and Kurt onstage at the MTV *Video Music Awards*, September 1992. (*PinkBeltRage*)

Kurt performing 'Heart Shaped Box' and 'Rape Me' on *SNL*, September, 1993. (Saturday Night Live / *NBC, publicity still via moviestillsdb.com*)

Nirvana, Germs and Foo Fighters guitarist Pat Smear performing with FF at Lolapallooza, Berlin in 2017. (*Ralph PH*)

Dave Grohl performing at Austin City Limits in 2009 with his band Them Crooked Vultures. (*Craig Carper*)

Krist Novoselic performing at Seattle's Experience Music Project in 2011 to celebrate the 20th anniversary of *Nevermind*. (*David Lee*)

The surviving members of Nirvana; Dave Grohl, Krist Novoselic and Pat Smear, attend the Grammy awards in February 2023. (*Axelle / Bauer-Griffin / IMAGO*)

The 'three wise men' of alternative rock production – Jack Endino performing in Seattle in 2015 (picture – Joe Mabel), Butch Vig at Smart Studios, Madison in 2006 (picture – Valdo Howell) and Steve Albini, approx mid 2010s. (Picture – Mixwiththemasters)

Kurt and Krist's mentor, Buzz Osborne of the Melvins, performing live in 2010. (*Peter Alfred Hess*)

Occasional Nirvana and eternal Melvins drummer Dale Crover, performing at Hellfest in 2023. (*Selby May*)

Bikini Kill's Kathleen Hanna, the sharpie-wielding coiner of anthemic song titles, pictured in 2016. (*Paul Hudson*)

Kim Gordon of Nirvana patrons Sonic Youth, Town & Country Club, Leeds, 1992. (*Greg Neate*)

Early promo photo for Screaming Trees produced by SST records, circa 1988. L-R: Mark Pickerel, Gary Lee Conner, Mark Lanegan, and Van Conner. Kurt considered Mark Lanegan to be his favourite singer. (*Naomi Petersen*)

Kurt Cobain's favourite band of all time, The Vaselines. L-R, Frances McGee and Eugene Kelly, pictured backstage at Shibuya WWW in Udagawa-chō, Shibuya-ku, Tokyo, Japan in 2015. (*Masao Nakagami*)

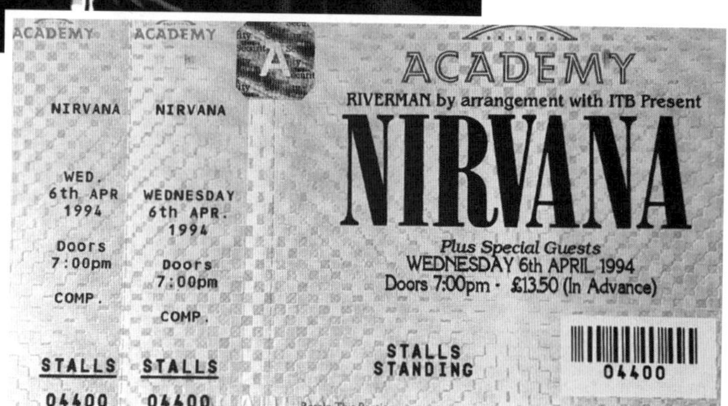

An unused ticket for Nirvana's cancelled show at Brixton Academy in London, dated 6 April, 1994. Kurt is thought to have died on either the fifth or sixth and the show would never take place. (*Gilian G. Gaar*)

September

- Guns N' Roses release their new single 'Don't Cry'. Singer Axl Rose does promotional interviews for the song and its epic[56] video wearing a blue baseball cap with the the Nirvana logo emblazened across it, which can also be seen (if you look very carefully) in the video itself, shoved on a couch next to him as he speaks to his therapist.[57]

---

in the final week of August (he was covered by 'Bates Mates', including Phil Collins and The Pet Shop Boys), meaning the earliest he could have played 'Teen Spirit' would have been Monday, 1 September. If that was the case, he'd have been beaten to the punch by roughly 12 hours by the far more on-brand John Peel. The reason for dwelling on this isn't just because of the delightful juxtaposition of Simon Bates and era-defining Punk Rock, but because of the size of the audience Bates would have given that song. Back in 1991, daytime Radio One shows were regularly getting listening figures between 16 and 20 *million*, with listeners drawn from all walks of life (within a few years the station would tighten its remit as a youth pop music station, deliberately shunting listeners to the more oldies-focused Radio 2, precisely because of old-school presenters like Bates hanging on to audiences they'd had since the 70s and blurring the lines of what those brands were for). The astonishing and undeniable fact is that Simon Bates would have exposed more people to Nirvana in one morning than *NME*, *Melody Maker*, *Sounds* and John Peel combined. He played the song often, too. Later he and Sturgess were, quite rightly, awarded gold discs by Geffen for their support.

56. And absolutely proposterous and oddly boring.
57. The relationship between Nirvana and Guns N' Roses, both in reality and in the public mind is an interesting one. The two bands, both on Geffen records, can be seen to represent two very, very different sides of music in 1991. GNR were bloated, they had just spent hundreds of thousands of dollars and over a year on two albums, released on consecutive weeks, full of over-long, pretty boring songs, overdubbed with strings and synths. Their world tour, calling at enormodome arenas and stadiums, involved fleets of trucks and private jets. Their million-dollar videos were full of awful cliches and conceptual nonsense. They were the epitome of hard rock excess. What was worse though, especially to Kurt who still loved Aerosmith, a band equally guilty of all of those excesses, was that Guns N' Roses behaved like assholes. They leaned into every rock 'n' roll cliche – strippers, groupies, drugs, bodyguards. They disrespected their fans by going on stage *hours* late. Their lyrics were often trite cliches and, at their worst, riddled with hate speech (I won't repeat them here but look up the lyrics for 'One In a Million' for evidence; although Axl Rose claims the song has been taken out of context. He's never defended the 'you get nothing for nothing ...' line from 'It's So Easy' though.) Nirvana were the ultimate contrast: feminist, pro-gay rights, socially aware and from the Punk Rock underground. Their first album had been recorded for $600 (ish). Guns' debut had a budget of $370,000. Axl had a mansion, Kurt Cobain was living in his car. To Nirvana, GNR were everything they were setting themselves against. As Dave Grohl said during a Q&A with SiriusXM in 2011, 'our whole world rejected that scene as something that was just not *real.* There were fundamental differences in what we did.' Michael Azerra, in the introduction to *The Amplified Come As You Are* says that Kurt himself dismissed the idea of an 'official biography', for which he would have final sign off, as 'too Guns N' Roses'.

    The interesting thing, though, is that Guns N' Roses didn't see it that way at all. Sure, Nirvana were from the underground, but as far as Axl Rose was concerned *so were Guns N' Roses.* Axl was a music fan, and he genuinely loved alternative rock, and Nirvana especially. He'd gotten Shannon Hoon, singer with LA alt rock band Blind Melon, to duet with him on several songs on the *Use Your Illusion* albums, and Hoon was featured heavily in the 'Don't Cry' video in which Axl himself is already dressed in the textbook grunge uniform of a plaid shirt, band tee and ripped jeans. GNR had become a bloated rock monster, but their roots weren't all that different from Nirvana's – bass player Duff McKagan had even started off in Seattle hardcore bands. Sure, Duff and guitarist Slash were known to do heroin, but so did Kurt. Guns had formed out of the underground rock scene, built a fanbase through hard touring and great songs and then signed to a major label. Just like Nirvana. Later, Axl Rose would pull out all the stops to try and convince Nirvana to tour with his band, and sure, you can interpret that as the rock dinosaur trying to glom on to some alt-rock cred, but then ... did Guns N' Roses, the biggest band in the world, actually *need* any alt rock cred? They were doing just fine. Rose, truthfully, had simply heard *Nevermind* and loved it, and thought the up-and-coming band would jump at the opportunity for the massive exposure a Guns N' Roses tour would provide, just as GNR themselves had when they'd opened for Mötley Crüe and the Rolling Stones in the 80s. He even begged Geffen publicist Lisa Gladfelter to get them to play his birthday party. He was pretty stung and a little confused by their rejection, and

September 3

- Back in the UK, on the eve of their return to the US, Nirvana play their third (and, as it turns out, final) John Peel session. The trio are exhausted after three weeks on the road, with Kurt seeming so weary and drained that engineer Dale Griffin worried he wouldn't be in a fit state to record the session. He is left to sleep on a couch in the control room at Maida Vale while everyone else sets up.[58] It is a markedly different experience to the band's first two Peel sessions as a result. Once Kurt recovers a little, the band record three songs – 'Dumb', 'Drain You' and 'Endless, Nameless'.[59]

---

simply couldn't see that to Nirvana, he was everything they felt was wrong with music. At a show the following year he introduced 'Double Talkin' Jive' with a rant aimed squarely at Kurt – 'He's too good and too cool to bring his rock 'n' roll to you, because the majority of you, he doesn't like or want to play to or even have you like his music.'

Still, as 'Smells Like Teen Spirit' did its work and Nirvana accrued a mainstream audience, there was definitely a subset of music fans for whom the two bands weren't just two sides of the same coin, they were on *the same side* of the coin. After Kurt made a crack about 'our next song is called 'Sweet Child O'Mine'' at a show in Portland in 1992, a kid jumped on stage to say 'Hey, man, Guns N' Roses plays awesome music, and Nirvana plays awesome music. Let's just get along and work things out!' *NME*'s Mary Anne Hobbs would later put her finger exactly on the issue, when she described Nirvana as 'the Guns N' Roses it's okay to like'. It was a reality Kurt was struggling to accept. In 1992 he would tell *The Advocate* 'there is a war going on in high schools now between Nirvana kids and Guns N' Roses kids … I'm really proud of that.' The truth was that for every Nirvana fan who felt they were in opposition to a GNR there were another thousand people who had bought *Use Your Illusion* and *Nevermind* and loved both of them.

58. In a correspondence with editor Alex Roberts, published on the *LiveNirvana* website, Dale Griffin very heavily implies that he believes Kurt was on heroin at the session. Griffin had been the drummer in Mott The Hoople and had seen more than his fair share of rock excess – he was particularly reminded of Free's Paul Kossoff, whose life had been blighted by heroin addiction and who eventually died from an embolism resulting from a blood clot that had been caused by heroin use. 'It was a hateful thing to see a young man like Koss wishing his life away on the dross of drugs,' he told Roberts. 'I hated to think that the same thing was happening to this likeable and highly talented young American, who was standing so unsteadily just inches from my gaze.' Kurt was using heroin regularly by this point and was now back in London, where pretty much anything is available if you know where to look, and where he now had friends. It wasn't out of the question that he could have found a fix. Committed users usually can. Kurt later wrote in his journal that it was after this tour that he 'decided to become a junkie', saying that 'heavy opiates' were the only thing he had found that provided relief from the painful and unidentified stomach condition that regularly plagued him. Accord to Charles R Cross, by the end of autumn his heroin use had become 'part of an ongoing daily addiction'.
59. The three Peel sessions all tell us something about the band at the point they were recorded. In 1989 they were earnest, glad to be there, showing off the two strongest songs on *Bleach*, 'Love Buzz' and 'About A Girl', and showcasing a nod to the future in 'Polly'. Returning the following year it was all smiles and cover versions, pointing the way to the influences on the upcoming *Nevermind.* Both sessions were professional and efficient and, crucially, recorded at the start of the tour when the band were fresh. This third session was at the other end of a tour, and showed a band a little jaded and a lot worn-through. The setlist choices are extremely interesting – conventional wisdom would have told them to play 'Smells Like Teen Spirit' and some of the other accessible moments of their upcoming album. Instead we get a version of 'Dumb', a song the band hadn't yet recorded and, tellingly, probably the most weary-sounding song in their repertoire. Here it sounds almost like *White Album* era-Beatles or John Lennon's early solo music. The session closes with an eight-minute, mostly improvised version of 'Endless, Nameless', as brutal as the one from the *Nevermind* sessions and arguably more chaotic and intense (and oddly, featuring a snippet of The Vapours' power-pop classic 'Turning Japanese'). The two songs showcase two very different but equally important sides of the band: the unhinged and the melancholy. They're balanced in the middle by a great version of 'Drain You' (complete with aerosol-can sound effects in the breakdown), the only song from *Nevermind* recorded at the session, and one of that album's more accessible moments. It's often said that no-one knew what was coming for Nirvana, but this session, seemingly done by a strung-out and burned up trio, almost suggests that *someone* was thinking of the

September 9

- 'Smells Like Teen Spirit' is released in the US & UK, with different formats in both countries (and elsewhere) using different b-sides. In the US, where the single comes out on CD, 7″ and cassette, all versions carry 'Even In His Youth' from the January sessions at Music Source, with the CD adding 'Aneurysm' from the same session. In the UK, all formats feature the album version of 'Drain You', with a 12" single adding 'Aneurysm' and the CD going for a value-busting four tracks with 'Drain You', 'Even In His Youth' *and* 'Aneurysm'.

September 13

- Chaos reigns at the *Nevermind* release party, held in Seattle at a club called the Re-Bar. The place is packed with friends of the band, plus some local media and a ton of music industry types, with Sub Pop's Bruce Pavitt DJing[60]. Someone makes the mistake of including a buffet spread, including chips and dip. The venue doesn't have a licence for 'hard liquor' (possibly someone at DGC thought ahead and selected it for that very reason) however, since it's their own party, the band have no trouble smuggling in a gallon of Jim Beam. The resulting, and entirely predictable, food fight eventually sees the three members of Nirvana thrown out of their own record release party by bouncers who either didnt know or didn't care who they were.[61] They, along with 20 or so friends, eventually had their own party at the house belonging to DGC's Susie Tennant, the label's NorthWest rep, where the band kitted themselves out in their host's dresses, built a domino rally from her CD collection and defaced a gold record for Nelson's *After The Rain* on the wall.[62]

future. The session wasn't due to be broadcast for two months, by which point no-one needed to hear a new version of 'Smells Like Teen Spirit', and *Nevermind* itself was well bedded in. Everyone thought they knew who Nirvana were. Anyone tuning in to John Peel because Nirvana were in session would hear 'Dumb' and 'Endless, Nameless' (which a lot of people missed … especially those who owned the cassette or LP or had dubbed a cassette from someone else's copy) and discover that there were other sides to the band, one wounded, one volatile, both equally damaged-sounding in their own way. It was probably accidental, but it worked out well. Perhaps understandably, but again in contrast to previous BBC sessions, the band don't stay for the mixing, leaving it to the in-house team. Despite (or maybe, because of) the state of the band, it's arguably the most interesting of three Peel recordings.

60. According to Michael Arezzad, the band soon talked Pavitt out of playing cuts from *Nevermind* in favour of 'the trashiest new wave and disco they could find'.
61. The party's invitation had promised 'Edible food, drinks, prizes you might want to take home, a few surprises, people to meet, the band to greet'. It certainly delivered on the food and drinks, and while the band being thrown out made them difficult to 'greet' it would definitely count as a surprise. Whether there were, indeed, 'prizes you might want to take home' is, alas, unrecorded.
62. Nelson are a justly-forgotten pop/rock duo, comprised of the twin sons of musician Ricky Nelson. Their debut album had been one of DGC's first hits. Charles R. Cross claims that Kurt wrote 'Affront to human kind' on it in lipstick and then microwaved it. In *The Amplified Come As You Are*, Azerrad corrects this – he actually fired the lipstick at it with a slingshot.

September 16

- Over 200 fans line up for entry outside Seattle's tiny Beehive Records (which holds about 50 people), where Nirvana are playing an in-store show to promote the album.[63]

September 20

- The North American tour to promote *Nevermind* begins at The Opera House in Toronto, Canada. The tour will take in 33 shows across six weeks. 'Smells Like Teen Spirit' is, by this point, being played heavily on radio stations across the US.[64]

September 21

- 'Smells Like Teen Spirit' debuts at number 27 on *Billboard's* Modern Rock chart, but doesn't trouble the mainstream Hot 200.

September 23

- The US leg of the tour begins in Boston, at a charity show hosted by local radio station WFNX, with support from local band Bullet Lavolta and Chigago's Smashing Pumpkins, who are touring their Butch Vig-produced debut album, *Gish*.[65] An MTV crew is on hand to film a game of Twister played between Kurt, Dave and Krist (who has stripped down to his underwear and smeared himself

63. Kurt would later cite this show, in which he was mobbed for autographs by fawning fans, amongst them people he'd been to high school with, as one of the first times he realised he was getting famous, and that fame wasn't going to be an easy ride.
64. Nirvana's meteoric rise hadn't quite caught fire in Canada in the same way. They were selling out 500-capacity venues, but it wasn't like another 500 people were clambouring outside to get in. That would change very soon.
65. Smashing Pumpkins are often lumped in with the grunge crowd, although in truth they have little in common with what was fairly loosely known as the 'Seattle sound' beyond fuzz pedals and a fondness for Led Zepplin and Black Sabbath. The four piece had formed around frontman Billy Corgan, a gifted guitarist with a distinctive but distinctly marmite singing voice. Corgan shared Kurt's love of the Beatles, Black Sabbath and Queen (and, ultimately, Courtney Love), and like Kurt he could write songs that ran from softly harrowing ('Disarm', 'Polly') to snarling monsters ('I Am One', 'Breed') to power pop ('Today', 'In Bloom'). The Pumpkins, like Nirvana, were also master improvisors, who could lose themselves in 20-minute jams ('Silverfuck', 'Endless, Nameless'). Where the two bands differed was over Punk Rock. Though Corgan, the son of a session guitarist, was a fan of *post*-punk, and loved Joy Division and The Cure, he hadn't grown up with the Punk Rock ethics of Black Flag and Minor Threat, and there was none of the DNA of Melvins or Bad Brains in his band, putting them at odds with the rest of the alt-rock set, who had almost all come from punk backgrounds. Instead, his tastes ran to prog and psychedelia. He and drummer Jimmy Chamberlin were also virtuoso musicians and perfectionists – to the point that Corgan almost all of the guitars and bass on their first two albums. Meanwhile, bass player D'arcy Wretzky and guitarist James Iha, a couple at this point, bought a fashionista cool to the band in much the same way Kim Gordon did to Sonic Youth. Onstage, however, the quartet had a monstrous chemistry and could be blistering live … when they weren't petulantly jamming for 20 minutes to punish a disinterested crowd. The pinwheeling, psychedelic and hugely promising *Gish* had come out in May on Caroline records, a subsidiary of Virgin, and was technically one of the biggest independent records ever released, although that's easy when there's major distribution looking over your shoulder. The following year the band would reunite with Butch Vig to make their major label debut, *Siamese Dream* which, like *Nevermind*, became a touchstone record for Gen X rock. 23 September was the only show where the two bands played on the same line up, outside of music festivals. For me, it's another of those 'if I had a time machine' gigs.

in Crisco vegetable fat), and Smashing Pumpkins' Billy Corgan and James Iha[66], with Pumpkins bassist D'arcy Wretzky spinning the wheel. After everyone has had one turn, Krist dives across the floor and the three members of Nirvana pull up the Twister mats and start throwing them at each other. 'We're slipping and sliding into the MTV Music News', Krist tells the camera.[67]

- That night, Nirvana debut their cover of The Vaselines' 'Jesus Doesn't Want Me For A Sunbeam'. The show is over-21s only and completely sold out, so the band plays a second, all-ages set the following day. That sells out too.

September 24

- *Nevermind* is released in the UK and US.[68] Anticipating modest sales, Geffen press 46,251 copies of the CD in the US and just 6,000 in the UK.[69] It very quickly becomes impossible to find a copy.[70]

---

66. Who both look like they'd rather be anywhere else.
67. Krist would later tell MTV that, while cleaning himself with an American flag hanging handily nearby (including dabbing Crisco out of his butt crack) he had inadvertently offended some ex-Army types who were in attendance, saying 'These patriotic jocks will probably be working me over within about half an hour!'. 'It's a good time to be running the camera', adds Kurt. 'They can play it in court'. 'We're like Rodney King,' says Krist.
68. To say reviews were kind would be putting it mildly. '*Nevermind* is the big American alternative record of the autumn. But better still, it'll last well into next year' said Steve 'King of Understatement' Lamacq in *NME*'s 9/10 write up. *Spin* was slightly more optimistic than *NME*, predicting, quite rightly, that 'you'll be humming all the songs for the rest of your life.' Meanwhile, Everett True was on review duties for *Melody Maker*, saying 'Nirvana have power oozing out of every guitar line and ripped snare ... Nirvana have emotion, raw emotion, the sort where the singer bares his soul all the way down the line ... When Nirvana released *Bleach*, all those years ago, the more sussed among us figured they had the potential to make an album which would blow every other contender away. My God, have they proved us right'. Everett was, by now, so deep in the Nirvana camp that anything less than a declaration of 'stone cold masterpiece' would have been seen as a great betrayal – it was lucky for him that that 'stone cold masterpiece' was a totally justifiable opinion. *Kerrang!*, which didn't have the same skin in the game, handed out its 'maximum five 'K's', calling it a 'brutally frank record with a wounded soul'. Not that everyone was convinced; *Rolling Stone* hedged its bets with a three-star review, '*Nevermind* boasts an adrenalised pop heart and incomparably superior material [to *Bleach*],' wrote Ira Robbins, describing the band as 'Scrappy garageland warriors setting their sights on a land of giants'. This *Rolling Stone* review has since been quietly bumped up to four stars online. At the far end of the scale was *The Boston Globe*, whose Steve Morse reckoned that 'most of *Nevermind* is packed with generic punk-pop that had been done by countless acts from Iggy Pop to the Red Hot Chili Peppers ... the band has little or nothing to say, settling for moronic ramblings'. You can't please everyone.
69. Often when researching a band like this you'll find conflicting accounts of the same event. It's not too surprising – memories fade and warp, people's agendas start to impact their telling and sometimes the polished version of a story is told so often it essentially replaces the true version, even in the minds of those present. Krist and Dave's trip to Newbury Comics in Boston to see kids buying *Nevermind* on 24 September 1991, however, is a doozy. According to Charles R. Cross's *Heavier Than Heaven*, they found a huge queue of fans waiting to get their hands on the album. Cross quotes Mark Kates of DGC as saying 'It was amazing! There were, like, a thousand kids trying to buy the record'. However, Kates was also interviewed by Paul Brannigan for his Dave Grohl biography, *This Is A Call*, written a few years later. This time, Kates says that 'we were expecting to see a line around the block ... [but] there was no vibe whatsoever'. According to Brannigan, they didn't see a single copy sold.
70. There's no small irony in this, given that one of Kurt's major issues with Sub Pop was hearing from kids who had tried to buy *Bleach* but couldn't find a copy. He could have reasonably expected this to not be an issue now he was on a major label. And yet ...

September 29

- MTV's late-night Sunday show, *120 Minutes* premieres the 'Smells Like Teen Spirit' video.[71] The show also features a quick ident by all three members shot backstage at Reading the previous month.[72] Somewhere between New York City and Pittsburgh, the three members of Nirvana are in a hotel room waiting for their TV debut, which doesn't come until the second hour of the show, following new clips from Morrissey, Titanic Love Affair, The Cult and The Farm. The experience is surreal. 'I screamed … and was simultaneously filled with both glee *and* the feeling of tripping on too much acid,' Dave will later write in his memoir *The Storyteller – Tales of Life and Music*. '*Holy shit!* I thought. *That's what we look like?*'.[73] The following day 'Teen Spirit' is added to medium rotation at the channel.[74]

October 12

- *Nevermind* charts on the Billboard Hot 200 at 144 (it will rise to 109 the following week). 'Smells Like Teen Spirit', though not troubling the mainstream singles chart yet, goes up to number 5 in the Modern Rock chart. In the UK it charts at 36, with almost all 6,000 copies selling out that week. As a result it will drop out of the top 40 the following week, not for a lack of demand, but a lack of availability. It's outsold by Mudhoney's *Every Good Boy Deserves Fudge*.[75]

---

71. MTV could, at that time, be career-making, though if you flicked over to it these days you'd find that hard to believe, since it's mostly tacky reality TV shows like *Jersey Shore*, *Ex On The Beach* and *Catfish*. However, back in the 80s the channel had pioneered the concept of 'Music Television' and had a huge audience essentially all to itself, since there were no other channels that did what MTV did. It was also, crucially, youth-focused and both a reflection and a driver of what young people were listening to. *120 Minutes*, however, was MTV's alternative rock show, and was often something of a dumping ground for songs that wouldn't have a hope in hell of getting onto the daytime playlist. That particular episode also featured Billy Bragg, My Life With The Thrill Kill Kult, Blue Aeroplanes, the Wonderstuff and Candyland – hardly chart-bothering stuff. The previous year, Sonic Youth's 'Kool Thing' had also debuted on the show before being added to 'medium rotation' (four to five plays a day) for a couple of weeks and then yanked off the station altogether. Nirvana's managers at Gold Mountain were expecting a repeat of that.
72. The ident has Kurt and Dave trying not to laugh on either side of Krist, who has made a sock puppet and is performing a bad ventriloquist act. 'These sods are Nirvana,' squeaks the sock as Krist struggles not to move his lips, 'and you're up very late on a Sunday night, and you're watching *120 Minutes*'. The sock then turns to Krist and says 'I can see your lips moving!' at which point the other two dissolve into giggles. Kurt has his arm in a sling after dislocating his shoulder during the day's onstage antics.
73. 'I was watching MYSELF on MTV,' Dave goes on to say. 'It was Krist, Kurt, and me, playing a song we wrote in a fucking barn. Dali's melted clocks had nothing on this.' Kurt, meanwhile, was on the phone to a girl he'd met a few nights previously in Boston, the singer/songwriter Mary Lou Lord, with whom he'd developed a fast and intense relationship, gleefully telling her every time he popped up on screen. In my head he looks exactly like Leonardo DiCaprio in Quentin Tarantino's *Once Upon A Time in Hollywood*, phone in one hand, beer beside him, pointing at the screen in disbelief.
74. MTV junior exec and Nirvana fan Amy Finnerty, one of the youngest people at the station, had put her career on the line over the video, telling her boss that she didn't feel her generation was represented by the channel's output and insisting 'Teen Spirit' be put straight into heavy rotation. 'If I was wrong and the record wasn't a hit, they could kick me out of the music meeting', she told Danny Goldberg. Unfortunately, thanks to that new Nirvana-hat-featuring Guns N' Roses video, there was no room for another track in heavy rotation, but she was promised the song would be moved up the following week.
75. Unbelievably, Sub Pop had managed to be more organised than DGC.

- Nirvana play a riotous and triumphant show at the 1,100-capacity Metro in Chicago, it is sold out and dozens[76] of people outside are attempting to get in.[77] Courtney Love[78] and Babes in Toyland drummer Lori Barbero show up toward the end of the show and hang out backstage.[79] After months of flirting Kurt and Courtney hook up.[80]

---

76. One estimate of the show claims that 5,000 people were outside, but that's unverifiable. It sounds unlikely, but then everything about the last few months of Nirvana's 1991 sounds unlikely.
77. 'The buzz in the air was unbelievable!' Butch Vig told Gillian G. Gaar. 'Kids were screaming and crying during the show, and almost everyone knew all the lyrics.' Danny Goldberg, head-honcho of Nirvana's management at Gold Mountain, who had flown in for the show, notes in his own memoir that 'decades later, Chicago rock writers still described it as one of the best shows they'd ever seen'. It was also the first time he had seen the level of onstage destruction the band were capable of. In fact, that night's destruction was a little more calculated than usual – tour manager Monty Lee Wilkes had been refusing to arrange a new drum kit for Dave, despite his becoming increasingly damaged night after night. The band hatched a plan to force his hand by smashing the kit beyond repair. It didn't work – Dave had to share support act Urge Overkill's kit for the rest of the shows.
78. I knew eventually I was going to have to write this annotation and I've kind of been dreading it. Courtney Love. Where to start? By October 1991, Courtney was already collecting notoriety like an avalanche collects snow as lead singer of Hole, the band she'd formed with ex-boyfriend Eric Erlandson with a remit of blending Black Flag, Sonic Youth and Fleetwood Mac (a pretty perfect summation of their first two albums), but that was far from the beginning of her story. Born Courtney Michelle Harrison in 1964, Courtney had spent the last decade or so causing trouble and breaking hearts across multiple continents. Her childhood saw her ping-ponging between divorced parents, struggling with behavioural issues, and being shuttled through various schools and correctional facilities. By her late teens, she had already travelled the world, working odd jobs and immersing herself in the punk and new wave scenes of Europe and the West Coast, and making ends meet as a stripper in Japan and the US (she adopted 'Love' as a surname while working in a Portland strip club). It took her until the early '80s to take the leap into music, briefly singing in an early incarnation of Faith No More in 1983 (William Martin – once known as Poppy Z.Brite – mentions in his Courtney Love biography *The Real Story* that Faith No More, at one point, denied that Courtney was ever a full member, despite her singing with them for several months. Try as I might, I can't find any source for this claim – the members of the band around at the time have acknowledged her role many times, however) and forming short-lived projects like Sugar Babylon with friends in Portland. She eventually landed in San Francisco, where she formed the Pagan Babies with Kat Bjelland (later of Babes in Toyland) before heading to Minneapolis and working as a concert promoter. Courtney was also an actor, studying at the San Francisco Art Institute, taking experimental theatre courses from Whoopi Goldberg, and landing roles in Alex Cox's films *Sid and Nancy* (she'd auditioned to play Nancy Spungen but lost out to Chloe Webb. It didn't matter – the public would soon cast her in that exact role in the production of her own life) and spaghetti western *Straight to Hell*, playing the lead in a film that no-one liked ... except, apparently, Andy Warhol. Obviously. Disenchanted with the celebutante fame she was gathering (being featured in Warhol's talk show, *Andy Warhol's Fifteen Minutes*, was pretty on the nose) Courtney retreated to Alaska in 1988 to strip and 'gather her thoughts', but within a year was back in LA with a renewed determination to make it in music. She'd been making a hell of a lot of noise, in one respect or another, ever since. Hole's debut album, *Pretty On the Inside,* had come out in spring 1991, co-produced by Sonic Youth's Kim Gordon; it was a viscerally brilliant record, full of bile and anger and pain. Later, in *Hit So Hard,* a documentary about future Hole drummer Patty Schemel, Courtney explained her agenda for the album: 'This is what I do, and I'm not going to back down from it. I am announcing my persona as a cunt'. Her ambitions ran a lot higher than pulverising art rock, however. Courtney loved pop music and fashion as much as she loved cathartic screaming and being a contrarian smart ass. Put that all together, and she was going to be a star.
79. Courtney was in town to visit Smashing Pumpkins' Billy Corgan, with whom she'd had a fairly tempestuous on-again-off-again relationship across the last year. She'd arrived at his apartment to find he was with another woman and stormed off to the Nirvana gig with a specific aim in mind – Kurt Cobain. As it turns out she got more than she bargained for, since she more or less sweet talked Danny Goldberg into signing Hole to Gold Mountain that night.
80. Mary Lou Lord, whom Kurt had been pretty infatuated with, had left the tour in Detroit as she had to go back to Boston to work, which was a stroke of luck for Courtney. Or a lucky escape for Mary Lou, depending on how you view it.

October 14

- 'Smells Like Teen Spirit' is added to MTV's 'Buzz Bin' (a playlist of songs the station believed deserved to break through[81]) and moved up to heavy rotation, meaning it will be played 10–12 times daily.[82]

October 17

- The band debut a new song, 'Curmudgeon' at a show in Lawrence, Kansas.[83]

October 19

- Nirvana play a dangerously oversold club in Dallas, Texas, called Trees, with fans already spilling onto the stage before the show even starts. The venue's security have no clue how to handle a Punk Rock show, let alone one full of screaming kids buzzed on the fact that they've scored the hottest ticket in town.[84] Nirvana had already endured one near-riot that week[85] and, channelling weeks of bottled frustration reflecting the absurd pressure cooker the band had been existing inside, Kurt lashes out at the monitor desk at the side of the stage, smashing it beyond repair with his guitar. Then during 'Love Buzz', he dives into the crowd, eventually colliding with a security guard who starts taking jabs at him, causing

---

81. This was a particularly good week for epoch-defining alternative rock classics – Nine Inch Nails' 'Head Like A Hole' and Red Hot Chili Peppers' 'Give It Away' were also added to *Buzz Bin* at the same time.
82. 'Once the video got played, I mean, it was really over,' Mark Kates told Gillian G. Gaar. 'This was that really amazing thing that occasionally happens in our business, where something has its own energy and momentum, and it doesn't really matter what you're doing.' The impact on the shows was immediate – suddenly a tour that had been booked for a moderately popular underground punk act was the showcase for the hottest band in the country, with a hit record on every radio station and a video playing on MTV several times a day. Every show was now oversold, some of them dangerously so, and often with hundreds of people outside hoping to get in (the band would meet fans and add as many names to their guest list as they could). Geffen's promo machine had gone into overdrive too. Just 18 months earlier, Kurt had been complaining (unfairly, as it turns out) that Sub Pop never arranged press and radio interviews. Now he was doing several a day, including top 40 radio stations he would never have wanted to listen to in his life, never mind appear on. And every radio appearance, every play on MTV, every piece of press pushed Nirvana higher. In his memoir, Dave describes the night 'Teen Spirit' debuted on MTV as 'an event that changed not only my life, but the world of music.' He wasn't wrong.
83. 'Curmudgeon' is one of the first musical signs that Nirvana were getting bored with the shiny power pop that was currently and with brutal efficiency making their name. Powered by a riff that would have sat happily on *Bleach*, it's a sludgy, almost discordant barrage, and a glimpse into a parallel world where Nirvana had gone straight from their first album to *In Utero* and skipped *Nevermind* and its build up entirely.
84. By this point slam dancing, moshing and stage diving was par for the course at punk shows, but less underground-inclined venues could still be taken by surprise by it. It can't have helped that the 'Smells Like Teen Spirit' video was now serving a generation of kids with a step-by-step playbook on how to riot at a punk show.
85. At a show in St Louis on 16 October, Kurt had gotten frustrated with the venue security's clumsy inability to handle the crowd, which was constantly invading the stage and interrupting the set. A speech by Krist had zero impact and the stage invasions and increasingly deranged slam dancing only intensified, with the security becoming more and more heavy handed with the audience – a full-scale, three-hour riot at a St Louis Guns N' Roses show the previous July, in which tens of thousands of dollars of damage had been done (Axl Rose would later be fined $50,000 and given two years probation after being charged with inciting it), had made jumpy local venues over compensate on crowd control. Kurt's way of retaliating was to simply invite the audience on stage. The mini-riot was finally quelled by another speech from Krist about how 'anarchy only works if we all accept responsibility'.

Kurt to react defensively and clobber his attacker with his guitar, leaving him visibly bleeding. The security guard, who is significantly bigger than Kurt, then socks him in the face, knocking him to the ground.[86] Dave dives from behind his drums to restrain the attacker, whom Krist attempts to talk down. The band abandon the stage, though come back to play a final brutal, bruised and bloodied version of 'Territorial Pissings' to placate the crowd and stop them rioting. Later the trio is smuggled out of the venue to avoid Kurt's new sparring partner, who is lying in wait with some buddies.[87]

October 25

- Krist and Kurt record a segment for MTV's hard rock show *Headbanger's Ball.* Kurt shows up 'dressed for the ball', wearing an over-the-top yellow ball gown with a huge collar.[88]

86. This particular security guard was not in the best of moods – he also happened to own the monitor desk that Kurt had just destroyed.
87. Video of this whole incident appears on Nirvana's home video *Live! Tonight! Sold Out!*, an attempt by Kurt to document the madness of the band's rise, completed after his death. You can see the whole thing play out on shaky camcorder footage. A delightfully lively description can also be found in Dave Grohl's *The Storyteller*, which adds a little colour.
88. The metal press wasn't really in DGC's original marketing plan for Nirvana. They'd never have pitched, for example, Sonic Youth to *Headbanger's Ball*, but the crossover appeal of *Nevermind* and especially 'Smells Like Teen Spirit' was absolutely undeniable and all bets were off. *Headbanger's Ball* itself was, at this point, caught in something of a transitional moment in music. The 80s old guard, including the preposterous hair metal of Warrant and Ratt as well as the ever-present Guns N' Roses and Metallica and the more parent-friendly likes of Bon Jovi and Aerosmith were still getting plenty of exposure on the show, but a change was definitely in the air – Soundgarden's *Badmotorfinger* was making waves and Alice In Chains' 1990 album *Facelift* had been a huge hit on the metal charts, as had Pearl Jam's debut, *Ten*. The ultra heavy Brazilian act Sepultura, whose *Arise* was one of the best metal albums of the year and whose image was about as far from hair metal as it's possible to be, were also on the show that day. MTV's flagship metal show, along with magazines and radio stations across the country, was having to cope with the end of spandex and make room for a new scene of much grubbier bands who'd never let a can of hairspray anywhere near them. In some cases, they barely used shampoo. The episode featuring Nirvana opens with host Riki Rachtman thanking Mötley Crüe's Vince Neil and Nikki Sixx for hosting the previous week, before promising new videos from cock-rockers Little Angels, Thunder and Ugly Kid Joe … but there's also an interview with Soundgarden's Chris Cornell, backstage at a show, discussing the band's new video for 'Jesus Christ Pose'. If you listen carefully in the background, you can just hear, very faintly, that the club PA is playing 'Come As You Are'. The changing of the guard was happening live on air.
    Nirvana's interview is not an all-timer, and while Krist and Kurt do their best, host Rachtman, who was close friends with Axl Rose and Poison's Brett Michaels, had absolutely no handle on their sense of humour. The interview starts with Kurt explaining he is 'dressed for the ball' in his yellow frock. '*He* wouldn't wear his tux,' complains Kurt, dryly, indicating Krist. 'He didn't give me a corsage either.' Krist's reply is brilliant – turning to Kurt and saying 'Well at least I ask you out, you know'. It's a lovely piece of comic improv, and the door was wide open for Rachtman to join in with a 'yes and …'. Instead he rides straight over it. 'It took me years before I even got that joke', he later told Mark Yarm for *Everybody Loves Our Town*, which just goes to show how much attention he's paying, because Kurt literally explains it at the start of the segment. His questions are all entry-level, asking the same bland queries about 'the Seattle scene' he'd asked Pearl Jam a few months earlier. He'd not exactly done in-depth research either – 'I wanna talk about the new album,' he says at one point. 'Is it new? Has it been out for a while and everyone's just getting excited, or is it pretty new?' Kurt and Krist are trying hard to be funny and interesting, but their host does a terrible job at giving the interview any focus, by turns ploughing over their answers and changing the subject or else leaving them hanging awkwardly when they've clearly finished speaking. It's a clash of people who simply don't get one another. Years later, he will complain that the interview was 'like pulling teeth' and that 'Nirvana didn't want to be on *Headbanger's Ball.* Then stand by your own rules and don't be on *Headbanger's Ball.*' The problem wasn't Nirvana, and it wasn't

- That night Nirvana headline the Rock For Choice benefit concert at The Palace in Hollywood, on a bill with Hole, L7 and Sister Double Happiness.[89]

October 26

- 'Smells Like Teen Spirit goes up to number two in the *Billboard* modern rock chart, while *Nevermind* jumps to 65 in the Hot 200.

October 27

- Nirvana play their own headline show at The Palace, the Hollywood venue where they played the Rock For Choice benefit just days earlier. At a capacity of 2,200 it was the band's biggest solo headline show yet[90], and it sold out quickly. Axl Rose is again in attendance, this time in the company of Geffen exec Eddie Rosenblatt, and asks to come backstage to meet the band. Danny Goldberg of Gold Mountain is at the show and suggests Kurt steals out the back door, guaranteeing he wouldn't be home when Axl Stops by. To Kurt, the idea of shaking hands with Axl Rose, the man who once wrote a song called 'I Used to Love Her but I Had to Kill Her'[91], was both deeply alien and a betrayal of his values.

October 28

- While in town for a show in LA, Nirvana do a photoshoot with underwater-photography specialist Kirk Weddle, who shot the image on the cover of *Nevermind.*[92] The shoot, involves the band playing their instruments underwater

---

the idea of being on a metal show – it was a host who didn't understand and seemed to vaguely resent the people he was interviewing. It may well have been an issue of prejudice – he'd taken one look at Kurt Cobain in the green room, napping on a couch, assumed it was because he was on dope and taken against him right there and then. It's an attitude Kurt would encounter a lot in the next few years, regardless of whether he was using at that time or not.

89. There's a lot written about how Nirvana were a changing of the guard for mainstream rock (and a change that happened at speed – the idea of Nirvana being 'mainstream' was preposterous just six months earlier) and this is an excellent example. No other rock band on the Hot 200 were playing benefit shows for abortion rights. Not Guns N' Roses. Not Metallica. Certainly not Skid Row. No-one. Political values were so common in the underground as to be almost cliche – *of course* a band like Nirvana were pro-choice, anti-homophobic, anti-racist. You couldn't show your face at a party in Olympia if you weren't. But the big rock bands in America kept their mouths shut on these issues because, well, racist, redneck assholes bought rock CDs too, and their money was as good as anyone elses. Not Nirvana, who may have been the the first rock band in the whole of history to look at elements of their fanbase and say 'we don't want you. Go away.' The trio were determined to use the platform they had, and both Kurt and Krist gave lengthy speeches on women's autonomy at the show. They were, in fact, the most outspoken band on the entire bill, which considering Courtney Love was fronting the opening act is quite some achievement. You wonder what some of the bigger names in the audience made of it ... for, while that particular show was a right-on benefit, it was also the hottest ticket in town and as such the LA rock glitterati all showed up, including reigning king of hard rock crossover W. Axl Rose and Mötley Crüe drummer Tommy Lee, neither of whom are known for their impeccable feminist credentials (according to Everett True, Lee spent the night complaining loudly about being forced to pay to get in rather than being put on the guestlist).
90. Although only just – the Astoria in London had a capacity of 2,000 and had sold out the previous year.
91. Axl, by the way, maintains that this slightly tongue-in-cheek piece is actually about a dog. Which isn't all that much better, when you think about it.
92. The *Nevermind* cover, of course, has become as much of a classic as the album itself. Originally Kurt wanted to call the record *Sheep* and wanted to use artwork showing a trailerpark full of identical

Winabagos, but after consulting with DGC's art department he decided the image felt cliched. During the recording of the album, he and Dave watched a late-night documentary on waterbirths and found it fascinating – simultaneously both deeply strange and extremely natural. Kurt found some graphic images of waterbirths to use, but it was decided they were a little *too* natural — instead DGC's art director, Robert Fisher, found an image in a stock photo book of a baby swimming underwater (very new born babies will instinctively hold their breath, open their eyes and swim when submerged). The plan was to add a dollar bill on a fishhook to the picture. In retrospect it all feels quite pointed; a symbol of innocence chasing the corporate buck – a fully conceived criticism of the juxtaposition between capitalism and the purest form of humanity, or possibly a metaphor for a band swimming wide-eyed toward some major label payola. It's an image that's powerful enough for the sleeve to be hanging in a 2024 exhibit on the depictions of money through the years at the British Museum. The reality, however, was far more haphazard. It was Kurt that came up with the idea of the fishhook, just to make the image more interesting and edgier. 'We spent the afternoon sitting around thinking of all the funny things we could put on the fishhook,' Fisher said in an article published by the Museum of Modern Art, where the image also hangs. 'One idea was a piece of meat, like a big raw steak. Another was a CD or something to kind of symbolise music. We went to lunch and we were like "How about a burrito?" "Oh there's a dog, what about a dog?" … it just went on for hours. I don't remember who said dollar bill but everyone was like "That's pretty good," and that's what it ended up being.' It was actually Krist who came up with the idea of putting a dollar bill on the hook. The band may have ended up with a subversive image undermining capitalist hegemony, but it certainly never started out that way.

Unfortunately the photographer behind the image Fisher had found wanted $7,500 a year, for as long as the album was in production, so it was decided that an original shot would be taken. Kirk Weddle, who specialised in underwater images, was engaged, and offered some friends $200–250 (it tends to change in the telling) to photograph their new born son, Spencer Elden, a kid (and now man) doomed to spend the rest of his life as 'the Nirvana baby'. There was, initially, some fuss around the inclusion of the baby's penis in the image; 'Man, it's such a dick shot!' Weddle told *The Guardian* in 2019. 'His unit was so prominent in the picture … he's a well hung kid for a four-month old, you know? I didn't know if the label would go for it.' There was, indeed, some hesitation; Geffen even photoshopped a version of the image without little Spencer's, um, Little Spencer on show, but ultimately the band insisted on using the image as was. Kurt claimed to Michael Azerrad that he would allow censorship only if the offending part was covered by a sticker saying 'if you are offended by this then you are a closet pedophile'. In the end the cover had remarkably little resistance from stores, though city officials in Ventury, California did demand a poster be taken out of a store window following a single complaint. It could certainly have been a lot worse.

In fact, the real controversy didn't kick in until the album's 30th anniversary, in 2021, when the now-adult Spencer 'Nirvana Baby' Elden filed a lawsuit alleging 'sexual exploitation', with his legal team claiming that the band and their label 'intentionally commercially marketed Spencer's child pornography and leveraged the shocking nature of his image to promote themselves and their music at his expense'. Elden, now 32 years old, argued that he suffered ongoing personal harm due to his depiction on the album cover as a naked four-month-old baby, despite recreating the image (with his underwear on) three times, for the 10th, 15th and 25th anniversaries, and having the word 'Nevermind' tattooed on his chest as a teenager. The lawsuit targets not only the surviving members of Nirvana (including, absurdly, Chad Channing) but also Kurt's estate, the band's record label (now Universal Music Group, following a complicated acquisition completed in 1999) and, despite being an old family friend, photographer Kirk Weddle. In all, fifteen different defendants have been named, with Elden demanding $150,000 from each – over $2 million in total. A federal judge initially dismissed the case, stating that Elden had waited too long to bring the lawsuit. However, a court of appeal overturned this decision in 2023, allowing the case to proceed based on Nirvana's more recent reissues, including the album's 2021 rerelease. Nirvana's lawyers are confident that the case won't come to anything, after all if the *Nevermind* cover is 'commercial child pornography' then over 30 million of us can be legitimately prosecuted for possessing it, which feels more than faintly absurd. The defense is pretty clear – to be considered 'pornography' an image needs to have a sexualised context, which this clearly doesn't. Naked children, after all, are included in personal, commercial and art photography all the time. Spencer Elden's participation in re-creations and his tattoo don't paint a picture of someone whose life has been made miserable by sexual exploitation, either. He's even given interviews where he's admitted to using his identity as 'the Nirvana baby' to pick up girls ('You'll hook up with a hot chick, and then they figure out you're not making any money from it and they'll dump you' he told *GQ Australia* in 2016). It's not quite open and shut, however. Elden is alleging that permission was never formally sought from his guardians that authorised 'the use of any images of Spencer or of his likeness, and certainly not of commercial child pornography depicting him.' The ridiculous 'child pornography' part aside, if true it still raises a lot of uncomfortable questions.

in a Pasadena swimming pool, and gear is hired especially, including a drum kit strapped to a ladder and floated upside down. No-one is especially happy with the shots.[93]

October 29

- Arriving at the Fox Theatre for the first of two co-headline shows with Mudhoney, Nirvana are told that *Nevermind* is now a gold record, with US sales of 500,000 in its first month — 10 times what DGC thought they'd need for the album's first CD pressing.[94]

October 31

- The US *Nevermind* tour comes to a close with a triumphant homecoming Halloween show in Seattle in a sold out, 2,800-capacity Paramount theatre. Again it is technically a co-headline show alongside Mudhoney (with Bikini Kill opening[95]), but again no-one seriously expected Mudhoney to be the closing band of the night.[96] The gig had actually been upgraded from the 1,800-seater Moore Theatre, which the two bands would probably have sold out even before 'Smells Like Teen Spirit', however the unprecedented demand created by Nirvana's sudden leap to 'coolest band in the country' meant that bigger premises were needed, and even then the gig had sold out comfortably. Yet again it was the biggest headline show they had played.[97]

---

93. The shoot was scheduled for 10am, which may as well be 4 o'clock in the morning in rock band time, especially as Nirvana had played a huge show the previous night. It was also a grey, chilly day – rare for California, even in October – and the pump in the pool had broken, leaving it murky. No-one had informed the band that they would be required to get in the water. Kurt, who was characteristically ill and understandably exhausted, needed some convincing and spent the first 90 minutes of the shoot napping. Krist insisted someone go out to find him Jack Daniels. Dave eventually walked away with photographer Kirk Weddle's wetsuit. Once in the pool, it was discovered that Kurt had an odd buoyancy problem and struggled to sink below the surface. In the end, DGC's art department were unhappy with the shots; 'They wanted something slicker,' Weddle told *The Guardian* in 2019. 'They said: "We don't like Kurt Cobain's hair!" I thought, man, there ain't nothing I can do about his hair!'
94. In that instant, of course, these stopped being 'co-headline' shows. Nirvana had *a gold record*. It was pretty clear who everyone had come to see. Just two years earlier Nirvana and Mudhoney's tours had converged in London for Sub Pop's Lame Fest UK, and Nirvana had gone on first of three bands. Those days had, long, long gone. Poor Mudhoney, the grunge pioneers who had paved the way for pretty much everyone were, like the Melvins before them, relegated to the status of support band. Not that that they really minded. 'Within two weeks of the tour starting it was obvious that's what would happen,' Mark Arm told Keith Cameron for his book *Mudhoney: The Sound & The Fury From Seattle*. 'And it wasn't like we were, "oh fuck them", it was amazing.'
95. Bikini Kill, who had just self-released their amazing debut tape *Revolution Girl Style Now*, played the show with their three female members in lingerie with the words 'SLUT' and 'WHORE' written on their skin in marker pen – they're a band that has always known how to use their platform. Not that the audience could necessarily see them. 'The venue, which was the biggest we'd ever played, didn't even turn the lights on for us,' Kathleen Hanna wrote in *Rebel Girl*, 'so we played in the dark.'
96. Mudhoney themselves were okay with the arrangement, since the agreement to split the ticket money 50/50 stayed in place.
97. Gold Mountain and DGC had decided to film the show for future release, so a large professional camera crew were planted around the stage, which did rather take the edge off the performance. Some clips were used for the 'Lithium' video the following year and for *Live! Tonight! Sold Out!* a few years after that,

November 2

- *Nevermind* breaks the Top 40 in the US, at number 36.[98] The band, having had just two day's rest, fly to the UK to begin a European tour.

November 3

- John Peel broadcasts the session recorded in September on his BBC Radio 1 show.

November 4

- The European tour begins at Bristol's Bierkeller.[99] Support for the UK shows is supposed to be from Captain America, the new band from The Vaselines' Eugene Kelly, but their van breaks down and they miss the first gig.

November 5

- Nirvana play the London Astoria for the third (and final) time. Captain America manage to get to the show in time to play and Nirvana blow Eugene Kelly's mind by opening with The Vaseline's 'Jesus Doesn't Want Me For A Sunbeam'. Never ones to leave a crowd satisfied if they can possibly bewilder and frustrate any casual

---

but the majority of the footage sat in the can until the 20th anniversary special edition of *Nevermind*, when it was also released as a DVD and a live album. Though it's not quite Nirvana at their most explosive (probably because of the cameras – 'It was so unfair to the home audience because it stilted the performance,' Charles Peterson told Everett True. 'It reeked of money.') the band were in the middle of a run of incredible form, well sharpened by months on the road and the show is still, especially with thirty years hindsight, a solid representation of everything that was great about the *Nevermind* line-up. It was also one of the last times Nirvana would play a headline show in Seattle (though there'd be a handful of benefit shows and guest appearance, the band would play just three more official headline shows in the city, all in arenas) and a capstone for a whole era of the band. Things could never be the same, and indeed they were already starting to change – Charles Peterson, the in-house photographer of the Seattle scene, wasn't allowed to shoot the gig from the pit, which left him feeling resentful. 'It was a great show,' he told Gillian G. Gaar, 'but it was frustrating to be standing there with my heavy camera bag watching it from the back while it seemed like there were at least ten cameramen with their little gizmo 16mils running all over the place.'

The presence of so many 'corporate goons' (Dan Peters' words) was causing all sorts of tension – Danny Goldberg remembers John Silva, having lost track of his charges, asking Mudhoney where 'my band is', and getting the reply 'they're not *your* fucking band'. Two of Kurt's friends, Ian Dickson and Nikki McClure, were asked to dance on stage through the gig (replacing 'skinny model looking dancers dressed as cats', according to Kathleen Hanna, who were apparently supposed to come out during 'Smells Like Teen Spirit' before Kurt replaced them with his friends from Olympia) but were taken aside by Silva before the show and told to stay out of shot. '[He] comes up to me and says "I didn't spend a quarter of a million dollars on this video for your to fuck it up!"', Ian told Everett True in *The True Story*. 'I'm like "Fuck you, John. I don't work for you. Kurt asked me to do this".'

98. It now sounds absurd that a record with half a million sales had only just broken the top 40. This was the peak of the music industry CD boom, however – CDs and tapes were selling in their millions, especially at this time of the year, wth Christmas just a month away.
99. 'The sound at the back is as blubbery as a distraught dentist' says *NME*'s Simon Williams. Nevertheless, the band's UK shows are met with raptuous responses from crowds of euphoric kids crammed into rooms that are universally too small to hold them or the band they've come to see. Nirvana had always done well in the UK, and that momentum had built and built. "Sliver' did the ground work', wrote Williams, 'Reading sowed the seeds, now … *Nevermind* is reaping the wild, wall-shaking harvest.'

observers, the trio encore with two songs from their two-years-in-the-future *In Utero*, 'Dumb' and 'Pennyroyal Tea', and the secret track from *Nevermind.*

November 8

- The band make their live TV debut on Channel 4's late-Friday-night party *The Word*,[100] performing 'Smells Like Teen Spirit'. Before starting, Kurt takes the mic and declares that 'Courtney Love, of the sensational pop band Hole, is the greatest fuck in the world'.[101]

November 9

- *Nevermind* moves up to number 17 in the Hot 200. It has sold another 100,000 copies in the previous week.
- Nirvana head to Maida Vale to record more songs for the BBC, this time for Mark Goodyear's Radio One show *The Evening Session.* They track versions of 'Been A Son', a super Punk Rock version of 'Polly' that will become known as '(New Wave) Polly', 'Anuerysm' and a dark, heavy version of 'Something In The Way'.[102]

---

100. *The Word* was an *extremely* 90s show. An example of what was, once upon a time, known as 'post pub TV, aimed at a late night audience that had either just come home from a night on the beers or else (and most likely) were too young to get into pubs in the first place, or too responsible to go to them much anymore but pined for the years when they could. The show, which was broadcast live, involved laconic interviews with edgy celebrities, weird audience challenges (like drinking your own sick or snogging an elderly woman) and fantastic live music, performed in front of a screen showing trippy projections. Live booker Jo Whiley, who would go on to find fame as a BBC radio DJ and TV host, had a knack for getting the most exciting acts in the world, and the show played host to electrifying early performances from Manic Street Preachers, Prodigy, Rage Against The Machine, Smashing Pumpkins, Oasis, Primal Scream, Snoop Dogg, Blur ... the list goes on. The show itself could be enormously grating, but the live music was incredible.
101. This was quite a shocking moment for the TV-watching audience at the time, not used to pop singers dropping the F-bomb on live telly, even of the scabrous late night variety. No-one, however, was more shocked than Mary Lou Lord who was under the impression that *she* was Kurt Cobain's girlfriend. She'd travelled to the UK with the band, unaware that Kurt had been seeing Courtney, and though she'd been left to her own devices she still thought her new relationship was a going concern. Courtney, meanwhile, had her own spies and had caught wind that Kurt was seeing someone else, and so phoned him the previous night knowing full well that Mary Lou was likely to be in the hotel room with him. The ode to Courtney on live television served a double purpose – impressing Courtney and letting her know, publicly, that she was his priority, and also saving him the trouble of having to tell Mary Lou to her face. The previous summer Courtney had apparently told another camera that 'Kurt Cobain makes my heart stop. But he's a shit', and that footage may or may not exist. It *was* however, and especially from the point of view of Mary Lou Lord, probably true.
102. This fourth BBC Radio session yielded what some might consider the definitive versions of 'Been A Son' and 'Anuerysm', since it was these takes that wound up on *Incesticide* rather than the official studio recordings. According to producer Miti Adhikari the band were in good spirits and were productive and creative, which is a marked difference from the John Peel session recorded a few months previously. Like the Peel session, however, the band were making savvy setlist choices, introducing new fans to the road less travelled with the *Blew* EP's 'Been A Son', one of their first forays into full buzzsaw bubblegum, 'Aneurysm', which was one of their heaviest and most dynamic songs and which had tightened considerably through consistent gigging since it was first recorded back in January, and radically reworked versions of two songs from *Nevermind.* The 'New Wave' version of 'Polly' blasts away some of the song's creepy seriousness, almost belying its subject matter. It had been in their set for two years now, so it's unsurprising that the band would want to mix it up a little. That kind of over-familiarity will allow you to have fun with even the most harrowing of subjects. Finally there's 'Something In The Way', which if anything, is even more intense than the quiet, contemplative take found on the album.

November 10

- The mainland part of the European tour kicks off in Berlin. The band will play 11 shows in five countries across just over two weeks. Where possible, shows have been upgraded to bigger venues (as with Amsterdam's Paradiso club[103]) but as in the US, many of the clubs were booked months in advance and are now almost comically small for the audience attempting to gain entry.

November 16

- Back home, *Nevermind* cracks the top 10 of the *Billboard* Hot 200, moving up to number 9.[104]
- Nirvana debut a new song, 'Talk To Me', at a show in Muggia, Italy.[105]

November 23

- 'Smells Like Teen Spirit' goes to number one on the *Billboard* Modern Rock chart, while *Nevermind* moves to number 4 on the Hot 200. Nirvana's album is now

---

Here the band beefs up the chorus into something towering and dark and huge. This is the only song from the session to remain officially unreleased, and it's surprising that, in an age where record labels are always looking for new 'product' for 'heritage' bands, a *Nirvana: Live At The BBC* hasn't come out. There's four sessions between 1989 and 1991 which give us 15 tracks, six of which have never been officially released, with a good mix of covers, songs from all three albums and deep cuts that show off the different dimensions and the development of the band.

103. This show, one of the high points of the tour (if you ignore the unlistenably out of tune version of 'Come As You Are' that Kurt maniacally leans into) will later emerge on the 30th anniversary reissue of *Nevermind*.
104. At this point the mainstream music industry had been taken completely by surprise. DGC's Ray Farrell told *Billboard* that the overwhelming response from record store chains was bafflement, saying 'we don't know who these guys are, but they're top five in our stores'. What was becoming clear is that America (and elsewhere) had a youth audience that simply hadn't been served by anyone else, and often comprised kids that would have gotten into underground rock if only they'd known it existed. The alternative and college rock crowds were already on board, and the commercial rock and metal fans had responded to the album's combination of genuinely great riffs and obvious authenticity. The momentum from those audiences was pushing 'Smells Like Teen Spirit' under the noses of mainstream music fans and casual listeners, who were responding on the basis that these were undeniably *great* songs that didn't sound like the normal, tired old hard rock they had been happily ignoring. Kurt's 'ultimate pop song' had become exactly that. Nirvana's underground authenticity had become a superpower that almost everyone found themselves responding to, even if they didn't realise what it was they were sensing. Danny Goldberg, interviewed in the same issue, explained that the marketing strategy for Nirvana was now simply 'get out of the way'.
105. Sometimes considered one of the white whales of Nirvana rarities, 'Talk To Me' was only ever performed four times and there is no known studio demo, though apparently there are studio-quality rehearsal recordings in the Nirvana archive. It's unsurprising that the song was never recorded properly – this was the last gasp of Kurt's power pop phase, and it has a very new wave, almost surf rock feel to it, influenced by The Wipers and Flipper. Kurt had perfected power pop with *Nevermind*, and was starting to feel increasingly embarrassed by how sugary and accessible people were finding his music. Captain America drummer Andy Bollen kept a detailed diary of the UK leg of the tour which he later published as *Nirvana: A Tour Diary* and in it he often noted how dismissive of their new album the band seemed to be. 'Nirvana were so fed up and frustrated, maybe even fearful, that their hardcore fans would hate them for "selling out",' wrote Bollen, 'that it almost became their default position to criticise the album … they were starting to think *Nevermind* didn't truly represent them artistically'. In their remaining three years or so as a band, Nirvana would focus on noisier and more discordant sounds, already represented by songs like 'Curmudgeon' or the BBC session recording of 'Something In The Way'. Something like 'Talk To Me' was a throwback to a version of the band they were now ready to move on from.

outselling the new records by Guns N' Roses and Metallica, two bands currently on massive stadium and arena tours, while Nirvana are playing 500–1,000-capacity clubs and aren't even in the country. Perhaps the biggest indicator yet that 'Smells Like Teen Spirit' has grown far, far past its expected audience, is that the song also appears in *Billboard*'s 'Hot Dance Breakout' chart – meaning it is being heavily played in dance clubs.

November 25

- The band records a session for two Dutch radio shows at once, VPRO Radio's *Nozems-A-Gogo* and VARA Radio's *Twee Meter De Lucht In*, booked months in advance. During a shambolic evening, Nirvana cut off-the-cuff and unrehearsed versions of 'Where Did You Sleep Last Night' and 'Here She Comes Now', plus some lengthy and formless jams with the trio swapping instruments. Only 20 minutes of the 45-minute recording is deemed usable.[106]

November 27

- Back in the UK, Nirvana record 'Smells Like Teen Spirit' for the TV show *Top of the Pops*, in what will become one of their most famous TV performances. Required to sing live vocals over an instrumental backing track, the band react predictably badly. Kurt sings in a comically lower register, making it clear he's only pretending to play the guitar by moving his hand up and down the fretboard as if he is a puppet. Dave is waving his hands in the air, bopping from side to side and only occasionally hitting the drums, while Krist keeps throwing his bass into the air and catching it. At the end of the song, in a slightly feeble nod to the 'Teen Spirit' video, fans invade the stage. The band decline a request to do a second take.[107]

---

106. VPRO's Lotje IJzermans, who had overseen Nirvana's last Dutch radio session back in 1989, had come to the recording with a list of songs she wanted the band to perform, including 'Polly' and 'Smells Like Teen Spirit'. This was a fatal error. Already pretty burned out from touring, and growing increasingly suspicious and troubled by their own unexpected ubiquity, the last thing anyone in Nirvana wanted to do was play 'Smells Like Teen Spirit' *again*. Kurt's natural petulance kicked in and he sabotaged the session. Not that there aren't highlights: 'Where Did You Sleep Last Night', which lies somewhere between the version on Mark Lanegan's *The Winding Sheet* and Nirvana's *Unplugged In New York* rendition has a stark and chilly power. 'Here She Comes Now', meanwhile, is messier though that does at least feel in the spirit of the Velvets original. The most interesting part of the session was a jam on a new song, nicknamed 'Horrified' by fans due to Dave Grohl shouting 'I STAND HORRIFIED', quoting a song of the same name by Daniel Johnston. It feels unfinished and formless, but it has a mesmeric, droning quality that could have been developed into something interesting, though it doesn't appear to have been taken any further. Nirvana jammed for two or three hours in total, with the engineers hitting record whenever they felt the trio might actually be about to perform a whole song. Ultimately only about 20 minutes were considered fit for broadcast. According to an interview conducted with IJzermans by *LiveNirvana*, Kurt and Dave fled the scene, leaving Krist to apologise, saying 'We know when we fuck up'.
107. British readers of a certain age won't need me to explain the importance of *Top of the Pops* at the time, though younger people and those in the US and elsewhere might. The show, which was broadcast weekly on Thursday nights for most of its run on BBC One, had begun in the mid 60s as a showcase for the pop charts. Its remit was always pretty simple: 'Here are the latest pop music hits from across genres'. Its audience was huge; an appearance could send a song into the stratosphere on the charts and many

- *Nevermind* is certified 'Platinum' in the US. It has sold one million copies in two months.

November 30

- *Nevermind* goes to number 9 in the Australian album chart.
- Over two months since its release, 'Smells Like Teen Spirit' enters the UK single chart, going straight in at number 9, while *Nevermind* slips into the top 40 album chart at number 40.

December 1

- Following shows in Edinburgh and Glasgow, Kurt and Dave perform an acoustic set in a tiny pub in the Scottish capital, with Dave on bass and Kurt on acoustic guitar.[108]

---

acts had created career-defining moments on screen, not least David Bowie's performance of 'Starman' in 1972 or The Smiths doing 'This Charming Man' in 1983. Doing the show was a rite of passage for British bands, most of whom had grown up watching it. It was a true democratisation of pop: if a song was popular, it went on, whether it was Iron Maiden or Bjork or the Bay City Rollers or the Prodigy or Cliff Richard. It could also be *incredibly* cheesy. Most bands mimed to a greater or lesser extent, sometimes singing live over backing tracks, sometimes lip syncing the vocals as well. Occasionally, a rock band would play fully live, but of course this was a substantially more complicated set up than merely miming, so the show tended to discourage it. In the 60s and 70s there were even dance troupes performing prepared routines for acts who couldn't make it to the studio. Things weren't quite that bad by the early 90s, but the show could still have the faint whiff of cheese to foreigners. To Nirvana, subverting such an orthodox and mainstream pop machine would have seemed an obvious move – they came from a culture completely removed from such fluff. Many in a British audience, however, would have seen their performance as disrespectful, even sacrilegious. *Top of the Pops* was an institution and every kid watched it. It was also one of the very few live music shows on television – MTV Europe was broadcast in the UK over satellite and cable, but very, very few had access to it in 1991, and most shows that had 'serious' music content, shows like *Rapido* and *The Word*, were late-night. *Top of the Pops* represented a chance for younger and more sheltered kids to have a transformational experience with Nirvana, as many had in the past with David Bowie, T.Rex, Happy Mondays, New Order or The Smiths. While the band's larking around was both hilarious and absolutely in character, and over the years has been celebrated as a pricking of the balloon of mainstream pomposity, in other ways it was a shame. Still, it didn't do the single's chart placing any harm – two days later 'Smells Like Teen Spirit' punched into the top 10, and then jumped a few more places the following week, peaking at number 7. The day of the broadcast, the band assembled in the common room at Sheffield University's Students Union, in service as a green room, to watch themselves on this most iconic of pop shows. 'Back in the common room, both Kurt and Dave are now cringing and sliding down their chairs so much that they are almost on the floor,' writes Andy Bollum in *Nirvana – A Tour Diary*. 'The look on their faces is one of vulnerability, shock and embarrassment.' 'They were worried they had gone too far', Captain America's Gordon Keen says in Nick Soulsby's *I Found My Friends*. 'We were reassuring them that it was just the right thing to have done.'

108. This was a charity show, organised by local band Joyriders, who had risen from the ashes of The Cataran, Nirvana's support band on their first UK tour. Nirvana were billed as 'special guests', although it seemed to be absolute common knowledge that they would be playing that night, and the pub was rammed way beyond capacity. The band dealt with this obvious health and safety issue by the simple and genius technique of not turning up until most people had given up and gone home, leaving only 30 or so fans to witness the duo playing 'Jesus Doesn't Want Me For A Sunbeam', 'Dumb', 'Polly' and a cover of Shonen Knife's 'Twist Barbie' (Shonen Knife, the Japanese power pop band, a favourite of Kurt's, were main support for the tour).

- 'Smells Like Teen Spirit' moves up two places to number 7 in the UK top 40, where it will peak.[109]

December 6

- Lying in bed in their hotel that morning, Kurt and Courtney decide to get engaged.
- Nirvana perform on *Tonight With Jonathan Ross*, a live TV show broadcast on Channel 4 at half six. The band are scheduled to play 'Lithium', and had rehearsed it on stage that afternoon so the crew could work out camera angles etc. After Ross introduces them ('Now, here with the song 'Lithium', probably the hottest band in the world right now, Nirvana!') the band launch into an abrasive 'Territorial Pissings', destroying their hired gear at the end of the song.[110]

December 7

- 'Smells Like Teen Spirit' goes top ten in Canada. In the US the single finally enters the point-of-sale singles chart[111] – it is the 19th best selling song in America. It's also, rather brilliantly, at number 40 in the 'Hot Dance Music' club play chart.
- Nirvana plays the Trans Musicales festival in Rennes, France. It is to be the final date of their European tour. Badly burned out and with Kurt's stomach issue flaring, the group cancel the remaining shows, set to be in Ireland and Scandinavia. The gig ends with a spectacular and cathartic trashing of instruments and Krist carrying Kurt off the stage, holding him like a baby.[112]

---

109. It's very likely that the single would have climbed higher and stayed longer if Nirvana hadn't deliberately sabotaged their two biggest UK TV appearances (the second of which would take place the following day). An important fact though, is that Nirvana didn't actually *want* the single to be a bigger hit than it already was. Its ubiquity was actively distressing them. It's one thing to *say* you want to be 'the biggest band in the world', but it's another entirely to live through it and Nirvana's life was becoming a kaleidoscopic headfuck, especially for Kurt. A few weeks later they would return to the US to find things were even worse. In his book *Sing Backwards and Weep*, Mark Lanegan describes hanging out with Kurt soon afterwards. Kurt was arguing over the phone over something business-related and, at one point, slammed down the receiver and pulled the cord out of the wall, yelling 'Fuck!' ... At which point MTV played 'Smells Like Teen Spirit'. 'Kurt grabbed my boot lying on the bed between us and threw a perfect strike at the television,' Lanegan writes. 'In that same instant, we heard ... a car rolling by three stories down blasting 'Smells Like Teen Spirit'. Kurt looked stricken and buried his head in the pillow'.
110. 'Hope we didn't wake the neighbours up', deadpans Ross as the camera returns to him. 'Nirvana would like me to tell you that they're available for children's brithday parties and Bar Mitzvahs'. This performance on the highly-rated *Tonight*, going out at peak time on Friday evening, would have had exactly the galvanising effect on young viewers that 'Teen Spirit' on *Top of the Pops* didn't, and on Nirvana's own terms too. It's brilliant.
111. At the time, *Billboard*'s charts, which essentially acted as the 'official' chart of the US, were compiled based on a myriad of factors – not only sales (as the UK charts were) but also plays on radio, TV and in clubs. *Billboard* had only been factoring true point-of-sale figures for a few months at this point, via a technology called SoundScan. Sales had never been accurately tracked across the country before that.
112. A review of the show in *Melody Maker* points to how utterly weary the band seemed. 'A lot of ... songs are severely lacking in sparkle', says the reviewer. 'It's as if they're worn thin and there's precious little Nirvana can do about it'. The band's exhaustion is understandable, and Kurt's stomach condition, though never fully diagnosed, was an undeniable reality. 'In Nirvana's dressing room if you sit too close to Kurt you can smell his stomach,' writes Andy Bollen in *Nirvana – A Tour Diary*. 'Sick, hungry, acidic, gaseous and in pain ... the smell of something you know just hurts like rotten burning flesh'.

December 21

- 'Smells Like Teen Spirit' goes to 17 in the *Billboard* Hot 100 singles, 7 in the pure-sales chart, 22 in the club chart and even enters the Hot 100 airplay chart, which monitors pop radio stations – the very definition of a crossover success.

December 27

- A run of four enormous arena shows as main support to Red Hot Chili Peppers, touring their own big league breakthrough, *Blood Sugar Sex Magik* begins[113]. Nirvana will be paid $10,000 per show. Opening the tour is Pearl Jam. It is the band's first taste of arena rock; a radical departure from the clubs and even festivals they're used to.[114] Kurt undercuts the macho, jock atmosphere of the tour by wearing one of Courtney's dresses; a velvet black number with a Peter Pan collar. It becomes clear fairly quickly to everyone present, that Nirvana are a bigger draw than the headliners.[115] The tour is a huge success. 'This was no

113. Red Hot Chili Peppers had popped and slapped their way through the 80s, making a succession of incredibly irritating funk rock records and dabbling in quite terrifying amounts of hard drugs, until founding guitarist Hillel Slovak died from an overdose in 1988. Out of the ashes of that tragedy, the group's fourth album, and major label debut, *Mother's Milk*, had gone gold, with their cover of Stevie Wonder's 'Higher Ground' giving them a bonafide radio hit. Like the similarly funky Jane's Addiction they were another of the crossover alt rock bands helping to end the dominance of LA hair metal; they were, however, a much straighter, less endearingly weird proposition than the Janes or someone like Faith No More, and were rather self-consciously macho and muscular. It's probably telling that their most famous gimmick was to play encores naked, with socks covering their assorted manhoods. *Mother's Milk* did well enough to prompt a bidding war for their next album and the Rick Rubin-produced *Blood Sugar Sex Magik* , featuring their classic line up of singer Anthony Keidis, virtuoso bass player Flea, oddball guitarist John Fruciente and drummer Chad Smith (a line up they would return to three times in the coming thirty years) had come out through Warner and gone Top 3 in the *Billboard* Hot 100. Their genuinely great, affecting ballad 'Under The Bridge' would become one of the defining alternative rock singles of the era when it was released the following March. In some ways they were a neat fit for Nirvana – both had come from the underground (*Blood Sugar Sex Magik* was even dedicated to Mike Watt of seminal Calipunks, Minutemen) both had a pervasive and perverse sense of humour, both had found themselves outsiders thrust into the mainstream and Kurt and John Frusciente were both reading William Burroughs while developing crippling heroin addictions and getting freaked out and uncomfortable with their growing fame. There was, however, something extremely *male* about RHCP that wasn't present in Nirvana, a jock-like cockiness. Keidis says that he and Flea were social outcasts when they met at school, but by 1991 they felt like the kind of guys more likely to stuff you in the locker and steal your dinner money because you'd looked the wrong way at their cheerleader girlfriends. Initially the tour had featured Smashing Pumpkins as main support and Pearl Jam opening, however as the popularity of the record grew and the venues got bigger it was thought that a bigger name was needed to open the shows, and a decision was made to swap out Pearl Jam for the ascendant Nirvana (according to Keidis' autobiography he had personally asked Dave Grohl, who had responded 'We love you guys! We grew up listening to you in Seattle!' which would be an odd thing for Dave to say considering he hadn't grown up in Seattle, and has never cited Red Hot Chili Peppers as an early influence). At which point Billy Corgan threw his toys out of the pram, refused to play with Nirvana and removed Smashing Pumpkins from the bill. Which was at least good news for Pearl Jam, who stayed on the tour.
114. 'Being in arenas was definitely like putting on some clothes that didn't fit yet. To be honest, it didn't ever really fit,' Dave Grohl told Paul Brannigan for *This Is A Call*. 'I don't think any of us were comfortable with it'.
115. 'I remember getting shivers every night from the whole place going crazy,' Nirvana drum tech Barrett Jones told Paul Brannigan. 'It was the first time I'd ever seen an entire arena jumping up and down in sync.' Anthony Keidis was blown away by his new support act, praising them in his memoir *Scar Tissue* for 'their raw energy, their musicality, their song selection, they were like a chain saw cutting through

longer the sound of the underground,' Dave would write many years later in his memoir, 'this was a fucking battering ram to the gates that guarded mainstream popular culture, and our three bands were spearheading the takeover.'

December 31

- At a show at San Francisco's Cow Palace, Pearl Jam tease the audience with the opening bars of 'Smells Like Teen Spirit'. 'Just remember,' says guitarist Stone Gossard, 'we played it first'. Nirvana are, reportedly, deeply unimpressed. [116]

---

the night'. The *LA Times* review of the the opening night at the LA Memorial Sports Arena, goes a step further – 'What if you gave a concert,' asks reviewer Robert Hilburn, 'and your special guests stole the show?' The review carried two photographs from the gig, one of the headliners and one of Kurt Cobain. Kurt's is about twice the size of RHCP's.

116. Pearl Jam are an interesting comparison with Nirvana, because ostensibly they came from the same scene. Formed from the ashes of Mother Love Bone (who were, themselves, formed from the ashes of Sub Pop band, Green River,) Pearl Jam had signed to Epic Records in early '91 and spent the summer recording their debut album *Ten*, which dropped in August, a month before *Nevermind*. Singer Eddie Vedder was originally from Illinois, but had moved to California as a child and then drifted around various LA bands for a while until he befriended former Chili Pepper's drummer Jack Irons. Irons had recommended him to Mother Love Bone's Jeff Ament and Stone Gossard, who were looking for a singer for their new project following the death of Mother Love Bone's Andy Wood. Vedder, more earnest than Wood and with a more powerful voice, was a natural fit and was invited to move to Seattle to form a band that was initially named after NBA legend Mookie Blaylock, though this was quickly swapped out for 'Pearl Jam'. If you're looking for a root-level difference between Pearl Jam and the punkier end of grunge, the fact that PJ were originally named after a sports star is pretty telling – it doesn't get more jock than that. Pearl Jam, though, were still lumped in with the 'Seattle sound', how could they not be? Their origins tied them to Mudhoney, Soundgarden (Gossard, Ament and guitarist Mike McReady had been in Temple of the Dog with Chris Cornell) and Mother Love Bone, and musically they sat comfortably next to Alice In Chains. The important difference, however, is rooted in a Seattle schism that happened way back in 1987, predating Nirvana even selecting a name. Green River had been one of Sub Pop's first signings, and had split before their Jack Endino-produced album was even out, due to a fundamental difference of ideology: punk purists Mark Arm and Steve Turner formed Mudhoney, while would-be rock stars Gossard and Ament hooked up with Wood and made a grab for the territory held by Guns N' Roses and Bon Jovi as Mother Love Bone. Seattle's underground rock community would follow one or the other path; Nirvana, Mudhoney, TAD and Screaming Trees on one side, Mother Love Bone/Pearl Jam, Soundgarden and Alice In Chains on the other. That's an oversimplification, of course, and there was plenty of crossing the streams (Nirvana and the more metal-indebted Soundgarden, for example, were always good friends), but it's true that Pearl Jam and Nirvana were approaching success from entirely different sides of the divide. Musically they had very little in common aside from heavy guitars and a distant root in Sabbath and Zeppelin – Pearl Jam were groove-based, highly polished and sounded like a Classic Rock band (capital letters intentional), Vedder's voice was a rich baritone; a 90s Jim Morrison, with some generic Robert Plantish crossover with Chris Cornell and Alice In Chains' Layne Staley. When the second-wave, watered down grunge copyists came along, the likes of Creed, Nickelback, Puddle of Mudd and Live, it was the Vedder/Cornell/Stayley version of the 'Seattle sound' they were aiming for. Nirvana, meanwhile, always had Black Flag and the Bad Brains and the Melvins at their heart. They had Flipper and the Wipers and Dead Kennedies. Sex Pistols and Buzzcocks. They weren't just alt rock, they were *Punk Rock*. Scuzzier, more irreverent, less musically flashy, way more chaotic and improvisational. Kurt's voice was far rawer, his scream far more primal. It's why Nirvana and Pearl Jam seemed to stare each other down across an ideological and musical chasm – the same chasm that had ripped Green River in two.

Pearl Jam's rockism clearly irked irked Kurt Cobain, who would take occasional jabs at them in interviews. A few months after the tour, a Singapore rock magazine called *BigO* asked Kurt about 'poseurs' jumping on the 'grunge bandwagon'. He didn't hold back. 'Yeah, and it's happening already!' he said. 'There are some bands that I absolutely despise and I'm not afraid to name them. They are [New Jersey rock band signed to Geffen] The Nymphs, Alice In Chains and especially Pearl Jam. They are just career-minded bands out to make big bucks and we've been unfairly lumped together with them.' In his first *Rolling Stone* cover feature a few months later he went even harder: 'I do feel a duty to warn the kids of false music that's claiming to be underground. They're jumping on the alternative bandwagon.'. It comes down, again, to that metaphorical 'Black Flag tattoo'. Kurt, of course, was overlooking that whatever Pearl Jam had become, the band's roots weren't that far from his own. As Jeff Ament told Mark Yarm, 'Fuck, man. We were putting out records on [DIY punk label] Homestead while Kurt was still going to Sammy Hagar concerts ... if you want to talk punk-rock credibility, I can back it up.' Mudhoney's Steve Turner agrees. 'For Kurt to say anything about Pearl Jam not having roots in Punk Rock – are you fuckin' stupid?' he says in *Everybody Loves Our Town*. 'Hello? Jeff was there from day one of the Seattle thing'. Within a few years Pearl Jam would pull ahead of Nirvana in sales, something which Nirvana always claimed to be relieved about (though Danny Goldberg remembers Kurt once phoning him to complain that he'd been watching MTV all day and they'd played three Pearl Jam videos and only one Nirvana. Kurt asked 'Have we done something wrong?' It clearly stung on some level). In an interview with counterculture travel magazine *Monk* in September 1992, Kurt was asked for a 'final message for the youth of America'. 'I'm bowing down gracefully and taking off my crown,' Kurt replies. 'I'm going to give it to Eddie Vedder of Pearl Jam. He's now the representative of the youth of America'. When the magazine's co-founder, Jim Crotty, pushed him on this, Kurt explained that it was 'because he stole my look ... and he uses it better than I.'

For their part, Pearl Jam were pretty baffled by Kurt's attitude. 'It was painful at times,' Stone Gossard told Mark Yarm. 'All those words that were being used ... poseurs ... more manipulation than talented, not the real thing compared to Nirvana – all it did was raise the bar for Pearl Jam. I think we took them as challenges.' Ultimately, they saw Nirvana less as bitter enemies and more as a reason to step up their game. Eddie Vedder remembers trying all sorts of frontman stunts; climbing stacks and crowd surfing (and playing Nirvana's most famous riff before they could) while the two bands were touring together with RHCP – 'We were playing before Nirvana, you had to do *something*,' Vedder said in *Everybody Loves Our Town*. 'Our first record was good, but their first record was better.' Which was true. As was, if we're honest, their second. And their third.

Part Five

A Denial

1992

January 4

- *Nevermind*'s success is inspiring newer fans to delve into the band's past and seek out their first record. Almost four years after 'Floyd The Barber' and 'Paper Cuts' were recorded, the album they appeared on, *Bleach*, which had been made for $600[1], enters the *Billboard* Hot 200 album chart.[2]

January 7

- The RIAA confirms that *Nevermind* has gone double platinum, selling 2,000,000 copies in less than four months.

January 8

- The Grammy nominations, America's most prestigious music awards, are announced. *Nevermind* is nominated in the 'Best Alternative Music Performance' category.

January 10

- An interview with Nirvana, conducted backstage at a Chili Peppers show the previous month, is published in *BAM* (*Bay Area Music*). In it, writer Jerry McCulley carefully, but very clearly, implies that Kurt is doing heroin, noting that 'he occasionally nods off in mid sentence, apologising blearily that he's had but an hour's sleep. But the pinned pupils, sunken cheeks and scabbed, sallow skin suggest something more serious than mere fatigue. Cobain's haggard visage and frail frame make him appear more like 40 than 24'.[3] It is the first clue the wider

---

1. Ish.
2. It went in at 185, but that was still a hell of an achievement. More people bought *Bleach* that week than Janet Jackson's *Rhythm Nation*, the Pet Shop Boys greatest hits or the soundtrack to the hit Macaulay Culkin movie, *My Girl.* The sound of champagne corks popping over at Sub Pop could probably have been heard as far away as Olympia. 'I was in a state of disbelief,' Bruce Pavitt told Mark Yarm. 'We went from not being able to pay our phone bill to getting a check for half a million bucks. Of course, after that, we were so happy they went to Geffen'. *Bleach* would stay on the chart well into the spring, peaking at 89.
3. Kurt's heroin use was becoming fairly indescriminate by this point. He and Courtney were spending every spare hour in one another's company, and had moved to LA together shortly after returning from their respective European tours, hotel-hopping with Kurt's newly acquired cash. Courtney had used heroin in the past but had been off the drug for a while – with Kurt's encouragement, that had gone out of the

public will have that Kurt is using. The same interview, incidentally, acknowledges Kurt and Courtney's engagement, which is soon announced on MTV.

- Nirvana play a nine-song mini-gig for MTV's *120 Minutes*, revealing Kurt's freshly-died raspberry-coloured hair.[4] Kurt and Dave's mothers are in attendance.

January 11

- *Nevermind* goes to number one on the Billboard Hot 100 album chart, displacing Michael Jackson's *Dangerous*. The album had sold 193,000 units in the US alone in the previous week – the single biggest sales week for *any* album in the United States since point-of-sale figures had started being tracked properly the previous May. *Bleach*, for good measure, goes up to 136. Elsewhere, *Nevermind* is at 19 in the UK, 11 in Germany, 9 in Australia, 7 in the Netherlands and 5 in Canada. [5]

---

window and with their eyes open, the two fell pretty willingly into a regular habit. Kurt maintained over and over again that his stomach condition was the primary motivation for acquiring an honest-to-goodness junk habit, despite being well aware of all the risks associated with it. 'I *wanted* to. It was *my* choice,' he told Michael Azerrad in 1992. He elaborated on it later in a journal he kept for a treatment program, republished in *Journals*. 'When I got back from our second European tour with Sonic Youth I decided to use heroin on a daily basis because of an ongoing stomach ailment that I had been suffering from for the past five years,' he wrote. 'The only thing I found that worked were heavier opioids … I decided, if I feel like a junkie as it is, I might as well be one.' Courtney Love, characteristically blunt, quotes an even clearer message from Kurt from this time in Brett Morgan's movie *Montage of Heck*: 'His fantasy was "I'm going to get three million dollars, and then I'm going to be a junkie". Those were his words.' Not that everyone believed the 'stomach problem' excuse. Photographer Michael Lavine, who had shot the band a few times, did a session with them in New York on 10 January, with Kurt clearly nodding out throughout the shoot, much to the silent disgustt of his bandmates. Lavine told Michael Azerrad the story: 'I asked him "why are you doing this?" He said "it's the only thing that helps my stomach pain." … I didn't have the guts to say, "Kurt, that's a bunch of shit."'

It was around this time that the other members of Nirvana realised quite how bad things were getting. 'He looked like shit,' Krist told Azerrad when he was interviewing the band for *Come As You Are*. 'He looked like a ghoul.' 'I remember walking into their hotel room and, for the first time, really realising that these two are fucked up,' Dave told the biographer. 'They were just nodding out in bed, it was disgusting and gross'. This was one of Kurt's most prodigious heroin periods, and that does make a certain amount of sense. Stomach issues aside, it was understandable that he needed a barrier between himself and a world that had in a very short space of time become inconceivably intense. Lots of books and articles about Nirvana focus on Kurt's stated desire that he *wanted* to be a rock star, that he invited his fame, and while there is obviously some truth in that, it's also clear that he, and Krist and Dave, were in no way prepared for this level of sudden-onset rockstardom. They wanted to be a popular rock band, sure, but nobody had signed up for *this*. Krist dealt with it by drinking two bottles of red wine a night, until he nearly brained himself cavorting in a drunken haze on New Years Eve and decided to take some time out from drinking. Kurt, though? Kurt already had his survival system in place. Kurt had heroin, which was comfortable, and made him feel like himself. He also had Courtney, who for all of her chaos provided something he badly needed in this period: someone to hold his hand, someone he could explain the plot to. Someone to bitch about everyone else with. For a while, things worked. The secret was out now though, despite Kurt's denials of his drug use to the press (the official line was that Kurt was 'tired from being on the road and that *BAM* had the wrong take' as the band's US press officer told Carrie Borzillo). However, it was becoming increasingly difficult for the other two members of Nirvana, the band's friends and their management to look the other way when it came to Kurt's self-destructive tendencies. Something was going to have to give.

4. Partly this was an acknowledgment of the role the station had in the band's success, partly it was to give them literally anything else to air instead of endlessly repeating the 'Smells Like Teen Spirit Video'. A live version of 'Territorial Pissings' from the show was soon added to rotation – mission accomplished.
5. The weeks following the holidays are always good for alternative music, and the reason is obvious when you think about it: many kids kicked off 1992 by heading to Tower Records or Kmart to spend their gift

- Nirvana performs two songs on *Saturday Night Live* (*SNL*)[6], bashing out versions of 'Smells Like Teen Spirit' and 'Territorial Pissings', after which the band cheerfully destroy their gear, Kurt puncturing his speaker cabs with his guitar, Dave hurling his drums one at a time onto the stage (and dodging when Krist throws a cymbal stand back at him). At the close of the show itself as host Rob Morrow, the somewhat smug star of the TV drama *Northern Exposure*, thanks the cast and guests, Krist grabs first Dave, and then Kurt and kisses them both full on the lips. The kissing is edited out of the show in subsequent broadcasts.[7] During the day, the band get a call from parody musician Weird Al Yanovic, who asks permission to do his own version of 'Smells Like Teen Spirit'. They are delighted.[8]

---

vouchers and exchange the Boyz II Men, Michael Jackson and Michael Bolton cassettes some remote aunt had given them for Christmas for Nirvana, Metallica, Red Hot Chili Peppers and REM.

6. Much like *Top of the Pops* in the UK, *SNL* was a *huge* deal. Only more so. Partly because it was on network television, broadcast live on Saturday night to an average audience of around 25 million people, and partly because, unlike *Top of the Pops*, *SNL* was *cool.* And, also unlike *Top of the Pops*, the band had no intention of sabotaging the opportunity, though they would of course try and do things their own way as far as possible. The weekly live comedy show had been running since the 70s, mixing straightforwardly silly sketches with genuinely subversive satire, and its alumni was a whose-who of US and Canadian greats: Andy Kaufman, Bill Murray, Dan Ackroyd, John Belushi, Eddie Murphy, Will Ferrell, Mike Myers, Kristen Wiig, Amy Pohler, Maya Rudolph, Tina Fey, Andy Samburg, Adam Sandler, Chevy Chase, Chris Rock … the list goes on. The movies *Wayne's World* and *The Blues Brothers* both came out of *SNL* skits. No *SNL?* No *Ghostbusters.* Every week had two numbers by a musical guest, and of course for an audience that big, only the coolest and biggest names would do. Everyone in *Nirvana* had grown up with *SNL*. Dave Grohl writes in his memoir of sitting down to watch it every week in his pyjamas, up past his bedtime; the B-52s' 1980 performance of 'Rock Lobster' was a seminal moment for him, opening the door to a weirder, wilder world of music and art. Everyone in Nirvana had a similar story. Hell, most young people in the United States have a relationship of some sort to the show. Nirvana, of course, were a perfect fit – they were the biggest band in the world at that point, certainly in terms of buzz. They were also about to have the number one album in the US and they were, themselves, just the sort of irreverent and subversive goofballs that had made *SNL*'s name. There had been some tension in rehearsals – the studio had been pushing for 'Come As You Are' rather than 'Territorial Pissings', but the band weren't to be pushed around. The camera crew and director also insisted on 'blocking' the performance, knowing exactly what the trio would be doing at any given time, including any instrument trashing they might indulge in at the close of the song … hardly the most spontaneous way of doing punk rock. The arguments got tedious and Kurt walked out of the rehearsal. For the taping itself, however, everyone was on best behaviour. That night's performance of 'Teen Spirit' is so tight it almost sounds like the CD, and though it's lacking some of the trademark Nirvana chaos, it's crackling with contained power. According to his memoir, Dave broke a drum stick during the opening of the song, though you can neither see nor hear it on the broadcast at all, so he covers it well. 'Territorial Pissings' is a little messier, as befits the band's most pure-punk moment, and the instrument trashing at the end is done with real glee rather than catharsis. The trio also make good on a vow they had made constantly in the press – to promote underground bands whenever possible. Kurt plays the whole show in a handmade Flipper t-shirt, Krist does the first number bopping in a Melvins shirt, which he seems to have handed over to Dave for the second song, while he himself dons L7's infamous *Smell The Magic* shirt. It's Nirvana at their best.
7. Gay rights were always extremely important to Nirvana, and Kurt would later go on record as saying this move was pre-planned to 'piss off the rednecks and homophobes'. However, Krist told Charles R. Cross that the kissing was far more spontaneous and purer in motivation. 'I walked right up to him and grabbed him and stuck my tongue in his mouth', Krist remembered. 'I just wanted to make him feel better. At the end of it all, I told him "It's going to be okay. It's not so bad".' He knew his friend was not in a great place. According to Cross's book *Heavier Than Heaven*, Kurt would overdose later that night, surviving only because of Courtney's intervention, though Everett True, in *Nirvana: The True Story*, is less certain, speculating that Courtney lifted a story from later in their relationship and moved it back in time, partly for dramatic effect and partly to make herself seem less culpable in his escalating addicton.
8. Weird Al had made a career doing musical parodies. His biggest hit was a warping of Michael Jackson's 'Beat It' called 'Eat It', accompanied by a video parodying Jackson's original, shot-for-shot. His popularity had been in decline for a couple of years, but his 'Teen Spirit' parody, titled 'Smells Like Nirvana', helped kickstart a revival. Kurt's reaction when he saw it was 'I laughed my ass off' (per Danny Goldberg's *Serving the Servant*). Al's songs are genuinely funny … at least on the first listen.

Mid January

- Around this time Kurt and Courtney discover that they are expecting a baby. Between the baby and Nirvana's upcoming tour of Japan and Australia, it is decided that the pair need to get clean. They book into a motel to hole up and work through withdrawal together.[9]

January 15

- Krist and Dave are the backing band for the Melvins' Buzz Osborne at a show at the Crocodile Cafe in Seattle.[10]

January 16, 19–20

- The video for Nirvana's next single, 'Come As You Are', is shot in Hollywood, directed by Kevin Kerslake who had worked on Hole's 'Garbage Man' video.[11]

January 23

- Nirvana arrive in Australia. They will be on tour in the country (plus a date in New Zealand) until 8 February before heading to Singapore, Japan and Hawaii. The tour will end on 22 February.[12]

---

9. Heroin withdrawal is far from pretty. It essentially means a couple of weeks of having the worst flu of your life, combined with something like norovirus. According to Charles R. Cross the couple got through it with 'sleeping pills and methadone'. There was certainly a lot of help available – the industry rumours about Kurt's heroin use led to Aerosmith's Steven Tyler contacting the band's friend, Janet Billig (Billig had signed Smashing Pumpkins and Hole to Caroline records and sorted a distribution deal with Sub Pop. She'd eventually join Gold Mountain and work with Hole and Nirvana on a management level) trying to get in touch with Kurt to offer help. Kurt wasn't interested. Billig told Mark Yarm that his response was 'Steven Tyler got to be a junkie for *18 fucking years*. I've only been doing drugs for an hour.' Danny Goldberg, who ran Gold Mountain, had also finally realised something was wrong – being asked to advance Kurt and Courtney $5,000 in cash for 'shopping' was probably a clue – and reached out to Aerosmith's manager, Tim Collins, for advice. Collins hooked Goldberg up with a drug counselor who helped him stage an intervention when the couple returned to LA. According to Goldberg's *Serving The Servants*, their highly-recommended counsellor spent a lot of time indiscreetly name-dropping famous clients, then bailed altogether during the intervention itself, saying 'I have never dealt with a situation like this with a husband and wife and a pregnancy'. He still invoiced Gold Mountain for $600 for his trouble.
10. The headline band that night, rather brilliantly, was called Bliss – one of Nirvana's early monikers. The show was supposed to be unannounced, but someone leaked the news, flooding the gig with Nirvana fans.
11. Just as 'Come As You Are' itself is a much less explosive song than 'Teen Spirit', the video couldn't be further from its predecessor. Where 'Teen Spirit' was incredibly direct, 'Come As You Are' is abstract, and has no narrative to speak of. It's an art piece. The band's faces are obscured behind transparent plastic and running water, or projected onto walls. There are no clear shots of any of them. Footage of Nirvana performing behind a sheet of water weaves in and out of clips of wriggling sperm, Kurt swinging on a chandelier while his own face is projected behind him, a baby (this time not Spencer Elden) swimming in a pool chasing a dollar on a hook (this baby, to the best of this author's knowledge, has *not* attempted to sue the band) and a gun sinking in the chlorine-blue water of a pool. It makes not a lick of sense, and it's probably the least immediately identifiable and interesting of all the band's videos. There's some sense behind that – Nirvana didn't want to repeat themselves, they also didn't really fancy getting any more famous than they already were. An artsy video where their faces are obscured would do the trick. There was also a darker advantage – obscuring Kurt's face meant obscuring his physical state. He came to the video shoot midway through his enforced rehab with Courtney and was looking far, far from his best. 'As we filmed the video, Kurt's fragility came as shock to me,' Dave says in his memoir. 'To this day, it's still hard for me to watch 'Come As You Are', knowing the state that Kurt was in at the time.'
12. This was a happier tour for the band. The sunnier climes and fun off-day activities (surfing, Koala-cuddling, camping in the outback – the full Aussie experience) making for a pleasant change. The shows,

January 27

- The *Hormoaning* EP is released as an exclusive for the Australia and Japan tour. [13]

February 1

- Spurred on by the band's performance on *SNL*, *Nevermind* goes back to number one in the Hot 200, while 'Smells Like Teen Spirit' becomes, once again, the top selling single in the US, having gone gold with 500,000 total sales. *Bleach* climbs to 106.

February 9

- Nirvana play their one and only show in New Zealand, at the Logan Campbell Centre in Auckland.

February 14–19

- The band arrive in Japan to play four shows.[14]

February 20

- A column in the gossipy but influential industry insider magazine, *Hits* is the most explicit press yet to reference Kurt's heroin use. 'Sources tell me that Nirvana's Kurt Cobain is slam-dancing with Mr. Brownstone[15]' says the magazine's Lonn Friend in his weekly metal column. 'Get real, dude! Need I remind thee of the

---

as was completely standard for Nirvana at this point, had been booked before the *Nevermind* explosion and were uniformly too small and oversold, but the band were far more at home in that environment than the shiny, controlled arenas they had played with RHCP. They were a messy band that thrived on chaos. They always had been. Spirits were relatively high – 'I started to have hope that we were going to make it,' Dave writes in *Storyteller*, 'that Kurt was going to make it.' Though Kurt had begun the tour in agony from his stomach pain and withdrawal, he had been given Methadone pills (Physeptone, as it's known in Australia) by an Australian doctor. The doctor had apparently assumed he was just another detoxing rock star and gave him the standard prescription. Kurt claimed later that, due to the different name, he didn't realise what he was taking. The pills were a great success and took the edge off his stomach pain which made the tour much easier and much more fun, but had the unfortunate yet another opioid addiction.

13. This is essentially the 'covers' EP Kurt had wanted to release over a year ago, and featured their Peel session recording of 'D-7', 'Turnaround', 'Molly's Lips' and 'Son of a Gun', plus the January 1991 recordings of 'Aneurysm' and 'Even In His Youth' that had appeared on the b-side to 'Smells Like Teen Spirit'. Alas, Kurt's original concept of having a cover featuring the band dressed as choirboys was never realised.
14. As many western rock bands, from the Beatles onwards, have discovered, Japan is a very different place to play shows. The audience were restricted to 10 x 10 blocks of seats, and though they were allowed to stand up and dance, they didn't move from their allocated spots. The level of politeness and obedience was absolutely disarming for Nirvana, who responded by playing as intensely as possible 'to try and provoke a riotous reaction by thrashing through the songs like never before,' as Dave writes in *Storyteller*. They would then watched horrified as any fan that broke ranks was ejected from the show. The first show, in Osaka, was crowned by a gleefully brutal instrument smashing, which apparently reduced a representative from Tama drums, who had supplied the drum kit, to tears. The poor man had assumed that Dave Grohl's wanton destruction of his drum set was an expression of how dissatisfied he was with the instruments they had supplied him with.
15. A reference to Guns N' Roses 'Mr Brownstone', one of the best moments on their *Appetite For Destruction* debut album – a song written by guitarists Izzy Stradlin and Slash about their own heroin use.

Stardog? (Okay, most of ya don't get it, but for those who do, it means somethin', I promise!)'[16]

February 21

- The band arrive in Hawaii for two gigs at Honolulu's Pink's Garage. These will be Nirvana's final shows until June.[17]

February 24

- Kurt Cobain and Courtney Love are married on the beach in Waikiki. Courtney wears a vintage silk dress, once owned by Seattle actress Francis Farmer[18] while her dashing groom is in green and white striped pyjamas.[19]

March

- Hole sign a seven-album deal with DGC.[20]

---

16. A very pointed reference, that those in the know will certainly have picked up, to Mother Love Bone's Andy Wood, who had died after a heroin overdose in March 1990. The song 'Stardog Champion' appears on their only album, *Apple*.
17. Conventional wisdom had it that a domestic success of the level of *Nevermind* should be followed by a big US tour, this time in proper arenas where the band's newly acquired fanbase could stand a hope in hell of getting tickets. Up to that point the biggest headline show Nirvana had played in the US was the 2,800-capacity Paramount in Seattle, and that was *significantly* bigger than most of the clubs they'd played on the autumn *Nevermind* tour, where the capacity hovered between 500 and a 1,000 on average. They were now an act that could play 10,000-capacity arenas, and the initial plan for spring 1992 was to do just that. However, what had become very clear was that the band, and especially Kurt, were entirely burned out. What's more, Kurt was a drug addict living under intense scrutiny, with a baby on the way, while the band themselves, as a trio, had become fractured and estranged. It was decided, quite sensibly, to shelve any touring plans until the summer and give everyone, and especially Kurt, a chance to recover and heal. Some in the Nirvana camp were alarmed by the downing of tools. 'I just saw it as unrealised potential,' soundman Craig Montgomery told Gillian G. Gaar. 'The band could be doing so much great stuff, but Kurt's got his Drug Problem and his They're Having The Baby problem and there's all this stuff in the way of what they could be doing musically.'. Still, given Kurt's knife-edge health, it was almost certainly a wise move.
18. More on her later.
19. The wedding was both a joyous and fraught occasion. Kurt cried, apparently Courtney didn't. Kurt had also scored heroin to keep himself from having withdrawals ('I just did a teeny bit so I didn't get sick,' quotes Everett True). Also present were Dave Grohl, tour manager Alex MacLeod, who had been with the band since their second UK tour, on and off, Earth's Dylan Carlson who was Kurt's closest friend, and a few members of the road crew (who had been banned from bringing girlfriends in case their plus-one's blabbed to the press later). Not present were Krist and Shelli Novoselic. Courtney had heard reports that Shelli had been criticising her for doing drugs while pregnant and was furious. As a result the Novoselics were not welcome at the wedding. Shelli later told Michael Azerrad that it was actually she and Krist that decided not to attend, saying 'I knew if she was pregnant and doing drugs, I didnt agree with it and I didn't agree with Kurt being so fucked up all the time.' For the record, Courtney has always denied doing drugs while pregnant once she'd gotten through the detox. The incident ripped a hole in the centre of the band – according to Everett True and Michael Azerrad, Krist and Kurt didn't speak for five months, including at rehearsals. Krist himself admitted that at the time his view of his old friend was 'Kurt's a fucking junkie asshole and I hate him'.
20. Hole consisted only of Courtney and Eric Erlandson at this point; rhythm section Jill Emery and Caroline Rue had walked after realising that the band was moving away from the brutal, noise rock of their debut into more melodic alt rock. They were also probably spooked by all the press attention Courtney was getting (Courtney's want-ad for a bass player was an all-timer: 'Someone who can play ok, and stand in front of 30,000 people, take off her shirt and have "Fuck You" written on her tits. If

March 3

- 'Come As You Are' is released in the UK and US. B-sides include live versions of 'Drain You' and 'School', with the UK vinyl releases (7″, 12″ and 12″ picture disc) adding the studio version of 'Endless, Nameless'.[21]

April

- 'Smells Like Teen Spirit', which was written and first performed live exactly one year earlier, goes platinum with sales of a 1,000,000 singles in the US.
- Sub Pop reissue *Bleach*, with distribution through DGC. The album is remastered with two bonus tracks tagged onto the end – 'Downer' from the January 1988 sessions with Dale Crover and 'Big Cheese', the original b-side to 'Love Buzz'. The tracklist is also standardised internationally.[22]
- At Kurt's insistence Nirvana's publishing royalties, which had previous been split equally between the three members of the band, are renegotiated. Kurt will now receive 75% of the royalties for the music and 100% for the lyrics. This is applied retroactively, meaning Krist and Dave have to pay back some of the royalties they have already received. The only exceptions are 'Smells Like Teen Spirit' and 'Aneurysm', the music for which is credited equally to all three members of the band.[23]

---

you're not afraid of me and you're not afraid to fucking say it, send a letter. No more pussies, no more fake girls, I want a whore from hell'. Hole found their drummer in Patty Schemel that spring, but it took another year for them to find a bass player that fit Courtney's exacting wishlist – Kristen Pfaff, the cool-as-all-hell bassist with Minneapolis punk Janitor Joe). Hole actually got a better record advance than Nirvana. *Nevermind* had kicked open the door for underground music, and every label wanted its own 'Nirvana', and were prepared to pay through the nose for it in the hope the investment would come back around. Hole's close ties to the biggest breakthrough rock band in a decade meant they felt like a safer bet than most – according to Courtney, in a 1992 feature in *Newsweek* titled 'Searching for Nirvana II', the president of Arista, Clive Davies, had marched into the office of Hole's lawyers and said 'I'm begging you, I'm begging you … I'll give them a million dollars' (Davies denied this later), while Charles R. Cross told the same magazine that an A&R had once admitted to him that 'sleeping with Kurt Cobain is worth half a million dollars.' Madonna had also tried to sign Hole to her Maverick label ('Madonna's interest in me was kind of like Dracula's interest in his latest victim,' Courtney told *Vanity Fair* in 1992) and it was Madonna's interest, so Courtney says, that sparked the bidding war. In the end, Courtney and her band stayed where they were comfortable – the label of Sonic Youth and Nirvana, safe in the knowledge they'd been paid more than either. The success of *Live Through This* and *Celebrity Skin* almost certainly justified the rumoured million dollars Geffen put up … even if they're presumably still waiting for the next five Hole albums.

21. One thing that possibly should have rang alarm bells for anyone paying attention, is that the single contains no unheard studio tracks as b-sides. This was the era of multi-format single releases, where fans were being encouraged to buy a song as many times as possible to collect all the bonus tracks, and it was common practice for bands to churn out quite a lot of extra material. Nirvana had a backlog of unfinished/unrecorded songs at this point – the fact no-one could throw them into a studio to record anything, or write anything new, went very much against the grain for a major label band. Of course we know why … exactly when were these recording and writing sessions supposed to take place? On Kurt's rehab sickbed? On a plane to Australia?
22. Previously the UK version, released through Tupelo, had replaced 'Love Buzz' with 'Big Cheese', depriving most UK fans of one of the band's best early tracks.
23. This, of course, would only widen the gulf between Kurt and the other two members of Nirvana. Kurt's reasoning was that the original three-way-split agreement was based on the assumption that they would never be making all that much money, and a royalty split that heavily favoured Kurt could leave his

- Dave Grohl's solo album, *Pocketwatch*, recorded under the name Late!, gets a quiet release on the cassette-only Simple Machines label.[24]

---

bandmates struggling financially. *Nevermind*'s utterly unprecedented success had blown such worries out of the water, as even a tiny percentage of those sales would provide a sizeable income for anyone. As the lead songwriter, Kurt could now ask for what he felt was his due. Talking to Michael Azerrad for *Come As You Are*, he is absolutely brutal in his assessment of his bandmate's contributions, saying that 'most of the time that I'm asking Chris [sic] and Dave their opinion it's just to make them feel a part of the band'. That had to have stung. The band's lawyer at the time, Rosemary Carroll, told Everett True that it was 'certainly the implication' that Kurt would split the band up rather than split the money evenly. Dave and Krist were both, quite understandably, horrified – especially by the suggestion that new terms would be applied retroactively. Grohl very nearly quit altogether over it. 'So the publishing issue came up … and I got close to nothing,' he told his biographer Paul Brannigan. 'Like, nothing at all … I considered bailing at that point.' *Come As You Are*, the semi-official biography that Michael Azerrad wrote in 1992 with full access to the band, includes the damning contemporary line: 'the bad feelings still simmer'. Ultimately, though, Kurt didn't give his band mates a choice. Nirvana was a once-in-a-lifetime deal. Neither Krist nor Dave expected to ever be in *another* multi-million-selling, globally successful rock behemoth (which turned out to be wrong, of course), and if they wanted to continue to have that career they were going to have to suck it up. Nirvana, after all, had always been Kurt's band. Jason Everman and Chad Channing could tell you all about the Nirvana dictatorship. Krist had once gotten so frustrated with Kurt's tight control of the music that he sounded Mark Lanegan out about joining Screaming Trees. And to an extent, Kurt was right – he *did* write the elements of the songs that made them, well, *songs*. His bandmates contributed hooks and grooves, sure, but they were *Kurt*'s songs … And yet … Nirvana were way more than *just* Kurt's songs. Krist Novoselic is one of the most distinctive bass players of the last thirty years; his gluey, syrupy style has a melodic genius all of its own, doing loop-de-loops around the rhythm and the melody with an apple-crisp tone. It gives Nirvana so much of its character. And as for Dave Grohl? It's not a coincidence that his arrival fired the starting pistol on the group's ascent. It's Dave's absolutely rock solid backing that allowed the songs to rise above the chaos they could be mired in with previous drummers. He gave them the space to shine. Nirvana was always a jam band – every rehearsal started with noise jams, full of improvisations and experiments out of which songs and grooves were formed. The trio's chemistry was part of what powered that. Without Dave and Krist, Nirvana couldn't be *Nirvana* – at least not the Nirvana that went eight-times platinum in less than a year.

Kurt's song writing gift was extraordinary but put him with two different musicians, swap the variables around, and would success come just the same? In another fairly conceivable universe, where Krist really did jump to Screaming Trees and was replaced with someone like Ben Shepherd, say, and Kurt recruited Tobi Vail or Danny Peters to play drums (all of which were on the cards at one point or another) would *Nevermind* still have been *Nevermind*? We can't know. Though in this author's opinion, probably not. *Nevermind* was lightning in a bottle. The right songs, the right moment, the right people, the right chemistry. I'm sure a different version of Nirvana would still have been very successful, but I don't think it would have been the same phenomenon. And maybe Kurt would still be with us now as a result.

Still. For the other members of Nirvana, this all stung. By Danny Goldberg's estimate, Kurt's power play left Krist and Dave with $3,000,000 each *less* than they would have recieved in 1992 and 1993, and while it's maybe understandable that Kurt would want to restructure the rights going forward, applying them retroactively feels, even now, petty and uncalled for. It's certainly not very punk. In the end, what saved the group was Kurt throwing them a particularly valuable bone (apparently at Courtney's suggestion, according to Goldberg) – equal split on 'Smells Like Teen Spirit'. It certainly helped, though given that 'Teen Spirit' is the ultimate example of Nirvana's collaborative process, it was also absolutely fair. More than anything the new deal signalled that things had changed, irrevocably. The multi-million selling band now had multi-million selling problems, and things would never be the same again. As Dave told Paul Brannigan in 2009: 'Okay, wait, this isn't just three guys in a van any more'.

24. The *Pocketwatch* album was released so quietly, and on such an obscure label – the cassette-only 'Tool Set' series of Virgina-based Simple Machines – that it was almost entirely ignored for months, though when word finally did get out the demand nearly overwhelmed the label, since its only two staff members, founders Jemmy Toomey and Kristin Thompson, manufactured their releases by dubbing them in their bedrooms, five at a time. It speaks to Dave's lack of confidence that he chose to release the record this way – had he approached his managers they almost certainly could have arranged a much more profitable record release. The project simply didn't evolve in that way, though: Jemmy Toomey, of the indie duo Tsunami, had popped into Barret Jones' studio in Washington DC during the first sessions Dave recorded back in December 1990 and was impressed enough by what she heard to ask if she could release something on her new label. Dave was flattered by the compliment from a girl he already had kind of a crush on and agreed. He hadn't been recording with a release in mind at all.

April 7

- Nirvana return to the studio for the first time since the *Nevermind* sessions, working with Barret Jones, Dave Grohl's roommate and drum tech, at his Laundry Room studios, built in his and Dave's basement.[25] In a single day, the band record two songs they've had knocking around for a while, 'Oh, The Guilt' and 'Curmudgeon' and a cover of The Wipers' 'Return of the Rat'.[26] The band also jams on new song ideas Kurt had been playing with.[27]

April 16

- The new issue of *Rolling Stone* features Nirvana on the cover, with a 5,000-word interview inside written by Michael Azerrad. The photograph on the cover, taken

---

The songs on *Pocketwatch* are genuinely great. Among them is a lovely, melancholy piece called 'Color Picture of a Marigold', which would later be re-recorded with Nirvana as the b-side to 'Heart Shaped Box' – the only Nirvana original neither written nor sang by Kurt Cobain. Also worthy of note is the beautiful 'Friend of a Friend', a Mark Lanegan-influenced reflection of Grohl's early days in Olympia, feeling homesick and isolated as he found himself in a new town, spending every day with two guys he barely knew. It's wonderful, and would later get a spruce-up on the Foo Fighters' 2005 double album *In Your Honour*, while 'Winnebago' would turn up on the b-side of the band's debut single 'This Is A Call'. The roots of Dave's post-Nirvana career were already planted.

25. Barrett Jones was an old friend of Dave's from Washington. He'd built his original studio in his parents house, with the control room in the laundry room, hence 'Laundry Room Studios'; a name he'd carried over when he'd moved to Seattle. When Nirvana broke big, Dave offered his old friend a job as his drum tech and he'd happily crossed the country and moved in with him. Kurt heard the work the two had done on the *Pocketwatch* tape and was impressed by the raw production. The last thing anyone in Nirvana wanted to do at that point was record more super-polished, sugar pop. It's telling that the first two original songs Nirvana recorded post-*Nevermind* were two of the most discordant and uncompromising in their entire canon. As had happened in the period following *Bleach*, Kurt was reacting against himself.
26. You might think this was Nirvana stocking up on b-sides for forthcoming singles from *Nevermind*, but you'd be wrong. 'Curmudgeon' did indeed end up on the flip of the 'Lithium' single, but the other two songs were tied into the band's stated aim to contribute to and support underground music. 'Oh, The Guilt' was intended for a split single on Touch 'N' Go records with Austin-based alt rock band The Jesus Lizard. Kurt was a big fan of the band and, besides, had wanted to put a record out with Touch 'N' Go since the inception of Nirvana – the 1987 'Dale Demo' was even sometimes referred to in his journals at the 'Touch 'N' Go Demo', though at the time the label wouldn't return his calls. He'd not told Geffen about the plan, which had been made over a year ago, and so ruffled some feathers at DGC, which Nirvana's managers had to smooth over. It was eventually agreed that the single could come out on condition it was a 7" only and capped on 50,000 copies in the US and 50,000 in the rest of the world (which was fine by The Jesus Lizard, who wouldn't sell anywhere near that on their own) and wouldn't appear on any albums or compilations. It also paved the way for Nirvana to donate 'Beeswax', another of the tracks recorded with Dale Crover back in 1988, to a compilation released through Slim Moon's kill rock stars label. The final track was recorded under similar assurance of a low key release – 'Return of the Rat', another Wipers cover, was intended for a vinyl-only box set, *8 Songs For Greg Sage and The Wipers*. The band had originally wanted to contribute the Peel Session recording of 'D-7' but rights issues meant it was simply easier to record a new track.
27. Dave Grohl believes these were early versions of 'Frances Farmer Will Have Her Revenge On Seattle', 'Very Ape' and 'Tourettes'. The unceasing torrent of new songs Kurt had been writing throughout 1990 and 1991 had slowed right down by 1992 thanks to the distraction of marriage and impending fatherhood, the day to day trials of fame, the pressures of a high profile career and, of course heroin. Kurt was using regularly again by May 1992 (according to Charles R Cross he had told a friend he was spending $400 a day on heroin). His bandmates had privately began to worry that there wouldn't actually *be* another Nirvana album. Dave Grohl saw the new material they jammed in his basement as a positive sign for the future.

in Australia earlier in the year, shows Kurt wearing a t-shirt with the slogan 'Corporate magazines still suck'.[28]

May 12

- Singer-songwriter Tori Amos[29] releases her EP *Crucify*, which is backed by emotive piano versions of songs written by men, among them 'Smells Like Teen Spirit'.[30]

June

- Two journalists, Irish-born Victoria Clarke and UK magazine editor Britt Collins pitch a book on Nirvana to the band's management, and are given the approval to go ahead with the project. The book, which has the provisional title *Nirvana: Flower Sniffin', Kitty Pettin', Baby Kissin' Corporate Rock Whores*[31] is bought by

28. The cover of *Rolling Stone*, like *SNL* and *Top of the Pops* was A Big Deal. It was a signal that you'd made it. *Rolling Stone* was the voice of mainstream American music fandom, and though a ton of bands from across genres were covered in depth within its pages, you didn't get the cover without being a commercial and cultural giant. Kurt had blown hot and cold over whether he wanted to be in *Rolling Stone* at all, since it was seen at the time as being a little past-it and associated with the Baby Boomer hippy rock of its 70s peak – it had very little to do with the Punk Rock culture that had birthed Nirvana. What's more, he was livid that the magazine had borrowed the phrase 'smells like teen spirit' for a recent cover feature on the tacky teen drama *Beverly Hills 90210*. Not to mention the fact that the magazine regularly printed letters from readers keen to rant about how much they *hated* Nirvana. On the other hand, it was also the rock magazine of note; The *New York Times* of pop. And Kurt, according to co-manager Janet Billig, was actually an avid reader. As Azerrad points out in his updated book *The Amplified Come As You Are*: 'He certainly knew my writing, and I had mostly written for *Rolling Stone*.'

    Predictably, Kurt did his best to have his cake and eat it. He was able to plug his favourite underground bands, publicly deny he was on heroin (a rumour some readers may only have been aware of because the *BAM* and *Hits* accusations from earlier in the year were repeated in the article), reaffirm his love for his wife, take potshots at Pearl Jam and show his disdain for the mainstream fame he had acquired – the full Cobain manifesto. In truth, *Rolling Stone* needed Kurt way more than he needed *Rolling Stone*, and he was well aware of the fact. As Danny Goldberg points out, 'They had a number one album without being on the cover of *Rolling Stone*' – a true rarity for a rock band. The 'Corporate magazines still suck' shirt was a reference to the SST (the punk record label founded by Black Flag's Greg Ginn) tagline 'Corporate rock sucks'. Waving a flag that says 'we are not a *Rolling Stone* band. We are not part of this world', while simultaneously being on the literal cover of *Rolling Stone* is either an amazing act of subversion or else a hell of a double standard. Possibly both.
29. 'The whips 'n' cleavage rawk bimbo turned kooky sensitive *artiste*' as she's described by Keith Cameron in *NME* that April.
30. The idea is a good one, but the execution is a little bloodless and anaemic. The problem for someone attempting a radical musical rearrangement of that particular song is that its power is almost all in its dynamics and performance. The lyrics themselves are fairly vague, cut and paste memes and slogans. There's not much there to really dig into, especially not for someone as expressive as Tori Amos. There are other Nirvana songs that can, and have, thrived as cover versions, especially sang by women – witness Amanda Palmer's cover of 'Polly', or St Vincent's version of 'Lithium', or Lorde singing 'All Apologies' at the Rock 'N' Roll Hall of Fame induction. 'Smells Like Teen Spirit', however, was, like its parent album, lightning in a bottle. You can't deconstruct lightning and then do your own version. There's a famous saying attributed to *New Yorker* columnist E. B. White: 'Analysing humour is like dissecting a frog. Few people are interested. And the frog dies.' Covering 'Smells Like Teen Spirit' is largely the same. Still, po-faced though it might be, the band got a kick out of Amos' rendition. Kurt told Michael Azerrad that he and Courtney danced to it every morning ('It's a great breakfast cereal version'), and it was used as warm up music as the band took the stage on their European tour dates that summer.
31. This slogan was taken from Nirvana's most famous post-*Nevermind* t-shirt, which referenced their own 'Fudge Packin' Crack Smokin' Satan Worshippin' Motherfuckers' shirt, making a typically self-satirising comment on their own move to the safe waters of a major label. The front of the shirt, yellow on black, featured the Nirvana logo, designed years before by the typesetters at *The Rocket* for Sub Pop, and a

the Hyperion publishing house in the US and Boxtree in the UK, and Clarke and Collins are given backstage passes for the upcoming European tour, with Clarke included in the touring party while Collins heads to Seattle to research and conduct interviews. Krist gives a lengthy interview for the book and hands the duo contact numbers for former Nirvana members and other key figures in their story.

June 12

- *Nevermind* goes 4x platinum in the US with sales of over 4,000,000.

June 21

- Nivana begin a short European tour at Dublin's Point Theatre,[32] covering the dates that had been cancelled the previous winter and playing some festival shows.

June 22

- At a show in Belfast, Kurt attempts to calm a fight between the in-house security and a fan. The security guard turns on him and (according to eye-witness Everett True) punches him repeatedly in the stomach. 'Backstage everybody seems pretty happy about Kurt's dust up,' reports *NME*, 'and the consensus is that the anger will translate itself into a stormin' show ... [and] Nirvana are indeed angsty and blamming[33].'

June 23

- Kurt collapses at breakfast and is taken to hospital. Anton Brookes, Nirvana's loyal UK PR man since their first visit in 1989, runs interference with journalists in the lobby at the hotel – 'it's a weeping ulcer, I've known him for three years and he's always had it. It's because he eats a lot of junk food'[34]. Kurt is dismissed from hospital and the tour continues.[35]

---

warped version of the famous 70s 'Smiley' design – a smiley face; its circumference now wobbly, its eyes replaced with crosses, its grin crooked. This design, which was created by Geffen's Robert Fisher, has become synonymous with the band.

32. Though it's called a theatre, The Point is really an arena venue with a capacity of roughly 8,000 at the time. This is the first time Nirvana would tour playing venues befitting a band of their size. One year earlier they had been opening for Dinosaur Jr in clubs holding a third of that, and Kurt was sleeping in his car. It had all happened *so fast*.
33. 'Blamming' – 'to be blasting and jamming to your music' according to *Definitions.com*
34. This quote from Everett True's *The True Story*.
35. Kurt later admitted that he had forgotten to take his methadone pills the previous night and had woken up with such intense stomach pains that he feared he'd just throw them up anyway. Michael Azerrad will later reflect on Kurt's excuses in disbelief in his *Ampified Come As You Are* – 'I had to be rushed to hospital – big deal,' says Kurt. 'What a remarkable thing to say,' comments Azerrad. The incident will colour the rest of the tour, with tensions stirred by a heavily pregnant and irritable Courtney Love. The band's management even hire minders to keep Kurt out of trouble (read – away from drugs). Kurt and Courtney respond by switching hotels without telling them. 'They were turning this band into everything it wasn't supposed to be,' he later complains to Azerrad.

June 26

- Backstage at the Roskilde festival, would-be Nirvana biographer Victoria Clarke makes the mistake of asking Courtney Love for an interview for her book. Though Courtney agrees, Kurt is furious and insists that Clarke is thrown off the tour.[36] That night's set is postponed so the festival can screen Denmark's European Championship football/soccer match, during the delay Kurt begs Mark Lanegan of Screaming Trees to headline in Nirvana's place so he can play earlier.[37]

June 30

- At a show in Stockholm, Nirvana open with a cover of Fang's 'The Money Will Roll Right In'.[38] Everett True, reporting for *Melody Maker*, is pretty withering about an audience who are only here because 'Guns N' Roses aren't in town until next week and Brian Adams was on yesterday', but even more withering about the show itself which is 'as bad as I've seen Nirvana play, in terms of spirit, excitement and inspiration (everything that Nirvana used to have in spades) ... and Oslo was way, way worse.'[39]

---

36. At this point, Nirvana's co-operation on the proposed book evaporates. Clarke and Collins however, having already signed publishing deals and begun work, have no choice but to plough on without any official support from the band. They will come to regret this. Gold Mountain, meanwhile, send out a letter to several people associated with the band asking them not to speak to the two biographers.
37. Kurt was, according to Mark Lanegan's *Sing Backwards and Weep*, wrapped backstage in a blanket suffering from 'dopesickness'. Lanegan absolutely begged Kurt to change his mind, arguing that Screaming Trees were in no-way as big a deal as Nirvana and would struggle to follow the biggest band in the world and hold the audience. Kurt insisted this was Screaming Trees' opportunity to show what they could do. It did not go well. 'When we finally took the stage in front of the disappointed 50,000 plus concert goers, I was beyond shitfaced,' Lanegan wrote. The set was so disastrous that Screaming Trees were pulled from almost every European festival they had scheduled for the rest of the summer.
38. Fang were a snotty, Brit-influenced Bay area punk band founded in 1980. Their 1993 song 'The Money Will Roll Right In' is a combo of sludgey riff, melodic grace and sneery lyrics and as such was basically already a Nirvana song. It also has a brilliant line about 'fucking Brooke Shields'. Its role as a set opener serves a double purpose, as both a withering acknowledgment of the sell out rock-star 'punks' some thought Nirvana had become, and as a way of wrong-footing a *Nevermind* audience with something unpalatably noisy.
39. Everett True is probably the person who writes most evocatively about Nirvana, and he saw the whole thing unfold, pinning and defining it forever in the pages of *Melody Maker*. It's worth remembering, however, that he was also the writer that was closest to the band. He was absolutely on the inside – this wasn't the usual rock anthropologist, parachuted in to spend a few days on the road with the travelling circus before scurrying away to write their fascinated field reports; he was every bit a part of it, getting messed up with the band members, joining them on stage and living the same moments. He'd also seen them at every stage of their career since 1988. What Everett True considers to be a bad Nirvana gig could still be a transcendental experience for an audience member who didn't have that level of context and emotional investment. This wasn't Nirvana's best ever run of gigs, sure, and a fairly toxic mood hung over the touring party which occasionally leaked onstage, mingling with the general uneasy feel of a punk band playing unfamiliar big rooms and resulting in some unsatisfying performances. ('I wonder if Nirvana really enjoys playing in such places?' one fanzine writer ponders, understandably, of a show in Paris that is full of 'screaming girls and fans of the Top 50') However, it's inaccurate to say that *every* show was a stinker – their set at Denmark's Roskilde is a doozy and stands up comfortably against the band's 'classic' Reading set later in the year. Nirvana were actually pretty consistent that summer – footage and recordings exist, of various levels of quality, for most shows on the tour and they show a tight enough unit and an explosive enough proposition to punch through the dampest of atmospheres, at least for the most part. Nirvana were capable of playing some genuinely dismal gigs. None of these fell into that category.

July 4

- Courtney starts having contractions shortly before Nirvana take the stage in Madrid. The band play the show, and the labour turns out to be a false alarm, but on the advice of a doctor she is sent home, and Kurt decides to cancel the remaining two gigs of the tour, not willing to miss his child's birth or be absent should any complications arise. When the pair return home they discover flood damage in their LA apartment has ruined Kurt's blue Mosrite guitar, plus two tapes full of song ideas and notebooks full of lyrics and poetry.[40]

July 13

- 'Lithium' is released as the third single from *Nevermind.* All versions are backed with 'Curmudgeon', from the Laundry Room sessions earlier in the year. The US 12", CD and cassette add a live cut of 'Been A Son' and the UK CD also has the Peel session recording of 'D-7'. The video, again directed by Kevin Kerslake, is a collage of live footage culled partly from the Halloween show at the Paramount Theatre in Seattle, and from footage shot for Sonic Youth's *1991: The Year Punk Broke*, including Kurt's now legendary shoulder-dislocating dive into the drum kit at Reading.[41] The artwork features a sonogram of Kurt and Courtney's baby. Responding to constant requests from fans, the 'Lithium' single also features all of the lyrics on *Nevermind*, absent from the album's own liner notes, printed inside the sleeve.

40. The couple had left some of their more valuable bits and bobs stashed in the bathtub of their apartment, reasoning that any thieves wouldn't think to look there. Unfortunately, their upstairs neighbour's bathroom had flooded, water dripping through the ceiling into the apartment below, filling up said bathtub and obliterating the contents of those journals and tapes. But what could have been on them? There were plenty of musical ideas knocking around from Nirvana's various jams – Dave had said that a lot of the pre-*Nevermind* rehearsals were full of unfinished bits and pieces that none of them would remember if they didn't record them on a boom box. Those cassettes, alongside stuff Kurt had recorded at home, apparently contained the only versions of several embryonic songs. It explains why Nirvana weren't as far along with the process of writing their next album as you'd think, and why the upcoming 'Lithium' and 'In Bloom' singles were lacking in new b-sides. Though Kurt had been hugely prolific through the back half of 1990 into summer of 1991, with half of *In Utero* already written by the end of that year, we have much less evidence of new songs written throughout 1992, and Kurt's output seems to have slowed to a trickle. It's easy to believe that losing so much material and having to start again from scratch would have a lot to do with that. Of course, having a persistent heroin addiction and a baby on the way, both of which were part of a tumultuous and extremely public life, would do that too.
41. Kim Gordon was extremely resistant to the band using a shot of Krist carrying Kurt around his shoulders, worrying that it would diminish its impact in the film. 'She was pissed at feeling pressured,' says Danny Goldberg, who had been given the task of talking her into it, 'especially by someone who until recently had been one of her managers, and, I suspect, a bit overwhelmed by the speed of the role reversal between the two bands.' Kurt originally had a much more involved idea for a bitter-sweet, stop motion animated fairy tale, but it was abandoned due to the complexities and time involved.

August 4

- Kurt enters a 25-day rehab at the Cedars-Sinai Medical Centre in LA in an attempt to get off heroin.[42] Three days later Courtney checks into a different wing of the same hospital.[43]

August 11

- The new issue of *Vanity Fair* hits stands. It features a frank, compelling and utterly spiteful feature on Courtney Love by the journalist Lynn Hirschberg. In a wide-ranging interview Courtney appears to casually admit to taking heroin for several months during her early pregnancy. 'We went down to Alphabet City and … we copped some dope,' she's quoted as saying. 'Then we got high and went to *SNL*. After that, I did heroin for a couple of months.' The article sparks an immediate uproar.[44]

August 14

- Kurt writes personally to David Geffen, the president of the Geffen group, assuring him that Courtney hadn't used heroin since discovering her pregnancy and stressing his support for his partner. 'We are capable of displaying a healthy attitude before our audience and the next record is easily as good as the last one but I'm so extremely pissed off about the piece of trash journalism that I'd lay anything on the line for the love of my wife and daughter.' He delivers the letter by hand.[45]

---

42. His stomach pain had become unbearable and he had written in his journal that upon regaining 'the familiar burning nausea' he had decided to kill himself to stop the pain. 'I bought a gun,' he said, 'but chose drugs instead'. This time the drugs didn't help and with fatherhood on the horizon and urged by his managers and wife, he checked into a formal rehab.
43. According to Charles R. Cross she was suffering from 'a complicated pregnancy and emotional exhaustion.'
44. Reading an early version of the piece is partly what put Courtney into hospital early ('my bones shook,' she told Michael Azerrad. 'I knew that my world was over. I was dead. That was it. The rest of my life.') She said later that she was scared of what she might do. The *Vanity Fair* feature, though entertainingly written, really is a nasty piece of work, in which writer Hirschberg gives Courtney enough rope to hang herself. It's full of unnamed sources expressing concerns about the couple's behaviour and the health of their child. And even if it *didn't* focus on that element, even if Courtney hadn't been pregnant at all, it would *still* be a nasty piece of work. Hirschberg paints Courtney as money grabbing and manipulative, implying that she turned Kurt onto heroin (which he had been dabbling in for years) and was driving a wedge between the members of Nirvana. Private discussions about Nirvana's internal politics are repeated verbatim ('"So," Courtney says, "what do you want to do? Why don't you start a new band without Chris?"') and Courtney is often referred to as someone with 'an agenda' or an 'ulterior motive' for her marriage. Kurt and, especially, Courtney didn't help themselves by talking far too frankly in front of an outsider. 'Courtney would phone me up and tell me all this stuff she was telling Lynn Hirschberg,' Everett True told Mark Yarm. 'I'd be like, "I'm not sure this is a good idea … this woman isn't a music critic [like me]; she's a professional journalist and there's a very big difference"'. In *Serving The Servant* Danny Goldberg remembers the wave of anxiety he got watching Courtney speaking animatedly to Hirschberg. 'Lynn seduced her, obviously,' he quotes Rosemary Carroll, Kurt and Courtney's lawyer, as saying. 'Courtney thought that she had charmed her. She thought that Lynn was eating out of her hand and that it was going to be a great article.'
45. It says a lot about Kurt's desperation that he would feel the need to reassure a label boss that handled Guns N' Roses, Whitesnake and Aerosmith that *his* band wasn't a bad influence on their audience. David

August 16

- Gold Mountain management, at that point representing both Hole and Nirvana, publish a statement from Kurt and Courtney which is quoted in the *LA Times*: 'The *Vanity Fair* article contains many inaccuracies and distortions, and generally gives a false picture of both of us, including our attitude about drugs.' In the statement the couple go on to 'unequivocally deny' that Courtney was intentionally doing drugs during her pregnancy. 'As soon as Courtney found out she was pregnant, she immediately contacted an obstetrician and a doctor specialising in chemical dependency,' the statement goes on to say, 'and has been under their care since then and has been assured that she can expect to have a healthy baby … Because we were stupid enough to do drugs at one time, we realise that we opened ourselves up to gossip by people in the rock world who want desperately to pretend they have some "inside" information on famous people. We never dreamed that such gossip would be reported as if it were true without us even having the ability to comment on it, especially when the gossip reflects on such a personal and important event as the birth of our first child'.[46]

August 18

- Frances Bean Cobain, daughter of Kurt and Courtney, is born at Cedars-Sinai Medical Centre in LA, a healthy, and normal seven pound and once ounce baby girl with her father's blue eyes.[47] The name 'Frances' was inspired by The Vaselines' Frances McKee, and 'Bean' was the nickname her parents gave her after their first sonogram, when she was a bean-sized blob on a screen. Kurt is present for

---

Geffen, for his part, was baffled and annoyed by the letter and called Danny Goldberg demanding to know why he was being dragged into a mess he clearly felt he was above … he considered all of this to be tawdry nonsense and had no time for it (probably *because* he handled Guns N' Roses, Whitesnake and Aerosmith). That 'easily as good as the last' line is interesting, though – Kurt, amid all this chaos, was still thinking about the next Nirvana record and his own career. Despite his irritation, Geffen did indeed reply, and graciously, sending a letter to Kurt and Courtney, courtesy of the hospital they were staying in. 'Kurt, I know you are upset about the recent article on Courtney and the attacks on her character,' he wrote in a note dated 18 August, reproduced in Courtney's published diaries, *Dirty Blonde*. 'Please know that I am here if you need me. This should be a time of joy and celebration … I'll help you get through it in any way I can.'

46. The *Vanity Fair* article was, unequivocally, the biggest disaster to befall Kurt and Courtney during Kurt's lifetime. It changed *everything* and had a dramatic impact on their lives and the life of their baby. The couple's drug use had been whispered about in industy circles, and then gossiped about in the music press, but it had never really ran amok in the mainstream's consciousness. Kurt had been the 'Smells Like Teen Spirit' guy. Now he was the 'heroin guy with the junkie wife'. Some of the nastier tabloids, the likes of *National Enquirer* and *Globe Magazine*, ran articles with headlines like 'Rock Star's Baby Born A Junkie'. It wasn't just the gutter press and celeb magazines though – despite a desperate attempt to intervene by Amy Finnerty, Nirvana's great champion at the network, MTV ran the quotes from *Vanity Fair* as a news bulletin, pushing the story into the world of the band's fanbase ('You can't just say, "I'm not going to cover this because Nirvana might be mad",' MTV News Anchor Kurt Loder told Mark Yarm.) Kurt wrote a letter to the station, which remained unsent but was reproduced in *Journals*. It read 'Dear Empty TV … how fucking dare you embrace such trash journalism … My life's dedication is now to do nothing but slag MTV and Hirschberg, who by the way is in cahoots with her lover Kurt Loder … We will survive without you. The old school is going down.'
47. Of course, lots of babies are born with piercing blue eyes. The difference is that Frances kept hers.

her birth, having come from the rehab ward, though he is still hooked up to an IV himself.[48]

August 24

- Following an anonymous tip from someone working in the hospital, the LA Country Department of Public Social Services successfully petition to have Frances Bean Cobain removed from the care of her parents. Frances is placed with Courtney's half-sister, Jamie Rodriguez while Kurt completes rehab. It will take until March 1993 for Kurt and Courtney to get full legal custody of their daughter. [49]

August 28

- Nirvana fly to London to prepare for their headline slot at the Reading Festival, the biggest gig they have ever played.[50]

---

48. 'I'm having the baby, it's coming out, he's puking, he's passing out, and I'm holding *his* hand and rubbing *his* stomach,' Courtney told Michael Azerrad.
49. I thought long and hard about the level of detail I would go into around *Vanity Fair* and Kurt and Courtney's experiences in its aftermath. As I said in the introduction, I always wanted this book to be about *Nirvana*. Not 'Kurt and Courtney' or the more lurid and scandalous parts of their story. I'm also not sure of the veracity of a lot of contemporary claims. Rock biographers have a habit of picking statements from one-another's books and replicating them without any fact-checking, leading to unprovable myths woven in as accepted truth. Did Kurt really escape hospital to score heroin and buy a gun the day after his daughter's birth and then try to instigate a suicide pact with his wife? It's repeated in several books and articles, but ultimately they're all referencing books and articles that only have Courtney herself as a source. Not even Eric Erlandson who apparently was actually there, has ever confirmed the story on record and has been extremely vague when directly asked about it. That's not to say it didn't happen, it may well have done. It probably did. But I'm trying to concern myself only with stories that are probably true and specifically relevant. Ultimately, though, the fall-out from the *Vanity Fair* affair drastically impacted Kurt's life and had a knock-on effect on his career and the career of Nirvana. It would cast a shadow over the next year that was unavoidable. I'm going to try to bring up the drama around Kurt's home life only when it's absolutely necessary after this, but it's important context to know that it's all going on in the background as Nirvana move into the next stage of their musical lives. Courtney Love, Frances Bean, heroin ... these are all huge parts of Kurt's day-to-day-existence that can't help but bleed over into his creative and professional worlds. Still, I have no wish to dwell unnecessarily. If you'd like to read the detailed ins and outs, I'd recommend Charles R. Cross's book *Heavier Than Heaven,* which is based around hours of interviews with Courtney herself, Michael Azerrad's *The Amplified Come As You Are*, which has long interviews with everyone involved annotated with the benefit of 30 years of hindsight, and Nirvana manager Danny Goldberg's *Serving The Servant*, as well as Brett Morgan's film *Montage of Heck.* The three books and film cover the key facts and timeline really well.
50. Booking Nirvana to headline Reading was a no-brainer. The band had stolen the show the previous year in a mid-afternoon slot, and that was *before* they'd made the biggest alternative rock album of all time. Their ascendence to headliners was inevitable, and they were due to close the final day. It was another one of those markers of success – *SNL*, the cover of *Rolling Stone*; headline the Reading Festival. Kurt had even handpicked that day's line up, with Nirvana topping off a juicy bill of Melvins, L7 (who added to their own myth when Donita Sparks responded to the audience's mud-hurling by reaching into her knickers and throwing her tampon into the crowd), Mudhoney, Screaming Trees (who, having been pulled from the line up following their disastrous 'headline' slot at Roskilde, were only allowed back on the bill after Kurt threatened to pull out if they didn't play), Pavement, Teenage Fanclub (featuring a guest spot from the Vaselines' Eugene Kelly), Nick Cave and the Bad Seeds and the brilliantly wry ABBA tribute band Bjorn Again (it was, as *Rolling Stone* put it, 'the Super Bowl of alternative rock'). Booking Nirvana paid off for everyone – Reading had its first total sell out in years, while the rival Monsters of Rock festival at Donnington, still waving the trad-metal flag with Iron Maiden, Skid Row, Thunder and Slayer, saw a plummet in sales. The changing of the guard was happening fast.

August 29

- Kurt, Krist and Dave rehearse for their set at Reading.[51]

August 30

- Nirvana headline the Reading Festival. Kurt is pushed onstage in a wheelchair by Everett True. He is wearing a hospital gown and a blonde wig. 'With the help of his friends and family he's going to make it,' says Krist, hamming it up superbly. A frail Kurt totters to his feet, grabs the microphone with both hands, sings the opening line of Bette Midler's sappy 1980 hit 'The Rose'[52] and executes a perfect prat-fall, before getting to his feet and slashing into the opening riff of 'Breed'. The band play a 26-song set, augmented by interpretive dancer Tony Hodgkinson who windmills his hair so hard he gives himself whiplash. The setlist is a true and triumphant snapshot of the band's career so far: they play almost all of *Nevermind*, including 'Lounge Act' which rarely gets an outing, the choicest cuts from *Bleach*, including a monstrous 'Blew', and even dusted off 'Spank Thru', one of the last times it would be performed. Clearly enjoying themselves, the encore includes messy covers of 'The Money Will Roll Right In', 'D-7' and a beautifully discordant version of 'The Star Spangled Banner' ('The tune still provides an ironic soundtrack for generational pain' notes *Rolling Stone*) played amid a brutal, gleeful ten-minute stage trashing post closer 'Territorial Pissings'. The band look to the future too – 'All Apologies' is a real highlight (preceded by Kurt getting the audience to say 'we love you Courtney!' in unison) and a new

---

The Reading rumour mill, however, had been pushed into overdrive and speculation was rife that Nirvana wouldn't make it to their performance. 'Every phone call and everyone I bumped into was feeling Nirvana was not going to play,' Anton Brookes, the band's UK spokesman told Danny Goldberg. 'There were rumours that the band was split up. It was just *assumed* that the band wasn't going to play.' Stories flew around everywhere: 'Kurt has gone home to be with his baby', 'Kurt is dead of an overdose', 'Nirvana have split up', 'the band have been thrown off the bill for doing drugs'. The stories were so pervasive that Dave Grohl, talking to *Kerrang!* in 2018, says that backstage 'some of my best friends in bands that were opening would see me and say, "What are you doing here?" And I'd go, "We're fucking headlining!" And they'd be like, "You're actually going to play?!" I didn't realise there was any question!'. Matters were not helped by an *NME* article by Keith Cameron, one of the band's early champions now bitterly disillusioned by Kurt's recent behaviour, that went deep into the *Vanity Fair* accusations, just in case any UK fans had missed them, and portrayed, more or less accurately, the current state of the band as a series of disasters. 'With the accountants still hiring bulldozers to gather up the money,' writes Cameron, 'they've begun to blow it all via smack, the biggest sucker punch of the lot. From nobodies to superstars to fuck ups in the space of six months?! That had to be a record.' The magazine then goes on to list recent heroin-based rock deaths, members of New York City's Unsane and Seattle's Seven Year Bitch. As a result of that piece, and many like it, fans were fully expecting a no-show. Keith Cameron, who had built his feature out of what he could cobble together after Kurt gave him basically nothing in an interview, would never repair his relationship with the band. Backstage at Reading, Kurt tore into him and Hole's Eric Erlandson poured a drink over his head.

51. 'It wasn't good,' Dave Grohl told the *Scotsman* many years later. 'I really thought, this will be a disaster, this will be the end of our career for sure.' It was the first time the band had rehearsed in months.
52. As brilliantly re-interpreted by Mudhoney on the *Sub Pop 200* compilation, sandwiched between 'Spank Thru' and Soundgarden's 'Sub Pop Rock City'.

song, 'Tourettes' is debuted[53]. It's Nirvana at their absolute best. 'This is our last show,' deadpans Kurt. '… until our November tour[54] … unless you guys wanna make a record?' 'Sure,' says Dave. 'Let's make a record.'[55]

September 8

- Rehearsals begin for the MTV *Video Music Awards* at the Pauley Pavilion, a giant basketball arena on the UCLA campus.[56] Kurt had returned from Reading and gone straight back to his court-appointed rehab, but has been allowed to leave hospital to rehearse and perform at the *VMA*s. Nirvana play through the two songs they intend to perform at the show, 'Rape Me' and 'Tourettes'[57], one a brutally uncompromising and lyrically nuanced (though extremely catchy) song about one of the most hideous crimes imaginable, and the other a short, spiky, noisy punker. Neither would be in the least bit familiar to a *VMA*'s audience.

53. 'We don't feel like putting this out ourselves, so this is for all you bootleggers to go ahead and GO!' says Krist. 'This is called 'The Eagle Has Landed,' says Kurt, making the tracklisting of all of those inevitable bootleg CDs extremely confusing once *In Utero* comes out. Strictly speaking it wasn't a *new*-new song, since the band had been knocking it around in rehearsals for a couple of years, but this was its live debut.
54. This is known in the craft as a 'pull back and reveal'.
55. Nirvana's headline performance at the 1992 Reading Festival – their last ever UK show – is rightly considered to be a high point in their career and, in what was an especially bleak year, a rare moment of real joy. The band were enjoying themselves so much that they just kept going – 'Tourettes' wasn't supposed to be on the setlist and 'D-7' and 'The Money Will Roll Right In' are obvious last minute additions. In the liner notes to *From The Muddy Banks of the Wishkah,* the Nirvana live compilation released in 1996, Krist calls the show 'the touring highlight of the year', saying 'hearing tens of thousands of people singing along to 'Lithium' was a very cool moment in the history of the band' (oddly, though *Wishkah* carries the Reading performance of 'Tourettes', presumably as a cheeky nod to how widely bootlegged it was and the version of 'Lithium' Krist specifically singles out in his liner notes is omitted in favour of a performance from a show in Amsterdam the previous year). 'It turned out to be a wonderful show,' Dave would tell the *Scotsman* in 2009, 'and it healed us for a while.' Nirvana, by their own admission, were never comfortable with being a 'big' band, feeling they were a Punk Rock act purpose built for sweaty, chaotic clubs, and sometimes that showed onstage. Reading 92, however, was one of those occasions where they stepped up and absolutely delivered. It became a communal experience. 'It was almost biblical,' Nirvana's press agent Anton Brookes told Danny Goldberg. 'Nirvana meant more to [the audience] than just a band … it was spiritual. It was cathartic … one of the greatest experiences of my life.' Reviews agreed – 'No-one lucky enough to have seen Nirvana do 'All Apologies' on this magical night will ever forget it,' says the *Independent On Sunday*'s Ben Thompson; 'The staggering energy and intensity radiating from the stage never let up' wrote soon-to-be Nirvana biographer Michael Azerrad in *Rolling Stone.* Azerrad would elaborate on this opinion 30 years later in his annotated *The Amplified Come As You Are*, saying, quite simply, 'it was the greatest rock concert I have ever seen'. The Reading performance, which had been widely bootlegged on both video and CD for years, was finally given an official release in 2009, though the editing out of all the stage banter is a shame that verges on criminal.
56. Since their inception in the mid 80s, the *VMAs* had become a fixture on the US musical calendar as a sort of teen-friendly, less stuffy Grammys. They also *specifically* highlighted videos rather than albums, which initially made them feel innovative, though as the years have gone by they've drifted closer and closer to every other award ceremony in tone. The awards were a huge part of MTV's brand and it was important for execs to represent the station properly to the show's audience of 7–10 million viewers. Thus Nirvana, such a big part of the previous 12 months, absolutely *had* to be there. Especially as they'd been nominated for four awards. Unfortunately, Kurt *really* didn't want to play the *VMAs.* He was going through rehab, and he and Courtney were trying to be parents despite being blocked by the courts from being alone with their daughter. They were under astonishing amounts of stress – he had a lot on his plate. MTV's president, Judy McGrath, personally called Danny Goldberg, begging him to get the band to perform, and Goldberg managed to talk Kurt into it.
57. At this point the song was unofficially known within the band as 'new poopie'. The title introduced at Reading, 'The Eagle Has Landed', was a joke played on the bootleggers.

MTV execs, who had been expecting the band to perform the widely-loved and celebrated 'Smells Like Teen Spirit', are now faced with their biggest stars singing about rape. They go into panic mode.[58] Eventually a compromise is reached and Nirvana agree to play 'Lithium' instead.[59]

September 9

- Nirvana perform 'Lithium' at the MTV *VMAs*, though not before playing the first eight bars of 'Rape Me', giving palpatations to the network execs who had to decide whether they would cut to a commercial break.[60] At the end of the

58. For Nirvana, this was a true clash of ideologies and an example of the central conflict at the heart of the band – they were happy to play at being big rock stars and pleased to be recognised as the important and successful band they were … as long as they were allowed to do so on their own terms. MTV wanted Nirvana? They could have them. But they couldn't control the Nirvana they got. Kurt, Krist and Dave were never going to play the game, do 'The Hit', as it was becoming known internally, and behave themselves. You can also see MTV's point – here's the biggest band in the world, a band whose album *everyone* owned, whose biggest hit had been ubiquitous on the channel and who, indeed, owed much of their success to MTV … and they were going to play two songs no-one had heard before, one of which was, if we're honest, pretty offensive at first glance. It took Kurt by surprise; he had thought MTV would be pleased about an exclusive new Nirvana song. MTV's top brass, meanwhile, immediately got it into their heads that 'Rape Me' was somehow about MTV itself, and while that wasn't exactly true, it also wasn't quite *untrue* either. When the song had been written back in 1991 its meaning had been fairly pure – at the Halloween show in Seattle Kurt had introduced it by saying 'this song is about hairy, sweaty, macho, redneck men', which was met with whoops from the audience. He left a beat for maximum impact before completing his introduction: '… who rape'. 'Rape Me' was intended as stark; a deliberate answer to *Nevermind*'s 'Polly' with the perspective switched from the attacker to a victim who is using her passivity as a shield and a weapon. It's made all the more subversive by being presented in the same quiet/loud format as 'Smells Like Teen Spirit' with an extremely similar riff. By 1992, though, the context had switched and the song had become more metaphorical – something that would become clear when a middle eight was added referencing the inside source that blabbed to *Vanity Fair*. (Kathleen Hanna of Bikini Kill, an old friend of Kurt's, took him to task over this in 1993: 'We were all in agreement that a guy making a comparison between being sold out by a friend to being raped wasn't the best idea,' she wrote in her memoir.) Kurt had shifted the perspective of his song, and rather than simply *empathising* with a rape victim he was now painting himself *as one*, and while Kurt's obvious feelings of exploitation and violation by media and industry were absolutely valid, the imagery he was using to express that felt uncomfortable to those who had actually been victims of sexual violence.
59. Under tremendous pressure from the network and their own management, the band ultimately compromised; at least they didn't have to play 'Smells Like Teen Spirit' again. The final straw had been a heavy implication that their friend Amy Finnerty, who had stuck her neck out for Nirvana to get 'Teen Spirit' on rotation the previous year, would be fired if the band didn't play ball. For her part, Finnerty has no idea where that implication came from and doesn't believe that would have happened. Many years later, she wheedled Dave Grohl into telling her the name of the person responsible: 'it was someone within their world, but outside of MTV,' is all she would tell Mark Yarm. Make of that what you will. Interestingly, Nirvana weren't the only band at the awards show fighting with organisers over their song choice – the same thing was happening with Pearl Jam, who wanted to cover Dead Boys' 'Sonic Reducer' but were being pushed into playing their hit, 'Jeremy'. Like Nirvana, Pearl Jam eventually gave in, though unlike Nirvana they didn't find a compromise – they just did as they were told.
60. MTV president Judy McGrath made it clear to Danny Goldberg that she didn't want the word 'rape' anywhere *near* the media narrative of their show and had been insistent that should Nirvana make a last minute switch the show would immediately cut to commercial. Years later, Amy Finnerty, interviewed by Mark Yarm for *Everybody Loves Our Town*, revealed that McGrath would actually have let the band get away with it, had they held their nerve and played 'Rape Me' in full. 'We're all looking at each other like, Are we gonna press this button [and cut to commercial] or not?' she said. 'And Judy said, "No, let them play."' Fortunately it was the best of both worlds – having made their point, the band switched smoothly into the planned song (the 20 seconds of 'Rape Me' they played, predictably, would be edited out of repeat broadcasts.)

song, Krist tosses his bass up in the air, accidentally hits himself over the head and pretends to knock himself out[61], while Kurt and Dave, somewhat predictably, destroy the stage. The performance ends with Dave Grohl at the microphone saying 'where's Axl? Hi Axl!'.[62] After winning an award for 'Best Alternative Video' for 'Smells Like Teen Spirit', the band send a Michael Jackson impersonator to accept it on their behalf.[63] Nirvana themselves accept their award for 'Best New Artist' in person, however, with Kurt thanking 'my family and our record label and our true fans ... you know it's really hard to believe everything you read'. Krist chips in with 'Remember Joseph Goebbels!'[64]

Back stage, Axl Rose and his supermodel girlfriend, Stephanie Seymour, have the misfortune to pass Kurt and Courtney, who are playing with baby Frances, leading to one of the all time great Courtney Love ripostes:

COURTNEY: 'Hey Axl, will you be godfather to our child?'
AXL: [to Kurt] 'Shut your bitch up or I'm going to knock you to the pavement.'
KURT: [to Courtney, deadpan] 'Shut the fuck up bitch'.
STEPHANIE SEYMOUR: [to Courtney, sarcastic] 'Are you a model?'
COURTNEY: 'No. Are you a brain surgeon?'[65]

Later, Kurt and Pearl Jam's Eddie Vedder slow dance while Eric Clapton plays 'Tears In Heaven'.[66]

September 10–11

- The band play a pair of benefit shows, one in Portland opposing a bill that would essentially enshrine homophobia in law in Oregon[67] and a huge show at the

61. Or at least that was his story, years later. His bandmates and crew believed he genuinely concussed himself.
62. A few days prior, Axl Rose had ranted onstage about alternative music in general and Kurt in particular ('Right now, "alternative?", the only thing that means to me is someone like Kurt Cobain in Nirvana, who basically is a fucking junkie with a junkie wife. And if the baby's born deformed, I think they both ought to go to prison'). Axl had taken Nirvana's refusal to play his birthday party or join his tour pretty personally.
63. The lookalike proceeds to 'announce my retirement as the king of pop and become the king of grunge rock'. The response in the room is pretty muted. No-one gets the joke. It would be delicious to think that this was the *same* Michael Jackson tribute who'd formed a band with his brother and sister and called it 'Nirvana' back in 1987 (see entry for August 16, 1991) but, alas, history doesn't tell us.
64. A reference to Hitler's propaganda chief during World War II. Almost certainly the only time Goebbels has *ever* been referenced in a major award speech on live US television.
65. Later on, Guns N' Roses bass player Duff McKagan, usually thought of as a good egg but in this case clearly the worst for wear, approaches Krist backstage with a camera crew in tow, filming for a GN'R 'behind the scenes' something or other and tries to pick a fight. Krist is too smart to get involved. Apparently McKagan and his entourage also shook Nirvana's trailer from side to side, with Courtney and the baby inside. 'Kim Warnick from the Fastbacks – the first real band I played with as a kid in Seattle – had called the day after the awards show and scolded me,' McKagan wrote later in hs memoir. 'I felt so low.'
66. 'We were slow dancing on the gym floor as if it was a seventh-grade dance,' Vedder says in *Everbody Loves Our Town*. 'Who led? That's a good question. That's the thing. Nobody led.'
67. The law would have amended the state constitution to declare homosexuality 'abnormal, wrong, unnatural, and perverse'. Thankfully, it was defeated. Queer rights was an issue close to Kurt's heart, partly because

15,000-capacity Seattle Centre Coliseum, their first in the city since Halloween 1991[68], fighting the introduction of a music censorship bill ('The Erotic Music Bill')[69] into Washington state law.[70]

September 26

- Kurt joins Mudhoney onstage in Castaic, California, where the band are on tour with Sonic Youth and Pavement, for a cover of 'The Money Will Roll Right In' and plays a solo, acoustic version of 'Where Did You Sleep Last Night'.

October 3

- Nirvana perform an unnanounced set opening for Mudhoney at Western Washington University in Bellingham. The only one of their singles they perform is 'Sliver', and they dust off 'Mexican Seafood' and 'Beeswax', songs dating back to the very early days of the band.[71]

October 4

- Mudhoney perform at Seattle's Crocodile cafe with a support band called Pen Cap Chew – one of Nirvana's early names. To the surprise of no-one, especially as they'd pulled the same trick yesterday, Nirvana are the opening band. This time they play no singles at all, but do include rare performances of 'Curmudgeon' and the unreleased 'Talk To Me'.[69]

---

his sister was gay, but mostly because homophobia is an abhorrent moral stance. Kurt, after all, had been spray painting 'GOD IS GAY' and 'HOMO SEX RULES' on buildings and cars since the mid 80s. In 1993 he would give an interview for gay magazine *The Advocate* in which he says he 'probably could be bisexual. But I'm married, and I'm more attracted to Courtney than I ever have been towards a person'. Compere and organiser Jello Biafra, formerly of Dead Kennedys, told Danny Goldberg that while wandering around the crowd he had overheard someone say, 'I thought this was just a Nirvana show. I didn't know it was gonna be about faggots.' Though this must have been depressing, Biafra had a more positive spin; he told Goldberg that he genuinely believed 'the concert helped open some eyes, turned some people around'.

68. Krist, who had been thrown out of the same venue for being drunk and disorderly at a Neil Young concert the previous year, claims he found a photo of himself on a bulletin board backstage of people 'banned for life', which he proudly announces onstage. The gig was also notable for Kurt's estranged father, Don Cobain, blagging his way backstage by showing his ID and fast talking the security guards, leading to a tense and uncomfortable family reunion in Nirvana's dressing room minutes before they were due to go on.
69. This law would have stopped under-18s from buying music with explicit lyrics. As Krist wrote in *Of Grunge and Government*, 'The state wanted to impose what could be considered an apartheid system on music' leading to a situation where 'musicians would have to go to court and prove that their art wasn't obscene ... you were guilty until proven innocent.' The law was judged 'unconstitutional' by the state Supreme Court in 1994.
70. This is generally considered to be another of the great Nirvana performances. 'The show itself is phenomenal,', writes Charles R. Cross in *Heavier Than Heaven*. 'The best Nirvana had ever done in Seattle.'
71. The show was part of a series called 'Hype The Vote', intended to prompt young people to vote in the upcoming US presidential election. Registered voters got in for $4, while unregistered voters had to pay $6. Which is still pretty good value to see Nirvana and Mudhoney, even in 1992.

69. It's the last time Nirvana would ever play 'Curmudgeon', 'Talk To Me' and 'Mexican Seafood'.

October 15

- The video for 'In Bloom', the final single to be taken from *Nevermind,* is filmed in Hollywood, with the band once again working with Kevin Kerslake.[70]

October 22

- Kurt and Courtney leave a series of abusive and threatening messages on would-be Nirvana biographer Victoria Clarke's answering machine after discovering she had interviewed *Vanity Fair*'s Lynn Hirschberg for her side of the story.[71] The tape of the messages will later be given to *Entertainment Weekly* who publish its contents in full.[75]

---

70. Of the band's four collaborations with Kerslake, 'In Bloom' is arguably the most successful, and in a way it leans into the personality of the band more authentically than even the 'Smells Like Teen Spirit' promo did. This isn't Nirvana the Punk Rock iconoclasts, or Nirvana the arty weirdos, as they were in 'Come As You Are'. This is Nirvana the subversive goofballs. Sending up The Beatles' appearance on the Ed Sullivan show in the 60s, with a host introducing them as 'three clean cut young men from Seattle' (itself an knowing wink to the media-created version of the band – no-one in Nirvana was 'from Seattle', and at this point Dave Grohl, who wasn't even from the same state, was the only member of the band living there). The band appear dressed in smart suits, Kurt's hair slicked into a sensible crop, his huge suit swamping him to the point he almost looks like David Byrne in *Stop Making Sense*, topped off with a pair of thick rimmed specs. He performs the whole thing with a wholesome, corn-munching grin plastered across his face. Dave is wearing a horrible blonde wig, and is even playing with his left drumstick reversed, jazz style. Midway through the video shots start to creep in of the band in dresses, pulling cock-rock poses, dry humping their instruments and destroying their gear and the set. The whole thing is filmed in black and white, using vintage, period-correct cameras with an audience of extras screaming like they're Kurt Cobain at a Vaselines show. It not only knowingly nods to, and sends up the media hysteria that had been churning around the trio for the previous year, it's also an absolute hoot. The band, of course, had no real wish to release yet another single from *Nevermind* and make yet another video, and the whole thing existed simply to feed the unceasingly ravenous demand for new content at MTV. Kurt's response, as usual, was to have his cake and eat it with a video that satirises media hysteria while, simultaneously reinforcing it by keeping Nirvana front and centre on the channel. It had the added benefit of projecting a version of Nirvana that was goofy, fun and likeable at a time when the tabloid stories risked making them feel too edgy and controversial. Dave Grohl was obviously paying attention – the thinking behind 'In Bloom' and its goofy likeability is the template for every video Foo Fighters ever made.
71. The messages are pretty horrible, and they don't paint either Kurt or Courtney in a very positive light. 'You fucking little parasitic cunts! If anything comes out in this book that hurts my wife I'll fucking hurt you. I don't care if this is a recorded threat. I'm at the end of my ropes … I've never been more fucking serious in my life.' Kurt goes on to say he could afford to have the writer killed but 'will try the legal way first'. Clarke and Collins had both been in the US researching their book, and Clarke had even been staying in Seattle with Charles Peterson, who had agreed to let her use his photography. At this point the pair found every door connected to the band, including Peterson's pictures, slammed shut. Stung and terrified by the *Vanity Fair* article, Kurt and Courtney were reacting in desperation and hurt, which explains their actions though doesn't really excuse them, particularly given the misogynist and violent tone. When Michael Azerrad asked Kurt about the incident for *Come As You Are* he doubles down. 'If I ever see [Clarke or Collins] in public, I'm going to beat the fucking shit out of either one of them.' Coming from someone so vocally opposed to violence against women, it is a pretty horrible thing to read. According to those who have read it, the book, which was never published, included a chapter (the longest in the whole book) on Courtney Love. The two authors had found that disliking Courtney was a common thread amongst old friends of the band. They'd even interviewed her ex husband, James Moreland, aka LA musician Falling James. It was a critical error on their part. The Cobains were terrified of anything, *anything*, that could jeopardise their chances of being given full custody of their child, and rawly sensitive about criticisms of their marriage. Their rage and hurt is understandable … still, it's hard to argue that Clarke and Collins weren't treated appallingly.
75. Nirvana's management bare-faced lied to the *New York Times* saying the tapes were a prank or a fabrication, as Danny Goldberg admitted in his memoir. 'I have never had any regret about trying to cover up for them in this way,' he says. 'I was doing my job and standing up for my client'. *EW* later called Courtney

October 25

- Work begins on demos for the new Nirvana album at Jack Endino's Word of Mouth studio (previously Reciprocal), the same room where Kurt and Krist had recorded *Bleach*. Krist and Dave arrive and set up, but Kurt never shows.

October 26

- The second day of recording is more fruitful, if a little tense.[76] Kurt is present, and the band track instrumental versions of 'Tourettes', 'Radio Friendly Unit Shifter', 'Dumb' and 'Frances Farmer Will Have Her Revenge On Seattle'. Only one song is completed fully, 'Rape Me', which has finished vocals and the sound of baby Frances screaming in her pram while her father sings.[77] Work is abandoned when the police arrived to complain about the noise and demand the session stop.[78]

October 30

- DGC announces the release of *Incesticide*, a new Nirvana album collecting early demos going back to the first tape the band cut back in January 1988, UK session

---

at home for a quote on the issue and she gave them both barrels, as Kurt had done with his biographer – 'I don't think [the messages were] that bad,' she said. 'I mean, I know we're right. I mean, we might have been mean to them, but they violated us and raped us, and it's just scary. I remember saying, like, "I'll fucking haunt you till you fucking die," and I meant it, because this kind of shit cannot go on.' The magazine published the full transcript. In 2011, Clarke wrote a blog about how she'd made her peace with the incident – she and her partner, the legendary Pogues singer Shane McGowan, had recently found themselves on the other side of the argument: 'Recently, Shane and I were sent a manuscript of a new Pogues biography,' she wrote. 'It was deeply unflattering, about both of us. After reading it, I was upset and angry for several days … I wondered what it must have been like for Kurt and Courtney, knowing that Britt and I could have been writing something that would affect their child, as well as them? Would I have been angry enough in their position to threaten the writers? Quite possibly!'

76. According to Jack Endino, who had known Nirvana for five years at this point, these were not happy sessions, and he was stunned that Kurt would simply not show up for a whole day of recording with no explanation – and that his band mates would just accept it. 'It was very tense,' he told Gillian G. Gaar for a 1997 article in *Goldmine*. 'There was something dark in the air. Just the idea of Kurt showing up 12 hours late – it wasn't like a band. It was dysfunctional in some way. People were not communicating with each other. Kurt was sort of in a different reality from everybody else. It made me very uneasy … It just wasn't the same band it had been.'
77. Nothing was done with these sessions during the band's lifetime, and they would stay in Endino's archive for many years before being dusted off for the *With The Lights Out* box set in 2004. Endino had been hoping that the band would record the new Nirvana album with him, but those hopes were dashed when Kurt spent much of the session asking his opinion about getting Steve Albini in to do it. As it turns out, the session itself was enough to convince Endino that he didn't want the job any more – not only was the mood in the studio tense, he was realising that the band wanted to make an unpalatably raw, deliberately un-commercial album, and felt instinctively that this would cause tension with Geffen and that whoever produced the record would end up taking the flack for it. 'Steve is gonna get blamed, and shit is gonna fly,' he told Gaar, 'and that's exactly what happened'. The tracks they recorded that day are all pretty close to the versions on *In Utero*. A warm-up improvisation Endino happened to record was later included on the 20th anniversary reissure of the album under the title 'Jam'. It's a great, loose, free flowing and super-heavy example of Nirvana's chemistry as a trio, even if it barely counts as a 'song'. As much fun as it is to hear the band cutting loose and feeling their way through the music, I always thought its inclusion on the *In Utero* reissue was the sound of the bottom of the barrel being scraped.
78. Dave was 'drumming was so loud, it was going right through the walls of the building,' Endino said. 'It was only the second noise complaint we'd ever had! It was kind of embarrassing. But they were almost done at that point.'

tracks and both sides of the 'Sliver' single. It's slated for release on 14 December in the UK and 15 December in the US.[79]

79. The idea came after Sup Pop mooted plans for their own Nirvana odds 'n' sods collection, provisionally, and with typical self-awareness, titled *Cash Cow*. Unhappy with the idea of a Nirvana album he'd have no control over, Kurt asked his managers to fix it. Geffen agreed to licence the Sub Pop tracks, meaning Kurt could take over the whole project and release it through DGC. His label were happy to oblige, of course – Nirvana had barely begun the very earliest stages of their next album and a stop-gap rarities collection, just in time for Christmas, solved a lot of problems. Sub Pop were also fine with the idea, since they got paid without having to put any work in, and Kurt was happy because he was able to showcase a full 360-degrees look at Nirvana's worldview and early music without any commercial pressure or anyone demanding hits. B-sides and rarities compilations are for fans, and they don't have any of the expectations for chart success that *Nevermind*'s follow up was inevitably going to be saddled with.

Initially his plan was to call the album *Throwaways* (Kurt shared a sense of humour with his former colleagues at Sub Pop) but he switched later to the more idiosyncratic and ambiguous *Incesticide*, a word that manages to be both a silly pun and oddly creepy without actually meaning anything. It's textbook Kurt Cobain. Everything in the vaults was up for consideration and reviewed, from the radio session the band had done for KAOS in May 1987 onwards. Kurt decided on the tracks himself – 'Dive' and 'Sliver' from the 'Sliver' single, 'Stain' from the *Blew* EP, 'Turnaround', 'Molly's Lips' and 'Son of a Gun' from the 1990 John Peel session, 'Been A Son', 'Anuerysm' and '(New Wave) Polly' from the 1991 Mark Goodyear session, 'Big Long Now' from the *Bleach* sessions and 'Beeswax', 'Downer', 'Mexican Seafood' (the inclusion of which absolutely enraged C/Z Records' Daniel House, who thought the track was exclusive to his *Teriyaki Asthma* compilation until Geffen's legal department trampled all over him), 'Hairspray Queen' and 'Aero Zeppelin' from the 'Dale demo'. Together the 15 tracks cover four years and as many drummers – Dale Crover, Chad Channing, Dan Peters and Dave Grohl. It's a great selection that gives a real snapshot of Nirvana's history. Side One is the pop Nirvana, the one in love with tweecore bands and sugar rush choruses, showing both their pop heart and their influences on their sleeves, while side two goes further back in time to their Melvins-loving sludgecore roots and their very earliest recordings, with the session version of 'Aneurysm' ending the record and essentially bringing it into the *Nevermind* era. The specifics of the selection is what confirms the Cobain personal touch – compilers at Geffen or Sub Pop wouldn't have reached for the BBC session versions of 'Aneurysm' and 'Been A Son' over the versions recorded at Music Source, nor would they have front-and-centred cover songs by a band as obscure as The Vaselines. Kurt knew his catalogue and he knew exactly what he wanted to say with it.

It's also interesting to consider what *didn't* make the cut here – the most surprising omission is probaby 'Spank Thru', which the band obviously had a soft spot for, considering they played it at Reading, their biggest ever show, not four months earlier. It is, however, the most juvenile and probably the most shallow of Kurt's songs, even if its melodic chops probably put it above something like 'Big Long Now' or 'Hairspray Queen' in the canon. Also conspicuous by its absence is 'If You Must', the opening song on the Dale demo and the track that first got Sub Pop's Jonathan Poneman's attention. Kurt had cooled on the song quickly, apparently considering it too metal ('He was embarrassed about it; it was too heavy,' Jack Endino told Gillian G. Gaar. 'He was just like that sometimes. I think it's a great song.' Endino is right; 'If you Must' is genuinely great, certainly when put against the inferior and equally heavy 'Big Long Now' and 'Aero Zeppelin', both of which made the cut. The other notable omission is 'Sappy', three versions of which were, by now, sitting in the vault. Either the 1989 version cut with Endino at Reciprocal or the mellower take done with Butch Vig at Smart the following spring could have sat perfectly on *Incesticide*. In this case, the reasoning is easier to see, however: Kurt was still hoping he could get a take of 'Sappy' strong enough for inclusion on his next album.

All in, *Incesticide* is a fascinating compilation that hangs together surprisingly well as a body of work. It shows that Nirvana's roots were always strong, and that the band they became had been imprinted in their DNA more or less from the word go. That said, the heavier songs would likely have been a culture shock for the band's new mainstream audience, and that's something Kurt would have both predicted and relished. Equally, though, the inclusion of so many pop gems in the first half meant that those fans wouldn't be utterly alienated. Kurt would have been well aware of *that* as well. He knew exactly what he was doing. Only four albums were released during Nirvana's lifetime, and *Incesticide*, despite being a compilation, holds its own against *Bleach*, *Nevermind* and *In Utero*. You could even argue that in poking into the nooks and crannies of the band's sound, it's a purer distillation of Nirvana's essence than the three studio albums, each of which contains an element of compromise of one sort or another. The album also prepared the way for Nirvana's next move. Kurt had once claimed that 'Sliver' was a way of getting *Bleach* fans into the idea of Nirvana as a pop machine. That same single now sat on an album that was doing a similiar job – showing *Nevermind* fans that Nirvana had a brutal side that was likely to rear its

- Nirvana perform a show at the Velez Sarsfield Stadium in the Argentine capital of Buenos Aires, in front of an audience of around 50,000 people. Outside of festivals this would be one of the band's biggest ever headline shows. Part of the deal for the show means Nirvana can pick their own support, and Kurt has invited Portland all-girl punk band Calamity Jane along for the ride. After the Argentinian audience react with hostility to Calamity Jane's set, Nirvana punish them by deliberately sabotaging their own performance, opening with a lengthy and formless instrumental jam before constantly teasing the crowd with the opening of 'Smells Like Teen Spirit' and cutting into another song. Kurt sings the first verse of 'Come As You Are' using only the word 'hey'. Dave, at one point, does a solo on a tiny children's drum kit, and toward the end of the set Kurt's guitar is dreadfully out of tune and he makes no effort to tune it, so several songs sound horrible. The band close with a ten-minute, cathartic and genuinely thrilling version of 'Endless, Nameless'. They never do play 'Smells Like Teen Spirit'.[80]

---

head on their next album. As Krist told *Rolling Stone,* 'maybe [after *Incesticide*] the next step we'll take won't be that much of a shock'.

80. There were a lot of dropped-balls here. Everyone had been in good spirits before the gig – the previous evening the whole party, *sans* Kurt who was sick again, went out drinking, ending up in a rock club enjoying local band Pirata Industrial playing a cover of New Order's 'Blue Monday' using motorcycle gas tanks as percussion. After their set, an impromptu jam band was formed of Courtney Love, Krist Novoselic, a local drummer called 'Louis' and members of Calamity Jane (there is some dispute about the make up of this one-off band, probably as a result of the free drinks the club's owner kept flowing all night – memories become rather fallable at that stage). Krist introduced Courtney as 'the most notorious woman since Marie Antoinette' and everyone had a whale of a time rattling out improvised nonsense. Courtney, however, did have to argue hard and talk fast in order to borrow a guitar from a man who, according to a tour diary Krist wrote for the British magazine *Raw*, 'probably thought she should have been at home baking pies'. This, possibly, should have been a red flag for what was to come.

The following day Nirvana were to headline a three-band bill with a hugely successful Argentine band, Los Brujos, as the opening act and the utterly unknown Portland punk band Calamity Jane as main support. You may have spotted a flaw in this plan. The huge stadium audience was already super familiar with the popular Los Brujos, and the band, who had a reputation for theatrical and crowd-pleasing performances, grabbed their opportunity and knocked their opening set out of the park. The crowd was now as primed as they ever could be to see Nirvana. Unfortunately, what they got first was an underground feminist punk act they'd never heard of. Apparently the reaction was not pretty – the Portland quartet were pelted with ice, coins and clods of earth. People were spitting at them. Men in the audience were exposing themselves and there were constant chants of 'Puta Madre!' ('Mother fuckers!'). Despite Courtney urging them on from the side of the stage, the band managed only a handful of songs before singer Gilly Ann Hanner basically told the audience where to go, smashed her guitar and fled for her life to a chorus of boos and yells. Backstage, Nirvana were so incensed by the treatment of their friends they tried to cancel their appearance ... until it was pointed out that they were getting $250,000 to play. Instead, Kurt, Krist and Dave tortured the audience with a long wait before their set, and then half-assed the performance on purpose.

Or at least that's the popular narrative, and the story that the band were happy to tell later. The reality, as is usually the case, is a little more complicated. Firstly the gig wasn't quite the car crash it's made out to be. There's some deliberate mischief – the teasing of 'Teen Spirit' and the mucking up of 'Come As You Are', plus the noise jam at the start and Kurt's out-of-tune guitar were all designed to punish the audience for the hostility Calamity Jane had been subjected to. Outside of that, however, the performance was, for the most part, merely fine. The problem wasn't the intentional messing around, it was the *unintentional* errors: Kurt messing up riffs and words, having to be shown the intro for 'Sliver' and the chords for 'Polly' by Krist on stage and occasionally checking he knows how a song goes by running through the guitar part for a few bars before it begins. The band hadn't bothered to rehearse for the show. Just a week earlier, Kurt had bunked off a recording session with no explanation – he wasn't taking his

November

- The December edition of *Spin* magazine hits the stands, with Courtney, Kurt and Frances on the cover, interviewed by Sub Pop's Jonathan Poneman. Nirvana are declared 'Artist of the Year'.[81]
- Nirvana approach Steve Albini about working on their new album.[82] Albini replies with a lengthy letter outlining his conditions and philosophy. 'I think the very best thing you could do at this point is exactly what you're talking about doing,' he says. 'Bang a record out in a couple of days, with high quality but minimal "production" and no interference from the front office bulletheads. If that is indeed

---

job especially seriously. We also need to remember that Nirvana were still not accustomed to gigantic gigs. Sometimes they pulled it off, as with Reading or Roskilde, but at others they felt and sounded a little lost in those huge spaces. Buenos Aires was one such show – the size and impersonal nature of the stadium sucked the joy and energy out of the performance. As Krist told *Raw*, 'We were playing with the passion of a cold fish … the limitations of such places creep up on us, fast'. Calamity Jane really did have an appalling experience (the band were so dispirited that they went home and *broke up*. Argentina was their last show) but it's pretty likely Nirvana's set would have had many of the same problems even if their main support had been rapturously accepted. The silver lining was that brutal performance of 'Endless, Nameless' which, for the members of the band at least, served up a timely reminder of why they loved being in Nirvana in the first place. It's probably the best version of that song ever performed; the trio's chemistry is almost telepathic. Krist summed it up beautifully in his tour diary – 'What they and we got during those last few minutes was total expression; something you can't create, something that grabs and affects you enough that you have to release it. Thirty thousand people were shovelled a mediocre performance for an hour-and-a-half, but 30,000 people, I hope, got to share with us for ten minutes the reason why we are in a band.'

81. This was entirely a puff piece, commissioned and approved with the intention of keeping Nirvana sweet. The choice of interviewer tells you everything – Poneman had known Kurt for years and wasn't about to roll over on the Cobains. The article is 100% wholesome and painted Kurt and Courtney as devoted, loving parents (true) whose various vices had been overblown by the media (occasionally true) and were very much in the past (absolutely not true). *Spin* magazine, like MTV, needed Nirvana. At the time *Spin* was the only music magazine that even got close to *Rolling Stone*'s influence, and it did so by being the default champions of alternative rock, a genre of which Nirvana were the definitive example. It was 'a jaw-dropping error in journalistic integrity,' *Spin* editor Craig Marks said in an interview with *Poyntor* years later. 'We were purely a PR mouthpiece for Kurt and Courtney at that time.' The mandate to softball Nirvana came directly from editor-in-chief Bob Guccione Jr, who knew on which side his bread was buttered and, for good measure, also went way back with Nirvana's manager, Danny Goldberg. He had also recently been immortalised in a particularly unflattering Guns N' Roses song on one of the *Use Your Illusion* records, so was presumably quite happy to stick it to Axl by supporting the band currently making him look like a petulant dinosaur. In all honesty, there's no real issue here. As Everett True himself pointed out to Courtney when she was spilling unwise beans to *Vanity Fair*, rock journalists don't operate in the same world or in the same way as other newspaper types. A rock critic's first responsibility is *not* to the truth. It's to the music. And the spirit of the music. And the world the music creates around it. A magazine interviewing a rock star does not have the same stakes as *The Times* interviewing the Prime Minister, nor does it have the same priorities or the same framework. No-one interviewing a world leader is entranced by the romance of political myth. Rock 'N' Roll, however? Very different. Your responsibility is to the art form, and sometimes that also means by extension to the artist. No-one was hurt by Poneman softballing the Cobains. No-one was brutally misled by *Spin*'s fulsome praises. No harm was done. Rock journalism is not the same as political journalism. It's way, way, way more important.
82. In typical Nirvana fashion, despite the fact that they had been talking about using Albini for some time, and even dropped his name in interviews, no-one had actually approached the man himself and *asked* him to do it (aside from a few slurred answerphone messages that he assumed were from Kurt). It got to the point where reports of Albini's involvement in the new Nirvana album were appearing in *Melody Maker* and *NME* and he was being asked about it in interviews ('I was having to contend with it on a daily basis; it was genuinely affecting my business, this notion that I was going to be doing this Nirvana record,' he told Gillian G. Gaar for her 33⅓ book on *In Utero*) but had never actually had a conversation with the band or their label about it. Eventually Kurt called to make the offer.

what you want to do, I would love to be involved … If instead, you might find yourselves in the position of being temporarily indulged by the record company, only to have them yank the chain at some point (hassling you to rework songs/ sequences/production, calling-in hired guns to "sweeten" your record, turning the whole thing over to some remix jockey, whatever…) then you're in for a bummer and I want no part of it'. Nirvana agree to his terms[83] and he sends them the recordings he'd just done for PJ Harvey's *Rid of Me* as an example of the studio he was proposing working in.[84] Albini also suggests that the band pay for the album themselves to minimise interference from Geffen, whom he suspects will be terrified by the combination of Nirvana's anti-commercial petulance and his own reputation for sonic nihilism.[85] He agrees a fee of $100,000 for himself (with no royalty, as was his custom). Recording is arranged for February 1993.

November 2

- Kurt records guitar for 'The "Priest", They Called Him', a collaboration with legendary beat writer William S. Burroughs.[86]

---

83. As discussed (see the entry for 2 January 1990) Albini had a specific and absolutely uncompromising attitude, which is outlined in his letter. He refused to take royalty points, suggesting an upfront fee and then a second, optional fee if the band are happy with his work. This was a big, ethical issue for Albini – partly he refused to take points because he felt a recording engineer should be treated 'like a plumber' would be and paid for a job well done, according to their value, and no more. More than that though, he felt royalty points were a trick of accounting that meant ultimately the cost of a producer was shifted to the band rather than the label, something he had no time for. He also outlines his personal philosophy: 'I consider the band the most important thing … I do not consider it my place to tell you what to do or how to play … I prefer to work on records that aspire to greater things, like originality, personality and enthusiasm. If every element of the music and dynamics of a band is controlled by click tracks, computers, automated mixes, gates, samplers and sequencers, then the record may not be incompetent, but it certainly won't be exceptional. It will also bear very little relationship to the live band, which is what all this hooey is supposed to be about'. Honestly, RIP Steve Albini. We will never see his like again.
84. I think there's an argument that this is the best PJ Harvey album. It's certainly the best manifestation of the original PJ Harvey trio – after this record, Polly Harvey split up her band and 'PJ Harvey' became, essentially, a solo project. There's a real magic to the early trio, however and Albini's focus on space and clarity makes the band absolutely sparkle.
85. He was right about this – Dave Grohl rememers their A&R, Gary Gersh, 'freaking out'. It was actually quite an unfair assumption, at least as far as Steve Albini was concerned. While his own musical output with Big Black and, unsurprisingly, Rapeman had been pretty brutal and uncompromising, Albini's whole thing was to make bands sound like themselves. As Kurt was fond of pointing out, he'd recorded both Pixies' *Surfer Rosa* and The Breeders' *Pod*, two albums full of pop accessibility. The worry was less that Albini would make Nirvana sound like Black Flag, and more that he'd allow them to sound like *Nirvana*. It can't have helped that the only finished new Nirvana songs anyone at DGC had heard were 'Curmudgeon' and 'Oh, The Guilt', or that they were well aware there was a song called 'Rape Me' floating around. If Kurt, Krist and Dave delivered an album of unpalatable sonic violence it would be because that was the album they wanted to make.
86. 'I've collaborated with one of my idols, William Burroughs' Kurt wrote the following year, bragging uncharacteristically in a particularly spiteful and ultimately unsent letter to Tobi Vail reproduced in *Journals*. 'And I couldn't feel cooler'. Kurt was a *huge* Burroughs fan. He'd discovered his work at high school and had been swept up in its weirdness and the odd, dark romance of its scrungy reality. It was an essay by Burroughs that had first turned him on to Lead Belly. According to Charles R. Cross, Kurt's only luggage on tour in Europe in 1991 consisted of a copy of Burroughs' classic 1959 novel *Naked Lunch* he'd found in London. Whenever a journalist would visit Kurt and Courtney at home they would invariably note that one of Burroughs novels, *Naked Lunch*, *Queer*, or *Junkie*, was lying around the place in their article. Burroughs' transgressive, boundary-pushing writing left an indelible mark.

November 15

- The *New York Times* runs an article on the 'grunge' phenomenon entitled 'Grunge: A Success Story'. 'This generation of greasy Caucasian youths in ripped jeans, untucked flannel and stomping boots spent their formative years watching television, inhaling beer or pot, listening to old Black Sabbath albums,' writes Rick Marin, 'and dreaming of the day they would trade in their air guitars for the real thing, so that they, too, could become famous rock-and-roll heroes'. The piece concludes with a lexicon of 'grunge' terminology apparently popular in Seattle,

---

Born William Seward Burroughs II, Burroughs was one of a handful of artists that comprised the 'Beat Generation', the loosely-linked literary contemporaries who pioneered freeform, experimental or sometimes hyper-realistic and unflinchingly confrontational prose and poetry styles. There was Ginsberg. There was Kerouac. And there was Burroughs, the most subversive and messed up of them all. Born in 1914 to a wealthy family in St. Louis, Missouri, Burroughs lived a life that, like his writing, was unconventional, unlikely and occasionally harrowing. He attended Harvard but was more interested in exploring Boston's many sexual and criminal vices than studying. In 1951, while living in Mexico City, he accidentally shot and killed his wife Joan Vollmer (who would later be played by Courtney Love in the 2000 film *Beat*, opposite Kiefer Sutherland of all people) during a botched and drunken William Tell game, a tragedy that haunted him as much as it energised his writing. Often his work, and indeed his lifestyle, with the twin vices of heroin and homosexuality featuring heavily in both, had been considered unforgivably scandalous and unpalatably weird. By the time he worked with Kurt, however, he was regarded as a postmodern pioneer who expanded the boundaries of literature, a reputation helped along by David Cronemburg's 1991 movie adaption of *Naked Lunch*.

It doesn't take a psychology degree to see what appealed to Kurt about *Naked Lunch*, a dizzying, nonlinear descent into the hell of heroin addiction that was so controversial in the 50s that it sparked an obscenity trial in the US. There was more to it than thematic crossover, though. Beneath the shock value, Burroughs was doing something truly innovative with the novel's 'cut-up' structure, which involved physically cutting up and rearranging pages of text to create a fractured, dreamlike narrative, a technique that Kurt, like David Bowie before him, borrowed heavily from. 'My lyrics are total cut-up,' he's quoted as saying in a piece in the *Chicago Sun Times*. 'I take lines from different poems that I've written. I build on a theme if I can, but sometimes I can't even come up with an idea of what the song is about.' It's trite to say that Kurt saw a kindred spirit in Burroughs, but his aura of an outsider artist who refused to compromise his vision for anyone was inspiring and relatable, certainly. When Nirvana played in Kansas in 1991 he'd even contemplated turning up on his doorstep. 'I had a Lead Belly record under my arm. I was ready to go,' he told *Monk*. 'But I was too nervous.'

For Cobain, who often felt suffocated, Burroughs was proof that it was possible to create art that was true to yourself, no matter how dark or challenging it might be. Both artists would go on to be touchstones for untouchably hip, subversive creativity – referencing Kurt now can feel like referencing Burroughs must have in the 80s and early 90s. Possibly more important than that, was the fact that Burroughs, at 79, had gone through pretty much everything Kurt had; overwhelming expectations and critical praise matched by outrage, depression and addiction, and had survived. As Nirvana's tour manager Alex MacLeod told author Casey Rae for his book *William Burroughs and the Cult of Rock 'N' Roll*, Burroughs was proof that there was a way out – 'It was "okay, I'm in this situation but I can last, I can get through".'

The pair's collaboration, which feels somehow both unlikely, given the generational divide, and a perfect match, had been instigated by Thor Lindsay of Portland-based label Tim/Kerr, who had recently worked with Nirvana on a Wipers tribute album, for which the band had contributed 'Return of the Rat'. The label had been founded originally with the specific purpose of releasing a collaboration between Burroughs and filmmaker Gus Van Sant called *Burroughs: The Elvis Letters*. Lindsay was probably the only person on earth who could bring William S. Burroughs and Kurt Cobain together, and had gifted Kurt a signed first edition of *Naked Lunch*, suggesting the pair could work on something. The then-77 year-old Burroughs was interested, and sent a recording he had made of his bleak short story 'The Junkies Christmas', originally published in the 1989 anthology *Interzone*. Kurt's guitar part, added at Barrett Jones' Laundry Room studio, was a discordant scratching through 'Silent Night' and 'The Star Spangled Banner', similar to the version he'd played at Reading a few months previously. Like a barely-honeyed take on Lou Reed's *Metal Machine Music*, Kurt's guitar feels isolated, abrasive uncomfortable and odd – the perfect accompaniment to Burroughs' dark story about a junkie priest looking for a Christmas fix. The piece would be released as a 10″ EP the following July.

including 'Swingin' on the flipperty-flop ("hanging out")', 'A Bloated Big Bag of Blotation ("drunk")' and 'Lamestain ("uncool person")'. All of the terms had been invented on the spot by Caroline Records sales rep and former Sup Pop receptionist Megan Jasper, who had received a call from a *Times* journalist and decided to mess with him.[87]

November 24

- Kurt asks *Rolling Stone*'s Michael Azerrad if he would be interested in writing an authorised biography of the band. Azerrad agrees on condition that he and his publishers, not Kurt and the band, have final sign-off on the book's contents. He will later spend hours interviewing Kurt, Krist, Dave, Courtney, Bruce Pavitt

87. 'If they're lame enough to scrutinise this stupid thing', she says in the documentary *Hype*, 'why not fuck with them?' Jasper's response is, in its own way, about as Gen X as it could possibly be, bringing to mind Mike Myers in the movie *Wayne's World* interviewing his fifty-something corporate sponsor with the words 'He blows goats, I have proof' written on the back of his interview cards with an arrow pointing at his guest, while the 'suits' producing his show have apoplexy. Thumbing your nose at the 'the man' was an age old tradition, and the *New York Times* was about as establishment as it is possible to be. That the *Times*, America's self-described 'newspaper of record', was writing about grunge, however, was a pretty clear indication of how huge the tiny scene that had grown around Sub Pop had become. Nirvana were, of course, the prime method by which its aesthetic had transmitted to the mainstream, but their peers were only a few steps behind them. Pearl Jam, Alice in Chains, Soundgarden ... these were some of the biggest bands in the US by the end of 1992, and any act looped into the same aesthetic was catapulted up with them, thus Stone Temple Pilots, Smashing Pumpkins, Blind Melon, Soul Asylum, Red Hot Chili Peppers, Lemonheads, Sugar, Nine Inch Nails ... they were all having hits. The major labels, meanwhile, were circling on their 'hunt for the next Nirvana', and pretty much any band tangentially related to the Seattle boom was getting huge deals. DGC, especially, emboldened by their success with Nirvana, went on an alt-rock spending spree; signing Hole, Weezer, Beck, Urge Overkill, Veruca Salt and Counting Crows all within a few years. Meanwhile Mudhoney and Babes In Toyland went to Reprise, L7 and TAD to subsidiaries of Warner and Screaming Trees to Epic. Even Melvins, probably the heaviest and most sonically uncompromising band in this story, had signed to Atlantic. 'Grunge', a genre made up on the spot to market Green River back in the 80s had *become* the mainstream.

   Grunge had even become a fashion movement, featuring the plaid shirts, ripped jeans and unwashed-looking hair that Seattle bands only favoured because plaid is cheap and warm, new jeans are expensive and Kurt Cobain was too lazy to wash his hair very often. They wore army surplus boots because they were hard-wearing and affordable, and Converse Chucks because, back then, they were simple and cheap. People didn't shop in thrift stores because it was cool. They shopped in thrift stores because *it was all they could afford*, and the outfits assembled were retro and mismatched because that's what happens when you assemble a wardrobe from second hand shops. Now those same outfits were being recreated by Marc Jacobs and sold for hundreds of dollars, while Perry Ellis was draping silk shirts that were styled to look like flannel around his runway models' waists. Even at the time, people were noting how weird this was. The *Times* article quotes the editor of men's fashion mag *Details* who seems pretty flummoxed by the whole thing. 'To me the thing about grunge is it's not anti-fashion, it's un fashion,' he says. 'Punk was anti-fashion. It made a statement. Grunge is about not making a statement, which is why it's crazy for it to become a fashion statement.' Charles R Cross said as much in the same article: '[Kurt] looked like (and was) a guy who slept on friends' couches or under a bridge, and bought his clothes at thrift shops.' Fashion mags talked about 'layering', ignoring that Kurt only wore several layers because he was scrawny and it bulked him out a bit, plus he lived in a cold and wet part of the country. Somehow, Kurt Cobain had singlehandily made looking cold and homeless into a fashion statement simply by being so charismatic and handsome that he looked good in anything. Back in the grunge heartland of Seattle, this was all viewed with suspicion. 'All things grunge are treated with the utmost cyncism and amusement,' Jonathan Poneman told the newpaper. 'Because the whole thing is a fabricated movement and always has been.' Which is, of course, a very grunge thing to say. Dave Thompson, in his book *The Grunge Diaries*, sums it up: 'Across the country regional papers and monthly magazines are sending journalists home with a pile of tourist brochures, a copy of *Nevermind*, and a photo of Tad, and demanding 2,000 words on the editor's desk by 9am.'

and Jonathan Poneman, former Nirvana members and anyone else he can find connected to the band.[88]

November 30

- 'In Bloom' is released as a single in the UK and US. The 7" and cassette are backed with a live version of 'Polly' recorded on the short tour opening for Red Hot Chili Peppers the previous December. The CD and 12" add 'Sliver' from the same show.[89]

December 15

- *Incesticide* is released.[90] It features original artwork by Kurt, who art-directed the entire project. The US version also includes liner notes in the form of an open letter to fans, in which Kurt celebrates what he felt were the big successes of the year: being sent a signed copy of the first Raincoats album, playing with Shonen Knife and the Vaselines, meeting Iggy Pop, collaborating with William Burroughs, opening for Sonic Youth, receiving drawings from Daniel Johnston[91] and being

88. This was an obvious attempt to neutralise the book Victoria Clarke and Britt Collins were writing (unnecessarily as it turned out – Gold Mountain were able to pressure both the UK and US publishers to drop the Clarke/Collins book, even after the authors offered the band full access to an early draft and the right of reply) by getting a fully endorsed biography on the market written by a sympathetic journalist who would have full access to the band. It's a smart move, and the decision to let Azerrad have an ostensible 'final cut' on the work was a better one. Azerrad is an exceptional writer with a genuine understanding of what made Nirvana unique and impactful, and he and Kurt instinctively connected – they were both underground rock fans who spent their lives revelling in that world. While the journalism in the book is mostly rigorous, the choice of writer achieved Kurt and Courtney's aim: Azerrad is largely loyal to his subjects, and while he doesn't always let them off the hook, he does always give them a right of reply and, often, the benefit of the doubt.

    The book, *Come As You Are*, was the first serious work on the band ever written and it stands as both a well-researched biography in its own right, and something of a time capsule, since, unlike most books on the band, it was written during their lifespan, hitting shelves around the time *In Utero* came out. Unlike most Nirvana biographies, it had a happy ending. There have been many, many books about Kurt and Nirvana since (usually more about the former than the latter), but most of them use *Come As You Are* in their base stock. Hell, even I'm guilty of that, although I've tried to give everything scrutiny. While Azerrad could be guilty, by his own admission, of indulging his subjects or not pressing them hard enough, *Come As You Are* still stands as an exceptional work. Better still, however, is *The Amplified Come As You Are*, an annotated edition released in 2023, in which the older Azerrad comments on his younger self and the band's responses with the benefit of thirty years of hindsight. While the original is a solid biography, the update is a fascinating look at journalistic ethics, personal bias and a vivid snapshot of a time and place. I'd recommend it highly.
89. You're right, this is an extremely uninspiring set of b-sides. What's more it breaks the accepted wisdom of the time – that a late single from an album that's been out for a while *needs* fresh b-sides to get fans to buy it. Nirvana, however, simply didn't have that many new songs, and what they did have were going to be needed for their next album.
90. With relatively little fanfare. Geffen were happy to have new product out, but also didn't want to oversaturate the market or burn out fans before the next true Nirvana album. Even so, the record still went gold within two months and has sold well over a million copies.
91. Daniel Johnston was the ultimate outsider artist. Based in Austin Texas, he churned out home-recorded cassettes of deceptively simple, almost child-like songs performed in a sing-song voice, with hand-drawn covers. Kurt had been introduced to him by Sub Pop's Bruce Pavitt, and he was, predictably, a favourite of the Olympia hipster set. Johnston's extremely lo-fi, oddly charming songs were almost absurdly influential

asked to produce the new Melvins album.[92] He also celebrates Courtney and Frances, emphasising his love for his wife and highlighting her smarts.[93] The note ends with a plea pretty-much unheard of in the annals of rock history, before or since: 'If any of you in any way hate homosexuals, people of different color, or women, please do this one favor for us – leave us the fuck alone! Don't come to our shows and don't buy our records.' The note is signed 'Kurdt (the blonde one)'.[94]

---

to several generations of artists, from Kurt and Beat Happening to Jeff Tweedy, Conor Oburst and the Mouldy Peaches. Kurt can be seen in *Rolling Stone* wearing a Johnston t-shirt featuring the now-iconic 'Hi, How Are You' frog design, gifted to him by Everett True. The endorsement was enough to get Johnston a deal with Atlantic.

92. With the possible exception of Iggy Pop, these are all names that wouldn't mean much to the wider *Nevermind*-buying fanbase. Kurt was specifically not mentioning Grammy nominations, MTV Awards, stadium shows or selling eight million records. It's not quite true to claim that this stuff didn't mean anything to Kurt, because he actively courted and felt he deserved that sort of mainstream success. He'd just never be caught admitting that to his fans. To them, he needed to frontload his outsider credentials. If you were being *really* cynical, you could say that such indier-than-thou posturing was as much about building up the brand identity of Kurt Cobain, underground art maverick, as it was about spreading the word about his favourite artists. Kurt's reputation as a super-authentic expert in outsider art was part of what got him a reputation as underground-overground king.
93. A later draft of the note contained a rant against *Vanity Fair* and Lynn Hirschberg. Kurt tried to get the album recalled so he could include his revised draft, but Danny Goldberg ultimately talked him out of it.
94. To this day I can't think of another band that has turned to their audience and said 'sorry, we don't want you listening to our music.' It was an aspect of Kurt's world-view that Axl Rose had identified in his rant against Nirvana earlier in the year, when he'd said, largely correctly, that Kurt felt himself 'too good and too cool to bring his rock 'n' roll to you ... he doesn't want you to like his music'. Even Courtney Love had called her husband out over that trait. 'If I was a kid, I'd spend my twenty dollars on Alice in Chains and the Chili Peppers,' she told Michael Azerrad. 'Because they *like* me – I'm not good enough for Kurt.'. In his defence, Kurt could easily say that no-one should have been surprised by this, because he'd been saying as much for years. 'We were the chosen rejects,' he'd told Danish radio station DR1 back in June. 'We chose not to be a part of the popular crowd'. It was just as true of his time in music as it was of his time at high school. On songs like 'Swap Meat' and 'Mr Moustache' Kurt was sneering at the people around him as early as 1988. The meathead jocks he met at Nirvana shows in 1989 were part of what led to his breakdown in Rome that year, feeding directly into 'In Bloom', which was written a few months later; his ultimate 'we don't want you as a fan' song. Kurt had been preparing to have mixed feelings about fame since way before they were justified. Which isn't to say that his feelings about homophobes, misogynists and racists weren't sincere. They absolutely were. It's just very rare for a rock star to truly have the courage to stand behind such convictions so absolutely.

Part Six

Oh Well, Whatever

1993

January/February[1]

- Kurt acts as a producer on the new Melvins album, *Houdini*; the band's major label debut.[2] However the sessions don't go well. Kurt's drug use meant he was nodding out often, but more seriously from Buzz Osborne's point of view, he simply wasn't showing up.[3] From Kurt's perspective, he felt the band were unprepared for the studio.[4] Kurt also contributes guitar on the song 'Sky Pup'.
- Kurt meets with Fender to develop a bespoke guitar – what would become the 'Jag-Stang'.[5]
- Kurt and Courtney move to Seattle.

1. Some work on the album was also done in the closing months of 1992. There's not a record of which sessions Kurt was involved with. He seems to have done the bulk of his work in January 1993, however.
2. As previously mentioned, there was a feeding frenzy going on around alternative rock bands at the the time, and Melvins were one of the progenitors of the form. They were not short of offers. In the end they went with Atlantic, which at this point was being run by Nirvana's manager, Danny Goldberg, who had left Gold Mountain, the company he'd founded, to take the job – though he was still involved in managing Nirvana and Hole. He signed Melvins essentially because Kurt told him to. They got a dream deal, too – full artistic control with a clause saying the label couldn't make them re-record an album if they didn't like it. Goldberg knew exactly what he was getting, and after four years of working first with Sonic Youth, then Nirvana and Hole he absolutely understood the importance of a few token outsider bands being allowed to do their own thing. He also knew that Kurt's name on the record as producer was always going to shift some copies. Kurt was evangelistic about the Melvins.
3. 'It wasn't the nodding off, I can deal with nodding off … I've dealt with drugs and things of that nature for years,' he told the *Life of the Record* podcast in 2023. 'What I can't handle is people not showing up … Finally, I went into Danny Goldberg's office and told him that we can't work with Kurt any more and basically fired him'. Goldberg remembers things differently. 'Was Kurt fired?' he asks Mark Yarm. 'I wouldn't have tolerated such a thing. He finished his work on it and he did an okay job.' This is the version that Courtney Love supports, but then Courtney and Buzz Osborne are, to say the least, not fond of one another.
4. 'He was very disappointed that, in his mind, they hadn't prepared for the record the way he prepared for his records,' Danny Goldberg told Mark Yarm. 'They didn't have the material.' Dale Crover holds his hands up to this as well. 'We didn't have any songs at the time,' he says in *Everybody Loves Our Town*. According to this account, Goldberg, Crover and Osborne all suggested that Kurt co-write some material for the album and that he simply didn't want to, eventually losing patience with the project. Buzz Osborne vehemently denies this: 'I don't need anybody to help me write songs. Clearly. I've written and recorded probably close to 500 songs,' he said on *Life Of The Record*. 'Last thing I need is for him to write songs.' Ultimately, everyone was aware of the real reason it was important to have Kurt's name associated with the record: 'Kurt was there in name, and that was obviously the important thing for the marketing department,' Jonathan Burnside, who engineered and mixed much of the album, told Nicholas Soulsby. 'Never mind if his head, heart, or soul weren't anywhere present. Never mind that he seemed very depressed.'
5. This was actually Kurt's second bespoke guitar. Kurt loved playing Fender Mustangs, but left-handed models were rare and Nirvana's road team were struggling to find parts, especially necks, to repair them after the inevitable nightly destruction they endured. In 1992 he'd had a craftsman called Danny Ferrington

January 1

- Kurt is photographed by Charles Peterson for the cover of gay magazine, *The Advocate*.[6]

January 7

- The Grammy nominations are announced. 'Smells Like Teen Spirit' is nominated for the 'Best Hard Rock Performance with a Vocal' category. Other nominees are Guns N' Roses, Faith No More, Pearl Jam, Alice in Chains and Red Hot Chili Peppers.[7]

January 16

- Nirvana play the first of a pair of huge shows in Brazil as part of the two-city Hollywood Rocks festival, beginning in São Paulo (a second show will be held a week later in Rio de Janeiro). Estimates of the crowd are between 80,000 and

---

create a new guitar for him, a bespoke modified Mustang (which Nirvana guitar tech Ernie Bailey later modified further) which he'd been really happy with. In February 1993, with a year as a huge rock star under his belt, he was able to swing a meeting with Fender themselves to get a new guitar especially made. The 'Jag-Stang', as it came to be named, was a hybrid of Kurt's two favourite Fender models – the Jaguar (a more high-end version of the Mustang, and Kurt's favoured guitar on the *Nevermind* tours) and the more common and budget friendly Mustang, using a Mustang-style 24" short-scale neck with a custom body shape that merged elements of both guitars into a garagey, 60s style. According to Fender's Larry Brooks, writing on the company's website, Kurt 'took photographs of each, cut them in half, and put them together to see what they'd look like.' Going back and forth with the Fender Custom Shop, Kurt specified the design and features he wanted. Two prototypes were built, one in 'Sonic Blue' and one in 'Fiesta Red'. The blue one was delivered to Kurt, who used it briefly on the *In Utero* tour in 1993 and 1994 … once Bailey had modified it further. The red one was still being finished when Kurt passed away in April 1994. The blue model was later gifted to REM's Peter Buck, who can be seen playing it in the 'What's The Frequency Kenneth' video. After Kurt's death, and with the permission of his estate, Fender put the Jag-stag into mass production, and it's been revived a few times. Ernie Bailey, however, has always been sceptical about some of Fender's claims regarding Kurt's involvement and enthusiasm for a 'signature' model, doubting that Kurt ever intended for the guitar to be mass-produced, believing he just wanted a custom instrument for himself. He also said Kurt didn't like the Jag-Stang that much when he received it, finding it unbalanced, as he had forgotten to have Fender do certain contours. Still, with some further modifications by Bailey, Kurt did use the Jag-Stang on rare occasions, including at Nirvana's last ever show. In 2015, Fender also produced a reproduction of Kurt's 1965 sunburst Jaguar, available with a 'road worn' finish intended to mimic the look of Kurt's original.

6. Kurt was being understandably choosy about the press he did at this point, and he had turned down almost everyone with the exception of *Spin*'s PR puff piece and *The Advocate*, the long-running gay magazine. Nirvana had gone from putting Kurt's personal phone number on press releases to a point where even local supporters like *The Rocket* had to go through either DGC or Gold Mountain to get access, yet Courtney Love instructed a mutual friend to hand over the couple's details to *The Advocate*'s Kevin Allman, explaining simply that 'gay people can have our phone number.' Queer advocacy was a serious mission of the band's. As Michael Azerrad puts it in *The Amplified Come As You Are*, 'Kurt made it clear that Nirvana shows were a safe space for gay people. And that was truly visionary … back then, rock stars defending gay people was very rare and very bold'. This was an era when Axl Rose sang homophobic slurs, when Sebastian Bach from Skid Row wore his 'AIDS kills fags dead' shirt, when even a film as harmless as *Bill & Ted's Excellent Adventure* had homophobic language built into its script. Nirvana took advocacy and acceptance further than any comparable sized act of their era.
7. If you're wondering how come 'Smells Like Teen Spirit' was nominated in 1993 while *Nevermind* was nominated in 1992, despite the single having been released *before* the album, then join the club. For reasons best known to the US National Academy of Recording Arts And Sciences, there are different rules for singles and albums. The machinations of the Grammys have long made absolutely no sense.

110,000 people – either way it is the biggest audience Nirvana will ever play to. The band play a poorly received, rambling set full of jams, instrument swapping and impromptu cover versions. Two new songs are debuted – early versions of 'Heart Shaped Box' and 'Scentless Apprentice', though neither is in especially sparkling form. Flea from Red Hot Chili Peppers provides a trumpet solo on 'Smells Like Teen Spirit'.[8]

January 19–21

- Having decamped to Rio (alongside the other bands on the bill[9]), Nirvana book time in a local studio to work on demos with soundman Craig Montgomery. Focusing (for the first time in a long time) entirely on tracks that haven't been demoed before[10]. The band track versions of 'Heart Shaped Box'[11], 'Scentless

8. This is another of those big pay-day shows that no-one particularly wanted to do. Again, they hadn't rehearsed and relations in the band had slipped again ('Nirvana totally wouldn't talk to each other,' L7's Jennifer Finch told Mark Yarm. 'Everyone was at the end of their rope with the drug and sickness situation with Kurt'.) Kurt didn't endear himself to his bandmates by taking valium and mixing it with booze before the show. The first half hour wasn't bad; not the most focused Nirvana show but absolutely fine. After that, though, things started to slip. Flea's trumpet on 'Smells Like Teen Spirit' is fun, but it's a sloppy rendition and Kurt's guitar is all over the place. By the end of 'On A Plain' he's fudging chords, and he forgets how to play 'Negative Creep' altogether – eventually Krist has to step in and start the song after which, fortunately, muscle memory kicks in. Kurt's semi-sarcastic shouts to the crowd ('is everyone having a good time tonight? ROCK 'N' ROLL!') and pleas to lighting designer Susanne Sasic to lower too-bright lights or change colours ('I don't look very good in blue') come across as borderline deranged, as do the improvised new lyrics to a dirgey and pretty horrible 'Something In The Way'. 'I could shit on stage and you would eat it up,' sings Kurt as he proceeds to do just that to one of his best songs. The show becomes increasingly difficult to listen to as it goes along, though Kurt seems to be trying to have a good time ('I'm going to be on the cover of *Guitar World* next month,' he drawls before attempting ironic widdley-widdley solo-ing on 'Blew', which would be funny if he wasn't messing up the song anyway). The band meander through terrible jams, Kurt playing tunelessly. 'It looked like three kids in a desperate attempt to stretch their time on stage,' said Brazillian magazine *Top Rock*. 'They played so badly that fans of the band began to leave in fury before the end of the performance.' At one point Krist, who has done God's work trying to hold things together, literally throws his bass at his singer and storms off stage – only to be dragged back so the band can do their contractual time and keep their fee. 'Spectators go from euphoria to despair in the space of one and a half hours,' one reviewer writes. At the end of the show, Kurt spends so long destroying instruments by himself, Krist and Dave having long walked off, that Courtney and guitar tech Ernie Bailey have to pull him off the stage. The destruction is so extreme that the band had to get new guitar cabs shipped from LA in order to play the Rio show the following week. Kurt, for his part, seems to be having a marvelous time throughout the set. Unlike his band. Or audience.
9. 'The one time I saw Kurt happy with his job was when we went to Rio,' Courtney told Mark Yarm. 'We had a bodyguard, we stayed at a four-star hotel. Hung out with Pearl Jam, Alice in Chains … he had fun mingling with his people.' Other accounts of the the Rio trip are nowhere near so breezy. According to Charles R. Cross Kurt 'had become suicidal that week' and was threatening to jump out of a window after a fight with Courtney. Cross quotes Nirvana production manager Jeff Mason – 'We checked into hotel after hotel, but couldn't stay because we'd walk into a room and there would be a balcony , and he would be ready to jump'. Meanwhile, Alice In Chains' Mike Starr, playing his last show with the band, remembers shooting heroin with Kurt and Courtney in Rio, a city where he himself later OD'd. It feels a little odd for Courtney to be so glib about the whole thing.
10. Much of Nirvana's upcoming record had been written at the same time as the later *Nevermind* material, or immediately after the album had been done, and the band had been playing with new ideas in dribs and drabs ever since, though with nowhere close to the level of output they'd hit in 1991. By this point 'All Apologies', 'Pennyroyal Tea', 'Dumb', 'Rape Me', 'Sappy' and 'Radio Friendly Unit Shifter' had been kicking around for a few years, having been set aside for later, while 'Tourettes' and 'Frances Farmer Will Have Her Revenge On Seattle' were also in pretty good shape. That's more than half an album, right there.
11. At this point known as 'Heart Shaped Coffin', and the most Courtney-influenced of all of Kurt's songs (Courtney collected heart-shaped chocolate boxes – make what you will of Kurt's allusions to

Apprentice'[12], 'Milk It'[13], 'Moist Vagina',[14] 'Very Ape'[15], a song known only as 'The Other Improv'[16], a Dave Grohl-led cover of 'Onwards Into Countless Battles' by Swedish metal band Unleashed[17], 'Gallons of Rubbing Alcohol Will Flow Through The Strip'[18], 'I Hate Myself and I Want to Die'[19] and an oddly affecting

---

being trapped inside one). Kurt had written this in the first half of 1992, and it continues the favourite Nirvana/Pixies trick of the quiet verse and loud chorus, but has more discordant sourness embedded in its bubblegum than anything the band had yet written. There's a lot of early-solo John Lennon here too in its deceptively simple, bitter pop. Even in this early demo, with half-formed lyrics, it's clearly a brilliant piece and an obvious single, somehow sounding perfectly Nirvana while simultaneously sounding like a stride forward from *Nevermind.* You can imagine a lot of people at Geffen breathing a sigh of relief when this was handed in. Legend has it (and by 'legend' I mean something Courtney has said in an interview), when Courtney first heard the riff she asked Kurt if she could have it for the Hole album, to which, according to a quote in *Rolling Stone*, he replied 'fuck you'. Courtney had also wanted to record 'Pennyroyal Tea' for *Live Through This*, which annoyed Kurt to the point that he asked Danny Goldberg to dissuade her from the idea.

12. One of only three Nirvana songs credited to all three members (the other two being 'Smells Like Teen Spirit' and 'Aneurysm'.) This one is based around a Dave Grohl guitar riff, and has the trio's inherent chemistry built into its core. The band's 2004 rarities box set, *With The Lights Out*, carries an astonishing nine-minute rehearsal demo of the song recorded in 1992 which begins as discordant riffage and builds, layer upon layer, into something very close to the finished song, as Kurt finds that nerve-damaged ascending riff and his screaming melody. It's the Punk Rock equivalent of that moment in Peter Jackson's *Get Back* Beatles documentary where we watch Paul McCartney writing the title track in real time. 'It's a good example of the Nirvana dynamic at work,' Krist told Gillian G. Gaar for her book *In Utero*. 'There's three players but there's a lot of stuff going on.' Initially Kurt hadn't been too impressed with Dave's riff ('It was such a cliché grunge TAD riff,' as he told Michael Azerrad), which itself had come out of a jam Krist and Dave had recorded the previous October with Scratch Acid/Rapeman drummer Rey Washam. Jamming on it, however, had given Kurt a solid base to scrawl over. The riff itself is what lent the song its working title: 'Chuck Chuck Fo Fuck'.
13. 'Milk It', along with 'Scentless Apprentice' gives us an idea of the band Nirvana were becoming. These are songs that couldn't have appeared on *Bleach* or *Nevermind.* They're acidic and uncomfortable, built around great riffs but spiked with a more dynamic sense of creativity. A lot of this is down to Dave Grohl. 'Milk It', especially, has a very Nirvana sense of bitter playfulness combined with a real muscularity. It's art rock, and a million miles away from anything their Seattle peers were doing … with the possibile exception of the Melvins, whose 1991 song 'It's Shoved' has a suspiciously similar riff, though none of the taut execution. Nirvana guitar tech Ernie Bailey remembers playing the song for Dale Crover – 'When it started, I saw the puzzled look come across Dale's face,' he told Everett True, 'which gradually changed as he realised it was a compliment, ultimately'. Buzz Osborne was a little more frank, talking to the long-defunct website *MP3.com* back in to 2011. 'Of course I like this song!' he says of 'Milk It'. 'Of course I like it because it's a total, TOTAL rip off of a song I wrote!'
14. Destined for b-sidedom, and one of the stranger pieces in the band's canon. There's something oddly beguiling about it though. It manages to be quite silly and knowing while also feeling … desolate? Courtney was, apparently, not a fan of the lyrics which here consist mainly of the title repeated over and over. The later version would swap 'Moist Vagina' for 'Marijuana'.
15. Known at this point as 'Pesky New Wave Number', one of *In Utero's* more straightforward Punk Rock moments.
16. This one was doomed to stay the formless jam recorded here – the idea doesn't seem to have been developed much further.
17. A Stockholm-based death metal outfit. This song, which is rather silly (as much death metal, rather knowingly, is) was taken from their 1992 album *Shadows In The Deep*. Dave plays bass, drums, guitar and lead vocal here, with Kurt doing backing vocals. Its very throwaway, done presumably just for fun.
18. Another lenghty noise jam, though more freeform and less angsty than 'Endless, Nameless'. This recording would eventually be tagged as a hidden track on *In Utero* (though curiously, not in the US). The band sound like they're having a lot of fun here, with Kurt free-forming poetry and cueing the trio into quiet and loud sections. It's Nirvana being their most Nirvanesque.
19. For a long time 'I Hate Myself and I Want to Die' was Kurt's working title for *In Utero*. It was meant to be dripping with sarcasm, but of course in the light of the events of the next year or so the title becomes substantially less funny. It's also wasted on this song, a grungey new-waver that feels a little art-rock by numbers.

cover of Terry Jacks' 'Seasons In The Sun'[20]. Some Hole songs are also demoed including 'Miss World'[21]. The sessions feel fruitful, and the band feels creative.[22]

January 23

- The second date of the Hollywood Rock festival[23] takes place at the Apoteose Stadium in Rio de Janeiro. Nirvana's set is far more consistent than at the São Paulo show. It's not without errors (Kurt playing the opening bars of 'Been A Son' while Krist and Dave are playing 'On A Plain' is a doozy) but they're nowhere close to as bad as they had been at the previous gig. 'Smells Like Teen Spirit', often lacklustre nowadays, is a delight with RHCP's Flea once again playing a flamboyant trumpet solo and moshing throughout. A hesitant version of 'Heart Shaped Box' slowly forms itself into something pretty wonderful, and a 17-minute improv around the new 'Scentless Apprentice' is as good a Nirvana noise jam as you'll find, though your tolerance will vary on those in general. It's during this song that an impish, if slightly stoned looking Kurt famously exposes himself to the live cameras on stage causing a minor scandal.[24] The show closes with Dave and Kurt in lingerie running through a solid encore of 'Dive', 'Lounge Act', 'Aneurysm' and 'Territorial Pissings'[25]. There is, however, no instrument smashing.[26]

February 12–26

- Recording begins on Nirvana's new album at Pachyderm Studios, a large residential studio in Cannon Falls, Minnesota, with Steve Albini behind the board.[27] To

---

20. 'Seasons In The Sun' was one of Kurt's all time favourite songs, and was apparently the first single he ever bought. He'd been delighted in 1991 when Television Personalities, the legendary UK post punk band, had closed their set supporting Nirvana at the Astoria with it. The original has always been an odd little thing, full of melancholy and regret and a sense of fading, told with a plaintive naivety. Nirvana's version, though knockabout, captures some of that. In the aftermath of Kurt's suicide it's absolutely devastating, of course. Here the band are having fun, though – Kurt is on drums, Dave on bass and Krist on guitar.
21. This early version of one of Courtney's very best songs would later appear on the compilation *My Body The Hand Grenade* (essentially Hole's version of *Incesticide*). In Carrie Borzillo's *Nirvana: The Day-By-Day Eyewitness Chronicle,* Craig Montgomery confirms that Kurt is playing bass on the track, with Courtney on guitar and Hole's new drummer, Patty Schemel on drums.
22. Though not everyone thought so at the time. Craig Montgomery, engineering the session, remembers feeling that the band didn't have enough material. 'My feeling at the time,' he told Mark Yarm, 'was 'Wow, good luck making an album guys, you're in trouble'. Which is a curious thing to say given the seven or eight really good songs Montgomery was well aware were ready to go and the obvious appeal of 'Heart Shaped Box'.
23. 'Hollywood' incidentally, was a Brazillian cigarette brand. The company had sponsored the festival since its inception in the 80s. Nirvana didn't actually know this when the gig was booked, since the name is fairly bland. Despite being prodigious smokers themselves, they were deeply uncomfortable with the idea of promoting smoking to young fans in such an overt way. Kurt had enough of a reputation for various vices as it was.
24. The footage is out there – you can decided for yourself if you can 'see' anything or not ...
25. Once Kurt remembered the chords.
26. Several clips from this show can be found on the *Live! Tonight! Sold Out!* home video. It's really not that bad a gig considering the car crash of the previous week.
27. The studio had been Albini's suggestion. Not only was it a great space that he knew well, with all the facilities the biggest band in the world would expectt to find in a residential studio ('Posh shit like a sauna and swimming pool and fireplaces and trout stream and 50 acres and shit like that' as Albini

maintain secrecy the booking is made under the name 'The Simon Richie Bluegrass Ensemble', Simon Richie being, of course, Sid Vicious' real name.[28] The band's management and label reps are banned from coming to the sessions.[29] The sessions go incredibly smoothly. Nirvana, knowing that time was limited, were extremely well rehearsed and prepared, and Albini's philosophy was always to record what a band actually *sounded* like.[30] The basic tracking for several songs is done on the first day of full recording, and almost all of the bass, drums and basic guitars are completed within a few days, mostly recorded live, with the remaining time left for overdubbing vocals, additional guitars[31], cello on some of the mellower numbers, and mixing. In all, 18 songs are recorded – 'Serve The Servants'[32] (which was the first song recorded on the first day), 'Scentless

---

had said in his letter), it also had a proven track record. Minnesota natives Babes In Toyland, who had known Nirvana for years, had made their major label debut *Fontanelle* there in 1992, and Soul Asylum's massive-selling *Grave Dancers Union* had been recorded there a little before that. Albini had recently used it for PJ Harvey's brilliant *Rid of Me*. The other big advantage is that Pachyderm is miles from pretty much anything. It was a fully residential studio without the temptations of LA or Seattle floating around within reach. Kurt was again trying to stay clean(ish) so this was big plus. The plan was to make an album in two weeks, which required a level of focus a messed-up Kurt Cobain wouldn't be capable of. The isolation was made more acute by the Minnesota winter – it snowed heavily for much of the sessions.

28. Kurt, a big Sex Pistols fan, had always been a little obsessed with Vicious and of course there *are* some parallels between the two – with the very obvious difference that Kurt was extremely smart and an astonishingly talented musician. Kurt and Courtney could sometimes be guilty of leaning into their Sid 'N' Nancy vibe, which since Courtney was constantly being cast by the media in the role of a 90s Nancy Spungen was only too tempting.
29. In truth, Geffen were indulging Nirvana with these recordings, and there was a general feeling that once they'd spent a few weeks getting all their noisy ideas out of their system with Albini, they could be bundled off somewhere with a proper big name producer to make the *actual* record. 'It was like, Go and have your fun, then we'll get another producer and make the real album,' Dave later told *Q*.
30. For all of Steve Albini's brilliantly quotable posturing and philosophising, all three of Nirvana's albums were made in a pretty similar way – intensive rehearsal, followed by a couple of weeks in the studio in which the basic tracks are knocked out live, with extra guitars, any other sounds and Kurt's vocals overdubbed. Alibini was very particular about how he recorded drums (apparently 30 microphones were used to record the drums alone), and tried his best to work with the sounds the band presented him with, rather than trying to build on them as Butch Vig had … but to all intents and purposes *Nevermind* and *In Utero* were not recorded in especially different ways. If anything, Pachyderm may have been a fancier studio than the sticky-floored and gaffa-taped together Sound City but both studios used vintage Neve consoles and both 'producers' (as much as Albini would hate the term) did their best to serve the songs they were presented with. Perhaps the most apt metaphor for the difference between the two experiences was happening outside the studio window: one album was recorded in the LA sunshine, the other in the Minnesota snow.
31. During a podcast interview for Spotify to mark the album's 20th anniversary, Albini talked about how Kurt never felt beholden to preserving Nirvana as a trio on record and was brimming with ideas for expanding the guitars, an interesting contrast to the *Nevermind* sessions, where Butch Vig had occasionally resorted to tricking Kurt into double-tracking his parts. 'Some of them were counterpoint, some of them were contrast, and some of them were just bolstering what was already going on,' he said. 'But he was adamant about having the three-piece band supplemented by this phantom fourth member pretty much all the time.'
32. The only song on *In Utero* to not be demoed properly and one of only two songs to not be played live prior to the sessions, 'Serve The Servants' is very much the album in miniature. Dave counts the band in and we open with a dischord – an absolutely unholy racket. So unholy, in fact, it pushed the needle into the red on the recording desk just for a moment, as Kurt had used a different effect to the one Albini had been expecting. Albini quickly pulls the fader and rebalances the sound, but that overdriven first beat is the first sound we hear on *In Utero*: a glaring, ugly sonic mistake. *Nevermind* began with the most accessible riff Nirvana would ever write, and it's not a coincidence that its follow-up goes in entirely the other direction. It's the band testing the listener: 'This is not necessarily what you were expecting.' It's

Apprentice'[33], 'Heart Shaped Box', 'Rape Me'[34], 'Frances Farmer Will Have Her

slightly undone by the fact that Kurt is just borrowing from The Beatles, who pulled the same trick with 'A Hard Days Night' 30 years earlier, and by the fact that the riff that emerges from that chaotic burst is super catchy. The chorus even more so. If the opening seconds didn't clue you into what Kurt was doing, then the lyrics certainly would. The first line on the entire album is an absolute all-time great; an acknowledgment of how Kurt feels he is seen by others versus how he sees himself. The whole lyric is sarcastic, even funny, very smart and utterly exhausted. The verses have references to the media witch hunt surrounding Courtney and also Kurt's relationship with his father, while the chorus simply complains about having to talk about his parent divorce all the time. It's quintessentially Kurt Cobain – he'd used his music to work through his pain, and now he was complaining that people had noticed. So he's using that too. Incidentally, this is one of Courtney Love's favourite Nirvana songs.

33. Kurt had completed his lyric by this point, with this song being inspired by Patrick Suskind's novel *Perfume*, about a serial killer *perfumier* who has no odour of his own, and uses his victims to create new scents.
34. Central theme aside, which we've discussed elsewhere, 'Rape Me' immediately became one of Nirvana's most subversive moments simply by *sounding a lot like 'Smells Like Teen Spirit'* while *being called 'Rape Me'*. Its intro is almost identical; the same rhythm circling four chords with that staccato scratch between the changes, all of which come in the same place, and the same quiet verses exploding into loud choruses. It's also monstrously catchy. It's the most straightforward song on *In Utero*, and would probably be the most obvious single on the album and a sure fire smash hit … if it wasn't called 'Rape Me', which also happens to be the opening line. You can imagine how frustrating that must have been for Geffen, and how gleefully Kurt would have welcomed that frustration. It's an act of commercial trolling so acutely well observed that you'd assume it was done on purpose… which, of course, it wasn't. 'Rape Me' was one of the oldest songs on the album, having been kicking around in Nirvana's live set since June 1991 – months before *Nevermind* was released. In fact, arguably, the shifting context of Nirvana's career rather rescued it from being a re-treading of old musical ideas. It made it look deliberate. New bands inspired directly by Nirvana were starting to mushroom across the globe, many of which would become major stars in the coming years – the likes of Weezer, Creed, Silverchair, Bush, Candlebox, Live, Seether and Puddle of Mudd were all just around the corner; some of them are great bands, some absolutely awful. All of them had songs with the same structure and form as 'Rape Me'. But none of them could have actually written it themselves. No-one else would combine *that* theme with *that* melody. It's pure Kurt Cobain.

Revenge On Seattle'[35], 'Dumb'[36], 'Very Ape'[37], 'Milk It'[38], 'Pennyroyal Tea'[39], 'Radio

35. Frances Farmer was a Seattle-born actress that shone brightly but briefly across 1930s and '40s Hollywood, all razor-sharp cheekbones, smoldering gaze, and attitude. On-screen, Farmer was a crackling force of nature, delivering raw, emotionally charged performances. She had a unique ability to convey both vulnerability and strength, often playing complex, independent women who defied societal norms. Off-screen, however, her disdain for the Hollywood system made her a handful to work with. As director William Wyler once famously said, 'The nicest thing I can say about Frances Farmer is that she is unbearable'. Courtney Love, who wore one of Farmer's antique dresses at her wedding, could surely relate. As compelling as Farmer could be, her career was overshadowed by her alcoholism and erratic behavior, leading to several arrests and an involuntary stay in psychiatric care, prompted partly by the press attention her behaviour attracted, where she was allegedly mistreated with insulin shock therapy. Though she lived until 1970 and worked fairly consistently, she never regained the promise of her early career.
36. The version of 'Dumb' done with Albini for *In Utero* is extremely close to the one recorded for the Peel session in September 1991, down to every line of the lyric, and Albini captures the lonely, desolate feel of the song beautifully, leaning into the feel Phil Spector got when recording the *John Lennon/Plastic Ono Band* album. Aside from the better production, the only notable difference is a lovely, sad cello on the album version played by Albini's girlfriend, Kera Schaley, whom he flew in especially. Cello, after all, had worked beautifully on 'Something In The Way', so it made sense to repeat the trick here. Schaley says she wrote her own parts for the songs on *In Utero*, under direction from Kurt ('he was like, "Yeah, that's good. Can you also mirror what I'm playing for this guitar line?"' she told *Rolling Stone* in 2023). Schaley also makes a guest appearance, courtesy of Courtney, in Azerrad's *Come As You Are*. While discussing her clashes with Albini (by all accounts Courtney was a huge pain during the short time she flew in for the *In Utero* sessions, though Albini, Grohl and Novoselic have always politely swerved the details when pressed), Courtney told the biographer that 'the only way Steve Albini would think I was a perfect girlfriend would be if I was from the East Coast, played the cello, had big tits and small hoop earrings, wore black turtlenecks, had all matching luggage and never said a *word*' – a dismissive but apparently accurate description of Kera Schaley at the time.
37. 'Very Ape' was exactly the sort of thing Geffen were dreading, and in a rougher form could be chucked in the b-side bucket with 'Curmudgeon' and 'Oh, The Guilt'. There's a bit more to it though; the verses are incredibly catchy and Kurt adds a really effective high-pitched riff that flips octave half-way through. It acts like a leash that tugs you through the whole thing. Albini gives this some real oomph – the boom of the kick drum and the growl of the bass absolutely carry it. Like 'Tourettes', it's throwaway, but *In Utero* kind of wouldn't be *In Utero* without it. Incidentally in *The Amplified Come As You Are,* Michael Azerrad points out how similar the riff to 'Very Ape' is to the song 'Kanishka' by Argentinian band Los Brujos, the opening act for Nirvana's 'legendary' show in Buenos Aires the previous year. He is, well … not wrong.
38. One of the big differences between *Nevermind* and *In Utero* was its complexity. Almost any high school garage band could nail 'Lithium' and have a descent stab at 'Smells Like Teen Spirit' – but try playing 'Milk It' from a standing start and you'll quickly see that it's a very different animal. *In Utero* was Dave Grohl's chance to shine; though his playing is a big part of *Nevermind*'s character, most of the songs on the album had been written before he joined, and many of the later ones were pretty straightforward. The structures and dynamics on *In Utero* are far more complex, and 'Milk It' is a perfect example. The verses feel like they could wobble apart at any second if not for Grohl's absolutely unshakeable tempo, around which the bass and guitars snake and shiver. Very little of what Grohl does on 'Milk It', and for that matter 'Scentless Apprentice' or even 'Heart-Shaped Box' are first-base choices. He always takes a less obvious route with his drum compositions, making choices that bring extra dimensions to Kurt's songs, and since Kurt himself was pushing into more complex structures and moods, the results are far more sonically interesting than anything the other grunge acts were doing at the time. No-one else would write such visceral, scatological lyrics either, which epitomise *In Utero*'s themes of bodily fluids, muck, effluence, milk and the viscera of birth.
39. The oldest song on *In Utero*, and one of Kurt's very best, was written somewhere in the back half of 1990, and premiered live on the same night as 'Smells Like Teen Spirit', at the OK Hotel in April 1991. It had been in and out of the setlist through the intervening few years, and hadn't really changed much in form since Kurt's original demo, recorded in the apartment he was sharing with Dave. It was writing 'Pennyroyal Tea' that convinced Dave of Kurt's absolute melodic gifts. Kurt had workshopped the lyrics with Courtney since then, which is probably why it's one of his most poetically accomplished songs. Courtney herself occasionally describes it as 'co-written' (she says as much to an *NME* journalist a few months later), though that's a bit of a stretch – the version on *In Utero* is certainly refined and honed, but its bones are still very, very similar to Kurt's original demo. Kurt certainly didn't think it was enough of a collaboration to give her a co-writing credit, despite the boost that would have given both her credibility and the legitimacy of their creative relationship. He even asked their manager (Danny Goldberg managed

Friendly Unit Shifter'[40], 'Tourettes'[41], 'All Apologies'[42], 'Sappy'[43], 'I Hate Myself and I Want To Die'[44], 'Moist Vagina'[45] and 'Marigold'[46]. Also captured are a jam

---

both – poor guy) to dissuade her from pushing to get it on *Live Through This*. That said, it's definitely the Nirvana song that sounds most like Hole, who added it to their setlist throughout 1993 and 1994. Kurt and Courtney would perform it together at a Rock Against Rape benefit in September 1993, with Courtney taking the lead vocals, and it's one of the best performances of the song you'll hear.

'Pennyroyal Tea' had been held back from *Nevermind* as Kurt didn't feel it was quite strong enough, and if you listen to the early version you can see his point. *Nevermind* didn't really need 'Pennyroyal Tea' anyway. It already had plenty going on. It fits magnificently on *In Utero* however, with its lyrics swimming in fluids and medication (the titular 'pennyroyal tea' is a reference to a herb said to bring about miscarriage). Like 'Rape Me' it sticks to the tried-and-true Nirvana format of quiet/loud/quiet, though here it sounds less formulaic. In the context of the band's career, the dynamics at play on 'Rape Me' feel knowing, even cynical. On 'Pennyroyal Tea', however, that roar into distortion on the chorus feels cathartic and utterly natural. It couldn't be less of a gimmick.

40. Kurt is really down on 'Radio Friendly Unit Shifter' in interviews. 'It could have been better,' he told his biographer. 'I know we could have had a few better songs on the album'. I'm not sure what the issue is – the riff is great, the arrangement is cool, the lyrics are actually really good, and that atonal feedback at the start and in the breakdown makes a gorgeously discordant racket. Plus the title is amazing. 'Radio Friendly Unit Shifter' would be Nirvana's default set-opener for the rest of their career, which isn't bad for a song Kurt considered 'throwaway'.
41. Another throwaway punk number, which could cynically be seen as someone in the band saying 'this album needs a 'Territorial Pissings' moment'. The lyrics are a tumble of disconnected words and screams, which is probably where the title comes from – sufferers from Tourette's Syndrome make involuntary noises and tics, which sometimes manifest in aggressive language or swearing. 1993 also saw the release of Manic Street Preachers' second album *Gold Against The Soul*, which features a song called 'Symphony of Tourette' that engages with the same disorder – though of course it's the Manics' third album, *The Holy Bible* that's often seen as a companion piece to *In Utero*.
42. This version is light years ahead of the Velvet Underground-aping instrumental recorded with Craig Montgomery back on New Years Day, 1991. Albini's recording is stark and powerful, and Kera Schaley's improvised cello weaves in and out of the melody. It's a brilliant album closer – noisy but incredibly poignant.
43. This final recording of a song Nirvana had been knocking about since 1989 is probably the best of the four full-band studio versions (one with Jack Endino, two with Butch Vig), though still wasn't thought good enough for the album. It's a shame, because it's a great recording of an underappreciated song. The key has changed again, and there's more sonic grit here than the abandoned take at Sound City for *Nevermind*, with Albini's textbook drums booming away, but broadly it's the same song with the same feel. You can see the band's point, though – it would probaby have sat oddly on *In Utero*; it doesn't feel of a piece with the rest of the record at all, possibly because it dated back to such a different era of the band. After all, Chad Channing was still around when the first version of 'Sappy' had been recorded. Eventually this recording would be released as a hidden track on a 1993 AIDS benefit compilation, *No Alternative*, though the song had been renamed 'Verse Chorus Verse' by this point, the title of another long-abandoned Nirvana track and briefly mooted as a title for both *Nevermind* and *In Utero*. Since the title doesn't actually appear anywhere on the *No Alternative* sleeve it was later changed back to 'Sappy' for future archive releases, presumably to avoid confusion. Which might be possibly be too late.
44. The slightest of all of the finished *In Utero* recordings, this version was later gifted to a compilation album, *The Beavis and Butthead Experience*, a tie-in with the popular MTV none-more-Gen-X animated show, which the band were fond of. It's not a tune anyone was especially keen on, however – it's one of the very few Nirvana songs to have never been performed live.
45. I *love* this version of 'Moist Vagina', from its ridiculous lyrics to the weird, dry, creaking noise Kurt makes at the back of his throat that closes the song, like some sort of odd, anti-feedback. There's very little going on here, it's all very simple but very knowing and very effective. It was eventually used as the b-side for the 'All Apologies'/ 'Rape Me' double A-side single, released in December 1993. Thurston Moore told Krist and Dave that he thought it should open the album and Sonic Youth did a brilliant, noisy cover on the b-side of 'Sunday' in 1998. Kim Gordon sang it with the surviving members of Nirvana onstage in 2014.
46. This version of Dave's 'Color Picture of a Marigold', previously recorded for his *Pocketwatch* album, might be one of the most low key and loveliest things the band ever did, and the only official Nirvana release to not feature Kurt Cobain at all – Dave covers everything except Krist's bass. A version with Kurt playing drums was tracked (it's rather loose. Kurt has a very light touch behind the kit and his tempo is a little wobbley), but wasn't used. Kurt presumably lost interest in having another attempt. He was certainly capable of playing the part if he'd really wanted to.

known as 'Lullaby'[47] and an instrumental Dave Grohl composition[48], on which he plays all of the instruments. The album is mixed with the band present once tracking is done, Albini racing through the mixes, spending (according to Kurt) just a couple of hours on each song. Recording is completed on 26 February, with everyone smoking cigars to celebrate. Playing the album back in the studio, everyone is pleased with how it sounds.[49]

February 16

- The Brit Awards in London award Nirvana the 'Best International Newcomer' gong.[50]

February 19

- *Incesticide* is certified gold with sales of 500,000 in the US.
- At Kurt's request, manager Danny Goldberg outlines Nirvana's projected income over the coming year. Kurt wanted to know whether he would be financially okay

---

47. This is an odd beast, featuring an off-key, swirling organ (that doesn't seem to appear anywhere else on the album) with some jazzy bass noodling and extremely basic drums. I wouldn't be surprised to find this was recorded with the occasional Nirvana jamming line up of Krist on keys, Kurt on drums and Dave on bass, though no details are known. Either way, it has very little going for it and has, perhaps not surprisingly, not surfaced on any subsequent releases or compilations. It can be probably be filed as a high-fidelity equivalent of Kurt's early art experiment, 'Beans'.
48. This sounds like Dave thrashing through some ideas. Since the majority of the drums on *In Utero* were recorded in the first three days of a two-week recording session, Grohl had found himself with very little to do aside from the odd vocal harmony. He and engineer Bob Weston, brought along as an extra pair of hands by Albini, would use other parts of the studio to try out some of Dave's songs. This short demo, marked only as 'Dave Solo', has some metallic riffing but no real form. It does, however, indicate that Dave Grohl was a much better guitarist than anyone realised at the time.
49. Recording *In Utero* seems to have been a pretty pleasurable experience, barring some friction when Courtney arrived at the sessions – though as I've said, everyone has been very tightlipped about what that friction was ('It sucked,' Albini told Mark Yarm. 'She's like a fucking lead weight on everything … I don't get any satisfaction talking about that person.' When asked about her by Michael Azerrad, his response was: 'I don't feel like embarrassing Kurt by talking about what a psycho hose-beast his wife is … especially because he knows it already'. And if anything tells you that the Nirvana camp didn't have final sign off on Azerrad's book, it was that.) Elsewhere though, spirits were good. The sessions involved plenty of goofing around, including dousing each other in rubbing alcohol and setting it on fire (apparently it burns off before it can cause any damage – according to Albini, Krist lit his celebratory cigar from Dave's flaming backside) and making prank calls. At one point they called Pearl Jam's Eddie Vedder, pretending to be David Bowie's legendary producer Tony Visconti who promised to get him 'a *real* band that could really play', on another they called Kiss's Gene Simmons, who wanted Nirvana to record another Kiss song, with Albini pretending to be Kurt, while Kurt sat next to him, tears of laughter streaming down his face. On another occasion they called John Silva, one of Nirvana's managers at Gold Mountain, with Dave claiming he'd been hitting a snare for three days while Albini moved mics around, seemingly confirming management's worst fears. Apparently Silva began to say 'Well you know, it's like we said…' and was hastily cut off by Dave before revealing Nirvana's apparent back-up plan. Albini, apparently, hung on to the prank recordings though they have never emerged.
50. Nirvana, of course, weren't available to collect the award in person but presumably would have gotten equal pleasure and bafflement from it being presented by comedians Paul Whitehouse and Harry Enfield in their personas as cheesy radio DJs Smashie and Nicey, and accepted by radio legend Alan 'Fluff' Freeman. They'd also, possibly, be a tiny bit peeved by being dubbed 'newcomers' in a country they had been touring in since 1989.

if the album did badly. Goldberg predicts that Kurt would likely make over two million dollars in the coming year *after* commissions and taxes.

February 22

- The long-planned Nirvana/Jesus Lizard split 7″ featuring 'Oh, The Guilt' is released on Touch And Go records.[51] Jesus Lizard's excellent 'Puss' is the flipside.

March

- Kurt and Courtney move their family to a house in the Sand Point area of Seattle, overlooking Lake Washington. Courtney will later tell a visiting *NME* journalist that most of their neighbours are Microsoft and Apple executives.[52]
- In interviews with Michael Azerrad for his biography, *Come As You Are*, Kurt talks about the new album, referring to it as *Verse Chorus Verse*.[53] Against the express wishes of the band's label, Azerrad is also given a cassette of the early mixes of the album in order to write about them for his book.
- The band make their fourth and final video with Kevin Kerslake, for 'Sliver', to help promote *Incesticide*. It's filmed in Kurt's home, and features Frances dancing to the song. Dave mimes to Dan Peter's original drum part.[54]
- Mid March, Kurt calls Steve Albini to tell him that his A&R and other figures in the Nirvana entourage didn't like the mixes of the new album, and asking if he'd consider remixing the record. Albini declines, telling Kurt that he feels he'd made the tracks sound as good as he ever could.[55]

---

51. This is a slightly different mix to the one found on *With The Lights Out*. The original mix has the sound of a zippo lighter being clicked as additional percussion, especially noticeable on the intro.
52. 'Kurt had his MTV Award in the bathroom,' Nirvana guitar tech Ernie Bailey told Everett True. 'You could either piss in the toilet or on the award.'
53. This was one of two working titles for the album, the other one being *I Hate Myself and I Want To Die*. Both are sarcastic and self-aware to the point of slightly irritating.
54. It's an absolutely perfect video for 'Sliver' and a genuine delight – super lo-fi, super simple, with the band surrounded by Kurt's toys and memorabilia. It's also the only Nirvana video to feature Kurt's brief period with black hair which, combined with his red-and-black striped jumper (which Courtney had literally bought from a fan she'd spotted wearing it in Belfast), makes him look like a goth Dennis the Menace. It's a shame it hadn't been around when the single first came out in 1990, when the UK's *The Chart Show* was forced to simply show the single sleeve while the song played.
55. There had indeed been some internal feedback that the album wasn't radio-friendly enough and the mix too uncompromising. In 2010 Dave Grohl told his biographer, Paul Brannigan, that Geffen's reaction to *In Utero* was immediatly hostile: 'When we turned the record in to the record company, the first listen, they called back and said, "Are you guys fucking kidding me? Is this a joke?".' As Kurt told Michael Azerrad, 'the grown ups don't like it'. Complaints were generally focused around the vocals being too quiet. While it's easy to draw a narrative that the out-of-touch suits at Geffen and Gold Mountain were pressuring Nirvana to compromise on their art in order to protect their bottom line (which is totally how Albini saw it), the truth was that Nirvana themselves also had some reservations about the mix. The recordings had sounded monstrous on the high-end speakers in the studio and everyone had gone away happy, but after living with the raw mixes for a while doubts were starting to creep in. Krist felt the bass wasn't distinct enough in the mix, and there was a general consensus that in places the vocal really was buried – which no-one familiar with Albini's mixing style should have been the least bit surprised by. He *always* buries the vocals. It's particularly obvious on The Breeders' *Pod*, and that's one of the touchstones Kurt had for how *In Utero* should sound. Kurt himself addressed the issue several times in the press that year. 'The first whole week I wasn't really interested in listening to it at all, and

March 26

- Dave Grohl records drums for the soundtrack album for the movie *Backbeat*, about the Beatles' early years.[56]

April

- *Spin's* May edition hits news stands containing a stunning piece of documentary journalism by Krist Novoselic, reporting from war-torn Croatia. In January Krist had travelled back to his parent's homeland in the disintegrating former Yugoslavia to write his report. Though the piece is printed under the name 'Chris Novoselic', it is around this time that he would revert to the traditional Croatian spelling of his name, Krist, in solidarity with his countrymen.[57]

April 9

- Nirvana headline a benefit show, organised by Krist, for Bosnian rape victims at San Francisco's Cow Palace, supported by L7, the Breeders and Michael Franti's Disposable Heroes of Hip-hopracy. It's the band's first major US show since September 1992. Kurt ends the set at the climax of 'Endless, Nameless' by climbing a speaker stack and diving straight into Dave and his drums. 'Serve The Servants' and 'Frances Farmer Will Have Her Revenge On Seattle' get their live debuts. Interviewed by MTV backstage, Krist talks about the woman's centre in Zagreb that will benefit from the show, while Kurt explains the band's hopes

---

that usually doesn't happen,' he told *Melody Maker*'s The Stud Brothers that summer. 'I got no emotion from it, I was just numb.' One of the problems was Albini's general philosophy of mixing – while other engineers would adapt a mix to account for people listening on low end systems, like cheap boom boxes, clock radios and (later) phone speakers, Albini always believed this was pointless. 'There's absolutely no way to compensate for something being played on a bad system by being in the studio and adding some compensatory badness,' he told the Grammy website in 2013. 'So the thing to do is to make the record sound as good as possible when you're listening to it on very good, accurate speakers in the studio.' As for having another swing at the mixes himself – for the uncompromising Albini, that was out of the question: 'I sat down and I played my copy of the master. And listening to it, I honestly felt like I couldn't do any better,' he told Gillian G. Gaar for her *Goldmine* article in 2007. 'If I had gone out there to remix this stuff, it would've been a compromise. Because it wouldn't have ended up sounding as good as it did already, and it would've been an indulgence. I felt like I would've been wasting their money in order to make a record that didn't sound as good. I just could not hear any room for improvement'.

56. In order to create the wild feel of the early Beatles, playing riotous shows in Germany, the album was recorded extremely quickly using underground punk musicians – Dave Grohl, Thurston Moore, Gumball's Don Fleming and (admittedly less punk) REM's Mike Mills. Vocals are handled by Afghan Whigs' Greg Dulli and Soul Asylum's Dave Pirner. It's a great soundtrack.
57. It's a fantastically written piece, distilling the turbulent recent history of the region and telling stories through the eyes of young people that American audiences could relate to. It opens with a former soldier in a wheelchair watching MTV and talking about how much he loved Nirvana and the Chili Peppers. Krist goes on to explore his own family connections in the area, interviewing teenagers and kids in their 20s who had a war thrust under their noses. Amid the personal stories, Krist does his best to explain the political background – the situation in the Balkans was as complicated as it was horrifying, with historical grievances, and political manoeuvrings culminating in brutal atrocities including tens of thousands of rapes primarily instigated by Serbian forces. The conflict was marked by horrific acts of genocide, and the images coming out of the region were chilling. It's what makes Krist's report in *Spin* so absolutely vital. He brought these complexities to light, connecting readers to people of their own age – music fans and oddballs, just like them.

for educating their audience.[58] 'Usually, when you attempt to make some kind of statement in a big place like this, people don't really understand what you're saying. That's why most bands … will resort to saying "How you people doin' out there?! Alright! Party!" I don't think it's gonna be very effective to have a long-winded speech. I think the fact that we're doing this and the literature that people are going to be able to read will be effective enough.'[59]

April 19

- An article appears in the *Chicago Tribune* claiming that 'Nirvana's new album, the most widely anticipated rock release of the year, has been recorded but may never be released by the band's Geffen label.' The article quotes anonymous sources at Geffen and the band's management, one of whom claims that Nirvana's new album is 'unreleasable'. The only statements made on the record by the band's team come from manager John Silva ('the band cut some tracks … there is no release date') and Geffen's Bryn Bridentha ('[it has been pushed back] due to a hang up with up with mixing and mastering'). The article quotes Steve Albini, who says confidently that 'Geffen and the band's management hate the record'.[60]

April 21

- Mastering engineer Bob Ludwig, who had mastered albums for everyone from Led Zeppelin and Hendrix to REM, Metallica and Crowded House, masters *In Utero*, working from Albini's mixes. The band are satisfied that Ludwig has been able to use careful EQing to fix many of their concerns.[61]

---

58. By this point there had been an estimated 30,000 rape victims in the Bosnian conflict. Rape was being weaponised by Serbian soldiers, who were deliberately assualting Muslim women in Bosnia in order to create a generation of Serbian children. In what is either a chillingly and boldly perfect choice or a completely inappropriate one, Nirvana open the show with 'Rape Me'. Where you fall on that issue will largely depend on how cynical you consider to the song to be. Oddly, 'Polly' – Kurt's most powerful song about rape – wasn't performed that night.
59. The show was a success for the band, getting rave reviews in the UK and US press. More importantly, however, it raised $50,000 for the Tresnjecvka Women's Group, a feminist and women's rights organisation based in Zagreb.
60. This article really set the cat among the pigeons, and it's never been fully clear who it was that spoke to the press. Albini blames DCG's Gary Gersh. 'The label started this whispering campaign about me and how I'd ruined the record,' he told Mark Yarm. 'I was getting calls from journalists saying things like "I just got off the phone with Gary Gersh. He said you've ruined the Nirvana album".' Though journalist Greg Cott had several unnamed inside sources, no-one was willing to go on the record with anything except boilerplate platitudes with the exception of Steve Albini who, as always, was happy to sing like a canary about his perspective.
61. 'We decided to take a chance on mastering, which we really didn't understand,' Kurt told *Melody Maker* later that year. 'We thought it was the last stage in the process where you just take the tapes in and run them through a machine that allows you to cut it onto a record, or whatever. So we went to the mastering plant and learned that you can actually take the vocals right out if you want to. It's amazing, it's practically like remixing.' He declared himself '100% satisfied' with the results.

May 2

- Kurt is rushed to hospital after an apparent heroin overdose. He is discharged later the same night.[62]

May 13–14

- Having decided that the album's key singles still weren't quite right, Nirvana spend two days at Bad Animal Studios in Seattle, recording additional parts and remixing 'Heart Shaped Box' and 'All Apologies' with Scott Litt.[63]

---

62. The incident report filed by the Seattle Police Department reads 'Cobain suffered symptoms associated with an overdose of a narcotic according to medical personnel on the scene. Cobain was conscious and able to answer questions, but was obviously impaired to some degree. Cobain was transported to Harborview Medical Centre by Seattle Fire Department'. Courtney had discovered Kurt dangerously out of it after visiting a drug buddy and had done her best to revive him, injecting him with Narcan, aka Buprenorphine, which can help counter the effects of opiates. She'd also summoned Kurt's mother and sister to help. When he started to turn blue, despite his previous slurred protestrations that they do no such thing, Courtney caved and called an ambulance. It was by no means Kurt's first overdose – by this point he was back to using on an almost daily basis. According to Charles R. Cross's *Heavier Than Heaven* Kurt overdosed 'as many as a dozen times in 1993 alone'. According to Kurt's friend Cali DeWitt, who worked as Frances Bean's nanny at the time, however, this wasn't actually an overdose, but 'cotton fever'. 'When you shoot drugs you rinse it through cotton,' he explained to Everett True. 'If the tiniest strand of cotton gets on the needle and into your bloodstream … you get flushed and achey and hot. It's physically uglier than an overdose'.
63. Litt had just finished working on REM's *Automatic For The People*, and since they'd been recording in Seattle, Krist had been hanging out at the studio and listening to their progress. It was Krist that had championed the producer as the right man to sweeten the *In Utero* singles. There had been talk of bringing in Andy Wallace, who had overseen the punchy, radio-ready and obviously extremely successful songs on *Nevermind*, which goes some way to showing how far the band had considered compromising – Kurt had been very vocal about his dislike of Wallace's work on *Nevermind* (according to *Billboard* the only reason Wallace wasn't used was because he was unavailable, but since *Billboard* tended to parrot the party line that can probably be taken with a pinch of salt. Using Wallace would have been a hell of a climb-down for Kurt). But he also knew that creating hit records was now his job, and that maybe the band had some responsibility to throw the commercial market a bone. Or, more cynically, as an unnamed source told *Newsweek* that same week, 'Kurt's incredibly fickle. He likes being your defiant, punk-rock, angry young man, but he also enjoys making millions and millions of dollars'. In the end Litt was a perfect halfway house; everyone in Nirvana loved REM, and he had a proven track record of radio hits. In the studio Kurt added an acoustic rhythm guitar part to both songs, smoothing out some of their more jagged edges, he also sang some harmony vocals. Remixing 'Heart Shaped Box', the key lead single on the album, Litt raised the vocal on the choruses, pushed the drums back a little and gave the whole thing some more punch and shimmer. He also reduced a particularly abrasive effect on the guitar solo, something which Krist had said at the time 'was just this horrible abortion on the floor of this really pretty song'. During the original recording, Kurt and Albini had been delighting in adding something so deliberately grating and noisy to the album's most obvious single. 'All Apologies' got a similar treatment.

    Steve Albini's original mixes of 'Heart Shaped Box' and 'All Apologies' were eventually released on the 20th Anniversary edition of *In Utero*, meaning fans could, for the first time, hear the versions that had worried everyone so much back in 1993. The biggest surprise is how incredibly similar the mixes are. The vocals are lower on Albini's, the drums louder, there's that uncomfortably discordant effect on the solo but really, that's about it. Would it really have been that bad if Albini's 'Heart Shaped Box' had been released? Would it still have been a hit? As with the Devonshire mix of 'Smells Like Teen Spirit' the answer is 'yeah, probably'. Albini's real gift wasn't as a mix engineer, it was a *recording* engineer and his work on *In Utero* was exceptional. The band gave great performances in a great room, using great equipment and playing great songs, and Albini recorded them really well. Everything else was just so much flannel. Litt's mix is the more commercial and immediate, but not drastically so, and he was working with the finest base ingredients. With 30 years of hindsight the whole thing seems something of a storm in a teacup, and one that Steve Albini would be answering questions about for the rest of his life. His position mellowed slightly – 'Whatever my concerns at the time, the record in the stores is the one the band wanted you to hear, and I'm totally fine with that,' he wrote on the *Gearspace* online

May 19

- An article with the headline 'You Call This Nirvana?' runs in the national magazine *Newsweek*, which takes the *Chicago Tribune* piece from the previous month and amps up the drama. In it, unnamed sources say 'everybody at the record label and everybody at the management company thinks that the record blows and gave it the big thumbs-down', and the article's writer, Jeff Giles, claims that any conciliatory statements from inside the Nirvana camp about tinkering were 'meant to hold off the press while both Gold Mountain and Geffen tried to prevent Nirvana from committing what they believe to be commercial suicide'. Again, the album is called 'unreleasable'. A source also claims that Andy Wallace would be parachuted in to rescue the album. The frustrating thing for everyone involved, of course, was that by the time this article hit stands, *In Utero* was essentially finished and the whole row had been put to bed.[64] The album would be remastered shortly in order to slot Litt's new mixes into the whole and make everything sound consistent, but that was all that was left to do ... *In Utero* (which was still being referred to as *Verse Chorus Verse* internally) was basically in the can.[65]

May 22

- Nirvana's response to *Newsweek*, which had been faxed to the magazine the previous week, is reproduced as a full page advert in the latest issue of *Billboard*. The letter, signed 'Kurt Cobain, Dave Grohl, Krist Novoselic[66]'. 'Most damaging to us', it says 'is that that [*Newsweek* writer] Giles ridiculed our relationship with our label based on totally erroneous information. Geffen records has supported our efforts all along in making this record'.[67]

---

forum in 2013. 'It's their record. It's not my place or anybody else's to say they were wrong about their own music.'

64. In the end, the only person who suffered from the whole affair was Steve Albini, who claimed he spent a couple of years in the wilderness as a result. 'I couldn't get arrested for about two years after I did that record,' he told Gillian G. Gaar. 'All the smaller bands I worked with were sort of frightened off [by the association with Nirvana] and all the big bands I worked with were frightend off by the political battle Geffen waged on me.' He told Gaar that on the day *In Utero* was released he had 50 cents in his bank account. Which does beg the question 'what happened to the $100,000 they paid you?' Albini's career, of course, recovered just fine and eventually his association with *In Utero* became a selling point rather than a problem for him. He'd go on to record massively successful albums for Bush, Low, Jimmy Page & Robert Plant, Manic Street Preachers, Godspeed You Black Emperor!, Joanna Newsome, Cheap Trick, Jarvis Cocker, The Cribs, The Breeders, Metz, Sunn O))) and Laura Jane Grace. The outpouring of love and admiration for him on his death in 2024 was overwhelming.
65. In his journals an impish Kurt speculates on the possibility of releasing the unmastered Albini mixes first, on vinyl, cassette and 8-track cartridge for the purists, under the title *I Hate Myself and I Want To Die*, with the properly mastered version coming out later on CD as *Verse Chorus Verse* ... and only *after* the inevitable terrible reviews the first version would garner. Gillian G. Gaar, in her book *In Utero* mentions that a version of this actually happened – a later vinyl pressing of the album in Germany did indeed use the original, unmastered mixes by mistake.
66. Note the first formal use of Krist's Croatian name.
67. Which is sort of true. Nirvana, as both band and label had consistently pointed out throughout this whole affair, contractually had 100% creative control over their music, so in truth Geffen didn't have much choice but to support them, and though they could decide not to promote the record properly, that would be far more of an act of 'commercial suicide' than Nirvana handing in 45 minutes of uncompromising

June 1

- Courtney, who is attempting to get clean, organises an intervention for Kurt. In attendance are Nirvana co-manager Janet Billig, Krist, Nils Bernstein, an old friend of the band's and the manager of the Nirvana fanclub, and Kurt's mother and stepfather. Kurt scrawls 'None of you will ever known my true intent' on the wall in magic marker.[68]

June 5

- Police are called to Kurt and Courtney's home in Matthew Beach after neighbours over-hear the couple fighting. According to the police report the couple had fought over Kurt having guns in the house. Courtney, ever volatile, had thrown a glass of juice in Kurt's face and he had wrestled her to the floor. The police report states, uncomfortably, that Kurt choked Courtney and left a scratch on her face. Seattle law specifies that in domestic disturbance cases one party *must* be arrested, so Kurt and Courtney then argue about who is going to jail. Eventually Kurt is taken to Seattle's King County Jail after being booked by the Seattle PD's North Precinct. Police also confiscate three guns belonging to Kurt from the house. Kurt spends three hours in jail, before paying $950 bail money to be released, and the charges are subsequently dropped.[69]

July 1

- 'The "Priest", They Called Him', by William S. Burroughs and Kurt Cobain, is released by Tim/Kerr records on one-sided 10″ vinyl. The second side is left blank with the artists' signatures etched into the vinyl: 'William S. Burroughs'

---

punk. Promoted properly, the new Nirvana album was going to sell in the millions regardless of how it sounded, at least initially, and everyone would get their bonuses. Even *Incesticide* had gone gold and they'd barely promoted that at all. It wasn't in anyone's interests to bury the album. On the other hand, where does Gary Gersh's (alleged) covert briefings to the press come under 'supported our efforts all along'? Later Courtney would claim that Kurt had deliberately created a 'the label hate the album' mythology in order to further his own legend. 'That was bullshit, he made that up,' she told Brett Morgan in 2015. ' He loved good myths about himself'.

68. Kurt's managers, friends and family staged a few interventions over the final years of Kurt's life. In all cases he reacted with petulance and sullen anger. Ultimately, although on some level he knew he *had* to, Kurt didn't *want* to get clean.

69. Both sides later played down this incident, as you'd expect. 'It started because we were playing loud music in our garage and we live in a quiet neighbourhood,' Courtney told the *Seattle Times*. 'Courtney and I were running around the house screaming and wrestling. It was a bit Sid and Nancy-esque, I have to admit, but we were having a good time,' was what Kurt told *Spin*. According to Charles R. Cross's *Heavier Than Heaven*, the Cobain biography he wrote with full cooperation from Courtney, the fight was actually about Kurt threatening to do crack cocaine. Also, apparently, Courtney didn't really throw juice – she threw a *juicer*. Just as concerning as Kurt's willingness to move into the skeeziest of street narcotics was the fact that he had guns in the house at all. Kurt said he kept them to protect his family from home invasions, which given he was a public-facing rock star with young child may seem understandable. But while that might explain the two .38 pistols the police discovered, it's less of an explanation for the Colt AR-15 semi-automatic assault rifle. Kurt's guns and ammunition were returned to him a month later. Most troubling of all is the fact that he named each of his guns after a different journalist he hated.

and 'Kurtis Donald Cöhbaine'. The cover image features Krist Novoselic dressed as the titular 'Priest'.

July 4

- Dave Grohl embarks on a 12-date tour with Scream, who have reformed to promote Dischord's release of their album, *Fumble,* which had been recorded in 1989 prior to Dave joining Nirvana, but had been stuck in a legal blackhole.[70]

July 7

- Mia Zapata, singer in The Gits, is raped and murdered while walking home, sending a shockwave through the local scene.[71]

July 14

- Kurt and Kevin Kerslake begin work on a video treatment for 'Heart Shaped Box'.
- Nirvana reconvene for the first time since April to rehearse for an upcoming surprise show at New York's New Music Seminar.

July 17

- *Nevermind* finally drops out of the Billboard Hot 200. It has been in the charts for 92 weeks and peaked at number one ... twice. It has sold over five million copies in the US and eight million worldwide. In the same issue, an interview with Jonathan Poneman of Sub Pop reveals that *Bleach* has now passed 470,000 sales and is on the verge of following *Incesticide* as a gold record.[72]

July 23

- Kurt experiences a heroin overdose in his hotel room in New York, with Courtney finding him lying motionless with his eyes open and a needle in his arm[73]. She is

70. This was a cleansing experience for Dave, for whom being in Nirvana had long stopped being fun, especially during a spring and summer full of inactivity, arguments over mixes and Kurt's ever-escalating addiction issues. After the tour he told *Q* magazine that 'humping our own gear into CBGBs and sleeping on friends' floors restored my faith'. *Fumble,* by the way, is a brilliant record. Notably, it also features Dave's first lead vocal an the unsurprisingly-Foo Fighters-sounding 'Gods Look Down'.
71. See entry for 18 January 1990.
72. The following issue, 24 July, features only one mention of Nirvana, and that's just a listing for the 'Lithium' video on MTV's video chart. It's the first time since September 1991 that the official magazine of the US music industry hasn't referenced Nirvana in any way at all. If Kurt had been paying attention, and once he'd gotten over his initial disappointment at being relegated, he might finally have glimpsed a future in which the mainstream pop industry stopped hounding him. Whether his ego could handle that was another matter. That said, *Nevermind* was back in the charts by 7 August, so maybe it's a moot point.
73. Cali Dewitt, the couple's nanny, who was witness to the incident, says this happened on the day of the band's New York showcase, though it's worth noting that Michael Azerrad, recalling the events for an article in *The New Yorker,* remembers it happening the previous evening. 'She sent word out to the band's crew,' he wrote. '"Pack up the equipment – there will be no show tomorrow, because Kurt is dead"'.

convinced he is dead. Her screams bring in Cali DeWitt, Frances Bean's nanny,[74] who revives Kurt with punches to the sternum.[75] Remarkably, Kurt appears fine when just four hours later, Nirvana play an unannounced showcase at the Roseland Ballroom as part of the New Music Seminar, the city-wide music showcase and industry schmoozathon Nirvana had previously performed at in 1989. It's their first show together in three months. For the first time since Jason Everman's departure back in 1989, right after a show at *that* year's New Music Seminar, the band is joined by a second guitarist for several songs – Nirvana guitar tech 'Big' John Duncan.[76] Nirvana also switch to an acoustic set augmented by a cellist, Lori Goldstein, toward the end of the show, which takes many people in the audience by surprise. They perform stripped down versions of 'Polly', 'Dumb', 'Something In The Way' and 'Where Did You Sleep Last Night'[77] before an electrified encore of 'Smells Like Teen Spirit' and 'Endless, Nameless'.

- During the show flyers are handed out revealing the artwork and title of Nirvana's new album, which has now been retitled *In Utero*.[78]

---

74. Cali was a teenage Nirvana and Hole fan who had fallen into the band's circle the previous year when Kurt and Courtney were living in LA. The couple adored him, and he became Frances' live-in nanny. He was also a heroin user. That's Cali pictured on the *In Utero* CD, dressed in drag.
75. 'I pulled the needle out of his arm and picked him up and started slapping him and punching his chest right in the sternum pretty hard,' he told Everett True. 'The second or third punch he blew out all of his air and started breathing again.' Whether Kurt was truly 'dead' or not is unknown, but it's pretty likely that Cali saved Kurt's life.
76. Glasgow-born John Duncan was the key member of seminal, snotty 80s punks The Exploited, and had later been in a band with future-Garbage singer Shirley Manson. Everett True describes him as being 'built like a barrel', although I'd suggest 'Sherman Tank' is closer to the truth. Dave introduces him as 'our friend Big John, a 29-stone cowboy' (Krist's intro is better – 'Big John won a competition to be here: "Write 500 words entitled 'What Is Grunge?'. You too can jam with Nirvana!"') Kurt felt that many of the songs on *In Utero* needed two guitars, and that since the band was now playing bigger rooms, a bigger stage sound was appropriate. Using their guitar tech for a handful of songs was a way of breaking the idea in.
77. This was Kurt trying to move Nirvana into another version of themselves. An acoustic performance meant he could represent his more melodic tastes in a way that would feel musically authentic without playing into the mainstream pop industry he felt he had been co-opted into with *Nevermind*. It also underplayed the extremes of Nirvana's image – as petulant, angry and (as Weird Al had noted) occasionally indecipherable. It certainly surprised people. 'What, really Nirvana?' said *NME*'s review. 'Ya know, *the* Nirvana? The gods of grunge? The saviours of rock? The Punk Rock band your mum would like?'. It was a smart move. Unfortunately that all went over the heads of the cooler-than-though industry crowd who chatted restlessly through the quieter moments. There's a particularly awful bit on one bootleg recording of the gig where Courtney Love can be heard in the VIP enclosure complaining about Dave Grohl, which isn't a *great* look for anyone involved. Despite the obnoxious industry types, the show was very well reviewed, with a lot of praise already being heaped on the new songs.
78. *In Utero* was the third title considered for the album, after *I Hate Myself And I Want To Die* and *Verse Chorus Verse*. The original title had been scrapped as being too negative; the worry was people simply wouldn't get the joke (which, of course, seems a lot less funny in retrospect.) 'I wasn't alone in hoping he [Kurt] would change it,' wrote Danny Goldman in *Serving The Servants*. Krist worried that the title would come back to haunt the band should a fan ever kill themselves, remembering the case, just a few years earlier, of an 18-year old Judas Priest fan, Raymond Belknap, who died by suicide and whose parents attempted to sue the band over 'subliminal messages' in their music. Kurt had then opted for the equally sarcastic *Verse Chorus Verse*, which had been considered as a title for *Nevermind* at some point. Eventually he settled on the far more creatively interesting *In Utero* meaning 'within the womb', a title taken from a poem Courtney had written while pregnant with Frances, further reinforcing the pair's incredibly creative form of co-dependence. It's a perfect title for an album that is positively swimming in bodily fluids, and full of references to births and wombs; subjects that had always fascinated Kurt (he'd doodled pictures of fetuses for years). He later told *Q* magazine that the album's themes were 'a coincidence'

August 6

- Nirvana are surprise headliners at a show at Seattle's King Performance Center, raising money to fund the investigation into Mia Zapata's killing. The band play a strongly-rumoured but unannounced set after TAD, using TAD's gear.[79]

August 30

- 'Heart Shaped Box' is released as a single in the UK, backed with Dave's song 'Marigold' and an album cut from *In Utero*, 'Milk It'.[80]

August 31

- The video shoot for 'Heart Shaped Box' takes place in Raleigh Studios, LA. The video is directed by Anton Corbijn[81], who has replaced Kevin Kerslake.[82] The

with no connection to his becoming a father since the last Nirvana album, though this feels a little like protesting too much. The front cover of the album, which had been in place before the title was settled, was another collaboration between Kurt and Geffen's Robert Fisher, the latter working at the former's direction. It featured an anatomical model of a woman, a transparent teaching aid showing the placement of organs, on which Kurt had drawn angel wings. It was placed over a background showing human cells.

79. This was Nirvana's final ever show as a trio.
80. None of the songs from *In Utero* were released as commercial singles in the US, where Geffen were panicking about taking sales away from an album they feared wasn't going to be a great seller anyway. Unlike the UK, which had a straightforward system, the US music industry had the strange phenomenon of 'radio singles' – songs that would be released for radio play, but not actually available to buy in stores. Since the *Billboard* Hot 100 was calculated on several factors, with sales only one of them, it meant it was possible to have a hit record without, technically, releasing it. Meanwhile, over in the UK, 'Heart Shaped Box' was put in the unusual position of being released as a single before its video had even been filmed.
81. Corbijn had one hell of a pedigree. He started his career as a rock photographer, known for evocative and moody black and white shots, who'd worked with Bowie, Siouxsie Sioux, Kate Bush, Dylan, Captain Beefheart and hundreds more. The shoot he did with Joy Division shortly before the death of Ian Curtis played a big part in crystalising their image for ever more, and he worked with them again to create the incredibly *atmospheric* video to 'Atmosphere' in 1988. He would also, of course, direct the movie *Control*, the stark and brilliant monochrome biopic of Joy Division's Ian Curtis in 2007. He was Echo & The Bunnymen's go-to video director for many years, and did classic promos for U2, Depeche Mode and Danzig. It was Courtney Love, who had known of his work since her time in Liverpool, who suggested him to Kurt when it became clear that a new director was needed for 'Heart Shaped Box'.
82. This was news to Kerslake, who only found that he had been dropped via Geffen a few days before this, and didn't know yet that shooting was even scheduled. Having worked up several treatments for the video with Kurt, he submitted a budget 'close to $500,000' according to Goldman, which apparently Geffen considered 'outrageous'. 'I reminded Kurt that half the video budget would be recoupable, meaning it would be deducted from from royalties otherwise payable to the band,' he writes in *Serving the Servant*. 'Kurt felt taken advantage of'. On 28 August, Kerslake had written to Anton Corbijn: 'I'm not sure if you're aware of the circumstances that predicted Nirvana choosing you … suffice to say that we had been awarded the job and Kurt became discontent about something (What? We still don't know.)' As usual, Kurt preferred to work through intermediaries and avoid confrontations. Kerslake also sent a letter to Geffen outlining his treatments for 'Heart Shaped Box', insisting that none of the imagery that had originated with him appear in the video. The following week Kurt would invite Kerslake to the MTV *VMAs*, since 'In Bloom' was nominated for an award. During the evening he assured him there that none of his work would appear in the new video. Of course, he was absolutely lying through his teeth – many of the images from Kerslake's original treatments, which the director had been canny enough to copyright, were indeed used in the video. Kurt, presumably, had felt that since Kerslake had been working under his direction, then the imagery was fair game. According to Charles R. Cross's *Heavier Than Heaven* Kurt claimed privately to friends that many of the images from the video came from his dreams, though Cross doesn't give any source for that. Kerslake would later sue Nirvana over the video. The case was settled out of court after Kurt's death.

video sees the band playing infront of an aging Christ[83], who hauls himself up onto his own cross while wearing a Santa hat, while two crows sit on the cross beam singing along. The video also features a little girl dressed in Ku Klux Klan robes, and fields of poppies, all shot to resemble classic 1930s/40s technicolour film.[84]

September 1

- Michael Azerrad's book, *Come As You Are* is published.[85]

September 2

- Nirvana attend MTVs *VMAs* where they collect an award for 'Best Alternative Video' for the 'In Bloom' promo. They accept the award in person, accompanied by director Kevin Kerslake, with Kurt being carried to the stage on Dave's back.[86]

September 5

- 'Heart Shaped Box' goes straight in at number 5 in the UK Top 40.[87]

September 7

- After watching a show by British post-punk art-rock geniuses The Fall at The Roxy in Hollywood, Kurt attempts to tag along with the band, asking if he can accompany them on their tour bus all the way to their next show in Dallas. [88]

---

83. Kurt offered this role to William S. Burroughs, who declined on the grounds of ill health.
84. Nirvana's final music video is, despite the popularity and ubiquity of 'Smells Like Teen Spirit', probably their most striking and effective, and the best distillation of Kurt's vision that the band would create on film. The video is dreamy, striking and deeply, *deeply* weird – it's full of intense and odd imagery, and the high contrast, super-bright faux technicolour (achieved by converting the film to black and white and then colourising it frame-by-frame) makes the whole thing pop. Those looking for imagery to decode will find plenty of material – Kurt knew exactly what he was doing when he set most of it in a poppy field, and it wasn't just to evoke *The Wizard of Oz*. There's trees hung with fetuses, there's the band sitting around the aging junkie Christ in his hospital bed, there's carrion and death, and eye-popping colour. You can read it as a series of hidden messages, or a tumble of disconnected, deliberately surreal imagery or (as was intended) a combination of the two.
85. You have to hand it to Azerrad, he turned around a detailed biography in super-quick time and managed, more or less, to navigate journalistic integrity and the fact that he was very much drawn into the inner-circle of his subject and felt real loyalty to them, especially to Kurt. *Come As You Are* has elements of propaganda that perhaps should have been examined closer by its author and is something of a time capsule, sure, and Azerrad would be the first to admit as much, but it's well researched, well constructed and compellingly written. As I've said, the annotated version, *The Amplified Come As You Are* is a must-read text.
86. There's a big difference between Nirvana's, and certainly Kurt's, appearances at the 1992 and 1993 *VMAs*. The previous year Nirvana had turned up as the *enfant terrible* of alternative rock, making no concessions whatsoever to the glitz of the event. This year, Kurt looks every inch the rock star; highlights in his hair, a striped designer top, immaculately patched jeans. That said, he'd worn exactly the same outfit in the 'Heart Shaped Box' video, filmed just two days previously. Courtney had been keen for Kurt to look amazing both in the video and at the awards, and her influence is definitely felt here, though it's also very, very possible that Kurt had simply been wearing the same clothes for three days straight. Still, he undeniably looks happier and more comfortable here than we're used to seeing him in public.
87. The single got excellent reviews. 'Huge, monstrous drums, gut punching bass. But the melody is as candy-apple as The Beatles,' raved *Melody Maker*'s Simon Reynolds, who had warmed to Nirvana after his evisceration of the *Blew* EP back in 89. 'Poppy enough for the casual passer-by, sufficiently hardcore to appease the rabidly self righteous … this really couldn't be a finer return,' said *NME*'s Simon Williams in what was clearly a big week for Simons in the British music press.
88. 'There's a scruffy blond-haired bloke at our bus door, standing on the steps, blocking the entrance just when we need a quick getaway,' writes Fall bass player Steven Hanley in his excellent memoir *The Big*

September 8

- Kurt joins Courtney onstage at Hollywood's Club Lingerie to perform versions of 'Pennyroyal Tea' (with Courtney taking lead vocals) and 'Where Did You Sleep Last Night'. Courtney introduces Kurt as 'my husband, Yoko'.[89]

September 13

- *In Utero* is released in the UK on vinyl and cassette.

September 14

- A limited clear-vinyl edition of *In Utero* is released in the US.[90] The CD version of the album is released in the UK.[91] According to sales data 300 CDs and cassettes are also this week as some independent stores the jump the sales embargo.

September 18

- 'Heart Shaped Box' enters *Billboard*'s Modern Rock chart at number 7 on radio play alone. The renewed interest drags *Nevermind* back into the Hot 200 at 188.

September 21[92]

- *In Utero* is released on CD and cassette in the US, though the super-mainstream Walmart and Kmart superstores aren't yet carrying it.[93] The stores had objected to the rear cover – a collage of models and artwork by Kurt which featured model fetuses, and also, unsurprisingly, the song title 'Rape Me'. An alternative version

---

Midweek. 'I loved your show tonight,' says Kurt. 'Let me come on your road trip.' The plain speaking Manchester band are having none of it. 'Having just scored a break from our own temperamental singer,' writes Hanley (combustible Fall frontman Mark E Smith had opted to fly to the next show). 'Do we really want to get saddled with someone elses?.' Hanley apparently reminded Kurt that they were about to embark on a forty-hour drive across America and perhaps he might not, when it came down to it, be all that up for it. Since the band have to push-start their tour bus in the middle of the desert the next day, it was probably for the best.

89. This is the only time the couple would ever perform together in public.
90. This was the last remaining ghost of Kurt's fantasy about releasing a rawer, vinyl-only verion. In order to reconnect Nirvana to their punk roots, it was decided that a limited edition vinyl version would get an earlier release (though it was the same version of the album as would be available on CD later). *Billboard* magazine reported that the vinyl release was 'in keeping with the alternative market' – the fact that *Billboard* felt the existence of a 12" LP version was unusual enough to report at all speaks to how little the format was regarded at the time. By this point in the 90s, many mainstream albums would only be released on CD and cassette. *In Utero*'s vinyl release sold just 2,600 copies in its first week.
91. This version included 'Gallons of Rubbing Alcohol Will Flow Through The Strip', recorded with Craig Montgomery in Rio at the start of the year, as a hidden track. Way odder and more rambling than 'Endless, Nameless', it was seen by some as a subversion of the 'arty, weird hidden track' trope that Nirvana had themselves ushered in, though that's unnecessarily dismissive of a piece that's actually kind of a hoot.
92. Initially there had been speculation that *In Utero* and Pearl Jam's new album, *Vs*, would appear on the same day, but both sides had carefully manoeuvered around each other, unwilling to force kids who could only afford one album in any given month to have to choose. *Vs* would eventually be released on 19 October.
93. 'It didn't fit within our merchandise mix,' a Kmart spokesperson told *Billboard*, presumably keen to highlight it as a business decision rather than a moral one. 'It was not something that would be in demand for our average Kmart shopper.'

was prepared that removed the fetus models from the rear cover and retitled the offending song 'Waif Me'.[94] The album's marketing campaign is deliberately low key.[95]

- The Melvins' *Houdini* is released on Atlantic records, part-produced by Kurt Cobain.[96]

September 25

- Nirvana make their second appearance on *Saturday Night Live*, performing 'Heart Shaped Box' and, despite some resistance from network officials, 'Rape Me'. The performance sees the band debut their new guitarist, Pat Smear.[97] After

94. This had taken the Nirvana team by surprise – they'd anticipated pushback for *Nevermind* that never really materialised, but *In Utero*'s cover, featuring anatomical models and obscure symbolism around fertility and female power taken from various cultures was thought to be relatively safe, though in retrospect the careless tossing of bones and model fetuses into the United States' ever-present tensions around abortion rights should have rung some alarm bells. They also should have seen the issue with 'Rape Me' coming a mile away. What was even more surprising, especially to Danny Goldberg who was prepared to fight his artist's corner tooth and nail, is that Kurt relented and allowed Geffen to issue a santised version of the album, though he did, briefly, push to rename his song 'Sexually Assualt Me', just make his point clear. It was important to Kurt to get the record into the sort of stores that ordinary people shopped in. He reminded his manager that when he was growing up, Kmart was the only place he could buy records, and he wanted to make sure his album was available to kids in similar towns, even if it meant compromising his vision a little. 'One of the main reasons I signed to a major label,' Kurt told Everett True, 'was so people would be able to buy our records at Kmart. In some towns, that's the only place kids can buy records.' Cynics might also suggest that it was in everyone's best interest to give Nirvana's deliberately uncommercial album the best possible chance that it could have.
95. 'We want this record to be discovered in the same way that *Nevermind* was – through the music and how powerful the band is,' Geffen's Robert 'Not-that-one' Smith told *Billboard*, once again saying that the label's plan was to 'set things up, duck and get out of the way'.
96. See entry for January/February 1993.
97. Pat Smear had previously been guitarist in LA gutter punk upstarts The Germs, a band everyone in Nirvana loved. He's probably the most instantly likeable person in this tale, with the most fascinating backstory, including as it does running away to join a cult-like Christian commune, bit-part acting, and seminal California punk. The Germs themselves had collapsed messily following the suicide-by-overdose of singer Darby Crash, so Pat had already seen his fair share of junkie drama. He was unshockable by this point. He was a great peformer (Dave Grohl, to this day, says that Smear was the best musician in Nirvana), and had an exuberant stage presence full of natural energy. He was extremely funny and was also mixed-race (African American, native American and Jewish) and, though straight, was delightfully camp, all of which appealed to Nirvana's inclusive, liberal credentials and desire to offend the worst of the American right wing. Pat himself (born George Ruthenberg in 1962) had been out of the major music game for a while and was currently working for minimum wage at a record store run by SST records, though he'd recently turned down a job offer from Red Hot Chili Peppers, amongst others. He was also a Nirvana fan, whose ears had pricked up when he heard Kurt say in an interview that he'd always thought of Nirvana as a two-guitar band who had never found the right fit (incidentally I've not been able to trace the interview this quote is from – I'm paraphrasing Pat Smear, here) and since he was vaguely acquainted with Cali DeWitt and Courtney Love, thought he might have a way in. It was either Cali or Courtney who suggested him to Kurt (Cali says it was him, Courtney says it was her). Kurt later announced to the rest of the band that he had 'found their new guitarist'. Neither Krist nor Dave was ever consulted on the issue, though both were pleased with the choice – 'He's got a lot of spirit and spunk that rubs off on the band,' Krist told *Billboard*. The fact that Dave would work with Pat on and off for the next thirty years also speaks volumes. 'We went from being fucking sulking dirtbags to kids again,' he told *The Ringer* in 2018. 'It changed our world. He's the sweetest person in the world. He became really close with Kurt. There was laughter.' 'Kurt wanted a fourth member, a happy person,' Courtney told Brett Morgan in the interviews for his film *Montage of Heck*. 'He wanted somebody to connect the band, somebody to make the band feel more like a band.' As Everett True

complaints about the band's sound on the show, Kurt decides to fire long-time Nirvana soundman Craig Montgomery.[98]

September 26

- *In Utero* debuts on the UK Album chart at number one, knocking Meat Loaf's' mega-selling *Bat Out of Hell II* into second place.

September/October

- Around this time Dave Grohl briefly quits Nirvana, having overheard Krist and Kurt on a flight discussing replacing him, with Kurt apparently saying, 'I think we need a drummer that's more rudimental, along the lines of Dan Peters'[99]. After confronting his bandmates, Dave tells tour manager Alex MacLeod that he will walk away after finishing up the currently-booked shows. He later backs down and agrees to stay.[100]

---

says in his memoir, 'It's almost impossible to stay miserable while Pat's around.' That's a quality that would become increasingly important for Nirvana and their crew.

98. This was a huge blow to Montgomery, who was gearing up for the *In Utero* tour, which he expected to provide a year or so of reliable, guaranteed work. It was also baffling – he had nothing to do with the sound mix on *SNL*, which was handled by the show's in-house team, and blamed any problems with the sound on Nirvana's performance and the fact they hadn't yet gelled with their new guitarist. Kurt appears to have relented, however; he fixed Montgomery up with a gig doing live sound for Hole, who would be embarking on their own lenghty tour the following year. For what it's worth, recordings of the performance sound absolutely fine.
99. As remembered by Dave during a 2021 interview with *Vulture*.
100. There would be a tension between Dave and Kurt for the rest of the band's lifetime, partly fuelled by Courtney Love, who seemed to dislike him greatly at this point – the fact she was openly bad-mouthing him for all to hear at Nirvana's New York showcase is pretty telling (and as it was caught on a bootleg of the show, all *did* hear). What's surprising, though, is Kurt's reported attitude that he somehow didn't *need* Dave and that any drummer could do the job. 'Kurt was really unhappy with the way I played drums,' Dave told *Rolling Stone* in 2005. 'I could hear him talking about how much he thought I sucked. But he'd never say it to me. If I'd confront him about it – "Is there a problem? If you want me to leave, just ask" – he'd say "No, no, no".' Kurt, however, would continue to complain about his drummer to his friends. 'Once, I stopped by Kurt's hotel room when he started yelling that he wanted to fire Dave for being an unsubtle and unspontaneous musician,' remembers Michael Azerrad in a 2021 article in *The New Yorker*. 'The thing was, Dave was staying in the room right next door.' 'Unsubtle and unspontaneous'? *Dave Grohl*? You could *possibly*, just about, make an argument for 'unsubtle' as Grohl after all is an animal behind the drums, belting the daylights out of his skins on every beat. This was the drummer who caused one of only two noise complaints in Seattle's Word of Mouth/Reciprical studio's eight-year history and whose battered and busted snare skin Kurt had proudly held aloft at the line-up's first show together. So subtle? Maybe not. But Dave was incredibly dextrous and creative; his disco flams are what makes 'Smells Like Teen Spirit' work – no other drummer would have approached that song in that way, and without 'Smells Like Teen Spirit' *everything* is different for Nirvana, and alternative rock in general. Listen to his choices on 'Heart Shaped Box', the way way he accents Kurt's riff with the high-hats at the end of each third bar of the verse; that's not obvious phrasing. Listen to how he holds 'Milk It' together, how his kick drum responds and accents Krist's basslines. Few drummers play with that sort of character. And as for 'unspontaneous'? Nirvana with Grohl were an incredibly improvisational band, able to pivot on a sixpence in the middle of lengthy, almost telepathic jam sessions in the studio and on stage. Dave had made himself a cornerstone of Nirvana's sound, and to talk of replacing him with someone 'along the lines of Dan Peters', a drummer they'd specifically passed over to get Grohl in, seems odd in the extreme. 'He was just saying that you should get a smaller drum set and play more like Danny or something,' was Krist's rather lame explanation, according to the interview Dave gave Paul Brannigan.

   In truth the differences were beyond music – musically Nirvana were in great shape. They'd delivered an amazing album that had moved the band forward in exactly the way they needed to, and shown

October

- Hole decamp to Atlanta to record their major label debut, *Live Through This,* with producer Paul Q. Kolderie, who had recently worked on Radiohead's debut *Pablo Honey.* Kurt records back-up vocals for several songs, but almost none of his contributions are used.

October 9

- *In Utero* debuts at number one on the *Billboard* Hot 200 album chart with first-week US sales of 180,000 copies, achieved without Walmart and Kmart, who haven't yet received their sanitised editions.[101] It is almost two years to the day (12 October 1991) since *Nevermind* debuted on the same chart at 144.[102]

---

that, despite how dysfunctional they could seem, they could knuckle down and put the work in. The problem was personal. By this point, Nirvana had split into two camps. On the one side was Krist, Dave and the band's entourage and road crew. On the other was Kurt, Courtney and their friends, including the members of Hole. 'You know, there were drugs around, and there was, like, the people who did the drugs, and then there were the people who didn't do the drugs,' Dave told *The Howard Stern Show* in 2011. 'And I didn't do the drugs, so I was just out of that world, you know. If you're in it you're in it. If you're not, you're out.' A decade or so earlier, Courtney had addressed the issue on *Howard Stern* herself – 'He [Kurt] hated his guts,' she told the host in 1999. 'Kurt loved him at first because he was sweet, funny and lovely. And then he turned into such a dick ... he really turned his back on Kurt.' Courtney, who would feud with Dave and Krist through the next decade or so, elaborated further on her *MySpace* blog, years later: 'Kurt loathed HIM more than anyone else (except a journalist). In his will he made a codicil that Grohl was no longer a member of Nirvana.' Which is depressing to read, though it's tricky to know how seriously to take any decisions Kurt made in those dark, final months.

101. This is obviously a lot of records and any artist would kill for those numbers these days. It's worth noting, however, that Pearl Jam's second (and vastly inferior) album *Vs,* which would appear a few weeks later, sold 950,000 in its first week alone. Even Smashing Pumpkins' shimmering and summery *Siamese Dream,* the album the quartet had made with Butch Vig, sold 130,000 units in its first week out the traps that August, and Billy Corgan and co were assuming Nirvana's mantle as the alt-rock poster children for those who found Pearl Jam and RHCP too macho and REM and Counting Crows too wishy-washy – the space that *Nevermind* had occupied throughout 1992. Nirvana had willingly given up their 'biggest rock band in the world' crown, since it never really suited them anyway, and settled for being the most vital one instead. The sanitised Walmart/KMart version of *In Utero* wouldn't make it into stores until the following spring.

102. All three of Nirvana's albums have their champions; hell, there are even those that claim that *Incesticide* is the purest distillation of the band, and you can see where they're coming from. The common view is that *Nevermind* is the definitive Nirvana record, which is a difficult position to argue with – it's the breakthrough, the one with the most iconic, anthemic songs, the most accessible and the one that *changed everything.* However, there has always been a hardcore (especially among music journalists and Nirvana obsessives) for whom *In Utero* is the truest artistic statement that the band created in its lifetime. Here was an album that truly was the sum of its parts, with all three members making musical contributions, leaning into their chemistry. Kurt's songwriting was at its peak here, both in the *Nevermind* era moments ('Dumb', 'Rape Me', 'All Apologies', 'Pennyroyal Tea'), which all have Kurt's sense of clean, defined poetic lines and punchy choruses, and on the more musically rich, complex and uncompromising pieces: 'Scentless Apprentice', 'Milk It', 'Frances Farmer Will Have Her Revenge On Seattle'. The two sides collide on 'Heart Shaped Box', perhaps the most distinctly *Nirvana* song in the band's canon, the one moment that no other group, not Melvins, not Pixies, not Mudhoney, not Sonic Youth, not Smashing Pumpkins, not Pearl Jam, not Soundgarden could have written. Albini did an exceptional job of capturing the performances, and though it's still a controversial issue, the decision to make the whole thing a little cleaner in the mastering and also remix the key singles paid off. The result was Nirvana's masterpiece. Critics largely agreed as well, recognising the melding of power and authenticity that defined the record. *Rolling Stone* dispatched editor David Fricke to deliver the key review, declaring that '*In Utero* is a lot of things – brilliant, corrosive, enraged and thoughtful, most of them all at once,' and praising its 'complex, gripping soundscapes' which showcased Cobain's genius at

October 18

- The *In Utero* tour kicks off at the 14,000-capacity Veteran's Memorial Coliseum in Phoenix, Arizona. That week, the venue is also playing host to Billy Ray Cyrus and some pro-wrestling. These were the pools Nirvana had to swim in. The band, augmented by Pat Smear and cellist Lori Goldstein, play a 21-song set covering all three of their albums and most of their singles. The stage set is far more elaborate than any they have previously used, with two 'transparent women' angel models and twisted trees nodding to the 'Heart Shaped Box' video. One of the two angels is smashed by Kurt during a closing 'Endless, Nameless', which is a pretty classic Nirvana move for the first show of a six-month long tour. The band will wind their way across the sports arenas of the United States and Canada until early January, playing a gruelling 48 shows.[103]

---

full throttle. *Melody Maker's* Sharon O'Connell (Kurt had asked *MM's* usual Nirvana correspondent, Everett True, to stop writing about the band and just 'be a friend' at this point) hit the nail absolutely on the head when she wrote that the album 'is not *quite* the rubbed-raw, confrontational, fan-alienating catharsis it's been talked up to be, but it's hardly KC and the Sunshine Band either', noting that the record's strength was in its ability to straddle the two poles as 'an almost perfect mix of inchoate rage and simple but eloquently expressed fury'. *Select's* David Cavanagh is equally eloquent about the album's fascinating contradictions and compromisies. 'It's not a horrible record, but it is an ugly one,' he writes. 'It's not a masterpiece, but it is a great one. It's not what anyone would call suicide on CD, but it has moments of stunning antimatter that demand newer and more descriptive words for the emotion that's left when all the others have dried up. Even when it's hard to listen to, it's impossible to take off. It is fantastically exciting music. It's as simple and complicated as that.' Across the board *In Utero* seemed to inspire critics to up their game just as the band had – most of the notices are beautiful examples of the record review as an art form in itself. 'The songs of *In Utero* are fractured, spasmodic, wrenched out of shape,' wrote *Spin's* Howard Hampton, 'notes pulled inside out, meanings stood on their pointy little heads and spun for kicks. Pushed to the brink, Cobain's mercurial guitar, Dave Grohl's self-contained drumming, and Krist Novoselic's split-the-difference bass have never been as cohesive.' There were dissenting voices however. *NME's* John Mulvey picked out the album's highlights, particularly 'Scentless Apprentice' and 'Heart Shaped Box', but felt it to be 'a document of a mind in flux – dithering, dissatisfied, unable to come to terms with sanity … as a follow-up to one of the best records of the past ten years it just isn't quite there.' Intellectually, it's hard to disagree with any of that. *In Utero* contains some staggering, perfect moments ('Heart Shaped Box', 'All Apologies'), but it has its share of throwaways ('Tourettes', 'Very Ape'). If you're feeling charitable then those moments are the band deliberately sabotaging the album from becoming a Great Artistic Statement that would further their legend and make their lives weirder. If you're feeling cynical, they're frantically padding out an album Kurt had had two years to write, and that was half written even before *Nevermind* came out. Still, there's something perfect about *In Utero* as an investigation of Nirvana as a trio and a snapshot of their development. It could have been a stepping stone to whatever came next. Alas, we can only ever see it as a final statement and epitaph.

103. The setlist for the *In Utero* shows would remain relatively stable across the tour. Some nights the whole album would be spread across the hour alongside staples like 'Blew', 'About A Girl', 'Sliver', 'School', 'Drain You', 'Lithium' and 'Breed', while 'Come As You Are' and 'Smells Like Teen Spirit' would be switched in and out of the setlist depending on the band's moods, though failure to play the latter would usually result in boos once the lights went up. An acoustic section was sandwiched in the middle of the set, a warm-up for the band's upcoming *MTV Unplugged* appearance (both 'Jesus Doesn't Want Me For A Sunbeam' and 'Where Did You Sleep Last Night' featured regularly). Later the band added a great cover of David Bowie's 'The Man Who Sold The World', a song Chad Channing had turned Kurt onto back in 1988. As the tour went on and the band warmed to their new role you could sense them relax – by November they had resumed all the instrument-swapping, improvised cover versions and onstage chaos that had been the hallmark of Nirvana club sets. The shows, with only a few exceptions (a second night at Chicago's Aragon Ballroom, witnessed by *Rolling Stone* editor David Fricke, was a notable stinker) were well received, and despite Dave Grohl's claim in his memoir that Nirvana 'never really' got comfortable with arenas, they were playing solid sets. In a lot of ways this was the band's first

October 16

- 'Heart Shaped Box' goes to number one on the *Billboard* Modern Rock 100.

October 20

- As the tour is passing through Lawrence, Kansas, Kurt visits the Learnard Avenue home of William S. Burroughs. Though the duo had collaborated and corresponded, this would be the only time they'd meet. The pair got on well, though afterwards Burroughs is quoted as saying that 'there's something wrong with that boy. He frowns for no good reason'.

October 23

- At the first of two shows at Chicago's Aragon Ballroom, Nirvana debut a new song, 'You Know You're Right'.[104]

---

real tour since the sudden-onset fame that came in the wake of *Nevermind.* The tour for that album had been of mid-sized clubs, booked before 'Teen Spirit' had broken, played out amid scenes akin to Beatlemania (Kurt would say it was his favourite era of the band), but an arena tour planned for spring 1992, which would properly exploit Nirvana's exploding fame, had been pulled as Kurt started to cripple under the pressure and his addiction. Since then the band had only played a handful of a mega shows (Reading, Argentina, Brazil) or unannounced club sets and benefits. Now they were on tour for real, and for the first time it was in real tour buses and nice hotels, playing regimented sets in huge venues with catering and people to hump the gear for them. Though everyone would, at some point, bemoan the distance from the audience and the impersonal experience, everyone was also enjoying the comfort ... and letting other people do all the difficult bits. No-one, except possibly Dave Grohl, actually enjoys carrying their own gear.

Spirits were largely high, especially in the non-Kurt-and-Courtney side of the touring party. Many of the band's favourite estalished and upcoming artists and old friends were drafted in as support (Mudhoney, Melvins, Chokebore, Butthole Surfers, Come, Shonen Knife, The Breeders, Jawbreaker, Half-Japanese, Boredoms, The Meat Puppets and brilliantly bananas comedian Bobcat Goldthwait, who acted as MC – the list was also due to include TAD, but they were booted from the line-up after Courtney apparently got into a confrontation with Tad Doyle's girlfriend and demanded Kurt fire them. 'People like to make stuff up about me,' Courtney told Mark Yarm when asked about it) which added to the sense of adventure and made them akin to a group of monkeys being given the keys to a banana plantation. The presence of Pat Smear (who travelled on a separate tour bus with Kurt, Cali DeWitt and, occasionally, baby Frances Bean) was an ever-present balm to any rising tensions. On Halloween they even played a show in fancy dress, with Kurt as Barney the dinosaur, Krist in 'white face' (sending up Ted Danson's recent blackface scandal) Dave as a mummy and, brilliantly, Pat dressed as Slash. 'It was full of joy and fun,' Meat Puppets drummer Derrick Bostrom told Danny Goldberg. 'The costumes, the joking, the interaction with the audience. In hindsight it's amazing that a band that big could put on shows that large that had that grassroots kind of small-club feel and have a good time.'

The good times, alas, were balanced by others that were pitch black. Kurt's moodswings were becoming the stuff of legend, and on more than one occasion a crew member would be fired for saying the wrong things in front of him. Shows would be pulled prematurely if something in the crowd upset him (though conversely Kurt could also extend the set, sometimes ending shows alone on stage smashing gear) 'Everyone was walking on eggshells,' Mudhoney's Steve Turner says in his memoir, *Mudride*, where he describes the atmosphere as 'awkward and unpleasant ... they had completely taken their hands off the wheel and were letting management and others steer the ship'. When Kurt was introduced to *Melody Maker* photographer David Baker he insisted, for apparently no reason, that 'he never be let near me again'. He was estranged from his bandmates, especially Dave, and fighting continually with Courtney, who was leaning hard into a celebrity lifestyle Kurt was increasingly becoming sickened with. The rest of the party learned to stay out of his way. When Courtney herself joined the traveling circus of the tour the atmosphere would change dramatically. 'All this negativity was based and directed at Courtney,' Cali DeWitt told Everett True. 'From the whole band. If she was there, it was bad. If she wasn't, it was a lot lighter.' Fortunately, Courtney was in the midst of recording Hole's *Live Through This* which kept her from the tour for long periods.

104. This was the only known performance of the song, and, jamming aside, the last time Nirvana would ever play a 'new' song at a show. The performance is a little uncertain, and Kurt appears to start it

October 26

- *No Alternative*, a compilation raising awareness of the AIDS crisis and money for research and treatment for patients, is released on Arista records. Smashing Pumpkins, Beastie Boys, Goo Goo Dolls, Soundgarden, Pavement, Urge Overkill and The Breeders are among the alternative rock names who contribute tracks. Nirvana's 'Sappy', recorded at the *In Utero* sessions is included as a hidden track.[105]

November

- Nirvana are offered somewhere between $6 and $8 million to headline the 1994 Lollapalooza tour[106], which will take place across the summer – more money than they could make touring by themselves. Kurt hates the idea, though the rest of his band, management and, crucially, Courtney, feel it's important for Nirvana to do it. Courtney, currently on tour with Hole, sends Kurt a fax stating her case[107], suggesting that should Nirvana turn the shows down they would likely be offered to Smashing Pumpkins.[108] Though the deal is never formally inked, Nirvana commit to the tour.[109]

November 18

- The band performs an acoustic set in New York for the *MTV Unplugged* series, for broadcast later in the year.[110] The setlist is light on Nirvana's biggest hits (no

---

without warning while Krist is attempting to introduce 'All Apologies'. There's a real power to the song, however, even in this scrappy rendition.

105. And thus a song Kurt had been attempting to get right since 1990, finally made its way into the world, though admittedly in a pretty low-key way. Confusingly, it had now been retitled 'Verse Chorus Verse', a name previously used for an unreleased *Nevermind*-era song and a working title for both *Nevermind* and *In Utero*. See entry for 9 May 1991.
106. The brainchild of Jane's Addiction/Porno For Pyros frontman Perry Farrel, Lollapalooza was Alternative Rock's annual travelling circus (quite literally – it always featured deliciously weird side-show The Jim Rose Circus as part of events), a full touring music festival that spent the summer trekking across the US. It's brilliantly parodied in the 1996 *Simpsons* episode 'Homerpalooza'. Nirvana's fee has been reported as $6, $7 and $8 million dollars in different sources.
107. This per Poppy Z. Bright's biography *Courtney Love: The Real Story*, which was written (at least initially) with access to Courtney and her papers.
108. Kurt was hugely jealous of Billy Corgan. Not only was Corgan the heir-apparent to Kurt's own Generational-spokesman crown, he was his wife's ex-boyfriend. According to several sources, Kurt was increasingly suspicious about Courtney and Billy hooking up behind his back, though Courtney has always strongly denied this.
109. According to his *Serving The Servants*, Danny Goldberg was dead-set against Nirvana doing the tour. 'I was worried … there would be much more liability in cancelling performances … than on a Nirvana tour. Given the number of shows Kurt had cancelled in the last couple of years, this was a significant financial downside.' Sensible words.
110. *Unplugged* had been running since 1989 and had become something of an institution. The premise was pretty simple – big name pop and rock artists performed a set of their hits stripped down to acoustic guitars in front of a small, invited audience. The series rests on a very rockist and somewhat self-conscious idea that, somehow, acoustic music is more 'authentic' and something that 'serious artistes' must be able to do. It wasn't a very punk concept. Most of the artists who had recorded sets for the series were the kind Nirvana would hate to be associated with – Mariah Carey, Eric Clapton, Sting, Roxette, Rod Stewart, Poison and Stevie Ray Vaughn. The day before Nirvana tracked their session, Duran Duran had recorded one. Recently, however, MTV had tempted some of Kurt's alt-rock contemporaries

'Teen Spirit', no 'Heart Shaped Box') and includes several pretty obscure cover versions, including The Vaselines' 'Jesus Doesn't Want Me For A Sunbeam' (a mainstay of Nirvana sets since 1991), David Bowie's 'The Man Who Sold The World', three Meat Puppets covers, 'Lake of Fire', 'Oh Me' and 'Plateau' (with the band's Cris and Curt Kirkwood on bass and guitar)[111] and a closing, definitive rendition of Lead Belly's 'Where Did You Sleep Last Night'.[112]

---

including REM, Pearl Jam, Stone Temple Pilots and Soul Asylum, while The Cure had played a great set for the show in 1991.

The band and their management were under no illusions about the debt they owed to MTV – its championing of the 'Smells Like Teen Spirit' video had been what put Nirvana on the map, and the network had remained consistently Team Nirvana ever since. More than that, though, for Kurt this was a chance to prove he was more than just 'the grunge guy', more than screaming and volume and smelling like teen spirit; something that was important to him if he was to have a future in music. He was also terrified by the thought of doing an entire set without volume and riffs and guitar smashing to hide behind, with his music rendered at its most basic. Once on board, however, Kurt took the show seriously; meticulously planning the stage set (candles and stargazer lilies, deliberately evoking a funeral) and choosing songs and collaborators that sent the right message – authenticity, songcraft, the underground. In a way, he managed to make the least punk show on TV pretty Punk Rock. Testimony to that seriousness is the fact that Scott Litt, producer for REM and remixer of 'Heart Shaped Box', was brought in to handle the sound.

111. The Meat Puppets were an early influence on Kurt, who saw them opening for Black Flag in 1983. The Phoenix trio, signed to SST and featuring brothers Cris and Curt Kirkwood, had started as a hardcore band, but like most of the early hardcore pioneers they soon learned to diversify and their second album, *Meat Puppets II*, twangs with noisy hoedowns and ramshackle rockabilly. What Kurt very smartly realised is that, at the heart of the band's oddball presentation, there was usually a robust and well constructed song, something which is proven pretty definitively when Kurt himself is singing them – under his laconic drawl the three songs Nirvana perform all sound like classics. *Unplugged* producer Alex Colleti was initially excited when he heard the band wanted to feature guests, assuming they'd bring Seattle contemporaries Pearl Jam (a pretty absurd idea, as almost anyone who knew Nirvana would have told him). He was less thrilled when he discovered Kurt wanted to showcase an obscure, lo-fi punk band; 'Oh great', he told Mark Yarm, dripping with sarcasm. 'I smell ratings!'

112. *Unplugged In New York*, as the recording of that night's performance would ultimately be titled, has, of course, become a classic and beloved album in its own right. Kurt's songs work beautifully stripped down, because *of course they do* and the choice of covers feel like genius. New content for the band to release showcasing overlooked artists they loved? *Of course that's a brilliant idea.* The warm and intimate environment absolutely suiting a raw but good humoured performance. *Obviously.* Except ... at the time, none of that was apparent and no-one was sure the set would work at all. Nirvana didn't want this to look and sound like any other *Unplugged* show, while the producers at MTV wanted it to look and sound *exactly* like their previous entries in the series, and it was creating tensions that could potentially wobble the whole thing off a cliff. Aaron Stauffer of New York band Seaweed remembers running into Dave Grohl before the show. 'He kind of gave this face and groaned,' he told Mark Yarm. '"It's not going to be good".' Rehearsals had been stilted, awkward and rambling to the point that Nirvana guitar tech Ernie Bailey was convinced the band were making a terrible mistake. 'By the end of the second day I was left thinking at this point it could be a mistake to proceed with the show,' he told *The Ringer* in 2018. 'The rehearsals were so loose, I don't remember them making it through a full set.' The Meat Puppets' Kirkwood brothers remember Kurt continually arriving at rehearsals late and obviously high, and if he'd been stoned for the rehearsals, the opposite problem was true of the day of recording – he turned up in withdrawal. MTV's Amy Finnerty, the band's biggest champion at the network, went out of her mind trying to track down valium to take the edge off Kurt's symptoms. Worse, his stomach problems had returned, and he was vomiting blood and bile on the morning of the show. Even the *Unplugged* format itself strained against Nirvana's instincts – Kurt's Martin DB-18 acoustic guitar had a pick-up fitted, essentially making it an *electric* guitar, which to producer Alex Coletti's annoyance needed to be ran through effects pedals and into a Fender amplifier disguised as a stage monitor. Krist didn't even *own* an acoustic bass and had to be leant one by producers, and Dave struggled to play his drums at anything like the level of delicacy necessary to give the performance the stripped-back feel the format demanded (presumably fuelling Kurt's view that he was 'unsubtle'). 'Kurt would turn to me and say, "Can you play quieter?"' he told *Rolling Stone* in 2007. 'Eventually I said, "Do you want me to just split?" I was barely touching the drums.' The worry was that his sheer volume would drive everyone

else to play harder, completely undermining the intended vibe of the music. At one point there was talk of Dave sitting the show out altogether.

The biggest issue, though, was that the band were terrified. Even after a month of playing mid-show acoustic sets on tour, specifically intended to prepare them for *Unplugged*, they weren't used to their music and performances being this exposed. It's one thing to busk some acoustic numbers at a gig; it's quite another to do it on TV with every wobble and mistake obvious for all to hear. If the taping was nothing but a succession of retakes and fuck ups then the show was going to be a frustrating experience for the live audience and the band alike – Stone Temple Pilots, who like Duran Duran had recorded their own *Unplugged* session just the day before, had taken *hours* to get it right, re-recording every song. Most of the press attending Nirvana's show had also been in the STP recording as well, and no-one was looking forward to sitting through more endless do-overs. Suddenly, the idea of including four songs the band had never played live seemed less than smart. Throw into that a combustible lead singer with a newly-developed tendency to turn full-on rock star diva when things didn't go his way, and a media hanging on his every move, waiting for him to mess up, and it was a recipe for disaster. The only blessing was that Courtney wasn't there to rock the boat (she and Cali DeWitt had intended to fly over from Seattle, but at the last minute decided to stay home and do drugs).

In the end, none of that mattered. Although it was a close run thing. Some problems turned out to have easy solutions – producer Coletti was no novice when it came to this acoustic thing, and provided Dave with a selection of alternative drum sticks, notably brushes and hot rods. The latter, which are comprised of dowling rods taped together, gave the feel of standard drum sticks while diffusing a lot of the power of the hits. Dave uses them on nearly every song and has gone on record as saying they're what saved the performance. Nerves were countered by hard rehearsal. Krist sat up late in his hotel room working out a bass part to Bowie's 'The Man Who Sold The World' (Tony Visconti's original, intricate line was a little beyond him, at least at short notice) and invited the Kirkwood brothers over to work on the Meat Puppets songs they planned to cover. Amy Finnerty ensured the front row was full of people Kurt knew and loved, herself included. Also in attendance were members of Sonic Youth, old friend turned-manager Janet Billig, members of the band's touring entourage like Bobcat Goldthwait and Half Japanese singer Jad Fair, familiar faces like Seattle journalist Gillian G. Gaar and, curiously, British supermodel Kate Moss. Kurt also asked to meet the audience queuing for the show, and knowing he had a crowd of genuine, appreciative fans in attendance seemed to bolster his confidence.

More than any of that, though, Nirvana – and especially Kurt – simply rose to the occasion, something which was by no means a given. The band were quite capable of pulling defeat from the jaws of victory; they had always been messy and on their worst days often felt on the verge of collapsing mid-set. They could also be *stunning*, however. When the stars aligned. When everything was in the right place. When everyone's moods were good. When it *mattered*, Nirvana could be absolutely magnificent. This was one of those times. Kurt was on wonderful form – belying his nerves, he seemed calm, relaxed, even enjoying himself. The stage setting might have felt funereal, but the performance itself had a lightness of touch that runs counter to the misery-and-addiction narrative often attached to the band. There's between-song jokes and endless self-deprecation. 'The reason we don't like to play these two songs back to back is that they're exactly the same song,' says Kurt of 'Dumb' and 'On A Plain'. 'If this doesn't work, well, these people are just going to have to wait,' he says before 'Pennyroyal Tea'. 'I don't think MTV would let us play that,' is his response to a frenzied request for 'Rape Me'. The show feels *fun*. And when it doesn't feel fun, it's because it's beautiful: Kurt's solo rendition of 'Pennyroyal Tea' is absolutely shattering. It's his definitive performance of the song, his voice cracking, wringing the raw emotion out of every note. Before the final verse it almost, *almost* falls apart, Kurt seeming to hesitate just for a second before descending into the final movement and raising goosebumps. The three numbers with the Meat Puppets are brilliant, the songs comfortably taking their place in the Nirvana canon and sitting shoulder to shoulder with the Cobain originals. Probably best of all though is the closing 'Where Did You Sleep Last Night', a song Kurt had been playing on and off since 1989, when he and Krist recorded it with Mark Lanegan and Mike Pickeral from Screaming Trees (see entry for 20 August 1989). That version featured on Lanegan's *The Winding Sheet* and is one of that album's highlights, but it's edged out as the definitive take (outside of Lead Belly's own) by the harrowing performance that capped Nirvana's *Unplugged* set. It's too easy, in retrospect, knowing what was happening in the background, knowing where Kurt was heading, to project any number of emotional resonances and unecessary context onto that rendition. You can insert your own interpretation of Kurt's pain into his howls and screams as the song hits its climax. It's hard to deny that he's channeling *something* in those moments. He seems to put his entire soul into that vocal, absolutely losing himself. Maybe he really was interpreting an ocean of pain. Maybe he just really, really loved that song. Either way, as he howls that final 'the whole ... night ... through' it brings absolute chills. An incredible moment. Beauty. Pain. Catharsis. Whatever – insert your own interpretation here. It's the capstone on a fantastic, definitive

November 23

- *The Beavis and Butt-head Experience* compilation album is released, featuring Nirvana's 'I Hate Myself and I Want To Die'. Elsewhere on the compilation are tracks by Anthrax, Megadeth, Red Hot Chili Peppers, White Zombie and a funny-the-first-time-but-you'll-never-play-it-again duet between Cher and Butt-head on 'I've Got You Babe'. The animated duo keep running commentary between every song.

November 26

- The tour resumes in Jacksonville, Florida.

December 1

- The band add an electrified version of 'The Man Who Sold The World' to the set. It will be played at almost every Nirvana show going forward.[113]

December 6

- The 'All Apologies'/ 'Rape Me' double A-side single is released in the UK, backed with 'Moist Vagina' on the CD version.[114]

December 13

- Nirvana record another gig for MTV, this time for the networks' *Live & Loud* show, to be broadcast on New Year's Eve. Amy Finnerty and her colleagues have pulled a lot of strings to put together a brilliant bill of Cyprus Hill and The Breeders, co-headlined by both Nirvana *and* Pearl Jam, playing a homecoming show at Seattle's Pier 48 and hosted by the Flea and Anthony Keidis from the Chili Peppers – a hell of a coup. Unfortunately, on the day Eddie Vedder calls in sick, and Nirvana headline the show alone.[115]

Nirvana performance that, thanks to its release as a live album the following year, has taken a place in the band's body of work that it absolutely deserves. Truly one of their finest moments. And they didn't have to do a second take of a single song.

113. Bowie himself was flattered that Nirvana had chosen to cover his work. 'I was simply blown away when I found that Kurt Cobain liked my work, and have always wanted to talk to him about it … why that song?' Bowie told Dutch TV show *Lola Da Musica* in 1996. It was, however, occasionally frustrating. 'Some of my recent albums have been picked up by the Nineties generation, but then they don't know the early stuff,' he told *GQ* in 2000. 'I think it's a surprise when they hear them all at once and think, "Did he write that?" I know that because, in America especially, when I do 'The Man Who Sold The World' the amount of kids that come up afterwards and say, 'It's cool you're doing a Nirvana song.' And I think, 'Fuck you, you little tosser!'" After Bowie's death in 2016, Dave, Krist and Pat reunited to play the song live with REM's Michael Stipe.
114. The title is abbreviated to 'MV' on the single's artwork. There's no video made for either of the A-sides, and neither are released as a commercial single in the US, though MTV do put the performance of 'All Apologies' from *Unplugged* into wide rotation. 'Moist Vagina' would be the last 'new', Nirvana original released until the posthumous 'You Know You're Right' in 2002.
115. This performance is later released on DVD as part of the *In Utero* 20th Anniversary edition and as an album in its own right. It's a great set, which captures and crystalises the *In Utero* tour and the final era of the band. It's well worth seeking out.

December 18

- The 'All Apologies'/'Rape Me' single charts at a disapointing 32 in the UK. It will drop out of the Top 40 altogether by 8 January.[116]

December 25

- *Billboard*'s End-of-year issue reports that *In Utero* has cleared a million sales in the US and a further 1.5 million overseas.[117] The album ends 1993 at 27 on the Hot 200, and at 74 on the over-all end-of-year album chart.

116. The band did almost no promo for the single as they were currently touring the US, there was no real video, one of the two sides was unplayable on day time radio and the CD contained only one song that wasn't on the album, so this isn't exactly a surprise.
117. However, it's interesting to note that the cover of the issue, which features album art from key releases of 1993 overlooks Nirvana ... despite showing Blind Melon, Stone Temple Pilots and Pearl Jam. Its evidence that the commercial shine was absolutely coming off the band. The 'industry bible' still struggled to know what to make of them, while their alt-rock peers fit more neatly into established boxes.

Part Seven

And Always Will, Until the End

1994

January 7–8

- Nirvana play a two-night residency at the Seattle Centre arena – the last date of the US leg of the *In Utero* tour.[1]

January 18

- Nirvana are garlanded with a Grammy nomination for the third year in a row with *In Utero* getting the nod for 'Best Alternative Performance' alongside the usual suspects – REM's *Automatic For The People, Star* by Belly, *Siamese Dream* by Smashing Pumpkins and *Zooropa* by U2.[2]

January 22

- 'All Apologies' hits number one on the *Billboard* Modern Rock chart, helped along by MTV's heavy rotation of the *Unplugged* performance.

January 24

- Kurt and Courtney upgrade to a bigger house on Lake Washington Boulevard East.

January 28–30

- Kurt, Krist and Dave are booked to record demos at Robert Lang Studios in Seattle, working with in-house engineer Adam Kasper.[3] Only Krist and Dave

---

1. These were, by all accounts, exceptional shows. The 7 January performance can be found on the 30th anniversary edition of *In Utero*. Sadly, 8 January was Nirvana's last show in Seattle and the last ever US Nirvana performance in Kurt Cobain's lifetime.
2. Nirvana were nominated for Grammys every year between 1992 and 1995, though they didn't win until their very last nomination: the posthumous *Unplugged In New York* saw off PJ Harvey, Bjork and, with no small irony, the debut Foo Fighters album to win the 1995 award for 'Best Alternative Music Performance', surely one of the few times in history that someone has been beaten to a Grammy by their own band.
3. 'It was to just do something,' Krist told *Mojo* in 2004.'That's how we got all those other weird little songs that came out on split singles and compilations or whatever. It was just, Let's do something.' January has always been a weirdly useful studio month for Nirvana, probably because no-one has much to do after the holiday period, especially in the dismal Seattle weather. The 'Dale Demo' was recording in January 1988, much of Bleach was recorded in January 1989, the first version of 'Sappy' was done in January 1990, the sessions with Craig Montgomery that yielded 'Aneurysm' and 'Even In His Youth' were done in January

show up for the first two days of recording, and work on some jams and a couple of Grohl-originals, including future Foo Fighters songs 'Exhausted', 'Big Me' and 'February Stars'.[4] Kurt turns up for the session on the final day, and the trio track their newest song, 'You Know You're Right' in full[5], as well as playing with a few other ideas, including Grohl songs.[6]

February

- Rumours start to swirl about Nirvana headlining Lollapalooza.

February 2

- The band departs for Europe for the next leg of the *In Utero* tour. Joining the touring party is cellist Melora Creager of neo-classical New York grunge-goths Rasputina.

February 4

- The band make a ferocious appearance on the French TV show *Nulle Part Ailleurs* performing 'Rape Me', 'Pennyroyal Tea' and 'Drain You'.[7] All four members are

---

1991, and several *In Utero* demos were tracked in Rio in January 1993. The Laundry Room sessions in April 1992 served a similar role – trying out ideas and seeing what stuck.

4. 'There was some word that hopefully Kurt would show up on Friday,' studio owner Bob Lang told *Mojo*. 'But I don't think they were really stressed about it. And they believed if he wasn't coming Saturday, he'd definitely be there Sunday. I thought it was a little odd that Kurt wasn't there, but Krist and Dave just went about their business and kept focused on what they were doing.' By now the Nirvana rhythm section had long accepted that they were at the mercy of their front-man's whims. He'd pulled the same stunt during the early demo sessions for *In Utero*. (See entry for 25 October 1992.)
5. 'You Know You're Right' is the last complete Nirvana song, and part of the tragedy of this is that it's *so damned good*. The band had been knocking it around in soundchecks and had tried it live just once, in Chicago the previous October, with its existence being the main motivator for recording that January. Though it still played in the mid-tempo, quiet/loud pool that the band had come to make their signature, it feels like a true progression, using the discordant heaviness of *In Utero* to springboard into a different expression of Kurt's pop instincts, this time pulled absolutely taut and rigid with tension. It means the choruses feel like pure release, and there's a wonderful trick in the refrain where Kurt continues his screamed melody as the band changes key beneath him, creating another moment of tension at the point the song is at its most melodic. The structure is relatively simple, but there's lots of noisy, interesting ticks happening with the guitars – this isn't Kurt sticking to the *Nevermind* powerchords or the meat-headed riffola of *Bleach*, and nor is it the wilfully awkward angles of *In Utero*. As they had with 'Heart Shaped Box', this was Nirvana's instinctive chemistry and natural creativity pushing themselves into new shapes. It was art rock, of a sort that sounded at once brilliantly, thrillingly like Nirvana while also feeling like a true step into their next era … an era which, of course, would never come. The song would eventually come out on the *Nirvana* best-of collection in 2002, though only after eight years of squabbling between Krist, Dave and Courtney on the best way to present it. The full tapes of the session have never been released.
6. Once Kurt turned up, this appears to have been a pretty fruitful day's recording in terms of throwing around ideas, opening with Nirvana's habitual noise-jam which at one point saw Kurt resurrecting the riff from the abandoned *Nevermind* track 'Verse Chorus Verse'. There's lots of musical experimentation here, especially on the two days Krist and Dave were killing time waiting for Kurt. They record with a harmonium organ for example, and a theremin played through an echoplex tape machine. Kurt plays drums on some Grohl stuff. Krist tries out some of his ideas. With the exception of the future Foo Fighters material, most of it sounds very half formed. That said, the sessions, when the band get down to business, sound fun and creative, and of course with 'You Know You're Right' the band absolutely nailed one final classic.
7. British viewers will recognise host Antoine de Caunes, who also presented 90s late-night shows *Rapido* and *Eurotrash*.

dressed in white shirts, black waistcoats and skinny ties in an attempt to look like The Knack. During 'Drain You', Kurt's guitar cuts out, and he finishes the song without it, leading to the rare vision of Nirvana, dressed in sharp suits, with Kurt singing without an instrument, hunched over the mic, grasping it with both hands.

February 6

- The European leg of the *In Utero* tour kicks off in Cascais, Portugal with British punk legends The Buzzcocks as support.[8] Across the next three weeks the band will play 16 shows in six countries: Portugal, Spain, France, Italy, Slovenia and Germany.[9] The plan is for the tour to then head through Belgium and the Netherlands and into a lengthy UK run, before heading back to the US for Lollapalooza in the summer.

February 14

- While in Paris, Kurt asks photographer and friend Youri Lenquette if the band could do an impromptu photoshoot.[10]

---

8. This was new cellist Melora Creager's first show with the band, with whom she hadn't even rehearsed. Kurt had told her to be creative and play whatever she wanted, so when it came to the gig itself, the rest of the band, who were assuming she'd be replicating Kera Schaley's parts from the album, were taken somewhat by surprise – anyone who has heard Rasputina will know that Creager has a fluid and creative approach to the cello. Before the next show she had to do a short bootcamp on the songs with Krist, bringing her parts closer to the album versions. There's still a lot of creativity in her playing, however – the part she creates for 'Dumb' is especially lovely.
9. This was not a happy tour and the good will that had sustained the US leg seems to have drained away. The band remained divided, travelling on separate buses with very different atmospheres. Kurt, who was in withdrawal and taking morphine in yet another attempt to kick his habit, was experiencing problems with his voice and was becoming more and more withdrawn and miserable as the shows continued. 'I thought I saw somebody seriously and dangerously depressed,' Melora Creager told Carrie Borzillo. Krist and Dave had both brought their partners on the road, and Kurt clearly missed Courtney deeply – however, she was in the UK doing promo for her upcoming album and unavailable. He was also, apparently, 'consumed with jealousy' (per Everett True) about Courtney sleeping with someone behind his back. 'I think he suspected her of cheating on him with Evan Dando and Billy Corgan,' Cali DeWitt says in *Nirvana: The True Story*. Courtney refutes that she ever cheated on Kurt – 'I almost [cheated] one time and he knew it,' she says in the interviews for *Montage of Heck*. 'I don't know how he knew it. The plan didn't go anywhere, so it was just – nothing happened ... I never, never cheated on him, but I certainly thought about it one time in London.' The evidence, of course, is totally circumstantial, but it's probably worth noting that Smashing Pumpkins were in London that February, playing a sold-out four night stand at The Astoria, at the same time Courtney was in town doing press. Cali DeWitt thinks something probably did happen between his boss and the Pumpkins frontman. 'I mean, define cheating?' he told Everett True. 'Did they get fucked up and make out one night? That counts to a husband who's wondering.' He remembers Kurt calling him and asking him directly (he denied any knowledge and kept his suspicions to himself.) In withdrawl, sick with jealousy and loneliness, in pain from his stomach and, as years of screaming over guitars and drums caught up with him, his throat; Kurt ploughed on with the shows. The amazing thing is that the gigs themselves are generally great – Nirvana were a well oiled touring machine with a team of techs to support them and organise everything. As long as the band could be shunted onstage at the right time, they would usually deliver.
10. The shots are deeply uncomfortable in retrospect. Kurt is back in his eyeliner era, trying to distract from how unhealthy his skin looks, and there's a sort of forced-whackiness about the whole thing – a band trying to look like they're having fun. Lenquette was unprepared for the shoot, Kurt's skin looks awful and there's a general sense that no-one really wants to be there. Most startlingly of all, at least with hindsight, is how many of the shots feature guns – pointed at the camera, tucked into Dave's waistband, and most horribly, stuck in Kurt's mouth. According to Lenquette this was all directed by Kurt.

February 23

- The band appear on Italian TV show *The Tunnell*, performing 'Dumb' and 'Serve The Servants'.[11]

February 25

- After a pair of shows in Milan, taking place over his wedding anniversary (which he is spending apart from Courtney), Kurt tells Krist that he wants to cancel the tour, though he doesn't go so far as insisting or demanding that they pull the rest of the shows.[12] The next few dates go ahead as planned.[13]

March 1

- The band play the 3,000-capacity *Terminal 1* in Munich, Germany, the first of two planned dates. Between the soundcheck and the show itself, Kurt leaves the venue and it's widely assumed he is heading into the city to score heroin. He calls Courtney and gets into another argument with her, then puts in a transatlantic call to Rosemary Carroll, the band's lawyer and Danny Goldberg's partner, and tells her that he wants a divorce. The show itself is plagued with technical difficulties, and at one point the power cuts entirely. Kurt's sore throat is also causing him problems. [14] The band open with a short cover of The Car's new wave hit 'My

---

11. This is Nirvana's final TV appearance and though musically, and even vocally, the performance is fine, it also has a weary quality. Krist's mugging for the camera has a forced energy, Kurt looks exhausted. It's easy to project these kind of things with hindsight, of course. The whole thing is on YouTube if you want to judge for yourself. Gear nerds will appreciate a rare sighting of Kurt playing his custom Fender Jag-Stang, the guitar he'd designed in collaboration with Fender's custom shop. (See entry for January/February 1993.)
12. Krist describes this conversation to Charles R. Cross for his book *Heavier Than Heaven*. It's not clear, however, if Krist talks Kurt into continuing (he certainly remembers pointing out to him that cancelling would cost them a fortune, since they apparently had no insurance), or if Kurt simply relents. Krist does theorise that the only reason his old friend didn't throw in the towel there and then, is that the band were due to play Slovenia next, the Novoselic's home soil, and many of Krist's relatives were going to be attending. 'He hung in there for me,' he said. 'But I think his mind was made up.'
13. The Milan show features Kurt's final ever performance of 'Smells Like Teen Spirit', the song that changed not just his life, but also thousands more. It's a surprisingly tight and energised run through a number the band could often be guilty of phoning in – the US tour was full of sloppy, half-assed versions. Here though, it sounds as vital as it ever did, punchy and muscular. I don't think there's anything particular to read into that; the band were just having a good show with a great crowd. It's satisfying that the final performance of Kurt's most important song is a good one, however.
14. This is the final Nirvana show of Kurt Cobain's lifetime, and the final live performance Kurt would ever give, so it's easy to project all sorts of meaning onto its various moments, finding poignancy in places that would otherwise be passed over in the grand scheme – 'This is the last time he plays the amazing solo to 'In Bloom'!' 'This is the last time he'll ever introduce 'About A Girl'!' 'This is the last time he'll ever scream the "yeaaah" on 'Lithium"… and on and on. All of those thoughts are valid, though they tell us more about how the context of a performance can be more meaningful than the mechanics of the show itself. If you didn't know this was the last show the band would ever play then Munich becomes just another solid Nirvana gig, with all the chaos and heart and triumph and mess found in pretty much any of the band's performances. There's a textbook Krist Novoselic comic riff in the middle where he says 'Grunge is dead! Nirvana is over!' which could take on some significance if it wasn't such an obvious bit of schtick ('Our next album is gonna be hip hop. We're going sing about bitches and sucking dick and guns and stuff!') Kurt's voice is certainly stuggling in places – we know he was suffering with a sore throat, but even so, his screams on 'School' and 'Lithium' are as blood-curdling as they ever were, though

Best Friend's Girl', a song Kurt first learned to play when he was 15 and teaching himself guitar.[15] After the show, Kurt tells his booking agent to cancel the next two gigs: a second date in Munich and a show in Offenbach, Germany. The plan, as far as everyone is concerned, is to resume the tour on 11 March in Prague.

March 2

- Kurt sees a doctor who diagnoses him with severe laryngitis and bronchitis, and prescribes four months off, though no more shows are officially cancelled yet. With time to kill before the next leg of the tour, Krist flies back to Seattle, Dave stays in Germany where he has promotional duties for the *Backbeat* soundtrack[16] and Kurt and Pat head to Rome, where Kurt has planned a reunion with Courtney.

And in a way, this is where the story stops. Munich was the last time all of the members of Nirvana were in the same room, the last time they worked together, the last time they made music. In the story of the band, as a functional, musical unit, as a creative partnership, as an entity that was more than the sum of its parts, the journey that began when Dale Crover and Kurt Cobain recorded a demo as Fecal Matter in Mari Freudenberg's house in 1986 ends on 1 March 1994, in Munich – and fittingly, Crover was present for it – the opening band that night were the Melvins. There's more story to tell of course – in many ways it's a story that's never really ended, though in another, more real sense, it will come to a horrible, shuddering and final conclusion the following month.

What follows is not the story of a band any more. That story ends here. I've tried to keep this book focused on the music, the achievements and the context of Nirvana … and there is no more music to be made. No more performances. Later, there are achievements of sorts – the sublime *Unplugged In New York* album and its deserved Grammy win. Box sets. Compilations. The Rock 'N' Roll Hall of Fame. The triumphant unveiling of 'You Know You're Right' in 2002. Millions and millions more record sales, and not just of the recognised anthems

by 'Territorial Pissings' you can hear him really starting to struggle, and in an encore performance of 'All Apologies' and 'Heart Shaped Box' he's audibly straining, occasionally ducking to a lower register. None of those moments are especially disastrous, however. Sure 'Heart Shaped Box' is a poignant closer ('All Apologies' would have been more so), but this particular performance doesn't feel especially poignant in itself, compared with any other. If anything, there's a sense Kurt just wants to get it over with and rest his voice. It's a shorter set, there's no 'Smells Like Teen Spirit' (always a sign that Kurt was unhappy), no noise jam or orgy of destruction, but it's unlikely anyone in the audience would have gone away feeling they'd seen anything of particular significance in the history of the band, as they might have done had the show ended in a brutal meltdown, or been particularly triumphant. It's just … another *In Utero* era Nirvana show. This will be a difficult show for some people to listen to, knowing the interior pain Kurt was feeling, but others will hear nothing more than a decent-enough gig from a great band. Context is everything.

15. Everett True notes that the significance of this song being about a cheating girlfriend; the reader is left to draw conclusions on this themselves. Probably more significant and characteristically passive aggressive is the return of 'Lounge Act' to the set; a song Courtney hated for its association with Tobi Vail.
16. See entry for 26 March 1993

like 'Smells Like Teen Spirit' and 'Heart Shaped Box'. *Bleach* and *Incesticide* will eventually sell two million copies apiece. The *With The Lights Out* box set will mean new fans, people not even born when the band were functioning, will come to know and love songs like 'Mrs Butterworth', 'Clean Up Before She Comes' and 'Ain't It A Shame'. Fans not only know the names 'Kurt Cobain', 'Krist Novoselic' and 'Dave Grohl', they also know Chad Channing, Aaron Burckhard, Dave Foster, Dale Crover and Dan Peters. They know Hole and the Melvins and Mudhoney. They know Beat Happening, Shonen Knife and The Vaselines. Those achievements are arguably more remarkable than getting a song called 'Rape Me' on *SNL*, or doing a Morrissey impression on *Top of the Pops*. That is the band's true legacy. That's the cultural footprint that matters – bringing the underground overground. That and the music.

What comes next has nothing to do with music. It's a different story to the one we're telling here. But it overlaps, and it's important. It's closure. What follows isn't the story of Nirvana any more. It's the story of Kurt. A horrible story. For all of those reasons, I'm not covering it in forensic detail – there are far more detailed accounts of the end of Kurt's tale that I can recommend, notably Charles R. Cross's definitive *Heavier Than Heaven* and Everett True's *Nirvana: The True Story*. Courtney Love's autobiography is apparently on the way. Many, many people have written about what happens next – it never has a happy ending. I didn't *want* to dwell on this part of the story. I wanted to write about life, not death. Music, not addiction. But the basics are important, and our story is incomplete without them.

And if all of that is clear, and it's alright with you ... read on.

March 3

- Kurt checks into the Excelsior Hotel in Rome to await Courtney and Frances' arrival. He has planned a romantic evening, has bought his wife diamonds and lingerie, strewn the room with roses and, according to Courtney, he has even stolen two huge candlesticks from the Vatican earlier that day. Courtney, however, is tired. She takes a pill and goes to sleep.[17]

March 4

- Courtney wakes up to find Kurt apparently dead on the floor. He has taken over 60 pills of the powerful tranquiliser Rohypnol, washed down with champagne. In his hand is a three page 'goodbye' note, in which he compares himself to Hamlet, having to choose between life and death. To be or not to be. 'I'm choosing death,'

17. 'Even if I wasn't in the mood I should have just laid there for him. All he needed was to get laid,' she later told *Rolling Stone*.

Kurt wrote. He is fully dressed, wearing an outdoor coat, and in his other hand is $1,000 in cash.[18] At 6.30am he is taken by ambulance to a local hospital, placed on life support and has his stomach pumped. He is declared to be in a coma.

- In the UK, BBC Radio One breaks the news that Kurt is an 'irreversible coma', while in the US the CNN news network reports that Kurt has died.[19] Nirvana's management issue a statement saying that Kurt has 'suffered a complete collapse due to fatigue and severe influenza ... complication arose after he combined prescription painkillers with alcohol. Doctors report he has made responsive signs'.[20] Dave Grohl receives a phone call telling him that Kurt is dead[21], and another shortly afterwards confirming that he is still alive.

March 5

- Kurt regains consciousness after 20 hours in a coma and is moved to The American Hospital.

March 9

- With some fairly insensitive timing, Kevin Kerslake files a legal complaint against Nirvana over the 'Heart Shaped Box' video, alleging that his treatment was used by Anton Corbijn. This would prey on Kurt's mind in the coming weeks, as he pondered both the betrayal from someone he'd considered a friend and the potentially catastrophic financial consequences should Kerslake win his case.[22]

March 12

- Kurt and Courtney return to Seattle. Nirvana's UK tour is pushed back to mid-April.[23]

---

18. These latter factors have led some to believe that Kurt was planning to simply leave, rather than end his life at this point, and that the overdose was a late decision.
19. This false report apparently originated from a hoax phone call made to David Geffen, though exactly how and why it got out has never been revealed.
20. Remarkably, Nirvana's team managed to hide the fact that the incident in Rome was a suicide attempt until after Kurt's death the following month. The official story of 'accidental overdose' was the one that stuck.
21. 'My knees gave out and I dropped the phone as I fell to my bedroom floor, covering my face with my hands as I began to cry,' wrote Dave in *Storyteller: Tales of Life and Music*. 'He was gone'.
22. Which he likely would have done, since he'd meticulously recorded his preparation. The case was eventually settled out of court later in the year. It must have felt like a hollow victory.
23. Nirvana's management were *very* loath to officially cancel shows. As late as 11 March, cellist Melora Creager was still being told that the mainland Europe dates beginning in Prague might happen, and even when the European shows were finally given up for lost, she was told to keep the summer free for Lollapalooza. The reason of course, was financial. Nirvana apparently *did* have insurance, but it wasn't a failsafe and Kurt's incident in Rome put things in a medical grey area – which was one of the reasons for keeping his true intentions under wraps. In the coming months there was pressure from all sides, from their management (though apparently not Danny Goldberg himself), Courtney, the rest of the band, for Kurt to agree to do the Lollapalooza tour, even though he hated the idea. No contract was ever signed, but negotiations were ongoing right up to the wire. There were also plans to tour South America and Japan. The whole organisation stood to lose money with Nirvana off the road, and it was in everyone's financial interests to play the tour. It put Kurt, burnt out from months on the road, worried

March 18

- Police are called to Kurt and Courtney's residence after a disturbance is reported. The couple has been arguing again over Kurt's drug use and the fact that he is keeping guns in the house ('for protection against home invaders'). A number of guns and illegally-obtained medicines are confiscated. Kurt is taken in by police but not charged.

March 24

- In the weeks following his return from Rome, Kurt's drug problems have spiralled to their most serious yet. Courtney, with the assistance of his managers and friends, stages another intervention. Nirvana's management are in attendance, though only Pat Smear is present from the band itself.[24] The intervention is something of a disaster – Kurt becomes angry and petulant and in the end he and Pat hide themselves away to play guitar and work on songs.

March 25

- Kurt, Pat and Hole's Eric Erlandson play music together and record some 4-track demos at Kurt's house. Among them is a new Cobain composition called 'Do Re Mi', an acoustic demo of which had already been recorded at his home earlier in the year.[25]

March 30

- Determined to make one last go at getting clean, Kurt checks into the Exodus rehab facility in LA. Gibby Haynes from Butthole Surfers is also a patient at the facility at the time.

April 1

- Kurt escapes rehab and flies back to Seattle.[26] On the flight home, by pure chance, he meets Guns 'N' Roses bass player Duff McKagan, himself recently clean of

---

that he couldn't continue to scream if he wanted to protect his voice, in the grip of addiction and hating every second of being in Nirvana, in an intolerable place.

24. Krist had already tipped Kurt off about a previous intervention, and had no wish to be involved. He didn't believe it would work, and thought it could well make matters worse.
25. These recordings have never been released, and are probably the most sought-after Nirvana rarities. 'Do Re Mi', an earlier acoustic demo of which was made available on *With The Lights Out,* is a beautiful piece, and Kurt's most obviously Beatles-indebted writing since 'About A Girl'. It was intended to be included on an EP to coincide with Lollapalooza, which would likely have also featured 'You Know You're Right', though it could also have been ear-marked for a planned project with Michael Stipe of REM. It is more or less the last Kurt Cobain song that we have.
26. In a move that says everything about Kurt's sense of humour, even in the bleakest times, he breaks out of rehab by climbing over the rear wall, even though there was nothing to stop him walking out the front door. He and Gibby Haynes had been laughing earlier about another patient who did exactly that, and Kurt must have gotten a kick out of the idea.

heroin, who is also returning to his native Seattle.[27] McKagan, who considers inviting Kurt to hang out more, loses track of him at Sea-Tac airport. Kurt doesn't inform Courtney that he is back in town, and she considers him missing. She begins a frantic search in LA, worrying that he will overdose or kill himself.

April 4

- Kurt's mother, Wendy O'Conner, files a missing person's report for her son with the Seattle police department. It states that Kurt has 'bought a shotgun and may be suicidal', but is not considered dangerous.

April 6

- The Lollapalooza line up is officially unveiled, with the surprise omission of Nirvana. 'Due to Kurt Cobain's ill health, we cannot confirm them on the bill,' a spokesman tells *Billboard*. Unknown to the media, Kurt hasn't been heard from for several days. *The LA Times* runs a story reporting that Nirvana has broken up.[28]

April 7

- Courtney Love is taken to Century City Hospital in LA after an apparent heroin overdose at the Peninsula Hotel, where she has also been attempting to get clean.

April 8

- A body is discovered by a workman, Gary T. Smith, in a green house above the garage at the Cobains' home near Lake Washington. It's later confirmed to be that of Kurt Cobain. Beside him is a suicide note and a Remington 20-gauge shot gun, which Kurt had purchased on his return to Seattle. REM's *Automatic For The People* has been played on the stereo.[29] It will later be discovered that Kurt had taken a massive, almost-certainly lethal overdose of heroin before shooting himself in the head with the shotgun. He also had traces of valium in his system. He is thought to have been lying dead for three or four days. Officially his date of death is 5 April, though it could have also been early on 6 April. The following day, a coroner officially rules his death a suicide. He was 27 years old; a father, a husband, an incredible artist. And he was gone.

---

27. 'I was in my hell and he was in his,' Duff wrote in his memoir *It's So Easy (and Other Lies)*. 'We both seemed to understand'.
28. 'They've been on the verge of breaking up forever and this doesn't sound more serious than the other 43,000 times,' the *Times* quotes an anonymous report as saying. 'Though this could be a signal from the other members of the band that Kurt needs to focus on taking better care of himself.'
29. I've always been haunted and fascinated by this detail. The last album Kurt likely ever heard, assuming he hit play, was REM's beautiful, melancholy and smart masterpiece. The album that includes 'Everybody Hurts', a song devastating in its simplicity and its message: I know it's hard. Everyone feels like this sometimes. 'Just hang on'.

Epilogue

There was more of course. There were the news reports, the statements, the piecing together of the details. Kurt Loder breaking the story on *MTV News*. There was the memorial service, a recording of Courtney tearfully reading from Kurt's suicide note. Kids with hands covered in wax from the candles they held. There have been the conspiracy theories (which I reject, by the way) and the obituaries, the tributes. There's the future careers of Dave Grohl, Krist Novoselic and Pat Smear. There's Hole's masterpiece *Live Through This*, released just weeks later, and the death of their bass player, Kristen Pfaff just months after Kurt's. There's *Unplugged In New York*, and its originally-planned second disc, *Verse Chorus Verse*, which would have featured more live Nirvana songs, if only Krist, Dave and Scott Litt, who had been tasked with mixing the record, had the heart and stomach to finish it amidst their grief. They did not. There's *Live! Tonight! Sold Out!*, the home-video Kurt had been working on, stitching together performances and interviews documenting the madness around the release of *Nevermind*.[1] There's the Rock 'N' Roll Hall of Fame induction twenty years later, when Krist, Dave and Pat performed Nirvana hits with brilliant female singers – Joan Jett doing 'Teen Spirit', Lorde doing 'All Apologies', St Vincent doing 'Lithium', Kim Gordon's thrilling, messy version of 'Aneurysm'. 20th and 30th anniversaries for *Bleach*, *Nevermind*, *In Utero* and *Unplugged*. Dave Grohl performing 'Heart Shaped Box' with his daughter, Violet. The death of Steve Albini in 2024. The deaths of Chris Cornell, Layne Stayley, Mark Lanegan, Dylan Carlson. The story doesn't end. Not really.

Except it did. Either with a flicker in Germany, or with horrible finality in Seattle.

What would have happened if Kurt had lived? The question is asked over and over, the evidence examined, the speculations logged. But Kurt *didn't* live. That's the point. He didn't want to. Living would have meant living clean, and Kurt couldn't do that. If he couldn't do that for his daughter, he certainly couldn't do that for his band.

Did Nirvana even still exist? That's a tricky one. Relations between the core trio had been toxic for a while. Sometime around March 1994 Kurt wrote a heartbreaking rant to Krist in the form of an unsent letter. 'You've done a lot

1. 'Before the stage is set. Before one lick of the guitar is heard …' Nirvana's best, deepest cut joke. If you know, you know.

for me sometimes,' it read, 'and mostly you've done less than nothing'. It goes on to call NIRVANA[2] 'an embarrassment'. First he says he will start another band, then he says he'll keep Nirvana going with other musicians. 'For years I had to sit and listen to your opinions about my songs my ideas my band,' he continues. 'I wasn't put here to please you … I have learned to hate the idea of this band with you and Dave.' That's pretty clear. Kurt never sent the letter, of course, but then he had fired plenty of people without actually telling them himself. Dave Foster got the same treatment back in 1988. On the other hand, the Kurt of spring 1994 was hardly in his right mind. Suicide, by definition, is rarely a sane act. Addiction does not allow for clear thinking.

It's clear what Nirvana needed, what Kurt needed, was space and time. And what he got was pressure and demands, from his band mates, his managers and his wife. To someone as petulant, as truculent, as stubborn and volatile as Kurt, that was a recipe for disaster. Maybe they could have taken a year off that dissolved into 'hiatus'. Kurt could have made a solo album, done what The Pixies' Frank Black did and cover himself in lo-fi obscurity. Would his ego have allowed that? Would his ambition? Dave could have gone off and done Foo Fighters and become the everyman classic rock star he was obviously always destined to be, and maybe in five or ten or fifteen years time they'd have drifted back together. Cobain/Grohl could have been the new Lennon/McCartney. They certainly fit those moulds. They would have headlined Glastonbury. Made a few more million. Done an album, and then returned to their differing poles again. Lots of bands have done it that way. The Police. Blur. Fleetwood Mac. Radiohead. We'd have had lots more Kurt Cobain music. Frances Bean would have had a father.

But that's another reality. That's not the timeline we live in. In *this* reality, Kurt Cobain had given up. You could argue that he'd fallen out of love with music years earlier, when *Nevermind* hit big. For two years he'd been a song-writing machine, but that had slowed to a trickle between 1992 and 1994. Half of *In Utero* dated back to 1990 and 1991. In the months that followed its release, there was little sign that Kurt was getting his songwriting mojo back, as brilliant as 'You Know You're Right' is, as beautiful as 'Do Re Mi' could have been. All he was left with was pressure and demands and things going wrong around him. The thing that gave him solace, heroin, was the thing everyone was trying to take away. His whole life had become incompatible, a mass of contradictions. It's horrible. It's unfair. It shouldn't have been like that.

2. Kurt always wrote the band's name in capitals.

That's why there's no point in playing the speculation game. In pondering what the 57-year-old, 65-year old, 80-year old Kurt would have been bringing to the table. He left us. He's gone. He didn't want that.

But what a legacy. What a footprint to have left. What songs. He mythologised Punk Rock and defined post-modern artistic credibility. He highlighted the contradiction inherent in celebrating someone for their underground sensibility and their pop heart at exactly the same time. He recreated the idea of the rock star, and made a ton of people look extremely stupid extremely quickly. And those songs. That glorious noise. He called it Nirvana. And he attained perfection.

Well, whatever. Never mind.

Marc Burrows
June 2024

Bibliography

Primary sources, photobooks and memoirs

Bollen, Andy. *Nirvana: A Tour Diary*. London: Omnibus Press, 2000.

Cobain, Kurt. *Journals*. New York: Riverhead Books, 2002

Cross, Charles R. *Cobain Unseen*. New York: Hodder & Stoughton, 2008

Goldberg, Danny. *Serving the Servant: Remembering Kurt Cobain*. New York: Ecco, 2019

Gordon, Kim. *Girl In A Band*. London: Faber & Faber, 2015

Grohl, Dave. *The Storyteller: Tales of Life and Music*. New York: Dey Street Books, 2021

Guzman. *Family Values: Kurt, Courtney and Frances Bean*. New York: Powerhouse Books, 2024

Erlandson, Eric. *Letters To Kurt*. New York. Akashic, 2012

Hanley, Steven. *The Big Midweek: Life Inside The Fall*. London: Route Publishing, 2014

Hanna, Kathleen. *Rebel Girl: My Life as a Feminist Punk*. New York: Ecco, 2024

Hughes, John and Novoselic, Krist. *Of Grunge and Government: An Oral History eBook*. Seattle: Washington State Legacy Project, 2009

Keidis, Anthony. *Scar Tissue*. London: Sphere, 2004

Lanegan, Mark. *Sing Backwards and Weep*. London: White Rabbit, 2020

Love, Courtney. *Dirty Blonde: The Diaries of Courtney Love*. London: Faber & Faber, 2006

McKagan, Duff. *It's So Easy (and Other Lies)*. New York: Touchstone, 2011

Moore, Thurston. *Sonic Life*. New York: Doubleday, 2023

Novoselic, Krist. *Of Grunge and Government: Let's Fix This Broken Democracy*. New York: RDV Books, 2004

Pavitt, Bruce. *Experiencing Nirvana: Grunge in Europe, 1989*. Seattle: Bazillion Points, 2013

Pavitt, Bruce. *Sub Pop USA: The Subterranean Pop Music Anthology, 1980–1988*. Seattle: Bazillion Points, 2014

Rollins, Henry. *Get In The Van, On The Road With Black Flag*. Los Angeles: 2.13.62, 1994

Thompson, Dave. *The Grunge Diaries*. New York: St. Martin's Griffin, 2004

Turner, Steve. *Mudride*. London: Omnibus Press, 2016

Books about Nirvana and related persons

Azerrad, Michael. *Come As You Are: The Story of Nirvana*. New York: Doubleday, 1993.

Azerrad, Michael. *The Amplified Come As You Are*. New York: Hachette Books, 2023.

Branigan, Paul. *This Is A Call: The Life and Times of Dave Grohl*. London: HarperCollins, 2011

Brite, Poppy Z. *Courtney Love: The Real Story*. New York: Orion, 1998

Borzillo, Carrie. *Nirvana: In the Words of the People Who Were There*. London: Carlton Books, 2000.

Burlingame, Jeff. *Nirvana: A Biography*. Santa Barbara: Greenwood Press, 2006.

Crisafulli, Chuck. *Nirvana: Verse Chorus Verse, The Story Behind Every Song*. London: SevenOaks, 2018

Cross, Charles R. *Heavier Than Heaven: A Biography of Kurt Cobain*. New York: Hyperion, 2001

Cross, Charles R. *Here We Are Now: The Lasting Impact of Kurt Cobain*. New York: HarperCollins, 2014

Cross, Charles R. and Jim Berkenstadt. *Classic Rock Albums: Nevermind.* New York: Schirmer Books, 1998.
Gaar, Gillian G. *Entertain Us: The Rise of Nirvana.* New York: Jawbone Press, 2012.
Gaar, Gillian G. *In Utero 33⅓* . London: Bloomsbury, 2006
Gaar, Gillian G. *Treasures of Nirvana.* Sevenoaks: Carlton Books, 2011
George-Warren, Holly (editor). *Cobain, By The Editors of Rolling Stone.* New York: Rolling Stone Press, 1994
Jovanovic, Rob. *Nirvana: The Recording Sessions.* London: Firefly, 2004
Luerssen. John D. *Nirvana FAQ: All That's Left To Know About The Most Important Band of the 90s.* Milwaukee: Backbeat Books, 2014
Morgan, Brett, Bienstock, Richard. *Cobain, Montage of Heck.* New York: Omnibus Press, 2015
Soulsby, Nick. *Cobain On Cobain: Interviews and Encounters.* London: Omnipress, 2016
Soulsby, Nick. *I Found My Friends: The Oral History of Nirvana.* New York: St. Martin's Griffin, 2015
Soulsby, Nick. *Dark Slivers: Seeing Nirvana in the Shards of Incesticide.* London: Running Water Publicatons, 2012
True, Everett. *Nirvana: The True Story.* London: Omnibus Press, 2006

General reference, oral histories and books about music
Azerrad, Michael. *Our Band Could Be Your Life: Scenes from the American Indie Underground,* 1981–1991. New York: Little, Brown and Company, 2001
Cameron, Keith. *Mudhoney: The Sound & The Fury From Seattle.* London: Omnibus Press, 2018
Garner, Ken. *Peel Sessions – Teenage dreams and one man's love of new music.* London: BBC Books, 2007
Prato, Greg. *Grunge Is Dead: The Oral History of Seattle Rock Music.* Toronto: ECW Press, 2009
Rae, Casey. *William Burroughs and the Cult of Rock 'N' Roll.* Austin: University of Texas Press, 2019
Yarm, Mark. *Everybody Loves Our Town: An Oral History of Grunge.* New York: Crown Archetype, 2011.

Newspapers, magazines, fanzines and other periodicals
Backlash (fanzine)
BAM (Bay Area Music) Magazine. San Francisco: BAM Media, 1976–1999
BigO. Singapore: BigO Pte Ltd, 1985–2003
Bikini Kill. Olympia: Self-published fanzine
Backlash. Seattle: Self-published fanzine
Billboard Magazine. New York: Prometheus Global Media, 1894–present
Chicago Sun-Times. Chicago: Sun-Times Media Group, 1948–present
Clot Self-published fanzine
Details Magazine New York: Condé Nast, 1982–2015
Dirt Self-published fanzine
Flipside. Los Angeles: Self-published fanzine, 1977–2000
Freiburger Nachrichten. Fribourg: Freiburger Nachrichten AG, 1863–present
GQ. New York: Condé Nast, 1931–present
Hits Magazine. Los Angeles: HITS Magazine, Inc., 1986–present
Kerrang!. London: Wasted Talent Ltd, 1981–present
Matt Lukin's Legs. Self-published fanzine
Maximumrocknroll. San Francisco: Self-published, 1982–2019

Melody Maker. London: IPC Media, 1926–2000
Mojo. London: Bauer Media Group, 1993–present
Monk Magazine. San Francisco: Monk Media, 1986–1998
Mucchio Selvaggio. Italian publication
National Enquirer. New York: American Media, Inc., 1926–present
Newsweek Magazine. New York: Newsweek Inc., 1933–present
NME (New Musical Express). London: TI Media, 1952–present
No Trend Press. German pulication
Offbeat. New Orleans: OffBeat, Inc., 1988–present
Option. Los Angeles: Option Publishing, 1985–2001
Q Magazine. London: Bauer Media Group, 1986–2020
Raw. London: EMAP, 1988–2001
Rockpool. New York: Rockpool Productions, 1985–1995
Rolling Stone. New York: Penske Media Corporation, 1967–present
Seattle Times. Seattle: The Seattle Times Company, 1891–present
Select Magazine. London: EMAP Metro, 1990–2001
Sleep Self-published fanzine
Sounds. London: United Newspapers, 1970–1991
Spin. New York: Spin Media LLC, 1985–present.
Subterranean Pop aka *Sub/Pop*. Olympia/Seattle: Self-published fanzine, 1979–1988
The Advocate. Los Angeles: Here Media, 1967–present
The Boston Globe. Boston: Boston Globe Media Partners, LLC, 1872–present
The Current. Tacoma newspaper
The Guardian. London: Guardian Media Group, 1821–present
The Independent. London: Independent Digital News & Media, 1986–present
The Irish Independent. Dublin: Independent News & Media, 1905–present
The New York Times. New York: The New York Times Company, 1851–present
The Observer. London: Guardian Media Group, 1791–present
The Rocket. Seattle: The Rocket, 1979–2000
Top Rock Magazine. Brazil
Uncut. London: TI Media, 1997–present
USA. New York: Gannett Company, 1982–2019
Vanity Fair. New York: Condé Nast, 1983–present

Online Resources

Beato, Rick. YouTube channel. https://www.youtube.com/user/pegzch
Conan O'Brien Needs a Friend. Podcast. Team Coco & Earwolf
Grammy.com. Recording Academy. https://www.grammy.com/
Life of the Record Podcast
LiveNirvana.com. https://www.livenirvana.com/
Moma.org (Museum of Modern Art, New York). http://www.moma.org
MP3.com (defunct)
Nirvana-Legacy.com. Nick Soulsby. http://nirvana-legacy.com/
Poynter.org. The Poynter Institute. https://www.poynter.org/
Reddit.com (AMA with Craig Montgommery, AMA with Aaron Burckhard) Reddit Inc. http://www.reddit.com/
The Ringer. http://www.theringer.com/
Vulture. http://www.vulture.com
Washington State Legacy. Washington State Department of Enterprise Services.

TV and Radio Shows
Classic Albums: Nevermind. Television series. VH1, 2005
Headbanger's Ball Television series. MTV, 1987–1995
Rapido. Television series. BBC Two, 1988–1992
The Chart Show. Television series. ITV, 1986–1998
The Howard Stern Show. WXRK (1986–2005) SiriusXM (2006–present)
The Word. Television series. Channel 4, 1990–1995.

Films
1991: The Year Punk Broke. Directed by David Markey. Geffen Pictures/Sonic Life, 1992
Hit So Hard. Documentary film. Directed by P. David Ebersole. Go Digital, 2011
Hype. Directed by Doug Pray. Helvery-Pray Productions, 1996
Nirvana: In Utero – Under Review. Produced by Thomas Walker. Chrome Dreams Media, 2006
Nirvana: Live! Tonight! Sold Out!! Directed by Kevin Kerslake and Kurt Cobain. MCA, 1994
Montage of Heck. Documentary film. Directed by Brett Morgen. HBO Films, 2015
When Nirvana Came to Britain. Television documentary. BBC, 2021
Sound City. Documentary film. Directed by Dave Grohl. Roswell Films, 2013
TAD – Busted Circuits and Ringing Ears. Directed by Adam Pease and Ryan Short. King Of Hearts productions, 2008

Required Listening
Note: This list albums and EPs combines key records mentioned in the text with albums the author feels are essential for understanding the era and albums listed as essential by Kurt Cobain in his journals. The latter are denoted with an *.

Aerosmith – *Rocks* (Columbia, 1976)*
Afghan Whigs – *Up in It* (Sub Pop, 1990)
Afghan Whigs – *Congregation* (Sub Pop, 1992)
Alice In Chains – *Facelift* (Columbia Records, 1990)
Babes in Toyland – *Spanking Machine* (Sub Pop/Twin Tone, 1990)
Babes in Toyland – *Fontanelle* (Reprise, 1992)
Backbeat – *Original Soundtrack* (Virgin Records, 1994)
Bad Brains – *Rock For Light* (Passport Records, 1983)
Beat Happening – *Jamboree* (K Records, 1988)*
Beat Happening – *Dreamy* (Sub Pop/K, 1991)*
Beat Happening – *Black Candy* (Sub Pop/K Records, 1989)
Big Black – *Songs About Fucking* (Touch and Go Records, 1987)*
Bikini Kill – *Revolution Girl Style Now* (Self released, 1991)
Bikini Kill – *Pussy Whipped* (kill rock starts, 1993)
Black Flag – *Damaged* (SST Records, 1981)*
Black Flag – *My War* (SST Records, 1984)*
Black Sabbath – *Master of Reality* (Island, 1971)*
The Breeders – *Pod* (4AD, 1990)*
The Breeders – *Last Splash* (4AD, 1993)
Butthole Surfers – *Locust Abortion Technician* (Touch and Go, 1987)*
Buzzcocks – *Singles Going Steady* (I.R.S., 1979)*
Calamity Jane – *Matha Jane Cannary* (SMR Records, 1992)
Credence Clearwater Revival – *Bayou Country* (RCA, 1969)*

Daniel Johnston – *Yip/Jump Music* (Self-released, 1983)*
David Bowie – *The Man Who Sold The World* (Mercury, 1970)*
Devo – *Q: Are We Not Men? A: We Are Devo!* (Warner, 1978)*
Dinosaur Jr – *You're Living All Over Me* (SST Records, 1987)
Dinosaur Jr – *Bug* (SST Records, 1988)
Dinosaur Jr – *Green Mind* (Sire Records, 1991)
The Dwarves – *Blood Guts & Pussy* (Sub Pop, 1990)
Earth – *Earth 2: Special Low Frequency Version* (Sub Pop, 1993)
Evel Knievel – *Evel Knievel* (Amhurst, 1974)*
Fang – *Landshark!* (Boner Records, 1982)*
Fear – *The Record* (Slash Records, 1982)*
Flipper – *Album: Generic Flipper* (Subterranean Records, 1982)*
Flipper – *Gone Fishin'* (Subterranean Records, 1984)*
Foo Fighters – *Foo Fighters* (Roswell/Capitol Records, 1995)
The Frogs – *It's Only Right and Natural* (Homestead Records, 1989)*
Fugazi – *13 Songs* (Dischord Records, 1989)
Fugazi – *Repeater* (Dischord Records, 1990)
Gang of Four – *Entertainment*! (EMI, 1979)*
Green River – *Dry As a Bone* EP (Sub Pop, 1987)
Green River – *Rehab Doll* (Sub Pop, 1988)
Half Japanese – *We Are They Who Ache with Amorous Love* (TEC Tones, 1990)*
Hole – *Pretty On the Inside* (Caroline Records, 1991)*
Hole – *Live Through This* (DGC, 1994)
Hole – *My Body, The Hand Grenade* (City Slang, 1997)
Huggy Bear – *Rubbing the Impossible to Burst* EP (WIIJA, 1992)*
Iggy Pop – *The Idiot* (RCA, 1977)*
Iggy and the Stooges – *Raw Power* (Columbia, 1973)*
Jad Fair – *Great Expectations* (Bad Alchemy, 1989)*
John Lennon – *John Lennon/Plastic Ono Band* (Apple Records, 1970)
Killdozer – *12 Point Buck* (Touch and Go, 1989)
Killing Joke – *Killing Joke* (E.G. Records, 1980)
L7 – *Smell the Magic* (Sub Pop, 1990)
L7 – *Bricks Are Heavy* (Sub Pop/Slash, 1992)
LATE! – *Pocketwatch* (Simple Machines, 1992)
Lead Belly – *Lead Belly's Last Sessions* (Folkways Records, 1953)*
Led Zeppelin – *Led Zeppelin II*
Led Zeppelin – *Led Zeppelin III*
Led Zeppelin – *IV*
Marine Girls – *Beach Party* (Cherry Red, 1981)*
Mark Lanegan – *The Winding Sheet* (Sub Pop, 1990)
Mazzy Star – *She Hangs Brightly* (Rough Trade, 1990)*
Meat Puppets – *Meat Puppets II* (SST Records, 1984)*
Meat Puppets – *Up on the Sun* (SST Records, 1985)
Melvins – *Gluey Porch Treatments* (Alchemy Records, 1987)*
Melvins – *Ozma* (Boner Records, 1989)*
Melvins – *Houdini* (Atlantic, 1993)
MDB – *Millions of Dead Cops* (R Radical, 1982)*
Minor Threat – *Complete Discography* (Dischord Records, 1989)

Mudhoney – *Superfuzz Bigmuff* (Sub Pop, 1988)*
Mudhoney – *Mudhoney* (Sub Pop, 1989)
Mudhoney – *Every Good Boy Deserves Fudge* (Sub Pop, 1991)*
Mudhoney – *Piece of Cake* (Reprise, 1993)
Nirvana – *Bleach* (Sub Pop, 1989, reissues 1992, 2009)
Nirvana – *Nevermind* (DGC, 1991, reissues 2011, 2021)
Nirvana – *Incesticide* (Sub Pop, DGC, 1992)
Nirvana – *In Utero* (DGC, 1993, reissues 2013, 2023)
Nirvana – *Unplugged In New York* (DGC, 1994, reissue 2023)
Nirvana – *From The Muddy Banks of the Wishkah* (DGC, 1996)
Nirvana – *Nirvana* (DGC, Geffen, 2002)
Nirvana – *With The Lights Out* (DGC, Geffen, 2004)
Nirvana – *Sliver: The Best of the Box* (DGC, Geffen, 2005)
Pearl Jam – *Ten* (Epic Records, 1991)
PJ Harvey – *Dry* (Island, 1991)*
PJ Harvey – *Rid of Me* (Island, 1992)
PiL – *The Flowers of Romance* (Virgin, 1981)*
Pixies – *Surfer Rosa* (4AD, 1988)*
Pixies – *Doolittle* (4AD, 1989)*
Pixies – *Trompe Le Monde* (4AD, 1991)*
Public Enemy – *It Takes A Nation of Millions To Hold Us Back* (Def Jam, 1988)*
Queen – *A Night at the Opera* (EMI, Elektra, 1975)
REM – *Murmur* (I.R.S., 1983)*
REM – *Green* (Warner Bros. Records, 1988)
REM – *Out of Time* (Warner Bros. Records, 1991)
REM – *Automatic for the People* (Warner Bros. Records, 1992)
Rites of Spring – *Rites of Spring* (Dischord, 1985)*
Roy Orbison – *Roy Orbison's Greatest Hits* (Monument, 1962)*
Saccharine Trust – *Paganicons* (STT, 1981)*
Scream – *Still Screaming* (Dischord Records, 1983)
Scream – *This Side Up* (Dischord Records, 1985)
Scream – *Fumble* (Dischord Records, 1993)
Screaming Trees – *Even If and Especially When* (SST Records, 1987)
Screaming Trees – *Buzz Factory* (SST Records, 1989)
Screaming Trees – *Sweet Oblivion* (Epic Records, 1992)
Scratch Acid – *Scratch Acid* (Rabid Cat, 1984)*
Sebadoh – *Sebadoh III* (Sub Pop reissue, 1992)
Sepultura – *Arise* (Roadrunner Records, 1991)
Sex Pistols – *Never Mind the Bollocks, Here's the Sex Pistols* (Virgin Records, 1977)*
Shocking Blue – *Shocking Blue* (Pink Elephant, 1969)*
Shonan Knife – *Burning Farm* (K, 1983)*
Shonan Knife – Pretty Little Baka Guy (Subersive Records, 1986)*
Slayer – *Reign in Blood* (Def Jam Recordings, 1986)
Smashing Pumpkins – *Gish* (Caroline Records, 1991)
Smashing Pumpkins – *Siamese Dream* (Virgin Records, 1993)
Smithereens – *Especially For You* (Enigma, 1982)*
Sonic Youth – *Daydream Nation* (Enigma Records, 1988)*
Sonic Youth – *Goo* (DGC, 1990)

Soundgarden – *Screaming Life* (Sub Pop, 1987)
Soundgarden – *Fopp EP* (Sub Pop, 1988)
Soundgarden – *Ultramega OK* (SST Records, 1988)
Soundgarden – *Badmotorfinger* (A&M Records, 1991)
Swans – *Young God EP* (K.422, 1984)*
TAD – *God's Balls* (Sub Pop, 1989)
TAD – *8-Way Santa* (Sub Pop, 1991)
Teenage Fanclub – *Bandwagonesque* (Creation, 1991)*
Television Personalities – *The Strangely Beautiful* (Fire, 1991)*
Various Artists – *The Beavis and Butt-Head Experience* (Geffen Records, 1993)
Various Artists – *No Alternative* (Arista Records, 1993)
Various Artists – *Deep Six* (C/Z, 1986)
Various Artists – *Sub Pop 100* (Sub Pop, 1986)
Various Artists – *Sub Pop 200* (Sub Pop, 1988)
Velvet Underground – *White Light/White Heat* (Verve, 1968)*
Violent Femms – *Why Do Birds Sing* (Reprise, 1991)*
Tales of Terror – *Tales of Terror* (CD Presents, 1985)*
The B-52's – *The B-52's* (Warner, 1979)*
The Beatles – *With The Beatles* (EMI, 1963)*
The Beatles – *Meet The Beatles* (Capitol, 1964)*
The Chipmunks – *Christmas with the Chipmunks* (Liberty, 1962)
The Clash – *London Calling* (CBS, 1979)
The Clash – *Combat Rock* (CBS, 1982)*
The Fall – *This Nation's Saving Grace* (Beggars Banquet Records, 1985)
The Fastbacks – *Very, Very Powerful Motor* (Sub Pop, 1990)
The Fates/Void – Split (Discord, 1982)*
The Fluid – *Glue* (Sub Pop, 1990)
The Germs – *GI* (Slash records, 1979)*
The Gits – *Frenching The Bully* (C/Z, 1992)
The Knack – *Get the Knack* (Capitol, 1979)*
The Raincoats – *The Raincoats* (Rough Trade, 1979)*
The Saints – *Know Your Product: The Best of The Saints* (Harvest, 1996)*
The Shaggs – *Philosophy of the World* (Third World Records, 1969)*
The Slits – *The Slits/Bootleg Retrospective* (Y Records, 1980)*
The Slits – *Typical Girls* EP (Island, 1979)*
The Stooges – *The Stooges* (Elektra, 1969)*
The Stooges – *Fun House* (Elektra, 1970)*
The Vaselines – *Dum-Dum* (53rd & 3rd, 1989)*
The Walkabouts – *Cataract* (Sub Pop, 1989)
The Wipers – *Is This Real?* (Park Avenue Records, 1980)*
The Wipers – *Youth of America* (Park Avenue Records, 1981)*
The Wipers – *Over the Edge* (Braineater Records, 1983)*
Urge Overkill – *The Supersonic Storybook* (Touch 'N' Go, 1991)*
Young Marble Giants – *Colossal Youth* (Rough Trade, 1980)*

Index